MOTHER CLAP'S
MOLLY HOUSE

Dedicated to
David William Allen

MOTHER CLAP'S MOLLY HOUSE

The Gay Subculture in England 1700 – 1830

RICTOR NORTON

◀◀◀‖‖GMP‖‖▶▶▶

First Published September 1992 by
GMP Publishers Ltd, P O Box 247, London N17 9QR

World Copyright © 1992 Rictor Norton

A CIP catalogue record for this book
is available from the British Library

Distributed in North America by InBook
140 Commerce Street, East Haven, CT 06512, USA

Distributed in Australia by Bulldog Books
P O Box 155, Broadway, NSW 2007, Australia

Front cover illustration: Confirmation or the Bishop and the Soldier.
A satirical print issued in 1822.
(Reproduced by permission of the British Library.)

Printed and bound in the EC on environmentally-friendly paper
by Nørhaven A/S, Viborg, Denmark

Contents

Illustrations

Acknowledgments

Several articles based upon the following research were first published in *Gay News*, *Gay Sunshine* and *The Advocate*, which I would like to acknowledge, with special thanks to *Gay News* editor Denis Lemon and *Gay Sunshine* editor Winston Leyland for their enthusiastic encouragement of studies of gay culture. I would like to thank Robert Cook, Louis Crompton, Jonathan Katz, and Randolph Trumbach for providing me with much helpful information. The late Robert Halsband kindly gave a critical reading of my study of Lord Hervey, and the late Brian Fothergill provided many stimulating ideas about William Beckford and the literary circles of the late eighteenth century. I am grateful to Keith Cavers for bringing to my attention and allowing me to reproduce the print of 'Ganymede & Jack-Catch' from his collection. The staff of the British Library and the Guildhall Library, City of London, have been most helpful in guiding me to the right documents, and they have kindly granted permission to reproduce several illustrations from material in their collections. I am grateful to Miss M. Boast of the Newington District Library, London, for her assistance with the Rev. John Church papers, and to the staff of the Bodleian Library, University of Oxford, for their assistance with the William Beckford papers.

Note on the Text

Until 1752 England used the old style of dating, in which the calendar year began on 25 March instead of 1 January. I use this old-style calendar throughout this study, citing the dates just as they appear in the contemporary documents. In several instances when it is particularly important to avoid confusion, I use a diagonal stroke to remind the reader of the new-style calendar, e.g. 'January 1694/5' to make it clear that January 1694 comes after December 1694.

I use contemporary spelling when citing documents, though I silently correct a few of the most obvious printing (rather than spelling) errors, e.g. the common printer's error 'goal' for 'gaol'. Early printers were excessively generous in their use of italicisation; in a few instances I have not followed this if it threatened to render a quotation nearly unintelligible for modern readers. I usually fill in the dashes left blank by prudent printers or publishers (if it seems clear to me what letters are missing), indicating this by the use of square brackets.

Introduction

'Molly' is the word which most gay men used to refer to one another for more than 150 years, a longer period of usage than the quasi-scientific modern term 'homosexual'. The nearest contemporary equivalent is 'gay', or, for those of a certain age, 'queen'. In a study of social interactions in which sex played only a part, albeit an important part, such terms as 'molly' and 'gay' are preferable to 'homosexual' because they have a greater resonance, and encompass a wider range of ambiguous references which is appropriate to the wider issues of social rather than specifically sexual behaviour. Narrowly defined, homosexuals have of course existed during all periods of history, but it was not until about 1700 that gay men began to gather together within a structured social organisation which we can properly call a subculture. What is not widely recognised is that 250 years ago there was a thriving gay subculture in England, and that there were actually more gay clubs and pubs in the heart of London in the early 1720s than there were in the 1950s when Parliament began to debate the consequences of reforming the laws against homosexuality.

Throughout this study, I will be using the term 'subculture' in its fairly precise sociological meaning, to define a body of social institutions and patterns of behaviour shared by a group of people who identify themselves as part of that group, who have several 'significant factors' in common, and who are viewed as 'deviant' by those in the mainstream of a larger, enclosing culture. Such subcultures usually have the following major characteristics: (1) social gatherings attended exclusively by members sharing the 'significant factor'; (2) a network of communication between members which is not generally recognised by the larger society; (3) specialised vocabulary or slang, used to reinforce a sense of membership in the group or to establish contact secretly; (4) self-identification with other members in the group, reinforced by common patterns of behaviour which distinguish the members from society at large, and (5) a self-protective community of shared sympathy caused by being ostracised by

9

society for being 'different'. This is the kind of subculture which we recognise in the black ghetto of Harlem, Jewish ghettoes in many capital cities, gypsies or travellers, thieves and criminals, prostitutes, and a host of religious and ethnic communities in modern Britain.

The following study is a history of the origin and development of the gay subculture in England, from the late seventeenth century through the early nineteenth century. The first organised gay community was born and grew up within the remarkably short period of a single generation. It probably did not exist prior to the reign of William III and Mary II (1689–1694) and William III alone (1694–1702), when it first emerged as a recognisable infant, but it rapidly attained adolescence during the reign of Anne (1702–1714), and grew to full maturity during the reign of George I (1714–1727). This subculture remained fairly stable for a hundred years, but became somewhat more secretive and more special-ised during the following generations, and I chart its progress through the remainder of the Georgian era to 1830.

The first chapter will look at the historical background and the quasi-subcultures during the English Renaissance, particularly in the court of King James, and the development of the anti-homosexual law and its first applications. The second chapter will attempt to unravel a mystery concerning London's first gay nightspot. In the remaining chapters my primary focus will be upon the subcultural aspects of homosexual life in England, primarily in London: the 'molly houses' or gay clubs, the first 'markets' or gay cruising grounds, the use of gay slang and 'maiden names', and the various activities such as 'mock births' and 'marriage nights' which took place in the clubs. Along the way I will offer some short biographies, including two or three of the great queens of history, but concentrating upon the less well-known figures such as the first minister to perform gay marriages. Throughout the study we will glimpse varying degrees of self-awareness, and the emergence of a gay identity and a gay lifestyle and the first stirrings of gay pride.

It must be acknowledged that the gay subculture during this period is by default a male gay subculture, for there is little evidence that lesbians either participated in this subculture or formed their own subculture until the mid-nineteenth century. That is, in England; in France the lesbian subculture began in the 1790s, and in Italy there were lesbian coteries at an even earlier period. I review the history of lesbians in eighteenth-century England in Chapter 15, rather than let it get lost by being scattered throughout the other chapters.

The first gay subculture which most fully exhibits all of the characteris-tics described above, developed during the Georgian period and inevitably reflects many of the features of Georgian society. I think many historians underestimate the importance of fashion when analysing socio-sexual behaviour. Homosexuals indeed are often said to be in the vanguard of fashion, or in any case seldom behind the times. The mollies began to club together when clubbing together was all the rage for men of all persuasions; they loved dressing up at a time when masquerades were the very height of fashion; they developed their molly dialect just at the time when middle-class society was enjoying the *frisson* of using thieves' cant and the vernacular in literature. The most prominent feature of the first gay subculture was the molly house, or club for homosexual gentlemen, an institution as characteristic of the eighteenth century as a coffee house. Indeed, in a letter to *The Tatler* on 9 June 1709, a writer remonstrated against a set of Pretty Fellows calling one another Betty and Nelly who frequented White's Chocolate-house and St James's Coffee-house, the very premises where Addison and Steele wrote their essays.

I avoid dogmatic theories as to why the gay subculture emerged when it did. It may be sufficient to see it as a natural result of urbanisation. At the beginning of the eighteenth century London had become the largest city in Europe, a result of a dramatic rise in population during the last quarter of the seventeenth century and the first quarter of the eighteenth century. There are no reliable statistics before 1800, but the population is believed to have reached about 750,000 by 1725; this was large enough to accommodate specialised subgroups of many sorts, and to provide greater opportunity for men of shared interests to associate with one another. Gay men naturally exploited the greater facilities provided by the metropolis: the arcades of the Royal Exchange and Covent Garden, and the public latrines of Lincoln's Inn, became ideal cruising grounds almost as soon as they were built, and I do not think we need a very sophisticated analysis to explain why they were so used. Most historians agree that a population of this magnitude is necessary to support this kind of subculture, but I would disagree with the view, based upon an analogy with the more furtive gay subculture of the 1950s, that this size of population was necessary to provide an anonymity deemed necessary for the subculture. On the contrary, this large population, with proportionally larger numbers of gay men, provided the opportunity and the publicity necessary for making contacts. The gay subculture seemed to burst full view upon the world, and was highly visible almost from the beginning; in fact it seems likely that the publicity given to it by its persecutors ironically helped to consolidate it.

The other factor which helped to develop the gay subculture so rapidly was its unified class structure. The urbanisation of this period, and especially the expansion of commerce, facilitated the creation of a lower-middle class of small shopkeepers and tradesmen, and the working class which served them. Although I will not ignore the role played by aristocrats and gentlemen, the gay subculture throughout most of the eighteenth century consisted almost entirely of members of these working classes, as illustrated by a list of their occupations: servants (messenger boy, chairman, coachman, footman, waiter, waterman), artisans or skilled craftsmen (cabinet maker, gilder, peruke maker, tailor, fan maker, upholsterer), tradesmen (fruit seller, butcher, hardware dealer, woollen draper), suppliers of services (barber, tavern keeper, porter, postboy), workers of various skills (candle maker, wool comber, silk dyer, blacksmith), and not a few foot soldiers, but relatively few schoolmasters and gentlemen of independent means. A certain amount of class exploitation did of course take place, particularly on the fringes of the court, and soldiers have always prostituted themselves to men with money, but the molly houses themselves catered almost exclusively for what are now called the respectable working classes.

The homosexual networks amongst the aristocracy will be examined in the first two chapters, but the majority of this study will demonstrate that the typical homosexual of the eighteenth century was a respectable tradesman rather than a fashionable libertine. In the nineteenth century the gay subculture came increasingly to service the upper-class homosexual's taste for rough trade, to function as a working-class pool into which wealthy gentlemen and aristocrats occasionally dipped. But during the eighteenth century there was far less crossing of the social boundaries: servants slept with servants more often than they slept with their masters; candle makers slept with upholsterers, and butchers slept with blacksmiths. Aristocrats would have been wholly out of place in a molly house; they sometimes used cruising grounds, particularly those near barracks, but they do not seem to have participated more actively in the molly subculture until towards the end of the eighteenth century.

It could be argued that upper-class gentlemen are not in much evidence simply because they had the money to escape justice. Most of my evidence is based upon trial records, and I cannot prove that wealthy homosexuals did not buy their freedom before any indictment was granted. But contemporary pamphlets and newspaper accounts also rarely mention any gentlemen customers frequenting the molly houses, even in those instances where the moralists and satirists would have something to gain by exposing the secret intrigues of the upper classes. And the gossip about upper-class homosexuals invariably connects them with soldiers rather than tradesmen.

A history of homosexuality necessarily entails a history of homophobia and a history of laws against homosexuality, though I have endeavoured to keep these brief, because I am more interested in how the mollies lived than what people thought about them. Some of the trials that I recount are relevant primarily for showing the background against which the mollies had to carve out their place in society, and it is also useful for us to understand how the law was interpreted and applied. A brief history of blackmail also seemed necessary, as is a look at prejudice against gays and the stereotypes created by the heterosexual culture at large. I have not delved too deeply into literary research — most of the imaginative literature is evidence of heterosexual prejudice pure and simple, and reveals virtually nothing about homosexuals. In any case, the literary evidence is meagre and fleshless compared to the richly detailed accounts in the trial records.

Sessions papers and newspaper reports form the basis of most of this study. The great virtue of the trial records is that gay men had their say in the dock, and this was the only time they were allowed to speak for themselves. Generally they were given a fair hearing, and their testimony usually gives a lot of information about their lifestyles as well as the sexual acts for which they were arrested. I have sifted the records not for statistics, but for any information with a cultural value and human interest. We will inevitably find some examples of crude fornication, for that is the very nature of their 'crime', but we will also find even more interesting descriptions of the ordinary social backgrounds to their lives.

The history of homosexuality in the early modern period necessarily depends heavily upon the scandals of the rich and infamous, and the criminal prosecutions of the unfortunate. The information we are searching for would never willingly be written down by the participants involved, for that would be self-incriminating. Those few letters, diaries and autobiographical defences that do exist are all the more to be cherished, but if it were not for gossip and rumour, we would know little about most homosexuals until quite recent times. The reader may complain that some evidence is mere hearsay, but that is all the evidence we are ever likely to find concerning 'important' people. Whenever evidence became fact rather than hearsay, a trial was the inevitable outcome, or flight abroad. Almost all of our evidence about homosexuals during this period was written by people who hated homosexuality. Pamphlets and satires and slanders are a specialised sort of evidence, and we must take due account of their limitations, but my own conclusions are based upon the principle that where there is smoke, there is fire.

Chapter 1

Queen James and His Courtiers

(1) The Buggery Act

The first significant reference to civil laws against homosexuality in England occurs in 1376, when the Good Parliament unsuccessfully petitioned King Edward III to banish foreign artisans and traders, particularly 'Jews and Saracens', accusing them of having introduced 'the too horrible vice which is not to be named' which would destroy the realm. But it was not until 1533 that a statute was actually enacted against homosexuals. The Act — 25 Henry 8, Chapter 6 — begins 'Forasmuch as there is not yet sufficient and condign punishment appointed and limited by the due course of the Laws of this Realm, for the detestable and abominable Vice of Buggery committed with mankind or beast', and proceeds to adjudge it a felony punishable by hanging until dead.

The Buggery Act was piloted through Parliament by Thomas Cromwell in an effort to support Henry's plan of reducing the jurisdiction of the ecclesiastical courts, as the first step towards depriving them of the right to try certain offences, which supported his policy of seizing Church property. It was a felony without benefit of clergy, which denied homosexuals in holy orders the right to be tried in the ecclesiastical courts, with the result that a conviction entailed loss of property to the Crown. The statute was re-enacted in 1536, 1539 and 1541 under Henry VIII; it was repealed in the first Parliament of Edward VI, along with all the new felonies established by Henry, but re-enacted in 1548 with amendments which no longer forfeited the felon's property to the Crown, and stipulations that indictments had to be framed within six months of the commission of the alleged act, and that no person who would benefit from the death of the accused could give evidence against him; with Mary's succession in 1553 it was repealed, along with many other statutes, thus giving jurisdiction back to the ecclesiastical courts; in 1563 it was revived by Queen Elizabeth I, in the harsh terms of the 1533 Act rather than with the amendments of 1548, because, according to the Preamble, since the repeal of the Act in 1553 'divers ill disposed persons have been the more bold to commit the said most horrible and detestable Vice of Buggery aforesaid, to the high displeasure of Almighty God.' Historical evidence fails to reveal any such excessive 'boldness' for the years 1553 to 1563, and the only circumstance which prompted this severe reaction of Elizabeth's ministers was probably Elizabeth's desire to establish her claim to the throne as direct heir of Henry VIII; always politically astute, she naturally re-enacted her father's laws rather than those of intermediate monarchs.[1]

The 1533 Act was on the books as a symbolic token of the supremacy of the secular courts over the ecclesiastical courts, and had no immediate effect, for homosexuals would not be prosecuted with vigour until the second and third decades of the eighteenth century.[2] The Essex Quarter Sessions for 1556–1680 do not show a single homosexual case; the Essex Assize records for 1560–1680 show only one, in 1669; the Somerset Quarter Sessions for 1601–1660 show only two; the Home Counties Assizes for 1559–1625 for Kent, Sussex, Hertfordshire, and Essex show only four indictments for sodomy.[3]

The first recorded instance of any legal action was in 1541 – one of the years in which the Buggery Act was re-enacted – with respect to Nicholas Udall. He was headmaster of Eton from 1534 to 1541, during which time the bachelor schoolmaster gained a reputation for administering corporal punishment to his boys. Being whipped by Nicholas Udall was one of the formative experiences of the English Renaissance. In *Five Hundred Points of Good Husbandry* (1580) one former pupil, Thomas Tusser, wrote:

> *From [St] Paul's I went, to Eton sent,*
> *To learn streightways the Latin phrase,*
> *Where fifty-three stripes given to me at once I had;*
> *For fault but small, or none at all,*
> *It came to pass thus beat I was.*
> *See, Udall, see, the mercy of thee to me, poor lad!*

In 1541, the same year that Udall's play *Roister Doister* was published, Udall was charged with committing both robbery and sodomy. The records of the Privy Council for 14 March 1541 read as follows:

> Nic. Vuedale, Scoolmaster of Eton, beying sent for as suspect to be of councail of a robbery lately commited at Eton by Thomas Cheyney, John Hoorde, Scolers of the said scole, and . . .

Gregory, seruant to the said scolemaster, and having certain interrogatoryes ministred vnto him, toching the sayd fact and other felonius trespasses, wherof he was suspected, did confesse that he did commit buggery with the said cheny, sundrey times heretofore, and of late the vjth day of this present moneth in the present yere at London, whervpon he was commited to the marshalsey.

Most scholars have argued that William Paget, Clerk of the Council, was writing so hurriedly that he misspelled 'buggery' for 'burglary'. The argument is specious, particularly since Udall's biographer, Thomas Edgerton, supports this view by pointing out that there are no homosexual passages in Udall's works — which is quite simply untrue.

Udall was free by September 1542, when he is known to have made a trip to the Scottish border; he also received his back pay at Eton, though he was not reinstated, and within a few years he was tutor to the youthful Earl of Devon. He became headmaster of Westminster school in 1554, the year of his death. All this in spite of the fact that conviction on a charge of buggery would have incurred the death penalty. But the possibility of a misspelled word is irrelevant to this line of argument, for even if it had been burglary, that was a serious enough felony in itself, and Udall should not have gone free. It is evident that the prosecution was somehow quashed, or that there were some misgivings about applying the Act for the first time, particularly in delicate circumstances. Thomas Wriothesley was a member of the Council at the time, and Wriothesley was both Udall's patron and a relative of Thomas Cheney by marriage. It is possible, even likely, that he kept the trial proceedings secret and had the charges reduced or dropped altogether, both because he was publicly connected with Udall and because he wished to avoid a scandal in the family.

The order says that Udall was committed to the Marshalsea prison, but there is no record of actual imprisonment. Udall later wrote a letter of remorse and contrition to an unspecified patron, probably either Wriothesley or Devon, promising 'to eschew and avoid all manner of excesses and abuses that have been reported to reign in me', and pleading for patronage because 'no man of honour or honesty will either receive me, or do for me, or favour, or look upon me.' These seem to be the words more of a repentant homosexual than a thief. 'Reigning abuses' suggest something that would be regarded as a vicious habit, applicable more to the Renaissance view of buggery than to burglary. It is certain that Udall was not stigmatised because of a spelling error.

As the author of *Roister Doister* (1541) — the first 'regular' drama in English literature to be divided into five acts — Nicholas Udall is something of an English Worthy; it is understandable, perhaps, that scholars should wish to whitewash the facts. But even in *Roister Doister* there is a homosexual theme that can be recognised as such without any prior knowledge of the buggery case. The plot is quite simple: Ralph Roister Doister loves Dame Custance, but Matthew Merrygreek, the puckish 'fun-maker', keeps putting forth mischievous impediments to their union. The tricks that he plays are motivated by jealousy. In the fourth scene of the third act, in particular, we seem to glimpse a brief but revealing tearing-away of the social mask worn by homosexuals even during the Renaissance. Matthew Merrygreek, alone with Ralph, suddenly adopts a most solemn demeanour, and mourns: 'That I am not a woman myselfe, for your sake. / I would haue you my-selfe, and a strawe for yond Gill!' Ralph is startled by this curious confession: 'I dare say thou wouldest haue me to thy husbande.' Matthew steps even further beyond the bounds of decorum, then just as suddenly retreats from this vulnerable position: 'Yea; and [if] I were the fairest lady in the shiere, / And knewe you as I know you, and see you nowe here / Well, I say no more!' No doubt the boys of Eton who performed in this play were more sensitive to this scene than modern professors of literature. The latter have simply ignored it, for they would prefer that Udall be branded as a thief rather than a homosexual. Surely this is a matter of misdirected moral rectitude.[4]

Homosexual prosecutions throughout the sixteenth century are exceedingly sparse; they are not limited to London, and they provide no evidence of a subculture; mostly they reveal relationships between servants and their masters, or sporadic cases of unwanted attentions from an older man to a youth. For example, in 1570 John Swan and John Lister, who were smiths and servants of the same master, with whom they lived, were charged with sodomy in Edinburgh.[5] In 1580 Matthew Heaton, a clergyman in East Grinstead, was prosecuted at the Sussex Assizes for a relationship with a boy in his parish.[6]

Homosexuals obviously existed in sixteenth-century England, both in court and in the country, but there was no 'cistern full of sodomy' as there was in Rome, and English gay or bisexual men did not band together and did not create those institutions that we will come to recognise as parts of the authentic gay subculture until the late seventeenth century. It does seem likely, however, that an embryonic courtly gay subculture began to emerge towards the end of the sixteenth century, when a high number of fops and dandies, including those who were not connected with the court, began strutting about town and may have availed themselves of the services of homosexual prostitutes. This at least is the claim of some satirists, though their observations are not altogether trustworthy. John Marston in *The Metamorphosis of Pigmalions Image* (1598) describes 'a dapper, rare, compleat, sweet pretie youth! / . . . / But ho, what Ganimede is that doth grace / The gallants heeles. One, who for two daies space / Is closely hyred', that is, secretly hired for sex. In *The Scourge of Villanie* (1598) Marston goes further and refers to 'male stews', i.e. male brothels, and satirises a character who has his Ganymede as well as his wench, though he prefers 'Cynick friction' or masturbation to 'faire Cynedian boyes'; he further remarks that 'the taste of Jesuit perversion' is rife at the schools of St Omer and Valladolid.[7] (Nearly a century later, Titus Oates was expelled from both St Omer College in France and Valladolid College in Spain, probably for sodomy.)[8]

The clearest description of male prostitution during this period is provided by Thomas Middleton in 1599. He devotes an entire satire to 'Ingling Pyander', from 'ingle', meaning a boy who gives himself to men for sexual purposes. This young man is characterised as 'a pale Chequered black Hermophrodite':

> Sometimes he jets [struts] it like a Gentleman,
> Otherwhiles much like a wanton Curtesan:
> But truth to tell a man or woman whether,
> I cannot say shees excellent in ether.
> But if Report may certifie a truth,
> Shees nether or ether, but a Cheating youth.

Apparently this 'lovely smiling Parragon . . . of Bewtie' was a transvestite, deceiving potential customers in his 'Nymphes attire':

> No Lady, with a fairer grace more grac'd,
> But that Pyanders self himself defac'd;
> Never was boy so pleasing to the hart,
> As was Pyander for a womans part.

The author for a time 'loved Pyander well', but, stung by the pricks of conscience, and the fact that Pyander spent all his money and then deserted him, he repents and confesses his sin by writing this 'snarling satire'.[9] This may well be a completely fictional creation based more upon Juvenal's satires than upon life in London, but the author seems to expect his readers to recognise such characters as Pyander.

In Marlowe's *Tragedy of Dido, Queen of Carthage* (1594), Ganymede is also portrayed as a prostitute, as when he asks Jupiter for 'a jewel for mine ear, / And a fine brooch to put in my hat, / And then I'll hug with you an hundred times.' Jupiter replies 'And shalt have, Ganymede, if thou wilt be my love.' Marlowe's own sympathies are easy to deduce from the frequency with which he explores the themes of homosexual love in such works as *Edward II* (1593) and *Hero and Leander* (1598), in which the beautiful boy rather than the maiden is the real object of desire:

His dangling tresses that were never shorn,
Had they been cut and unto Colchos borne,
Would have allur'd the vent'rous youth of Greece
To hazard more than for the Golden Fleece.

Leander was probably modelled upon Marlowe's beloved boy actor Thomas Walsingham, and Jupiter might have been a man of power in the government. In 1593 Marlowe was stabbed through the eye-socket by Ingram Frisar in a private room above a tavern in Deptford, under mysterious circumstances that have been variously explained as a tavern brawl, as a political assassination because Marlowe was a spy, or as a lovers' quarrel. Had he not been murdered, he may well have been tried for sodomy. He was under suspicion for treason, and a warrant had already been issued for his arrest. The Privy Council had so far obtained testimony from Thomas Kyd that Marlowe 'wold report St John to be our savior Christes Alexis J cover it with reverence and trembling that is that Christ did loue him with an extraordinary loue', and from Richard Baines, who accused Marlowe of saying not only 'That St John the Evangelist was bedfellow to Christ and leaned alwaies on his bosom, that he vsed him as the sinners of Sodoma', but 'That all thei that loue not Tobacco & Boies were fooles.'

(2) The Court of King James

The Buggery Act was enforced with no greater frequency during the seventeenth century than it had been during the sixteenth century, and only a few trials took place. At the Hertfordshire Assizes in 1607 James Slater, a barber, was charged with sodomy with the son of a neighbour.[10] In 1613 one Alban Cooke of Hoxton was indicted for buggery 'with a man under 20 years of age.'[11] Queen Elizabeth's cousin Lord Hunsdon seems to have supported a male brothel in Hoxton, to judge by Marston's satiric lines: 'at Hoxton now his monstrous love he feasts / for there he keeps a bawdy house of beasts.'[12] In 1622 George Dowdney, a married innkeeper in Somerset, was charged with a homosexual offence, and the evidence brought forward revealed a succession of homosexual encounters for the previous fourteen years.[13] In 1643 John Wilson, the vicar of Arlington in Sussex, was ejected from his benefice on charges that 'divers times [he] attempted to commit buggery with Nathaniel Browne, Samuel Andrewes, and Robert Williams his Parishioners . . . *that* (as he shamed not to professe) *they might make up his number eighteene;* . . . and hath openly affirmed, *that Buggery is no sinne.*'[14]

The scarcity of prosecutions in England may have been partly because King James I was himself homosexual, and the court during his reign (1603–1625) was very nearly a gay subculture unto itself. The King had his favourites from the age of fourteen, such as the elegant French courtier Esme Stuart, Earl of Lennox, of whom a fervid clergyman bluntly said: 'the Duke of Lennox went about to draw the King to carnal lust.' Another of James's early companions was George Gordon, who married Lennox's sister Lady Henrietta Stuart in order to be elevated to the rank of Captain of the Guard, and he proceeded to lodge himself in the King's own chamber. The Scots chronicler, Fowler, commenting on this irregular barracking, concluded that 'it is thought that this King is too much carried by young men that lie in his chamber and are his minions.' Other minions of the early 1580s included Alexander Lindsay, Lord Spynie, the boy nicknamed 'Sandie' whom James appointed as his Vice-Chamberlain, and Francis Steward Hepburn, Earl of Bothwell, whom James nonchalantly kissed and embraced in public, causing great scandal to the prudish French ambassador.

James's greatest favourite was George Villiers, Duke of Buckingham; their relationship sparked a moral debate in the Privy Council in 1617. Sir John Oglander testified before the Council that 'The King is wonderous passionate, a lover of his favourites beyond the love of men to women. He is the chastest prince for women that ever was, for he would often swear that he never kissed any other woman than his own queen. I never yet saw any fond husband make so much or so great dalliance over his beautiful spouse as I have seen King James over his favourites, especially Bucking-ham.' James responded with what may well be the first defence of homosexual love in modern history, as elegantly brief as would be Oscar Wilde's defence of platonic love at his own trial nearly three centuries later:

> I, James, am neither a god nor an angel, but a man like any other. Therefore I act like a man and confess to loving those dear to me more than other men. You may be sure that I love the Earl of Buckingham more than anyone else, and more than you who are here assembled. I wish to speak in my own behalf and not to have it thought to be a defect, for Jesus Christ did the same, and therefore I cannot be blamed. Christ had his son John, and I have my George.

One cannot help but feel that James may have been aware of the heresy then current in some quarters, and that Marlowe was not the only one who held such views about Christ and St John.

The love letters from James to Buckingham, extending over a period of

nearly ten years, are the earliest examples of what might be considered a
homosexual literary genre, since most love letters between men before
and since that time have been either destroyed or suppressed. They
suggest that James was the 'dominant' partner in the relationship; usually
he signs himself 'Thy dear dad and husband' and addresses Buckingham
as 'my sweet child and wife'. The relationship was interchangeable, though
its meaning for James was clear: 'I desire only to live in the world for your
sake, and I had rather live banished in any part of the world with you, than
live a sorrowful widow-life without you.' Their love for one another was
expressed not only in private letters, but in public shows of affection.
According to the contemporary Francis Osborne: 'In wanton looks and
wanton gestures they exceeded any part of womankind. The kissing them
after so lascivious a mode in public and upon the theatre, as it were, of the
world prompted many to imagine some things done in the tyring house
[dressing room] that exceed my expression no less than they do my
experience.'[15]

This is not the place to assess Buckingham's motives or his personality,
or James's lack of political tact. Their drunken riotous feasts contributed
to the nation's steadily rising national debt and civil unrest, but if power
had not been invested in Buckingham, it would have been invested in some
other favourite, possibly possessing less statecraft than either. Most
members of the nobility were eager to steal James's favour from Buckingham, and they pursued their self-interest with what was laughingly referred
to as 'the mustering of minions'. Every day some aspiring lord, such as Sir
William Manson, would hire a troop of handsome young ragamuffin
boys, scrub their faces clean with curdled milk, curl their hair, powder
them and perfume them, dress them in silk and lace, and lead them in
procession around the throne in order to seduce the King's favour.
Marvellously delighted by this display of prime mignon, James nevertheless grew weary with surfeit, and when he realised that he was being made
a fool of, he gave Buckingham orders to clear the court in 1618. This
marked the end of the riotous period and the beginning of a period when
James would mellow, and, eventually, slide into a state of depression. But
the country was verging upon civil war, and when James dissolved
Parliament in 1621 he effectively lost his control over the kingdom. The
date coincides with the fall of Sir Francis Bacon.

Sir Francis Bacon was born into a middle-class family in 1561, became
a practising lawyer in 1582, and was appointed Queen Elizabeth's Counsellor in 1591. His career remained static until King James assumed the
throne. He was knighted in 1603, made Solicitor General in 1607,
Attorney General in 1613, and Lord High Chancellor in 1618 — thus
occupying the highest public post next to the throne itself. He received the
titles of Baron Verulam in 1618, and Viscount St Albans in 1621. Bacon

was undoubtedly a man of uncommon abilities, but people did not rise in James's court on that count alone; it is very likely that Bacon's preferment was due in part to his personal friendship with the King, and particularly with Buckingham.

Similarly, he fell from power just when James was no longer in a position to offer much support. In 1621 Bacon was found guilty of having accepted bribes while serving as a judge. Actually, it was common practice during this era for all judges to accept gifts from the winning parties — no scholar investigating this affair has challenged Bacon's assertion that such gifts never influenced his judgments — and the trial was more for a breach in politics than a breach in law. A strong faction in Parliament disliked Bacon's friendship with James and they seized the opportunity to pretend moral outrage, with the result that Bacon's public career was ruined.

If this ploy had not succeeded, undoubtedly his opponents would have attacked him as a homosexual. John Aubrey in his *Brief Lives* says quite bluntly that Bacon 'was a pederast' and had 'ganimeds and favourites'. Even his mother, Lady Ann Bacon, in a letter to her other son Anthony complains of 'that bloody Percy' whom Francis kept 'yea as a coach companion and a bed companion', as well as other boyfriends including Jones, Markes, Edney, 'and his Welshmen one after another'. Lady Ann's major distress was not that her son was homosexual, but that it seriously violated the class barrier for a servant to sleep in the master's bedroom.

The Puritan moralist Sir Simonds D'Ewes in his *Autobiography*, in the entry for 3 May 1621 — the date of Bacon's censure by Parliament — reveals the full extent of Bacon's homosexuality, and is worth quoting extensively if only because it has been suppressed in the only printed edition of the autobiography, and has been studiously ignored by most of Bacon's modern biographers:

> . . . the favour he had with the beloved Marquis of Buckingham emboldened him, as I learned in discourse from a gentleman of his bedchamber, who told me he was sure his lord should never fall as long as the said Marquis continued in favour. His most abominable and darling sinne I should rather burie in silence, than mencion it, were it not a most admirable instance, how men are enslaved by wickedness, & held captive by the devill. For wheeras presentlie upon his censure at this time his ambition was moderated, his pride humbled, and the meanes of his former injustice and corruption removed; yet would he not relinquish the practice of his most horrible & secret sinne of sodomie, keeping still one Godrick, a verie effeminate faced youth, to bee his catamite and bedfellow, although hee had discharged the most of his other household sevants: which was

the moore to bee admired, because men generallie after his fall begann to discourse of that his unnaturall crime, which hee had practiced manie yeares, deserting the bedd of his Ladie, which hee accounted, as the Italians and the Turkes doe, a poore & meane pleasure in respect of the other; & it was thought by some, that hee should have been tried at the barre of justice for it, & have satisfied the law most severe against that horrible villanie with the price of his bloud; which caused some bold and forward man to write these verses following in a whole sheete of paper, & to cast it down in some part of Yorkehouse in the strand, wheere Viscount St. Alban yet lay:

	*alluding both to his
Within this sty a *hogg doth ly,	sirname of Bacon,
That must be hang'd for Sodomy.	& to that swinish
	abominable sinne.

But hee never came to anye publicke triall for this crime; nor did ever, that I could heare, forbeare his old custome of making his servants his bedfellowes, soe to avoid the scandall was raised of him, though hee lived many yeares after his fall in his lodgings in Grayes Inne in Holbourne, in great want & penurie.

Sir Francis Bacon's relationships — like those of his King — closely followed the pattern of patron/favourite. More specifically, he had a preference for young Welsh serving-men. The roll of attendants for Bacon's household in 1618 lists a total of 75 attendants, of whom some 25 were gentlemen waiters. There was Francis Edney, who, upon Bacon's death in 1626, received '£200 and my rich gown'; Henry Percy (Lady Ann's 'that bloody Percy'), who received a legacy of £100 (as well as a letter to the Secretary of State, recommending him to His Majesty's service on 26 January 1626, nearly Bacon's last letter); young Thomas Meautys, who was to become Bacon's secretary-in-chief; a Mr Bushell, 'gent. usher', who came to the household in 1608 as a lad of 15, and who remained until Bacon's death; Edward Sherburn, groom of the chamber; and, above all, young Tobie Matthew, who was left only a ring to the value of £30, but who had become Sir Tobie through Bacon's efforts, and who was well able to care for himself.

Tobie, widely acclaimed for his charm and good looks, had appeared in a play at Gray's Inn in 1595, and he quickly became Bacon's most particular friend, intelligencer and confidant. Tobie had previously served as a spy on the Continent, where he had met and been befriended by Buckingham. A contemporary observed that Tobie, while lodging with

Bacon at York House, had 'grown very gay or rather gaudy in his attire, and noted for certain night walks to the Spanish Ambassador.' Tobie was the inspiration for one of Bacon's most famous essays, 'Of Friendship', wherein he says that although 'nuptial love *maketh* mankind, friendly love *perfecteth* it', and 'If a man have not a friend, he may quit the stage.'[16]

Francis Bacon's brother Anthony (1558–1601) was also homosexual, and his relationships took a similar pattern. His favourite page was Isaac Burgades, who himself would forcibly 'mount' a still younger page in the household, David Boysson, and who told another page, Paul de la Fontayne, that there was nothing wrong with sodomy. One of the lackeys, Barthelemy Sore, had left Anthony's service because his master was wont to bugger all the boys and then bribe them with sweetmeats to keep quiet. These events occurred in Montauban, where in the summer of 1586 Anthony Bacon was charged with sodomy. In France, convicted sodomites were sentenced to death by *le bucher* (in 1563 Benoist Grealou, a priest at nearby Moissac, was so convicted and *brulé tout vif*), but in September Henri, King of Navarre, personally intervened, with the result that the charge — though evidence was heard again in November 1587 — was not pressed. The case was so effectively suppressed that no knowledge of it came to light until 1973, after the diligent researches of Daphne du Maurier.

Anthony returned to England in 1592, to live in Gray's Inn with his brother Francis, and attended by the young Gascon Jacques Petit. Other of his most particular friends included his travelling companion Ned Selwyn, and Thomas Lawson. A bachelor establishment was set up at his estate in Redbourn, and he died a bachelor in 1601, having faithfully served both Essex and Sir Francis Walsingham as an intelligencer.[17]

There were many other homosexuals in the court as well. According to Anthony Weldon in 1651, 'Above all the miracles of those times, old Sir Anthony Ashley, who never loved any but boyes, yet he was snatched up for a kinswoman [of Buckingham], as if there had been a concurrency thorow the kingdome, that those that naturally hated women, yet should love his kindred as well as the King him.'[18] Weldon succinctly noted that King James 'was not very uxorious', and his phrase 'a concurrency thorow the kingdome' suggests a courtly gay network, a series of connecting links at court that might reasonably be termed a subculture. Other homosexuals at court included Lord Henry Howard, who had dealings with Antonio Perez, the homosexual Secretary of State to Philip of Spain (and probably the Spanish Ambassador with whom Tobie Matthew and Anthony Bacon had connections), and the homosexual Anthony Standen, who in turn also had dealings with Anthony Bacon in the latter's intelligence gathering. Then also there was the Earl of Oxford, who preferred his pages over his wife, and who held that 'Englishmen were dolts and nitwits not to realise that there was better sport than with women.' And of course we must not forget to mention the Earl of Southampton, Shakespeare's patron and possibly the addressee of the Sonnets, who, when in Ireland with Essex, lay in his tent with Captain Piers Edmonds and 'would cull and hug him in his arms and play wantonly with him.'

There is nothing particularly surprising about the gay households of the brothers Bacon. What is worthy of note is the apparent link between such homosexual groupings and a widespread spy network. It seems likely, for example, that Anthony Bacon used Jacques Petit — just as Francis may have used Tobie — to seduce and then draw out information from the Spanish Ambassador. The secrecy perfected by the homosexual to evade public detection may serve him well as an intelligence gatherer, but lest this lead us too far astray into speculation about the interrelationship of espionage and homosexuality even up to modern times, let us remember that virtually everyone in the courts during the sixteenth and seventeenth centuries was actively engaged upon 'intelligence' work.

(3) Earl of Castlehaven

As we have seen, prosecutions under the Buggery Act were virtually nonexistent, but with both King James and Sir Francis Bacon out of the way, it was only a matter of time before a suitable victim could be chosen, preferably one who had few resources to fight back. The first notable victim was Mervyn Touchet, Earl of Castlehaven, and it cannot be mere coincidence that he was Francis Bacon's brother-in-law.

On Monday, the 29th day of April, in the year of our Lord 1631, about the hour of ten in the morning, the Lord Keeper Coventry, being by special commission duly appointed Lord High Steward of England, with 26 members of the Nobility, proceeded into Westminster Hall, attended by a Herald and six Sergeants at Arms. The Lord High Steward being seated in a Chair of State, and the Peers of the Realm being seated round a table covered by a cloth of green velvet, proclamation was made for Silence! Thus began — amidst all the dread-inspiring pomp and circumstance of a solemn rite of degradation — the trial and condemnation of Mervyn Touchet, the trial which would remain the legal precedent for all homosexual court cases for the next 200 years. It was a sensation, and pamphlets describing it were reprinted every time there was a gay scandal during the next two centuries.

Actually, it was only partially a homosexual trial, for the indictments against Castlehaven included one count of rape as well as two counts of sodomy. The evidence (which we have little reason to doubt, for even

Castlehaven admitted to much of it) illustrates a quasi-subculture within the highly circumscribed boundaries of a private estate, where Castlehaven endeavoured to collect a group of lusty Irish lads to fulfil his fantasies, even going so far as to recruit vagabonds and out of work sailors from the ports.

Mervyn Touchet was the 12th Lord Audley in the peerage of England, and the second Lord Audley and Earl of Castlehaven in the peerage of Ireland. When only about 24 years old, he inherited a goodly fortune from his father, which augmented the estate at Fonthill near Tisbury in Wiltshire which he had inherited from his mother. He proceeded to marry an heiress, by whom he begot his son James, and when she died he became wealthier still and married another heiress. His second wife was Lady Anne Stanley (heiress of the Earl of Derby, widow of her first husband, Lord Chandos), and a marriage was arranged between Lady Ann's daughter (also previously married) and Lord Audley's son — just to keep the money in the family.

The alleged orgies are supposed to have begun on the first day after Castlehaven married Anne. According to her, he called upon each manservant to come into their room, one by one, 'to show their Nudities, and forc'd me to look upon them, and to commend those that had the longest.' On succeeding days, he brought into their bridal chamber three of his menservants, including Henry Skipwith and Giles Broadway, who lay between them, being husband before and wife aft, and upon one occasion he held Anne tightly while Broadway ravished her against her will. Another servant named Amptil (or Antill in some accounts) sometimes also participated in these odd nuptial rites, though he was usually busy elsewhere. Amptil had originally been a beggar and a vagabond, until Sir Henry Smith picked him up and made him his footman. Castlehaven eventually acquired Amptil as his personal page, and found his services so agreeable that he made him his master of the stables. For thus tending his horses, Castlehaven gave Amptil a salary of £500 per year, compared with a yearly allowance of only £100 given to his own son James. James was furious when Castlehaven arranged for Amptil to marry his daughter by his first marriage, giving Amptil a dowry of £7,000. As will appear throughout the tale, Castlehaven was a kind master, though an unkind father and a vicious husband.

Henry Skipwith had been fetched over from Ireland to be the page to Lady Anne. Like Amptil, he also had come from a very poor background, and he was similarly rewarded by Castlehaven with an estate in Salisbury worth £260 per year. According to Skipwith, 'For the most part I lay in Bed with the Earl.' At other times he lay with Amptil. At still other times Skipwith was persuaded by Castlehaven to sleep between himself and Lady Anne. Eventually Lady Anne gave birth to Skipwith's child, but the child disappeared, and Skipwith, believing Lady Anne had foully done away with it, grew to hate her. Castlehaven then coerced the young Lady Audley, his stepdaughter Elizabeth Brydges, to lay with Skipwith in the presence of himself and other servants. Elizabeth was but twelve years old, and the first time Skipwith lay with her, Castlehaven had to apply to Skipwith's member some oil to make penetration easier. It required two applications. Elizabeth was already married to Castlehaven's son James, himself hardly more than a child, but his resentment at this paternal unkindness eventually led to the court action. Castlehaven in court admitted that he often lay with Skipwith, 'and being a good Servant I gave him good Rewards'.

Meanwhile, Florentius (sometimes called Lawrence) Fitz-Patrick and Castlehaven were buggering each other in the mansion at Fontain (later Fonthill) Gifford in the County of Wilts. Amptil *et al* were not actually involved in the trial, and Castlehaven was charged with perpetrating the *crimen sodomiticum (inter alios non Christiandos)* specifically upon Fitz-Patrick on 1 June and 10 June 1630, when they were overseen. Florentius was also a vagabond who one day happened upon the Fonthill estate, and lingered on, in spite of his misgivings, 'through frailty, and because I was not furnished of another place.'

Eventually Giles Broadway was brought into this sociable circle. Broadway was a sailor: 'I came not to my lord with a desire or intent any ways to serve him, but was rather inclined for the sea: only Mr Skipwith had drawn me thither for society sake; and not hearing from my friends concerning my intended voyage, and being more kindly respected by the earl than I looked for, I staid from week to week, and from month to month, contrary to my intention, and my lord made me his bed-fellow.' Castlehaven, who had already married off his daughter and stepdaughter to his other servants, had further plans for Broadway. One day while they were strolling in the garden, he said to Giles, 'Thou art young, lusty, and well-favoured. I am old, and cannot live long, my wife wholly delighting in lust, which I am neither able nor willing to satisfy, thou mayest do well to lie with her: and so pleasing her, after my death marry her, and thereby raise thy fortune.' He continued to so solicit Giles as they lay in bed together, with Florentius lying at the foot of the bed to keep their feet warm. Broadway finally agreed, and lay with Lady Anne on only one occasion, not quite successfully penetrating her while Castlehaven held her arms behind her back. This resulted in the charge that Castlehaven had caused the rape of his own wife.

On 1 November 1630, James, Castlehaven's son, who had recently come into his majority, wrote a letter remonstrating Castlehaven for parental unkindness, and soon thereafter he brought the matter to the attention of the courts. Six weeks later Castlehaven was arrested and confined in the Tower of London pending formal arraignment. He appealed to be tried by a local jury of Wiltshire men, but was informed that as a nobleman he must be tried in Parliament, and the House of Lords duly heard the indictment in April 1631. The outcome was a foregone conclusion because of Castlehaven's suspected Roman Catholic allegiance; in the words of the Attorney General: 'when once a Man indulges his Lust, and Prevaricates with his Religion, as my Lord Audley has done, by being a Protestant in the Morning, and a Papist in the Afternoon, no wonder if he commits the most abominable Impieties.' He was the ideal victim to be prosecuted for what many regarded as the 'Jesuit perversion'.

Castlehaven was sequestered without benefit of counsel for more than six months. When he finally appeared in Westminster Hall, pale and haggard, he requested that a solicitor be permitted to speak for him since his voice was so weak after the confinement and poor treatment. The Lord High Steward courteously replied that the long imprisonment 'hath been to you a special favour; for you have had time enough to bethink yourself', and refused to grant his request. The charges were read, containing such rhetoric as 'seduced by the Instigation of the Devil, he Wickedly, Devilishly, Feloniously committed that Detestable Abominable Sin', to which Castlehaven pleaded Not Guilty. One might almost think that he was being tried for witchcraft.

The Attorney General, Sir Robert Heath, began with a harangue about the Sodomitical Sin, including its history since the degenerate times of Rome, and became so carried away with his theme that Castlehaven rightly interrupted him to urge him to stick to the specific charges of the indictment. The Lord High Steward politely bade Castlehaven to let the Attorney General complete his opening statement. Eventually Heath finished quoting Scripture, and Castlehaven was permitted to proceed with his defence. Castlehaven also quoted Scripture in defence of his love of Skipwith (his exact reference is not cited, but it was probably an allusion to the love of David and Jonathan, perhaps even the 'heresy' about Christ and St John). He went on to argue that Lady Anne was a lusty whore who wanted to replace him with a younger husband, and that his son was 'gaping after my estate' and was paying the servants to lie against him. He argued that a wife could not testify against her husband, but the court decided to accept her testimony since she was the aggrieved party. Castlehaven then emphasised the legal point that since Broadway testified that Castlehaven had emitted between his thighs rather than actually penetrated him, technically there was no sodomitical rape, but the court replied that it still came within the definition of buggery. Castlehaven then protested that Broadway by his own testimony was a participant in the crime, and could not therefore be a legal witness against him. The Lord Chief Justice argued that such a conspirator or participant could be a legal witness until he himself was convicted of the felony, 'for otherwise,

Facts of this nature would seldom or never be discovered.' It is this precedent in particular which would lead to the convictions of numerous homosexuals throughout the following centuries (although, during the next century, proof of actual penetration would be required for conviction of a felony and the ultimate penalty of death, while attempted but incompleted penetration would be a misdemeanour, punishable by the pillory, fines and imprisonment).

Lady Audley, young Lady Audley, Giles Broadway, and Florentius Fitz-Patrick testified, and after two hours of deliberation the jurors unanimously found Castlehaven guilty of rape, and 15 of the 26 jurors found him guilty of sodomy (a majority was enough to convict). He was sentenced to death. Castlehaven appealed for mercy to King Charles, who granted only a postponement of execution so he could repent. Castlehaven's coffin was prepared, and placed in a corner of his prison room, where he prayed daily with Dr Wickham, Dean of St Paul's. On Saturday, 14 May, Castlehaven ascended the scaffold on Tower Hill, wearing a plain black Grogram suit and a black hat. He knelt and prayed, then stood up and made his dying speech protesting his innocence, declaring himself a member of the Church of England, and requesting the spectators to lift up their eyes to heaven and to pray for his soul. His hands were then tied behind his back, a handkerchief was placed over his eyes, he knelt again and placed his head upon the block, and at a sign from him the executioner at one blow divided his head from his body. Undoubtedly Castlehaven deserved punishment for having assisted in the rape of his wife, but he would never have been prosecuted for that had he not been a homosexual and a suspected Papist.

Six weeks later, on Monday, 27 June 1631, Florentius Fitz-Patrick and Giles Broadway were brought to trial in Westminster Hall on charges of rape and sodomy. Lady Audley appeared to give testimony against Broadway, and then 'departed with as much privacy as might be into her coach.' Fitz-Patrick pleaded Not Guilty, and asked who were his accusers. Sir Nichols Hyde, the Lord Chief Justice, replied that he was his own accuser, because of his former testimony against Castlehaven. Florentius protested that it was against the laws of England for a man to be required to testify against himself, but Hyde countered that since his testimony had already served to take away the life of a lord, it should serve to take away his own life also. It was catch-22. Both men were found guilty and sentenced to death. King Charles requested a stay of execution, to allow more time to consider the grave legal question of self-accusation. Sir Thomas Fenshaw, one of the judges, wrote up a report virulently attacking Broadway as a liar and Fitz-Patrick as a fool, and he urged that the land be rid of such miscreants as soon as possible, never mind the finer points of the law. Thus persuaded that the legal niceties need not be examined too closely, the King set a date for execution one week hence. The legal precedent therefore clearly established the principle that homosexuals can be convicted and executed for acts which take place between consenting adults in private, even if penetration cannot definitely be proven, and even if the only accusation comes from the confession of one of the men involved.

The turnkey of Newgate Prison noted that the prisoners behaved themselves civilly and religiously. On Wednesday, 6 July, Broadway and Fitz-Patrick were brought in a cart to Tyburn. The executioner tied the rope about Fitz-Patrick's neck, and he began to pray to Christ, Mary, and the Saints. An anti-Catholic among the spectators rebuked him for praying to Mary, but he persisted, saying 'O yes, the blessed Virgin never forsook or failed any that trusted in, or called upon her.' Then he turned to Broadway to exhort him to die proudly in the Roman Catholic faith. Broadway, sitting in a corner of the cart, did not respond. Fitz-Patrick then gave his dying speech, confessing that everything he had said was true, but that Lord Dorset, one of the judges, had falsely promised him immunity from prosecution if he would testify. But he forgave all, and asked all assembled to pray for his soul, and began his private prayers.

Broadway, who had been intermittently meditating upon Fitz-Patrick's speech and nodding to the crowd in appreciation for their sympathy, then stood up so that the rope could be placed around his neck and his hands tied behind his back. The executioner granted his request that his hands be untied so he could read the confession he wrote in prison. It was a formal confession, ending in three short prayers from *Learn to Die*, a pamphlet given to all condemned men while in Newgate. He finished, and handed it to the minister, Mr Goodcoate, a kinsman who was seated on horseback near the cart, and began with a more specific confession about his relationship with Castlehaven, ending with regrets that he had been the cause of his kind master's death. Concluding his speech, he pulled out a lace handkerchief and asked the executioner to tie it about his head. Then he pulled off his garters and unbuttoned his doublet, and joined with Goodcoate in cheerfully singing the 143rd Psalm. He made a confession of faith as an Anglican, and requested burial in his own country. The executioner again tied his hands behind his back. As Giles said 'Lord Jesus receive my spirit' and Florentius commended himself to God, the cart was drawn away, leaving them to hang by their necks until dead.[19]

Chapter 2

The Birth of the Subculture

(1) The Late Seventeenth Century

The first gay cruising grounds and gay brothels may have appeared in London towards the middle of the seventeenth century, but the evidence is scant. Michael Drayton in *The Moone-Calfe* denounced the theatres as the haunts of sodomites; Edward Guilpin in *Skialetheia* said that the plays were frequented by sodomites, who went to sup with their 'ingles' or young male prostitutes after the play;[1] and Stubbs in his notorious *Anatomie of Abuses* claimed that the theatres were the meeting places of sodomites. Clement Walker in 1649 referred to 'new-erected sodoms and spintries at the Mulberry Garden at S. James's' — it is amusing to note the possible existence of gay brothels on the site now occupied by Buckingham Palace, but the heterosexual brothels of Salisbury Court were called 'Sodom' and 'Little Sodom' by satirists such as Dryden and Rochester, so this may refer to places of debauchery in general.[2] The names of some streets in London such as Maiden Lane and Gropecunt Lane (better known as Grub Street) are clearly derived from the prevalence of female prostitutes along their thoroughfares, so one might be tempted to deduce male homosexual prostitution along Cock's Lane and Lad Lane (directly across from Maiden Lane).

However, as we shall see in the following chapters, homosexual prostitution was of only marginal significance during the eighteenth century, and I find it difficult to believe that it was thriving in the seventeenth century, lay dormant in the eighteenth century, and blossomed once again in the nineteenth century. The commentators upon morality probably could not deal with the concept of homosexuality except by labelling its practitioners with terms borrowed from the underworld of heterosexual prostitution, and misleadingly use terms such as 'He-Strumpets' and 'He-Whores' even for quite ordinary gay men who would never think of soliciting payment for their pleasures.

This is not to say that low-paid lads would not accept favours pressed upon them by Restoration libertines such as John Wilmot, Earl of Rochester: 'There's a sweet, soft page of mine / Does the trick worth forty wenches.' Wilmot candidly admits to being bisexual: 'Nor shall our love-fits, Chloris, be forgot, / When each the well-looked linkboy strove t'enjoy, / And the best kiss was the deciding lot / Whether the boy fucked you, or I the boy'; the 'linkboy' is the lad who carries the torch to light street lamps at night, and no doubt such boys were game for some pretty diversion.

Wilmot's play *Sodom, or The Quintessence of Debauchery* (1684) is the first work in English literature ever to be censored by the government on the grounds of obscenity and pornography, primarily because of its homosexual nature. King Bolloxinion declares that 'with my Prick, I'll govern all the land', and he decides that sodomy shall be the rule of the realm. Borastus, Buggermaster-General, persuades the King to abandon Queen Cuntigratia for either Prince Pockenello or Pine, a Pimp of Honour:

> It could advise you, Sir, to make a pass
> Once more at loyal Pockenello's arse.
> Besides, Sir, Pine has such a gentle skin,
> 'T would tempt a Saint to thrust his Pintle in.

Cuntigratia arranges heterosexual orgies for all, but Bolloxinion is obdurate:

> Since I have bugger'd human arse, I find
> Pintle to Cunt is not so much inclin'd.
> What tho the letchery be dry, 't is smart;
> A Turkish arse I love with all my heart.
> . . . .
> May as the Gods his name immortal be
> That first receiv'd the gift of Buggery!

His brother King Tarsehole of neighbouring Gomorrah sends him a present of 40 young striplings to celebrate peace between their countries. The women, tired of their dildoes, plot rebellion, but too late; half the cast is destroyed by an epidemic of venereal disease while Bolloxinion perseveres in his mad attempt to bugger the gods out of heaven. As the last curtain falls, fire and brimstone descend upon the sinful Cities of the Plain. Cunticula reappears from behind the curtain to deliver the epilogue, encouraging the audience to renounce masturbation and buggery, which is the moral (!) of the play. Wilmot died at the age of 33, exhausted by a life of libertinage.[3]

Bolloxinion's sodomitical conspiracy seemed to have its real-life counterpart with the discovery of the Titus Oates hoax, for Oates had been not only a Roman Catholic and a traitor, but he was suspected of being homosexual as well. He was a religious fanatic who convinced the authorities that there was a Roman Catholic conspiracy upon the life of Charles II. During his reign of terror from 1678 to 1681 he lived at the palace, and his false accusations against others of treason brought about the deaths of about 35 men. Finally he was exposed as a bigot and a liar, and was convicted of perjury in 1685, fined 1,000 marks (a mark was two-thirds of a pound sterling), whipped from Aldgate to Newgate, stood in the pillories at Tyburn, Westminster Palace Yard, and Charing Cross, and imprisoned.[4] As an example of contemporary satire on him, here are some excerpts from *Titus's Exaltation to the Pillory, upon his Conviction of Perjury. A Ballad* (London, 1685):

> *IV. There once was a Time, Boy, when to the Worlds wonder,*
> *I could kill with a Breath more than Jove with his Thunder;*
> *But, oh! my great Narrative's made but a Fable,*
> *My Pilgrims and Armies confounded like Babel:*
> > *Oh they've struck me quite dumb,*
> > *And to tickle my Bum,*
> *Have my Oracles turn'd all to a Tale of Tom Thumb.*
> *Oh! weep all to see this ungrateful Behaviour,*
> *In thus ridiculing the great Nation-Saviour!*
> > . . . .
> *VII. A curse on the day, when the Papists to run down,*
> *I left buggering at Omers, to swear Plots at London;*
> > . . . .
> *VIII. With what Homage and Duty to Titus in Glory,*
> *Had the worshipping Saints turn'd their Bums up before me.*

Oates was eventually released from prison, and his pension was reinstated by King William; he continued intriguing until his death in 1705, but people stopped paying attention to him.

(2) Love Letters

During the reigns of Cromwell and Charles II the court was either austere or predominantly heterosexual, but in the reigns of William and Mary, and Anne, we find not only the quasi-subculture of the court, but also the earliest evidence of a fully formed gay subculture in London. There are many clues to its emergence during the closing decade of the seventeenth century, and it might even be possible to pinpoint the birth of the gay subculture in England as occurring in the year 1694, at the Earl of Sunderland's house, Piccadilly. That at least is the substance of the claim put forward in three documents written in the early eighteenth century. The most explicit statement is found in the diary of Rev. Robert Wodrow, the Scottish antiquary who recorded the following observation in the entry for 20 September 1727:

> Profaneness never abounded more at London, and throu England, than nou. The abomination of Sodomy is too publick. My Lord Ross tells what he heard; but, as he is highly dis-oblidged, so it's probable it was a story of his enemies, of whom he had many, that the Earle of Sunderland was the first who set up houses for that vile sin, and, when this was like to break out, poisoned himself, to prevent the discovery. This is so horrid, that it's not to be belived till vouched.[5]

William Ross, Lord Ross of Halkhead, worked with Charles Spencer, 3rd Earl of Sunderland, on the commission to consider the question of Union in 1689, and again on the commission to debate the Act of Toleration in 1704. Though he was an enemy of Sunderland, his accusation may be based upon personal knowledge, and it becomes more believable when we begin to piece together the rest of the story.

The mysterious intrigue really began in 1693, when Sunderland seems to have seduced Edward Wilson, whose handsome looks and extravagant style earned him the sobriquet Beau Wilson. The Beau lived at the astonishing rate of £4,000 per annum, without any visible estate.[6] A mere commoner, Wilson's meteoric rise to public splendour, with a magnificent equipage and a display of wealth more lavish than the court, quite amazed society. John Evelyn wondered in his diary how the younger son of a man of only middling wealth had managed to live 'in the Garb & Equipage of the richest Noble man in the nation for House, Furniture, Coaches & 6 horses, & other saddle horses; Table & all things accordingly; . . . But the Mysterie is, how this so young gentleman, a sober young person, & very inoffensive, & of good fame, did so live in so extraordinary Equipage; it not

being discovered by any possible industry, by any his most intimate
Friends.'[7]

Speculation reached fevered pitch when Wilson was murdered in a
sword fight in April 1694. *The Plot Discover'd* published later that year[8]
revealed that Captain Wilson had spent a short time in Flanders serving
under his uncle who was a colonel of a regiment, who sent him home
because 'he was much fitter for a courtier than a soldier because of his
comeliness and presence.' After only six months in England, he was
observed to 'appear in that Pomp and Grandieur becoming the Quality of
a Peer', living in ever-increasing magnificence until his death, leaving vast
riches behind him. According to our author, some suspected Wilson of
being involved in a recent theft of diamonds from some Jews, but he had
not sufficient boldness for such an adventure; some believed him to be a
spy in the pay of France, but he knew little of state affairs; the Royal Society
speculated that he had discovered the Philosopher's Stone; many believed
he was maintained by a woman, but 'there is but one Dutchess in the
Kingdom able to support a Gallant in the expensive Grandeur of his
Living.' After he received his mortal wound, he gave his keys to a friend
with instructions to burn his writings, but 'all they found was a recipe from
his grandmother for the cure of a tooth ache.'

Wilson was obviously a kept man, but who was keeping him? The
mystery as to how he supported such a lifestyle was not revealed until 1723,
with the publication of an astonishing packet of homosexual love letters
which were claimed to have been discovered in a cabinet in his room upon
his death, which were published as *Love-Letters Between a certain late
Nobleman And the famous Mr. Wilson.*[9] In a copy of this book in the British
Library, the Nobleman is identified, in a late eighteenth-century style of
handwriting, as 'the Earl of Sunderland'. Sunderland died in mysterious
circumstances in 1722, so he was 'late deceased' when the love letters were
published, and other evidence to be discussed below will support this
identification. There is no internal evidence which clearly demonstrates
that the love letters are not authentic documents from the 1690s. It seems
clear to me that the letters were not written by the same person who
published them and who wrote the editorial preface and observations in
1723. The observations were written by a journalist, and his breathless
style does not suggest that he had the skill necessary to concoct letters
supposed to have been written in 1694. The letters themselves have an air
of arrogance which one would associate with an aristocrat such as Sunderland, and an insinuating sycophancy one might associate with Wilson. The
observations are very moral and earnest, while the letters are quite amoral
and typically libertine.

Why do we have letters from both parties, instead of just one side of the
correspondence? If Wilson intended to blackmail Sunderland, then

keeping copies of his own letters is just what he would have done. And blackmail would certainly account for his conspicuous wealth, even more than being a kept man. It is not difficult to imagine Sunderland arranging for Wilson's murder when the latter's demands grew too large. A secret man-mistress is one thing, but someone as conspicuous as the Beau was bound to lead to scandal.

According to the letters, the first meeting between Beau Wilson and his Nobleman took place 'behind Flamstead's House' in Greenwich Park (the Royal Observatory, built for Flamsteed, the first Astronomer Royal, in 1675), but later meetings were more private. In 1693/94 at the time of these letters, Sunderland was 20 years old and Wilson was a year or two older than him. Passion and money were commingled in the affair, as shown by the third letter addressed to Mr Wilson:

> I had not above a hundred Pieces by me when I receiv'd yours, which made me send, swift as the Minutes, to the Bank to fetch this. I would have my *Willy* believe, I am never so delighted, as when I am doing that which may convince him, how very dear he is to his nown Love: Then come away, the Bath is ready, that I may Wrestle with it, and pit it, and pat it, and — it; and then for cooler Sport, devour it with greedy Kisses; for *Venus*, and all the *Poet's* Wenches are but dirty Dowdies to thee.
>
> Put on the *Brussels* Head and *Indian* Atlas I sent yesterday.

So Wilson was a type of the 'ingling Pyander', even to the extent of putting on a woman's Brussels lace headdress and Indian silk gown to satisfy his client. While keeping a later assignation, Wilson was carried off by a crew of ruffians, while still in his female dress, and 'a Fellow who had discover'd my Visits to you, endeavour'd, first with flattering Means, and then by bullying me with a Pistol at my Breast, to make me reveal what those private Meetings between us meant.' But Wilson promised him money and implied that 'a certain Great Lady who knows all her Actions are back'd by a superiour Power, had a Hand in it', and he asks his lord to help him make this story more feasible. The lord doats on 'my dearest Boy' and is obsessed by an 'unruly Passion' for him. Wilson spends some time in the country recovering from some illness, and misunderstandings arise. Wilson returns, and goes to the theatre, where 'sometime to disguise my secret affection, I survey Beauty with as much seeming Delight as other Men.' But there he discovers his lord with a mistress and flies into a jealous rage. The lord protests that he has taken a wench 'to stop some good natur'd Reflections I found made on my Indifference that way. But thou alone art every, and all the Delight my greedy Soul covets.' 'When I have Thee in my Arms, thou shalt see how I despise all the Pleasures that changeling Sex can give compared to one Touch of thine.'

Sunderland in turn becomes jealous of Wilson, whom he sees being slobbered with kisses from another man named G—n, and he accuses Wilson of behaving like a Harlot in 'the Trade' that Sunderland 'taught' him. Wilson protests he is innocent of infidelity, and that if he ever ceases to be grateful to the lord, may the world 'hate, despise, and brand me, for the most villanous of all that black and loathsome Herd you have already rank'd me with.' Presumably Sunderland has taught Wilson the ropes of homosexual prostitution, and introduced him to a circle of sodomites. In one of the letters, Wilson makes a veiled threat of blackmail: 'remember, it is a Crime you first descended to encourage me in.' Several complete sentences in letters from the lord are deemed by the editor to be too obscene to be published and are omitted, but other passages in Sunderland's letters to Wilson make their relationship clear: 'for one melting Extasy, thou alone can'st give. . . . D—n this confounded Hurry of Business, which has debarr'd me of Thee these five Days, and forced me last Night to make use of my Pillow which was as insipid as a —.'

The letters come to an abrupt end (as did Wilson's life), but the background is explained by the writer of the 'Observations'. He says that society was conspiring to find out where Wilson got his money from, so 'a Certain Late Nobleman' (i.e. Sunderland) and Wilson spread a rumour that there was an intrigue between Wilson and Elizabeth Villiers, sister of the first Earl of Jersey (afterwards Countess of Orkney), mistress of William III. When she heard this rumour, she hired spies to search out the truth, led by 'Mr L—' or 'Johnasco' (i.e. 26-year-old John Law). He and his assistants discovered that Wilson very regularly took a chair around 10.00pm to a private house near Hyde Park Corner, which he entered with his own key, and from which he returned home about 5.00am the next day. This house was kept by a woman who advertised lodgings, but when Law and his assistants tried to take rooms she refused, and they concluded that her establishment was a front.

Mrs Villiers was herself a great intrigante, and she told her agents not to give up. Eventually they discovered that this house had a back passage, and whenever Wilson entered at the front door, about 45 minutes later a woman left by the back door, got into a chair, and went to the Lord's house, where she stayed for three or four hours. Sunderland's house was in Piccadilly, east of Burlington House, just a short drive down the road from Hyde Park Corner (in 1707 he would buy the house right next to Burlington House, on the site now occupied by the Albany, and build his magnificent Sunderland House with its five-room library, but the Dowager Lady Sunderland probably still lived in the former residence next door). In due course the mysterious lady returned by the back passage to the house at Hyde Park Corner, and Mr Wilson issued from the front door shortly afterwards. One night Law and his men laid in wait and arrested the 'lady' in her journey; Wilson was revealed, and he paid them money to keep quiet. Law readily shifted his loyalty to Wilson and his gold, and to further confuse matters, they (perhaps with Sunderland's help) devised a counter plot which persuaded Mrs Villiers that Wilson was conducting an affair with the young daughter of Sunderland's French Steward. She laughed at the intrigue and gave up her efforts at further discovery. So by the end of the intrigue, as explained by our editor, John Law is in the pay of Wilson and Sunderland, and I would speculate that he may have attempted to blackmail both of them.

To leave speculation and return to documented fact: there was a quarrel between Law and Wilson, and a heated exchange of letters between them. The court dismissed as nonsense the claim that Wilson had taken his sister from a lodging house in which Law's mistress resided, thereby casting aspersion upon the latter's virtue by suggesting that the house in question was a brothel. In the event, one day Law forced a quarrel with Wilson as he was drinking with his friend Captain Wightman at the Fountain Inn in the Strand; Wightman and Wilson left the tavern and got into a carriage; Law followed, and stopped the carriage in Bloomsbury Square; Wilson alighted and drew his sword; Law drew his sword and killed Wilson with the first thrust.

Some accounts described this as a duel, but it was in fact a premeditated assault, and unfairly fought, without any of the niceties of a formal duel. The jury convicted Law of murder. He was sentenced to death at the Old Bailey on 20 April 1694.[10] The sentence was commuted to a fine, but Wilson's family appealed that decision; while awaiting the outcome, Law filed through the bars of his prison window and fled abroad. In a book published in 1708 there was speculation that Wilson was secretly supported by Villiers, and when he became too acquisitive she arranged his murder and subsequently helped Law to escape from prison.[11] This is more likely true if we substitute Sunderland for Villiers.

Law worked for a while as an officer of the Bank of Amsterdam, then roamed the Continent, gambling and trying to persuade European powers to adopt his financial projects for state banking and paper money. With the help of the Duke of Orleans he founded the first bank in France, which was very successful, and established the preeminence of paper money over metallic, resulting in the expansion of French industry by his system of credit. In due course he controlled all the non-European trade of France and became a famous fiscal administrator and financial theorist; even today his theories of money supply are given serious study. But his plans for the Mississippi Scheme collapsed in 1720, ruining the economy of France. He died in relative poverty in Venice in 1729. John Law was on familiar terms with many of the Scottish lords, and he probably knew his fellow Scotsman Lord Ross, so perhaps Lord Ross heard the story about Sunderland direct from John Law.

Sunderland was a connoisseur of the arts, an avid bibliophile and a great patron to young scholars, and by 1699 he had assembled a large collection of rare books. He came of age in January 1694/5 and married the great heiress Lady Arabella Cavendish, worth £25,000, who is probably the mistress of whom Wilson was jealous in the letters. In another copy of the *Love-Letters* in the British Library, at shelfmark C.115.d.15, which bears the ownership signature of Charles Kirkpatrick Sharp (1781–1851), a Scottish historian who may have collected this book because of his interest in his compatriot John Law, there is a handwritten note doubting the authenti-city of the letters because they contain no allusion to Sunderland's marriage. But the letters would have been written shortly before Wilson's murder in April 1694, and Sunderland did not marry until January 1694/5, that is, January 1695 in the new-style calendar, nearly ten months after Wilson's death. On the back end-paper of this copy is another note, presumably by Sharp, speculating that the nobleman might have been the first Earl of Portland, 'who it is alluded obtained his honours in consequence of being one of K. Williams Pathics . . . the letters however are not like those of a foreigner and I am not aware either that Bentinck could read write or speak English fluently or grammatically.' The Lord could not have been Bentinck, for he died in 1709, and would not have been called 'late deceased' when the letters were published in 1723.

Lady Arabella died in 1698, and though Sunderland did not wish to remarry, his father forced him to marry another great heiress Lady Anne Churchill, worth £20,000, in 1699, daughter of the Duke of Marlborough.[12] This marriage was one of the major political alliances of the century, incidentally creating a line of descent which would lead to Winston Churchill and Diana, Princess of Wales. He married for a third time in 1717, another great heiress Judith Tichborne, from whom he separated in 1720. A man of fiery passions and an ultra Whig, Sunderland was regarded as a great political intriguer, and he held much power at court. In 1718 he became First Lord of the Treasury (i.e. the Prime Minister). In 1720 he formed the South Sea Company, using Law's Mississippi Scheme as a model, and he was held guilty for the collapse of this bubble in 1721, which ruined the British economy. The business of Parliament during 1721 to 1722 was almost wholly occupied with unravelling this crisis and laying the guilt at the doors of the South Sea Directors, whose estates were threatened with confiscation, and some of whom were eventually imprisoned. Sunderland repeatedly had to defend himself against charges of conspiring, first, to make a great deal of money from the affair, and, second, of deliberately destabilising the nation in order to support the Jacobite cause.[13]

We now come to the last document which supports the belief that Sunderland quite literally established a sodomitical club in which transvestism played a significant role, and which was frequented by a circle of sodomites from the middle echelons of the government. In 1721 a political journalist under the name of Britannicus published *The Conspirators: Or, The Case of Catiline*, with a dedicatory preface to The Right Honourable The Earl of S— d. Sunderland was immediately recognised in the character of Catiline, and his conspirators were recognised as the Directors of the South Sea Company. The bribery, corruption, and political sins of the conspirators are catalogued, but what stands out is the detailed charge of homosexuality brought against them. Sunderland and his Directors are characterised as a troupe of eunuchs who dress in women's clothes and promote all effeminate and sodomitical tastes in order to weaken the nation. Catiline was the greatest sodomite amongst them: he 'married several times, but chiefly, as People suspected, for the Convenience of strengthening himself by Alliances with Great Men, rather than out of any Affection for the Ladies.' Sunderland's string of heiresses was clearly being alluded to, but his real tastes are revealed: 'For if we may believe some Authors, he had a most unnatural Tast in his Gallantries: And in those Hours when he gave a Loose to Love, the Women were wholly excluded from his Embraces. . . . 'Tis certain, however odd and unnatural his Lewdness was, (yet it was a notorious Practise among some great Men of that Age) and some of his Ganymedes were pamper'd and supported at a high Rate at his Expence.'[14]

It is likely that Beau Wilson was intended to be seen as one of his Ganymedes. The character of Cornelius seems to be modelled upon Captain Wilson: an army officer of mean birth full of pride, vanity and ostentation, who 'generally wore his Vest richer than any of the Patricians' in order to impress the vulgar and to obscure his mean origins. Sunderland laid on pleasures for his conspirators: 'Catiline was publick and preposterous in this Sort of Gallantries: Nor was he alone or singular in the Practice of it. For the Pathicks, and Cinaedi, began to be in the greatest Request in those Times, and to be look'd upon as the fine Gentlemen of the Age. Of these, Numbers resorted to Catiline's House, and found Entertainment, who were publickly reported not to have any regard to their Modesty.'[15] This was the substance of Lord Ross's accusation.

Catiline's cunning and great intriguing, plus his medium stature, inclination to corpulence, and 'fixt and settled Sowreness in his Face' were recognised as descriptions of Sunderland, and the printer of the pamphlet (Mist, who printed the *Weekly Journal*) was imprisoned for libel, though the publisher (named as Peele) absconded, and the author (named as Thomas Gordon) 'kept out of the way'; the pamphlet went through at least eight editions, and it was loudly denounced in Parliament.[16] It was not uncommon to slyly hint that one's political enemy was homosexual, but never before had such an accusation been so specific and alleged at such length.

Sunderland was forced to resign as Prime Minister in favour of Sir Robert Walpole, but he remained First Gentleman of the Bedchamber and continued to have great influence upon George I. The national crisis gathered momentum and was exacerbated when John Law suddenly returned to England in November 1721, and was granted a royal pardon for the murder of Beau Wilson.[17] Then, at the very height of the crisis, on 19 April 1722 Sunderland was found dead, at the age of only 47. It was believed he had poisoned himself, and an autopsy was ordered, which published its findings of pleurisy in the left lung, a polyp in the heart, and an inflamed kidney, in a vain effort to remove the suspicion of suicide.[18] The court was more than disconcerted by this unexpected event, and the government was thrown into a panic, for Sunderland was the greatest intriguer of his day and there were fears about what might come to light; the ministers ordered that the seals of his papers be broken and they were examined, and no doubt certain revelations were prevented thereby.

Many pieces of this puzzle seem to fit together, though ultimately there is no real proof. Why did John Law return to London in 1721? Perhaps he wished to exploit the moment when Sunderland was at his weakest, and perhaps he threatened to expose him as a sodomite unless he obtained the king's pardon for his murder of Wilson, which Sunderland accomplished. But Sunderland realised that his crimes were coming home to roost, so he killed himself rather than face the ignominy of moral as well as political ruin. Why were the Love Letters kept for 29 years without being published? Because Sunderland was a powerful man whose retribution was something to fear. Why were they published in 1723? Because Sunderland was now dead, and under British law the dead cannot be libelled, and one cannot be imprisoned for slandering the dead. Who published them? Almost certainly Thomas Gordon, revealed as Britannicus and the author of *The Case of Catiline* when a warrant was issued for his arrest in 1721. Gordon was also the author of *Francis, Lord Bacon: Or, the Case of Private and National Corruption*, 'Address'd to all South-Sea Directors', which went through several editions in 1721. The printer's decorative border surrounding the letter 'I' beginning the Preface to this book is identical to the same border containing the letter 'I' beginning the Observations in *Love-Letters*. Gordon probably also wrote *A Collection of the proceedings in the House of Commons Against the Lord Verulam*, 1721, also 'Address'd to all South-Sea Directors', in which the decorative portrait in a cartouche flanked by winged cupids in a rectangle at the beginning, is identical to the decorative head-piece at the beginning of the first letter in *Love-Letters*. The printer's devices for all three books come from the same store. Gordon's colleague was John Trenchard, a political writer with an independent income, who employed Gordon as his amanuensis from 1719. The two men grew to be great friends, and Gordon married Trenchard's widow, and was taken into Walpole's pay. I would speculate that the letters were in Trenchard's possession, and passed to Gordon when Trenchard died — significantly in the year 1723. The 'deceased' mentioned in the Preface may actually be Trenchard rather than Sunderland: 'the Originals were found in the Cabinet of the Deceas'd, which had pass'd thro' some Hands, before the private Drawer, the Lodgment of this Scene of Guilt, was discover'd. How, or by what Means this was done, or from what Hand they are made publick, is a Point too tender and consequential to relate.' The 'too tender and consequential' point must relate to something in Gordon's own domestic affairs, and it may well be the death of his closest friend and marriage to his widow. But I have no clues as to how the letters passed from Captain Wightman (who must have been the man to whom Wilson gave his key, and who would have concealed them and pretended to find only a remedy for toothache) to Trenchard, or who other intermediaries may have been.

Whether or not the letters are genuine, the author of the observations upon them clearly intended the reader to recognise Sunderland as 'a Certain Late Nobleman'. The time was ripe to exploit the Catiline controversy and the mystery of Sunderland's death, even if the only motivation was to make some money from publishing them. But if the letters were not genuine, it hardly makes sense for anyone to have taken such great pains to concoct such a hoax, for it would lead nowhere and achieve nothing that had not already been achieved — Sunderland was already dead and discredited, and the Walpole faction was firmly in power. If it is difficult to understand why letters should be published after a gap of 29 years, it is even more difficult to understand why someone should seize upon such an old story that most people had forgotten. If one was going to fabricate a story, it is strange to have chosen an intrigue that until then was believed to be thoroughly heterosexual. Gordon was not the kind of man to set for himself such an uphill struggle.

One last piece of circumstantial evidence: Sunderland arranged for his daughter Lady Anne to marry William, Viscount Bateman, whom Horace Walpole revealed to be homosexual ('Another Bateman shall debauch the boys'), and who was to be forcefully 'separated from his wife, by her brother Charles Spencer Duke of Marlborough, for his amours of this sort.'[19]

(3) Captain Rigby

During the late 1690s there were many anti-Williamite and anti-Jesuitical tracts attacking the court for popery, absolutism and sodomy; one satirist saw little change 'to find old Popery / Turn'd out and replaced by Allmighty Sodomy / But here content with our own homely joys, / We had no relish of the fair fac'd Boys. / Till you came in and with your Reformation, / Turn'd all things Arsy Versy in the nation.'[20] This sort of debauchery was something that had to be rooted out, particularly among the lower classes. To accomplish this, the Societies for Reformation of Manners were formed in Tower Hamlets in 1690, with their primary goal being the suppression of bawdy houses and profanity. A network of moral guardians was set up, with four stewards in each ward of the city of London, two for each parish, and a committee, whose business it was to gather the names and addresses of offenders against morality, and to keep minutes of their misdeeds. By 1699 there were nine such societies, and by 1701 there were nearly 20 in London, plus others in the provinces, all corresponding with one another and gathering information and arranging for prosecutions.

As early as 1700 the Reformers were being satirised as parasites and mercenaries: 'A Modern Reformer of Vice; Or, A Reforming Constable, Is a Man most commonly of a very Scandalous Necessity, who has no way left, but *Pimp* like, to Live upon other Peoples *Debaucheries*. Every Night he goes to Bed, he prays heartily that the World may grow more *Wicked*; for one and the same Interest serves him and the Devil. . . . He searches a *Bawdy-* house, as a *Church*-Warden does an *Ale*-house, not to punish *Vice*, but to get Money.'[21] By 1710 the Informer had become the hated symbol of the Reformers. The Society for the Promotion of Christian Knowledge (SPCK) was formed at the same time, and its members helped to distribute guidelines on the giving of information to magistrates, with specimen forms and advice on how to present prosecutions. King William himself declared 'We most earnestly desire and shall endeavour a general reformation of manners', and there followed several great waves of enthusiasm for moral regeneration, and a veritable army of informers.[22]

Their first homosexual victim was Captain Edward Rigby. Early in 1698 he was tried for sodomy at a court-martial, but acquitted. But Thomas Bray, a member of the Society for Reformation of Manners, believed him to be guilty, and worked out a plan with the constabulary to entrap him, using as bait a servant who had previously been approached by Rigby (whose master Rev. Charles Coates was a parishioner of Bray).[23] William Minton, age 19, had previously met Rigby in St James's Park to see the fireworks on the 5th of November (Guy Fawkes Night), 1698, where Rigby 'took him by the hand, and squeez'd it; put his Privy Member Erected into Minton's Hand; kist him, and put his Tongue into Minton's Mouth.'[24] A meeting was arranged for the following Monday at the George Tavern in Pall Mall. When Rigby joined Minton in the private back room, No. 4, on the day, little did he know that in the adjoining room had been stationed a clerk of the court, a constable, and two assistants, who were ready to burst in upon him as soon as they heard Minton shout the agreed code word 'Westminster!'

Rigby told Minton he 'had raised his Lust to the highest degree', to the point that he had already ejaculated in his breeches but had regained sufficient firmness to proceed further. He sat on Minton's lap, began kissing him and asked 'if he should F— him.' When Minton said only women were fit for that sport, and asked how could he do it with a man, Rigby said 'I'le show you, for it's no more than was done in our Fore fathers time.' To further incite him, Rigby asserted 'That the French King did it, and the Czar of Muscovy made Alexander, a Carpenter, a Prince for that purpose, and affirmed, He had seen the Czar of Muscovy through a hole at Sea, lye with Prince Alexander.' Rigby must have observed this incident during Peter the Great's visit to England from 11 January through 21 April 1698, aboard the royal yacht, or perhaps during Peter's two month stay in Deptford to examine the shipyards, where he caroused with the English sailors, or perhaps in the course of the sham naval battle that was staged for Peter's entertainment on a visit to Portsmouth.

Peter hired John Evelyn's house at Says Court in Deptford for his stay, and Evelyn's servant wrote to say that the house was 'full of people, and right nasty';[25] the Russians behaved in a brutish fashion, and the house was wrecked and in need of repair when they departed. Captain Rigby might well have had some official role to play during this state visit of a monarch whose obsession was the building of ships. Rigby had been made captain of the *Mermaid* fireship in 1693, and from 1695 until his arrest he commanded the *Dragon*, a 40 gun man-of-war in the squadron under Commodore Moody; he had taken two valuable prizes in the Mediterranean, and was an officer of some small fame. The 26-year-old Czar was accompanied on this trip by Alexander Danilovich Menshikov, the handsome lad picked up in the slums of Moscow, possibly as a prostitute, who had become his constant companion, and who was to become the virtual ruler of Russia during Catherine's brief reign, and then Prince Regent during the reign of Peter's grandson. Peter sailed back to Europe on the *Royal Transport*, a gift from King William.

Rigby's claim about Louis XIV may have been misunderstood by Minton; perhaps Rigby had referred to the King's notoriously homosexual younger brother Philippe, Duc d'Orleans. Hearsay or no, even in the seventeenth century gay men were developing a sense of identity supported by reference to great men and to earlier periods of history, probably ancient Greece. By 'our Fore fathers' Rigby might just possibly be referring to a gay subculture of the very recent past (which is a tantalising theory), but he is more likely referring to classical history. He may even have known the satire *A Dialogue Concerning Women* published in 1691, in which there were learned references to Socrates' love for Alcibiades, Plato's love for the boy Aster, and defences of homosexuality in the works of Plutarch, Lucian, Anacreon, Tibullus, Martial, as well as travellers' reports on homosexuality in Turkey, Italy, and Spain.[26] Rigby may well have conceived of himself as one of the homosexual military heroes of antiquity.

In due course Rigby pulled down Minton's breeches, 'put his Finger to Mintons Fundament, and applied his Body close to Mintons', whereupon Minton reached round and took hold of Rigby's privy member and exclaimed loudly for those in the next room, 'I have now discovered your base Inclinations, I will expose you to the World, to put a stop to these Crimes.' Minton ran towards the door, Rigby pulled his sword to stop him, Minton stamped his feet and cried out for assistance. At the sound of that fateful word 'Westminster!' the four officers rushed in and seized Rigby, who vainly proffered some money to be set free.

At his trial in December, Rigby pleaded neither Guilty nor Not Guilty, but 'demurred' to the indictment for attempted sodomy, on the understanding that such a plea would avoid public disclosure. But he was misled by his lawyer; this was tantamount to pleading guilty, and the evidence was read out to the court, without any opportunity for cross examination or character witnesses. He was convicted, and sentenced to stand in the pillories near the George Tavern in Pall Mall, in Charing Cross, and in Temple Bar (from 11.00am to 1.00pm each day), to pay £1,000 fine, and to spend one year in prison.

A 'pillory broadside' called *The Women's Complaint to Venus* was printed, intended to be distributed to the crowds while he stood in the pillory; the ballad is humorous enough to be quoted in full:

> *How happy were good English Faces*
> *Till Mounsieur from France*
> *Taught Pego [the penis] a Dance*
> *To the tune of old Sodom's Embraces.*
>
> *But now we are quite out of Fashion:*
> *Poor Whores may be Nuns*
> *Since Men turn their Guns*
> *And vent on each other their passion.*

In the Raign of Good Charles *the Second*
  Full many a Jade
  A Lady was made
And the Issue Right Noble was reckon'd:

But now we find to our Sorrow
  We are overrun
  By Sparks of the Bum
And peers of the Land of Gommorah.

The Beaus too, whom most we rely'd on
  At Night make a punk
  Of him that's first drunk
Tho' unfit for the Sport as John Dryden.

The Souldiers, whom next we put trust in,
  No widdow can tame
  Or virgin reclaim
But at the wrong Place will be thrusting.

Fair Venus, thou Goddess of Beauty,
  Receive our Complaint.
  Make Rigby Recant
And the Souldiers henceforth do their duty.

Lotteries were common at this time, and Rigby is referred to in the satirical advertisement published to promote a lottery called 'The Ladies Invention'. One of the gentlemen who is described as buying a ticket for this lottery is caricatured as if he were a ship: 'A *Dutch Merchant* of the *Italian* humour, known by name of the *Queen of Sheba*, frightened over to *Germany* upon Capt. *Rigby's* fate, put in Forty shillings just before his departure, and what Benefits arise are to be spent in drinking his Health, amongst all the handsom Prentices that frequent *Paul's* on a *Sunday* Afternoon.'[27] This may well have been aimed at a real Dutchman, for the bookseller, printer, and publisher of this lottery were arrested and found guilty of libelling a host of gentlemen, and were sent to Newgate prison.[28]

Another man was indicted for aiding, abetting, and assisting Rigby in his sodomitical attempts, and was therefore not allowed to speak in Rigby's defence; but he was not named at Rigby's trial, and I have not discovered his fate with any certainty.[29] He probably was Edward FitzGerald, one of two men with the same name, both of whom accused William Tipping, a clergyman, of suborning them to falsely charge Rigby with sodomising them. Tipping was indicted for this conspiracy in July 1699, but the

FitzGeralds' charge was not believed, and the Grand Jury threw out the bill, with directions to seek out the two FitzGeralds to try them for perjury.[30] Tipping was probably another Reforming clergyman and friend of Bray, who was overzealous in building a case against Rigby.

Rigby in fact did not serve his sentence. Upon conviction, he fled to France, where he became a Roman Catholic and entered the enemy's service. In 1711 the French man-of-war the *Toulouse* was sighted by two English ships that were returning to Port Mahon in the Mediterranean. They engaged and captured her, and towed the badly damaged ship into port. The 'second captain' of the *Toulouse* turned out to be none other than Edward Rigby. At Port Mahon the resourceful Captain Rigby found means to get on board a Genoese ship lying at anchor in the harbour, and by that means he again escaped to France. He was highly regarded in France for his marine skills, and very well paid, though his pleasures were said to be expensive.[31]

In May 1699 William Bentinck, Earl of Portland, resigned all his offices including his place as First Lord of the Bedchamber, and went to Holland.[32] No public explanation was given; possibly he feared being implicated in the Rigby affair. Reasonable evidence has been gathered to confirm the existence of a gay court circle, consisting of more than a dozen members including King William, Charles Talbot, Duke of Shrewsbury (who resigned his seals as Secretary of State in January 1697/8), Bentinck, Van Keppel (the 20-year-old page who accompanied William to England and eventually received the title of Earl of Albemarle), Blathwayte, Wentworth, Ross, Roberts, Villiers, Cornwall, and Queen Mary and Frances Apsley.[33] In 1698 the Duchesse d'Orleans wrote to a friend that 'nothing is more ordinary in England than this unnatural vice',[34] and she was amused by the description of the English court as *un château de derriére*.[35] William was widely believed to belong to the sodomitical brotherhood, but he defended his fondness for one of his courtiers: 'it seems to me a most extraordinary thing that one may not feel regard and affection for a young man without its being criminal.'[36] Later, Queen Anne was openly accused by Sarah Churchill, Duchess of Marlborough, of 'having noe inclination for any but one's own sex' (not that this prevented her from bearing seventeen children). Anne was called 'the squire queen', and she devoted all her attention to her servant Abigail Masham (cousin of Sarah Churchill), who dressed her hair and nursed her.[37]

(4) Reformation of Manners

But of course the Reforming Societies dared not attack the aristocracy, at least not directly. The trial of Mervyn Touchet, Earl of Castlehaven, previously discussed, which occurred in 1631, was published in full in a tract printed in 1699. This old story was publicised partly to capitalise on the interest aroused by the Rigby affair (which was referred to in its preface), and partly to cast aspersions upon the nobility. In the same year in another tract called *The Sodomites Shame and Doom*, the Societies for Reformation of Manners threatened to reveal more lowly sodomites' 'places of abode' and 'scandalous haunts' if they do not reform — and this is precisely what happened.

By carrying out their threat, the Societies for the first time revealed the gay subculture, to modern historians as well as to contemporaries. Information was given, and in Windsor a 'gang' of sodomites was rounded up and committed to Newgate; they had formed a 'beast-like confederacy among themselves for exercising this unnatural offence'.[38] In August 1699, at the Kingston Assizes, 'a nonjuring parson who taught school' was convicted of attempted sodomy, fined £100, and sentenced to stand in the pillory.[39] In September 1699 Monsieur Fournier, a French engineer in the Ordinance, was indicted for sodomy; the trial lasted for a considerable time, but the evidence produced against him was rejected as being malicious, and he was honourably acquitted.[40] Later that same month, 'an eminent Citizen, who being on the point of consummating a great Marriage, was by the Lord Mayor committed for indeavouring to commit the Sin of Sodomy with his Barber's Boy', but the case was not brought to trial.[41]

In 1702 the Reforming Middlesex justices issued an order encouraging justices and constables to prosecute those guilty of moral crimes, for fear of the brimstone of Sodom and Gomorrah;[42] and Lord Chief Justice Colt, the magistrate who had convicted Captain Rigby, ordered the execution of four sodomites at the Maidstone Assizes. The Society for Reformation of Manners bragged about their success in this part of their moral crusade in their annual report for 1703.[43] Their work was cut out for them, according to a ballad of 1703: 'Such cursed Lewdness does infect the Town, / 'Tis a meer Sodom, or Gommorrah grown.'[44]

The movement gathered momentum, and in 1707 there was a veritable pogrom. Eight or nine members of the Society acted as *agents provocateurs* and set about the systematic entrapment of homosexuals, and in October 1707 at least eight gay men were convicted on the basis of their evidence. Thomas Lane, a Foot Soldier, was standing on London Bridge, and went up to Mr Hemmings (one of the Society's agents), 'and pulling out his

Nakedness offer'd to put it into his Hand, and withal unbutton'd the Evidences Breeches, and put his Hand in there'; Hemmings later returned with Mr Baker, another agent, and they apprehended Lane when he approached them again, separately. Also on London Bridge, Charles Marriot similarly went up to Hemmings, and later his co-agent Robert Bokins, 'pulled out his nakedness, and unbuttoned their breeches', and said 'a Gentleman in black' had offered to commit sodomy with him one week previous.

The Royal Exchange was the main cruising ground. There William Huggins, a porter carrying coffee into Leadenhall Street, approached Hemmings and another agent Thomas Jones, separately, while they were 'walking upon Change, with design to detect such wicked Persons'. Also at the Exchange, John Williams approached Thomas Jones and John Jones, separately, and 'had his Nakedness out, which he offer'd to put into their hands'; he confessed 'he had first been seduc'd to that Practice, by one Fish, in May-Fair last.' Also caught soliciting on the Exchange were Paul Booth, Benjamin Butler, John Blithe, and James Brooke — all on virtually identical evidence. All the men confessed at their initial examination, but Brooke was the only one to plead guilty at the actual trial; all were convicted.[45]

The Royal Exchange had been publicly identified as a gay cruising ground as early as 1700. It was full of traders and hawkers, fruit sellers, chemists, and stalls to buy and eat fruit or confectionery and drink coffee. The pillars of the arcade were pasted over with advertisements, mostly for quack nostrums, and strolling up and down were tough types called Water Rats offering themselves for casual work in the dockyards, and homosexuals attracted by rough trade: 'We then proceeded and went on to the *Change*, turn'd to the Right, and Jostled in amongst a parcel of Swarthy Buggerantoes, Preternatural Fornicators, as my Friend call'd them, who would Ogle a Handsome Young Man with as much Lust, as a True-bred English Whoremaster would gaze upon a Beautiful Virgin.'[46]

John Dunton in *The He-Strumpets: A Satyr on the Sodomite Club*, which was published in 1707,[47] claims that sodomy was becoming popular because so many female prostitutes were infected by the clap:

> *Lewd Cracks repent, for 'tis the News,*
> *Your Tails have burnt so many Beaus,*
> *That now He-Whores are come in Use.*
> *Yes Jilts! 'tis prov'd, and must be said,*
> *Your Tails are grown so lewd and bad,*
> *That now* Mens Tails *have all the Trade.*

. . . .

All Cracks are found so full of Ails,
A New Society *prevails,*
Call'd S[o]d[om]ites; *Men worse than Goats,*
Who dress themselves in Petticoats,
To Whore as O[s]born *did with* O[a]tes.

He repeatedly asserts that these sodomites are members of a gang, club
and society, that there are exactly 43 members of the gang, that they 'Do
Ply (that's Whore) near the Exchange', and that 'there's a Club hard by the
Stocks*, / Where Men give unto Men the Pox' (*Stocks-Market). He calls
them He-Strumpets and He-Whores who indulge in He-Lechery and He-
Lust and address one another as '*Sukey*, (for so 'tis said you greet / The
Men you pick up in the Street).' He refers to an incident in which at least
40 sodomites were arrested, three of whom hanged themselves in the
Compter including one named Jones; he also names 'Ber—den' and
Jermain, Clerk of St Dunstan's in the East, who cut his throat with a razor.

Another broadside called *The Women Hater's Lamentation* also publicised the raids of 1707, and illustrated several men who cut their own
throats or hanged themselves while awaiting trial, including Mr Gant,
woollen draper, and Mr Jermain:

A Hundred more we hear,
    Did to this Club belong,
But now they scatter'd are,
    For this has broke the Gang.

Shop-keepers some there were,
    And Men of good repute,
Each vow'd a Batchelor,
    Unnat'ral Lust pursu'd.[48]

Zealous members of the Society had entrapped nearly 100 sodomites that
year, though not all of them were brought to trial. Reformers such as Rev.
Bray were obsessed with sodomy, which he called 'an evil force invading
our land' in the sermon he preached at St Mary's Le Bow before the Society
for Reformation of Manners on 27 December 1708.[49] Through the efforts
of Bray's Society, in 1709 nine sodomites were apprehended at a brandy-
shop near 'German Street', and brought to the Gatehouse of St James's.
Jermyn Street runs parallel to Piccadilly, a few minutes' walk from
Sunderland House; perhaps this brandy shop was the first sodomitical
house set up by the Earl of Sunderland. Officers were sent in search of the
men who frequented it, but only two were committed to Newgate, the
keeper of the shop and 'a Foot-Boy belonging to his Grace the Duke of

O—' (probably James Butler, second Duke of Ormonde, who was impeached in 1715). Skelthorp, a soldier executed the previous year, 'gave a private Intimation of some of them, and the Houses they met at.' Despite the example made of sodomites in the previous year, 'several Knots, and Gangs of them still Associate themselves together.'[50] Nevertheless the Society for Reformation of Manners at its 15th annual meeting in 1710 could boast that by its means 'our streets have been very much cleansed from the lewd night-walkers and most detestable sodomites.'[51]

In 1720 the Society was strong enough to cause prostitutes to be publicly whipped by the police,[52] and they were preparing themselves for their second major onslaught upon the gay subculture. Scapegoats were necessary at a time of political crisis. The South Sea Bubble had burst, and the Directors of the Company were being attacked as a company of sodomites. A hellish conspiracy by the Earl of Sunderland was being exposed in the newspapers: 'we are ruin'd by *Footmen, Pimps, PATHICKS, Parasites, Bawds, Whores.'*[53] On 28 April 1721 the King received information that there existed certain scandalous clubs and societies in London where young people met to blaspheme and corrupt each other's morals, and a few days afterwards the newspapers reported the discovery of notorious assemblies of persons of figure who had formed the Hell Fire Club to commit shocking practices and make mock of religion. It was suspected that the Directors of the South Sea Company were in charge of these clubs. A Bill was put forward in Parliament to re-enact William III's statute for the suppression of blasphemy and profaneness, but Sunderland was among those who voted against the bill and caused it to be dropped.[54]

The Societies for Reformation of Manners were themselves responsible for stimulating the growth of the gay subculture, which coalesced under the pressures of this reforming environment. The publicity given to homosexuality by the Societies must have made gay men aware of the cruising grounds where they could pick one another up. The attempt to suppress vice actually may have facilitated the expression of homosexuality. And the pressure of persecution may have persuaded gay men that it would be in their interest to form associations to meet in less public places. Self-preservation is a powerful impetus to the formation of a subculture.

---

1. *The Women-Hater's Lamentation*, a broadside printed in 1707, following raids at which some 40 sodomites were arrested. Two mollies kissing one another (centre), one cutting his own throat and one hanging himself (left) and one being cut down (right).

The Women-Hater's Lamentation:

OR

A New Copy of Verfes on the Fatal End of Mr. *Grant*, a Woollen-Draper, and two others that Cut their Throats or Hang'd themfelves in the *Counter*; with the Difcovery of near Hundred more that are Accufed for unnatural difpifing the *Fair Sex*, and Intriguing with one another.

To the Tune of, *Ye pretty Sailors all.*

I.
YE injur'd *Females* fee
  Juftice without the Laws,
Seeing the Injury,
  Has thus reveng'd your Caufe.

II.
For thofe that are fo blind,
  Your Beauties to defpife,
And flight your Charms, will find
  Such Fate will always rife.

III.
Of all the Crimes that Men
  Through wicked Minds do act,
There is not one of them
  Equals this Brutal Fact.

IV.
Nature they lay afide,
  To gratifie their Luft;
Women they hate befide,
  Therefore their Fate was juft.

V.
Ye *Women-haters* fay,
  What do's your Breafts infpire,
That in a Brutal way,
  You your own Sex admire?

VI.
Woman you difapprove,
  (The chief of Earthly Joys)
Yoh that are deaf to Love,
  And all the Sex defpife.

VII.
But fee the fatal end
  That do's fuch Crimes purfue;
Unnat'ral Deaths attend,
  Unnat'ral Lufts in you.

VIII.
A Crime by Men abhor'd,
  Nor Heaven can abide
Of which, when *Sodom* fhar'd,
  She juftly was deftroy'd.

IX.
But now, the fum to tell,
  (Tho' they plead Innocence)
Thefe by their own Hands fell,
  Accus'd for this Offence.

X.
A Hundred more we hear,
  Did to this Club belong,
But now they fcatter'd are,
  For this has broke the Gang.

XI.
Shop-keepers fome there were,
  And Men of good repute,
Each vow'd a Batchelor,
  Unnat'ral Luft purfu'd.

XII.
Ye *Women-Haters* then,
  Take Warning by their Shame,
Your Brutal Lufts reftrain,
  And own a Nobler Flame.

XIII.
Woman the chiefeft Blifs
  That Heaven e'er beftow'd:
Oh be afham'd of this,
  You're by bafe Luft fubdu'd.

XIV.
This piece of Juftice then
  Has well reveng'd their Caufe,
And fhews unnat'ral Luft
  Is curfs'd without the Laws.

Licenfed according to Order.

LONDON: Printed for *J. Robinfon,* in *Ftteer-Lane,* 1707.

Chapter 3

Mother Clap's Molly House

(1) The Raid

In the preceding chapter we have seen that during the first decade of the eighteenth century there were not only private intrigues and public cruising grounds, but also meetings of groups of men in private houses and the beginning of a network of communication amongst themselves: the emergence of the gay subculture in England. In this chapter we will see how the gay subculture blossomed and fully developed all of its distinguishing features by about 1720, and how its members interact with society at large. The story begins with a raid.

On a Sunday night in February, 1725/6, a squadron of police constables converged upon the molly house kept by Mother Clap in Field Lane, Holborn, tucked away between an arch on one side and the Bunch o'Grapes tavern on the other. All the avenues of escape being blocked, by the early morning hours the rooms had been emptied of 40 homosexual men — 'notorious Sodomites' in the language of the day — who were rounded up and hauled off to Newgate prison to await trial. By the end of the month several more molly houses had been similarly raided, and more mollies imprisoned. None of the men were actually caught *in flagrante delicto* — though a few were discovered with their breeches unbuttoned — and eventually most of them were set free due to lack of evidence. A number of them, however, were fined, imprisoned, and exhibited in the pillory, and three men were subsequently hanged at Tyburn.[1]

Mother (or Margaret) Clap's molly house was nothing out of the ordinary, for molly houses — public houses and alehouses or taverns where homosexual men kept their rendezvous — had existed in London since 1700, and apparently were thriving when they were first described in detail in Ned Ward's *The History of the London Clubs* in 1709.[2] Her house, however, was one of the most popular molly houses during the 1720s, for she catered well for the wishes of her customers. According to the testimony given in the trials, for their greater convenience and entertainment 'she had provided beds in every room of the house', and with such an attraction it is not surprising that 'she had commonly 30 or 40 of such kind of Chaps every Night, but more especially on Sunday Nights.'[3]

The main room was large enough to accommodate dancing and fiddling as occurred in other molly houses — but the flow of spirits was generous, the fire cheerful, and the company convivial. Samuel Stevens, a Reforming constable who became a member of her club by pretending to be the 'husband' of a homosexual informant, reports on his visit on Sunday, 14 November 1725:

> I found between 40 and 50 Men making Love to one another, as they call'd it. Sometimes they would sit on one another's Laps, kissing in a lewd Manner, and using their Hands indecently. Then they would get up, Dance and make Curtsies, and mimick the voices of Women. *O, Fie, Sir! – Pray, Sir. – Dear Sir. Lord, how can you serve me so? – I swear I'll cry out. – You're a wicked Devil. – And you're a bold Face. – Eh ye little dear Toad! Come, buss!–* Then they'd hug, and play, and toy, and go out by Couples into another Room on the same Floor, to be marry'd, as they call'd it.

And what did Mother Clap, presumably heterosexual, and of course a woman, think of such goings on? 'As for Mother Clap, she was present all the Time, except when she went out to fetch Liquors. The Company talk'd all manner of gross and vile Obscenity in her hearing, and she appeared to be wonderfully pleas'd with it.'[4]

Her special room was also a feature of other molly houses; it was sometimes referred to as 'The Marrying Room' or 'The Chapel', and usually contained a large double bed. Though no ordained minister seems to have officiated at the nuptials celebrated therein, in Mother Clap's molly house there was at least a kind of marriage attendant, by the name of Eccleston.[5] He stood guard at the door to guarantee the occupants' privacy if they so desired. Often, however, the couples did not bother to close the door behind them — allowing the others to witness the carnal rite — and as a general rule, 'when they came back they would tell what they had been doing, which in their Dialect they call'd *Marrying*.'[6] Although Eccleston was called a 'pimp', it is not certain that either he or Mother Clap regularly procured male prostitutes for the services of their customers. Unfortunately Eccleston died of old age or gaol fever (at least there is no clear suggestion of foul play) while awaiting trial in Newgate, and we have no particulars of those activities which might have been revealed during his trial.

The portrayal of Mother Clap suggests that she was in the business more for pleasure than for profit. She was fond of joking about the time when a molly named Derwin was brought before Magistrate Sir George Mertins on charges of 'Sodomitical Practices' with a linkboy (a boy who carries a torch to light the street-lamps at night), and how her testimony as to the 'good Character' of Derwin so befuddled Magistrate Mertins that Derwin was freed.[7] From the evident humour wherewith she recounted this incident, one assumes she was more mischievous than mercenary. But of course this had occurred many months before her own honour was to be impugned. In so far as Mother Clap went out to fetch liquor (probably from the Bunch o'Grapes next door), her house — which bore no specific name — was probably a private residence rather than a public inn or tavern. Hints that it may have been specifically organised as a house of prostitution are very slim, and it is likely that she provided for herself simply by letting out rooms, by taking a percentage on the spirits she procured, and perhaps by accepting the occasional gift from a grateful guest.

Mother Clap and her company would have gone unmolested were it not for the jealousy of an embittered homosexual turned informant. He was so helpful in aiding the police to carry out their successful raids that they returned the favour by not prosecuting him and by carefully guarding his identity: he is still known only as 'P—'. He may have been Thomas Phillips, a molly who actually lived at Mother Clap's for two years, but who 'disappeared' after the raid and was never tried; or he may have been a certain P—e mentioned in a satirical poem which was printed in *The London Journal* during the trials. Be this as it may, sometime during October 1724, P— had a quarrel with his lover Mr Harrington (whose first name is also lost). What we can piece together from confusing court testimony (which is scattered throughout several trials since neither P— nor Harrington were themselves tried) is that Harrington revealed to someone that P— was his lover, and that P— when he heard of this betrayal was angry at being revealed as a sodomite, so he proceeded to revenge himself by spreading the (true) rumour that Harrington was an habitué of a number of molly houses. The rumour got out of hand, that is, it spread outside the confines of the molly subculture and soon P— was contacted by the police. With remarkable alacrity he was either persuaded or coerced by them into becoming an informer.[8]

So by late 1725, P— was leading various constables to all of the London molly houses that he knew of, introducing one or the other of them as his 'husband' so they could be admitted as *bona fide* members of each group. On Wednesday, 17 November for example, P— took constables Joseph

Sellers and William Davison to another molly house, one kept by Thomas Wright in Beech Lane, where there was a very big row because the others had heard that the rumour was out. They called P— a 'Treacherous, blowing-up, mollying-Bitch', and threatened to kill anyone who would betray them. P—, however, was able to mollify them by arguing that it was Harrington who let out the secret in the first place. So they forgave him and kissed him — and kissed the constables too, little suspecting who they were, and little knowing how treacherous P— indeed was.

But P— was not the only informer, and perhaps the greatest villains in the piece were the two hustlers Thomas Newton[9] and Edward Courtney.[10] Both men were rogues long before this, though harsh economic poverty contributed to their becoming queer-bait and *agents provocateurs* for the police.

Thomas Newton, 30 years old, was a hustler in the employment of Thomas Wright, first at his home in Christopher's Alley in Moorfields, later at his own molly house in Beech Lane. According to Newton, Wright 'has often fetch'd me to oblige Company in that way', an indication that the former was a prostitute, although there is no explicit testimony during the trials that money exchanged hands. Beyond this, Newton seems to have been bedded in nearly every molly house in London. Of course no man is black all the way through, and soon after the February raid Newton kindly went to the police station with money to bail out Mother Clap. The source of this money is unknown — perhaps it came from his earnings, perhaps he was returning a favour to a woman who had procured business for him, or perhaps he was acting as a middle-man. But unfortunately he was met at the station by constables Williams and Willis, who 'told me they believed I could give Information; which I promised to do.'

Newton's testimony may be inaccurate as to the actual date when he agreed to become an informer, for he was himself arrested at the end of the month, and it was not until he was set at liberty in March that he became an active informer. The likelihood is that the condition for his release and subsequent immunity from prosecution was his agreement to give evidence to help convict others. Constable Willis testified that the day after Newton was set at liberty he returned to the station and 'made a voluntary Information'; Willis's testimony is transparently designed to rebuff the suspicion that the police may have used unorthodox methods to assemble their case. Williams and Willis were probably members of the Society for Reformation of Manners.

For the most part Newton simply gave testimony concerning those men who had slept with him — testimony which would lead to their imprisonment or death. But the police were overzealous and Newton acted upon occasion as their *agent provocateur* to entrap homosexuals who had not been apprehended in the actual raids. For example, there was a notorious

cruising area in Moorfield Park — near Wright's molly house — that was
called 'The Sodomites' Walk', and when Newton told the police about this
they obtained a warrant for the apprehension of homosexuals in the area.
One night constables Willis and Stevenson followed at a discreet distance
while Newton lured his prey. 'I was no stranger to the Methods they used
in picking one another up. So I takes a Turn that way, and leans over the
Wall. In a little Time a Gentleman passes by, and looks hard at me, and at
a small distance from me, stands up against the Wall, as if he was going to
make Water. Then by Degrees he sidles nearer and nearer to where I
stood, 'till at last he comes close to me. — '*Tis a very fine Night*, says he. *Aye*,
says I, *and so it is*. Then he takes me by the Hand, and after squeezing and
playing with it a little (to which I showed no dislike), he conveys it to his
Breeches, and puts [his penis] into it. I took fast hold, and call'd out to
Willis and Stevenson, who coming up to my Assistance, we carried him to
the Watch house.'

The gentleman so awkwardly apprehended was William Brown, who,
when 'asked . . . why he took such indecent Liberties with Newton, . . . was
not ashamed to answer, *I did it because I thought I knew him, and I think there
is no Crime in making what use I please of my own Body*.' This answer is
strikingly modern in its similarity to the basic principle behind the desired
reforms of laws concerning 'crimes without victims', such as abortion and
homosexuality, but it meant little to an early eighteenth-century court of
law. At the actual trial, in July 1726, Brown's defence was that he was
innocently making water, and that he had been married for 12 or 13 years.
The jury nevertheless found him guilty of attempted sodomy, a misdemeanour, and sentenced him to stand in the pillory at Moorfields, to pay
a fine of ten marks, and to suffer two months' imprisonment.

The other hustler-turned-informant was 18-year-old Edward (Ned)
Courtney, who may have begun plying his trade when he was an alehouse
boy at the Yorkshire Grey tavern in Bloomsbury Market. Eventually he
went to live with Thomas Orme, a silk dyer at the Red Lion in Crown Court
in Knave's Acre, and there performed his services in Orme's private back
rooms. By the time of the raids he was a bondservant to George Whittle
(or Whitle), who was charged with keeping a molly house at the Royal Oak
alehouse at the corner of St James's Square in Pall Mall.

Ned was an habitual rabble-rouser. He had already been sent to
Bridewell Prison on three occasions: once for drunkenly hitting an old
woman when he was an alehouse boy at the Curdigan's Head at Charing
Cross (he was sacked, since the woman was the tavern-keeper's mother);
a second time for stealing goods from Whittle's establishment; and a third
time for disturbing the peace at an unnamed molly house in Covent
Garden. Ned apparently turned informer as a means to spite Whittle, who
had caused him to be arrested for theft. The jury's realisation that this may

have been the motive behind his testimony, eventually led to Whittle's acquittal.

The giving of information also may have been a means for obtaining money, which Ned desperately lacked, and for which he was not above prostituting his own younger brother or extorting his customers. During the time when he was working in a cook's shop, in July 1725, after he left the Yorkshire Grey and before he went to live with Orme, Ned claimed that he let George Kedger bugger him in a back room. Kedger claimed that Ned 'asked me to do it, . . . but I told him I would not. *What*, says he, *am not I handsome enough for ye? That's not the Case*, says I, *but I have got an Injury. That's only a Pretence*, says he, *but if you don't like me, I have got a pretty younger Brother, and I'll fetch him to oblige ye.*'

Kedger again met Ned later at Thomas Orme's, and again claimed that 'Ned solicited me to do the Story, and would fain have had me to have gone into the Necessary-House [outside toilet] with him, for he said he could not rest till he had enjoy'd me. And afterwards, when he was turn'd out of his Place, I met him by chance in a very poor and ragged Condition, and he told me that he had nothing to subsist upon but what he got by such Things. I advised him to leave of[f] that wicked Course of Life; but he said he wanted Money, and Money he would have, by hook or by Crook; and if I would not help him to some he would swear my Life away.' Whether or not Kedger was homosexual — his excuse of an injury implies that he would have slept with Ned otherwise, and he travelled in the regular molly circuit — Ned's credibility as a witness was not above suspicion, and although Kedger at his trial in April 1726 was found guilty and sentenced to death, he was later reprieved.

(2) The Trials

In April 1726 five men were brought to trial. The first to be tried was Gabriel Lawrence, 43 years old, indicted on charges of having sodomised Thomas Newton on 20 July 1725, and of having sodomised P— on 10 November 1725. Newton and constables Stevens and Sellers testified that Lawrence was a frequent visitor at Mother Clap's. Newton specified that Lawrence and his friend Peter Bavidge (who was never caught) often expressed a desire to sleep with him. 'They buss'd me, and stroked me over the Face, and said I was a very pretty Fellow.' But Newton apparently refused except upon one occasion when Lawrence, in the presence of Bavidge, took him upstairs and slept with him.

Lawrence in his defence acknowledged that he often drank ale at Mother Clap's, but denied knowing that it was a molly house. Lawrence was a milkman, and Henry Yoxam, the cow-keeper who had supplied him with milk for the past 18 years, said that Lawrence was a decent sort of chap, and that when they once got drunk at the Oxfordshire Feast and were coming home together in a coach, Lawrence made no advances toward him. Samuel Pullen, another cow-keeper, offered similar testimony on behalf of Lawrence's character. Margaret Chapman said that Lawrence often drank at her alehouse, and that he appeared to be a good man. William Preston said he often got drunk with Lawrence, who always kept his hands to himself. Thomas Fuller offered similar testimony, and added that Lawrence had married his daughter — now seven years dead — and had a 13-year-old daughter still living. Charles Bell, Lawrence's brother-in-law, said 'I never heard the like before.'

The jury nevertheless found Lawrence guilty as charged, and he was sentenced to death. The second charge, that he had slept with P—, was not pressed in view of the conviction on the first charge. While awaiting execution in Newgate, Lawrence, according to the ordinary, made no confession, and steadfastly maintained that Newton had committed perjury. He attended the prison chapel regularly, and generally exhibited a grave demeanour.

William Griffin, a 43-year-old furniture upholsterer, was tried in April on charges of having also sodomised Thomas Newton. Newton testified that Griffin had lived for two years at Mother Clap's, and that he had slept with him on the night of 20 May 1725. Constable Stevens added that Griffin was often to be seen amongst the company, that he saw him accompany another man into the Marrying Room, and that on one occasion Griffin 'put his Hand into my Breeches.'

Griffin weakly testified on his own behalf that although he had lodged for a year and three-quarters at Clap's house, he had never realised it was a molly house. He brought forward no character witnesses. The jury found him guilty and he was sentenced to death. While awaiting execution, he spoke to the ordinary about how he had squandered his money and was forced to seek lodgings wherever he could. He maintained his innocence, and claimed to have a wife and two children, though they were separated.

Also in the April trials, Thomas Wright, a 32-year-old wool-comber, was charged with having sodomised Thomas Newton as well. According to Newton, Wright had been in the business of selling ale to various molly houses before he set up his own molly house in Beech Lane. There he supposedly slept with Newton on 10 January 1725, and afterwards regularly fetched Newton to sleep with his customers, particularly one Gregory Turner (never caught), who considered Newton his especial sweetheart.

Wright's molly house was nearly as popular as Mother Clap's, at least its lower floor. Constable Sellers testified that he went to Wright's house on 17 November 1725, 'and there I found a Company of Men fiddling, and dancing, and singing bawdy Songs, kissing, and using their Hands in a very unseemly Manner.' At Sellers' departure, Wright 'kiss'd me with open Mouth.' Constable William Davison, who went there the night the mollies threatened P—, reported that 'in a large room there, we found one a fiddling, and eight more a dancing Country-Dances, making vile Motions, and singing, Come let us [bugger] finely.' (Unfortunately this ditty has been censored by the court reports, and the full text is lost.) 'Then they sat in one another's Laps, talked Bawdy, and practised a great many indecencies. There was a Door in the great Room, which opened into a little Room, where there was a Bed, and into this little Room several of the Company went; sometimes they shut the Door after them, but sometimes they left it open, and then we could see part of their Actions.'

Edward Sanders, on Wright's behalf, said that he had known Wright for many years and 'never heard the like before.' Mary Cranton and Mary Bolton, who lived in the rooms above the house, said that 'indeed we had sometimes heard Musick and Merry-making, but we knew nothing of such Practices, and believe him to be a sober Churchman.' (Were these two women 'fag-hags', or prostitutes, or lesbians? It seems doubtful that they could have been unaware of what was happening below-stairs, but we know nothing else about them.) The jury brought in a guilty verdict, and Wright was sentenced to death. While awaiting execution, he confessed to the ordinary that he was indeed homosexual and that he had in fact kept a molly house, though he maintained that Newton's specific charges against him were false.

The last of the April round of trials were those of George Kedger and George Whittle, both charged with having sodomised Ned Courtney, which we have already mentioned. We should add that part of Kedger's defence was his assertion that he visited Thomas Orme not because Orme kept a molly house, but because Orme was an old school chum. One Francis Crouch testified that 'I believe he loved a Girl too well to be concern'd in other Affairs', and another woman testified to the same effect. (Again, we know nothing about these two women.) Kedger, as noted above, was found guilty and sentenced to death. He was sent to the Gatehouse, Westminster, but later reprieved.[11]

The trial of George Whittle, briefly mentioned above, merits our greater attention because the actual facts are very much open to question. According to Ned Courtney, Whittle's tavern, the Royal Oak, was itself a molly house, and there 'he helped me to two or three Husbands' in a small room called 'The Chapel'. The specific charge was that on the night of 1 December 1725, Whittle had said to Ned, 'there's a Country Gentleman of my Acquaintance, just come to Town, and if you'll give him a Wedding-Night, he'll pay you very handsomely.' So Ned, always eager for money, 'staid 'till Midnight, but no Gentleman came, and then it being too late for

me to go Home, the Prisoner [i.e. Whittle] said I should lie with him, which
I did. He put his Hand upon — and promised me a great deal of Money,
if I would let him — which I agreed to, and he —.' (The charge was sodomy,
so these prudent dashes were felt to be necessary in the published version
of the court recorder's transcript.) But what was Ned's surprise and
anguish when 'in the Morning he gave me no more than Six-pence!'

A certain Mr Riggs testified that Whittle's Royal Oak tavern had an ill
repute in the neighbourhood, and was regarded as a popular molly house
for the past two or three years. Drake Stoneman, a neighbour, also testified
that the Royal Oak was known as a molly house — with a Chapel — for the
past two or three years. He added his first-hand account: 'I have seen Men
in his back Room behave themselves sodomitically, by exposing to each
other's Sight what they ought to have conceal'd. I have heard some of them
say, *Mine is the best. Yours has been Battersea'd.* — I don't know what they
meant by the Expression.'

'Battersea'd', nowhere else recorded in this verb form, probably is
related to the common slang injunction 'you must go to Battersea, to be
cut for the simples.'[12] 'Simples' were medicinal herbs grown in large
quantities at Battersea Park at this time, and this phrase meant 'to be cured
of one's folly.' In the context of the trial, it would seem that one man's
penis bore evidence of having been treated for venereal disease, but the
slang term more likely meant that his penis was a ripe candidate for being
treated for venereal disease, and 'Battersea'd' is probably a synonym for
'clapped'. The man's penis is more likely to bear the physical marks of the
pox, than the visible evidence of being treated for it. Venereal disease
during this period was treated either with mercury, rubbed in or taken
internally, or with balsalmic salves containing rhubarb, juniper, sassafras,
saffron, cinnamon, nutmeg, mace, and various astringents and diuretics,
taken internally, or rubbed in, or injected into the urethra by a syringe. The
compounds of polygonum, tomentilla, thyme, and *rosa rubra* would
probably be gathered at Battersea. Many of the ointments to be applied
externally also contained a mercury dilution to cause the ulcers to
discharge their contents. If the testicles began to swell, fenugreek had to
be applied morning and evening. Purgatives were generally favoured over
balsams, and salivation was increasingly common (the ingestion of mercury to provoke spitting and slavering).[13] It is just possible that 'Battersea'd' means 'covered with curative ointment', but these ointments
were not visually remarkable; it is far more likely that the 'Battersea'd'
penis was covered with the pustules, tubercles, shankers, ulcers, nodes,
tumours, swellings, inflammatory buboes and blotches associated with the
clap.

Whittle, quite undaunted by the charges, was certainly the most
resourceful of the mollies, and he proceeded to mount a brilliant defence.

First he undermined the credibility of the major witness by drawing the jury's attention to Ned's earlier imprisonments in Bridewell. Then he asserted that the rumours about him being a sodomite and running a molly house were spitefully started several years ago by a certain Mrs Johnson, 'a cursed Bitch', who, when drunk, which was often, would call him a 'Sodomite Dog!' because he had her husband arrested for non-payment of half-a-year's rent on the barber shop he leased to him. He added that Mrs Johnson had once been sent to Newgate for perjury. The *coup de grâce* was his explanation for what Drake Stoneman had seen in his back rooms: 'There is nothing in it but this: I was acquainted with several young Surgeons, who used to leave their Injections and Syringes at my House, and to bring their Patients who were clap'd, in order to examine their Distempers, and apply proper Remedies. I have had them there on that Account eight or ten times a Week.' Whittle topped this off by bringing forward an array of character witnesses. His servant Peter Greenaway said that Ned simply wanted to get revenge for Whittle's having once refused him a free pint of beer late one night. Amey White and Ann Cadle, also his servants, said that the Royal Oak had no such room as the Chapel, that the middle and back rooms were public and had no locks or bolts. They added that surely they would have known if Ned had slept with Whittle in December, but that Ned had not been seen on the premises since Amey began working for Whittle on 13 October. William Baylis and Nicholas Croward deposed that they had lain with Whittle several times while his wife was still living, but they had never noticed anything in his behaviour to make them suspect him of sodomitical intentions. Elizabeth Steward and her husband confirmed that they had heard the scandal from Mrs Johnson, and Alexander Hunter and William Brocket said they likewise had heard the rumours but never saw any foundation to them.

None of this evidence is conclusive one way or the other, but it should be noted that Whittle's wife was deceased, that three of the defence witnesses were in his employment, that Whittle's testimony about an apparently private examining room seems to contradict his servants' testimony about there being no other rooms besides the public ones, and that no 'young Surgeons' ever came forward to confirm their giving of medical examinations. If this really was an early clap clinic, the man whose penis 'was the best' had no reason to be there, or to show it off to his fellow patient. The jury nevertheless acquitted Whittle of the sodomy charge, and by implication cleared the reputation of the Royal Oak.

On Monday, 9 May 1726, Gabriel Lawrence, William Griffin, and Thomas Wright were taken in a cart to Tyburn and hanged together at the same time. Three persons could be hanged at one time at Tyburn, because the gallows consisted of three uprights with three cross beams forming an equilateral triangle. At the same time, three other felons arrived in another cart to be hanged, and the notorious Catherine Hayes (to become the subject of Thackeray's novel *Catherine*)[14] was brought to be burned for the murder of her husband. Before the hangman, Richard Arnett, could strangle her with a rope (as was customary), the flames reached his hands and he had to let go of the rope. The spectators were horrified by her screams as she struggled to kick away the burning faggots; she failed, and people watched in dismay as the eyes in her sockets melted from the heat; it required three hours for her body to be reduced to ashes.[15]

Such mass executions as these were quite popular, and the wealthier spectators could afford to sit in the viewing stands specially erected to accommodate them. On this particular occasion, the stands collapsed under the weight of 150 spectators, six of whom were killed. All that is necessary to conclude this bizarre episode in gay history is to note that, as was customary with hanged felons, Gabriel Lawrence's body was dissected at Surgeon's Hall on Tuesday, 10 May.[16]

A new round of trials began in July 1726. Martin Mackintosh, a young orange-seller, was charged with an attempt to commit sodomy — a misdemeanour — with constable Joseph Sellers. Sellers testified that on the night of 12 November 1725, P— took him to a molly house owned by a certain Mr Jones (never caught), a candle maker, at the Three Tobacco Rolls alehouse in Drury Lane, where an argument occurred between P— and Gabriel Lawrence. Mackintosh, because of his profession, 'went by the Maiden Name (as they call'd it) of Orange Deb.'[17] On that night, Mackintosh 'came to me, thrust his Hand into my Breeches, and his Tongue into my Mouth, swore he'd go forty Miles to enjoy me, and beg'd of me to go backwards [to the back room] and let him. But I refusing, he pull'd down his Breeches and offer'd to sit bare in my Lap, upon which P— snatched a red hot Poker out of the Fire and threatened to run it into his Arse.' Three men testified on Mackintosh's behalf that he had a wife and child, and that on occasion they had lain with him but that he always kept his hands to himself. (It was common practice for men to share the same bed as well as the same room in a public house or inn, partly to save money, partly because of limited accommodation during this period, and partly because it simply was not thought to be out of the ordinary; such overnight sleeping arrangements are frequently put forward as evidence on behalf of the accused in sodomy cases.) Unconvinced, the jury found him guilty, and he was sentenced to stand in the pillory in Bloomsbury Square, to pay a fine of 10 marks, and to suffer one year's imprisonment.

---

2. Catherine Hayes being burned for murdering her husband (the crime of 'petit treason'). In the background two of the three sodomites who had just been hanged have not yet been taken down from Tyburn gallows.

Dodd delin.   J. Lodge sculpt.

The manner of **BURNING** a **WOMAN** *convicted of Treason.*

Finally Mother Clap herself was brought before the bar of justice — on charges of keeping a disorderly house. Much of the evidence we have already covered was cited against her. Having only one defence, Mother Clap, with great presence of mind (and no little sense of irony), indignantly addressed the jury thus: 'I hope it will be consider'd that I am a Woman, and therefore it cannot be thought that I would ever be concern'd in such Practices.' Nevertheless, the jury found her guilty, and she was sentenced to stand in the pillory in Smithfield, to pay a fine of 20 marks, and to suffer two years' imprisonment. During her punishment, she fell off the pillory once and fainted several times.[18] It is not known what became of her, if indeed she survived prison.

By August 1726, three men had been hanged at Tyburn, two men and one woman had been pilloried, fined and imprisoned, one man had died in prison, one had been acquitted, one had been reprieved, and several were forced to go into hiding. The court may have sensed a witch-hunt atmosphere in the proceedings, not so much because the victims were innocent, but because the accusations came almost solely from only two men, both of whom were *participes crimen* in every instance, and both of whom were demonstrable rogues of dubious credibility. Whether or not the judges fully appreciated the disrepute into which they may have precipitated the administration of British justice, the trials ceased, there were no more convictions (although in December 1727 Samuel Roper, alias Plump Nelly, died in prison while awaiting trial for keeping a molly house in Giltspur Street[19]), and this particular episode of homosexual history came to an end.

(3) Public Outrage

The molly subculture revealed by the trials prompted a public outcry. Outrage and indignation were vented in the weekly *London Journal, or The British Gazetteer* and was picked up on the subsequent publishing dates of other journals. The front-page editorial of *The London Journal* for 7 May 1726, expressed appropriate horror, and proceeded to expose the major cruising grounds in London: 'besides the nocturnal Assemblies of great Numbers of the like vile Persons at what they call the Markets, which are the Royal-Exchange, Moorfields, Lincolns-Inn Bog-houses [privies], the South Side of St James's Park and the Piazza's of Covent-Garden, where they make their Bargains, and then with draw into some dark Corners to *indorse*, as they call it, but in plain English to commit Sodomy.' This term comes directly from contemporary boxing slang, meaning 'to cudgel upon the back' or 'to knock down one's opponent upon the back'; ultimately it is derived from the Latin *dorsus*, the back.[20] The editorial concludes with the hope that prosecution of the mollies will 'avert from these Cities those just Judgments, which fell from Heaven upon Sodom and Gomorrah.'

The same issue contains a letter signed by 'Philogynus' (Latin for 'woman-lover') exposing more details of this vice. According to him, the mollies commonly refer to each other as 'Madam' and 'Miss Betty', and in a quarrelling mood will say such things as 'Oh you bold Pullet, I'll break all your eggs.' (In the heterosexual underworld, a Game Pullet was a young whore-to-be.)[21] He cites another slang phrase, 'bit a Blow', which is equivalent to the modern gay slang 'score a trick'. Although Philogynus graciously acknowledges that the mollies 'are really very good Customers where they frequent', he denounces their 'effeminacy', suggests that they 'despise the Fair Sex', and concludes this uncomplimentary personality profile by suggesting that they are 'brutish People . . . harden'd in Iniquity.' He reinforces the editor's allusion to Sodom and Gomorrah by quoting Genesis 18.20–21. Especially worth noting is his comment which illustrates that the general public regarded homosexuality not merely as a great crime, but as a crime so terrible that it occupied a unique category unto itself: 'The greatest Criminal has some People that may drop some pitying Expressions for his unhappy and untimely Fate, and condole his dismal Circumstances, whilst those Persons convicted by the Laws for Sodomy, can neither expect Pity or Compassion, because they die for Crimes detestable both to God and Man.'

To describe this period as the Age of Enlightenment somewhat strains one's credulity. The early eighteenth century is noted as an era of unusually severe punishment, and we would misrepresent the facts if we did not acknowledge that very minor crimes such as the theft of a cap, as well as major crimes such as highway robbery and assault, were equally subject to sentences of hanging. Hogarth's illustrations of boys torturing animals are witness to this Age of Cruelty. The man in the street would not blench at any punishment meted out to homosexuals, and would no doubt welcome the unsigned modest proposal printed in the next issue of *The London Journal*, for 14 May 1726:

'tis humbly propos'd that the following Method may not only destroy the Practice, but blot out the Names of the monstrous Wretches from under Heaven, viz. when any are Detected, Prosecuted and Convicted, that after Sentence Pronounc'd, the Common Hangman tie him Hand and Foot before the Judge's Face in open Court, that a Skillful Surgeon be provided immediately to take out his Testicles, and that then the Hangman sear up his Scrotum with an hot Iron, as in Cases of burning in the Hand.

Philogynus contributes another letter to the issue for 14 May, wherein he suggests that men become mollies because they engaged in the vice in their juvenile years, and 'find it an hard Task to shake it off' when they come to maturity. Perhaps his acquaintance with mollies is not so extensive as his earlier letter pretended, for he now goes on to castigate Pumpers (masturbators) and practitioners of heterosexual vice — Shackling Culls (fornicators) and Flogging Culls (disciplinarians), and several heterosexual scatological types as if he's run out of information on the mollies. (In 1698 the Flogging Cullies in a club in Billingsgate were described as members of 'the Black School of Sodomy', but they were in fact men who wished to be caned by women, and were not homosexual.)[22]

The Covent Garden prostitutes apparently feared for their livelihood if this vice were allowed to progress untrammelled. In the issue for 21 May was published a letter purporting to have been sent in by an official delegation of the Drury Lane Ladies. These 'honest whores' report their feelings: 'The other Night we had a general Meeting at a Gin-Shop, where it pass'd, *Nemine contradicente*, to return you our hearty Thanks for endeavouring to suppress the notorious Practice of the *Mollies*, by which Abuse of Nature we may properly call ourselves the greatest Sufferers: for of late, several of our Christian Acquaintance have resorted to the Jews, and in particular my old Friend Mr. P—e, who . . . has left me and learnt a Way to go to the D[evi]l backwards.' This is accompanied by a doggerel verse 'To that Sodomitical Villain, P—e', with couplets such as the following:

> *You stand indicted in the publick News,*
> *For Innovations offer'd at the Stews,*
> *What cursed D[evi]l brought this Trick in vogue,*
> *To spite a W[ho]re, and doubly damn a Rogue?*
> *To change the Laws of Nature, vice versa,*
> *And set a W[hor]e to Prayers — the Lord have Mercy!*

I suspect the author of this poem is a witty male journalist, but it is not beyond the powers of an aggrieved woman, and the letter and poem may both be genuine. This letter from the Drury Lane Ladies — whether hoax or not — does express a malevolence genuinely felt by the female prostitutes of London towards the mollies (as we shall see in chapters 4 and 7).

Of course the Societies for Reformation of Manners were immensely satisfied by the success of their good work. Richard Smalbroke, Lord Bishop of St David's, gave their annual sermon in January 1727/8 and congratulated the members on their zeal: 'that those abominable Wretches, that are guilty of the *Unnatural Vice*, have been frequently detected and brought to condign Justice, is very much owing to the laudable Diligence of the Societies for Reformation.'[23] He urges the magistrates to vigorously execute the laws that have justly made this practice a capital crime; zealous efforts must be exerted by the Brethren to inform upon any one pursuing such behaviour; they must advance the glory of God by routing out such vices, particularly among the lower ranks of society.

The 33rd 'Account of the Progress' made by the Societies celebrates the fact that due to their efforts 'the Streets were very much purged from the wretched Tribe of Nightwalking Prostitutes, and most detestable Sodomites.' From December 1726 through December 1727 the Societies prosecuted 1,363 offenders for disorderly practices, drunkenness, and keeping gaming houses, and for the past 36 years they prosecuted a total of 94,322 offenders; they also assisted in the discovery of offenders to be prosecuted by the magistrates. In particular, 'the said Societies have also been assistant in bringing to Punishment several Sodomitical Houses, as well as divers Persons for Sodomy, and Sodomitical Practices, who have been prosecuted by the Direction, and at the Charge of the Government.'[24]

But the Societies were increasingly being attacked for their methods of gathering evidence and for being informers rather than reformers. As early as 1714 they were characterised as 'sly reforming hirelings',[25] and by 1727 they had prosecuted so many people before the civil magistrates that they had to defend themselves from charges of being officious meddlers. They also had to defend themselves against charges of accepting bribes and extorting money from offenders.[26] The fashion for reform had passed, and people grew sick of the reformers and increasingly attacked them for being as corrupt and vicious as those they attempted to suppress. Amongst the members themselves there was widespread disillusion that they had failed to halt the spread of vice — there was clear evidence that it had in fact increased since they began their work. By 1738 only a few Societies were left, and in that year they formally gave up their work, and all remaining Societies were disbanded.[27] In the 44th and final Account of their Progress, the Societies once again credited themselves for having instigated the prosecution of numerous sodomites and molly houses, then wound themselves up.[28] Their only success story was the SPCK, the Societies' essentially religious (and specifically Anglican) rather than reforming arm, which continues to distribute its literature today.

Chapter 4

The Sodomites' Walk in Moorfields

(1) Cruising Grounds

A subculture cannot develop without a large and cohesive minority population to support and patronise those institutions — such as molly houses — which cater to its members' needs. Relatively small subcultures can emerge in highly circumscribed associations such as a ship, a college, a convent or a royal court, but their continuity and growth is unstable due to the frequent turnovers in population or to the degrees of tolerance of the persons in authority from one period to another. Only within a densely populated urban area such as London does a subculture have a chance to thrive and continue over a period of decades. Such metropolitan subcultures often become clearly recognisable ghettoes — such as the Jewish community in Prague or the black community in Harlem — as members of ethnic groups tend to 'choose' to live only in those areas of the city where they are allowed to live in relative peace, but also in relative poverty or exploitation. Unlike other ethnic groups, however, homosexuals have no differentiating physical or racial characteristics, with the result that they are far less likely to be recognised and then herded together into such residential subcultures; most of their daily lives will be spent within the heterosexual culture-at-large, going to subcultural 'haunts' either infrequently or not at all.

The mollies lived in the same areas as everyone else; but the areas where they sought their pleasure and socialised — the molly house districts and cruising grounds — do form a distinctive subculture, one which tended to coincide with the more 'permissive' areas notorious as the haunts of thieves and prostitutes. There were six or seven such areas in central London in the eighteenth century. An editorial in the *London Journal* more specifically identified the 'Markets' in the Royal Exchange, Moorfields, Lincoln's Inn, the south side of St James's Park and the piazzas (arcades) of Covent Garden.[1] Some of our evidence is necessarily circumstantial: for example, the specific pillory in which a molly is placed is usually a reliable guide to the area in which the 'crime' was committed; so also are the areas in which extortion attempts were frequently made. But even the more direct evidence in the following survey demonstrates that the molly subculture was very extensive, large enough to support the claim by some that homosexuality was growing apace in London. Or at least public manifestations of homosexuality, for it is not proper to conclude that it was a common practice among homosexual men to engage in sex in public places: evidence consisting mostly of court trials necessarily records the most public aspect of their sex lives, and should not be confused with the no doubt discreet conduct of the homosexual population in general.

***

Let us begin with the area around Mother Clap's molly house, which was in Field Lane, Holborn, northwest of St Paul's. Part of Field Lane survives today as the southern end of Saffron Hill, and the smaller branch of Shoe Lane, parallel to Farringdon Road. The area was heavily redeveloped with the building of the Holborn Viaduct from 1863 to 1869, and the actual site of her house is probably beneath Charterhouse Street or the Viaduct itself. Directly east was West Smithfield, which has a long history of notoriety. The actual site in West Smithfield where Mother Clap was pilloried was an ancient site of execution, at least since William Fitz Osbert and his fellow devil worshippers were hanged from the gallows of the Elms in 1196. As early as 1290 the red light district had spread from the Cripplegate area to West Smithfield, especially Cock's Lane just outside Newgate. 'Nightwalkers' were frequently imprisoned in The Tun in Cornhill, then whipped and deposited outside the New Gate through the city walls (Newgate prison would eventually be built nearby). In 1483 King Edward V's ordinance 'For to Eschewe the Stynkynge and Orrible Synne of Lechery' was specifically designed to clean up areas like Farringdon, Cripplegate, Holborn and Finsbury. A Roxburgh Ballad of the mid-sixteenth century boasts 'At Cowcross and at Smithfield / I have much pleasure found / where wenches like to fayres [fairies] / did often trace the ground.' In 1622, King James was compelled by the high rate of pimping to issue an ordinance 'Touching on Disorderly Houses in Saffron Hille', which 'of longe tyme hath bene and is still much pestered with divers immodest lascivious and shameless weomen generally reputed for notorious common whores.' And in 1624 he issued another ordinance, listing the areas that were raided: Cowcross, Cock's Lane, Smithfield, St John Street Clerkenwell,

Norton Folgate, Shoreditch, Wapping, Whitechapel, Petticoat Lane, Charterhouse, Bloomsbury and Ratcliffe. By the 1680s the great arc containing these areas still encompassed the 'underworld', though the red light district was gradually moving towards King's Cross, Holborn, and Lincoln's Inn.[2]

In the latter part of the eighteenth century the area comprising Field Lane, Chick Lane, Black Boy Alley, Turnmill Street, Cow Cross and other back alleys was collectively known as Jack Ketches Warren. 'Jack Ketch' (or 'Catch') was the name given by the public to every hangman, ever since the time of the real Jack Ketch who was the executioner at the death of Lord Russell in 1683, and Monmouth in 1685, and who helped with the punishment of Titus Oates and his colleagues. This maze of alleys and buildings had become one large den of thieves: 'These places constitute a separate town or district calculated for the reception of the darkest and most dangerous enemies to society. . . . The houses are divided from top to bottom, and into many apartments, some having two, others three, others four doors, opening into different alleys. To such a height is our neglect of police arrived, the owners of these houses make no secret of their being let for the entertainment of thieves.'[3]

After the raid upon Mother Clap's premises in 1726, the area acquired notoriety as a molly district. Thus when James Whitmore in 1731 saw two men going down Saffron Hill, one very much in liquor and the other grabbing at him, he followed them because he suspected they were 'Molleys'. He traced their career past Mr Cross's brew house, then towards Black Mary's Hole, near Hockley-in-the-Hole, then towards the house of one Colchester. The men were apprehended, and it transpired that they were not mollies, but that one had stolen the clothes from his drunken acquaintance.[4] In the nineteenth century Field Lane acquired a particularly notorious aura for lovers of English literature. We may recall that, in Charles Dickens' novel *Oliver Twist*, Oliver is conducted by John Dawkins from Islington, down St John's Road, past Sadler's Wells Theatre, through Exmouth Street and Coppice Row, across Hockley-in-the-Hole, and thence into Little Saffron Hill and Saffron Hill the Great:

> A dirtier or more wretched place he had never seen. The street was very narrow and muddy, and the air was impregnated with filthy odours. There were a good many small shops; but the only stock in trade appeared to be heaps of children, who, even at that time of night, were crawling in and out at the doors, or screaming from the inside. The sole places that seemed to prosper amid the general blight of the place, were the public-houses; and in them, the lowest orders of Irish were wrangling with might and main. Covered ways and yards, which here and

there diverged from the main street, disclosed little knots of houses, where drunken men and women were positively wallowing in filth; and from several of the door-ways, great ill-looking fellows were cautiously emerging, bound, to all appearance, on no very well-disposed or harmless errands.

And finally, at the bottom of the hill, Oliver is pushed through the door of 'a house near Field Lane': Fagin's kitchen.

But it is not likely that the building which contained Mother Clap's molly house would have survived to become a neighbour to the fictional arch-villain, for this area suffered the worst during the Gordon Riots of June 1780. The fire which began in the houses of Fleet Market west of Farringdon Road was fed by streams of burning spirits from Langdale's Distillery, and a fierce conflagration raged through the district of low sensuality around Holborn Hill. The flames were somewhat checked by the river Fleet (which still flows in a vast tunnel beneath Farringdon Road), known as Fleet Ditch in the eighteenth century because it was 'a filthy sewer into which much of London's refuse was discharged.' Often it was merely a thick sludge: in 1763 a man fell in and was suffocated by the mud; one winter a barber from Bromley got stuck in head first and froze to death.[5]

(2) City of London

Holborn was equidistant between two other molly districts in London, Lincoln's Inn Fields and Covent Garden to the west in Westminster, and St Paul's and the Royal Exchange to the east in the City. Let us first of all trace the mollies' movements through the City. If we were to leave West Smithfield and go south along Little Britain Street, we could turn left into Cox's Court, and then right into a very small mews called Cross Key Court, and trace in reverse a route followed by Charles Banner beginning from Wood Street several blocks east. On 12 March 1723, about midnight, 15-year-old Nicholas Burgess, postboy, was walking along Wood Street about his father's business, when Charles Banner, gentleman, overtook him and they fell into pleasant discourse. When they came to the Cross Keys, Charles ran Nicholas up against a gate, called him 'My Dear' and 'My Precious', unbuttoned his breeches, and acted several indecent things. Nicholas declined Charles' invitation to go with him to a nearby public house for the night, but said he would meet him again next week at the same time, for his father and he worked for the Post Office and he carried letters along Wood Street every post-night.

Young Nicholas, a sneaky rogue, informed his father and two friends of his strange encounter, and they set about making plans to capture Charles at the time and place appointed. Sure enough, on the next post-night Charles appeared at the Post Office, clapped young Nicholas upon the shoulder, and told him he would be waiting near the gate as before. Come midnight, and Nicholas sets out to deliver the mail, with his father and friends dogging his heels. Nicholas met Charles near the gate, and they moved off towards a shallow ditch, where Charles began to ready himself for a bit of buggery by pulling out his Yard. Just as he began to renew his indecencies, the three men leaped out of the bushes and seized the scoundrel. They hauled him off to the nearest magistrate, and in early April he was brought to trial on charges of attempting to commit sodomy. Nicholas testified to the facts of the matter, and his father described the circumstances of the capture, but admitted that they seized the prisoner 'I believe a little too soon', since no overt sex act had taken place. Charles Banner testified in his defence that he had never seen the postboy before, that he was guilty of no indecency, and that 'I was only standing to make Water.'

The honourable court replied, 'It's very odd the Boy should inform his Friends of such an Appointment, and that you should afterwards, by meer Accident, be found with him at the very Place and Time appointed.' Banner made no reply, but a witness testified that Banner 'always bore a good Character.'

Banner lived in Swedeland Court, near East Smithfield, where he kept a school. The court was surprised that anybody would trust their children with him, but heard testimony that 'he is looked upon in the Neighbour-hood as a very honest, sober Man.' In spite of the judge's great reservations and reasonable doubts, Banner was acquitted by the jury.[6] For a change, heterosexual justice seems to have been foiled, and no doubt the postboy and the schoolmaster continued to harmlessly serve their community as before.

Cross Key Square survives today as a very small enclosed courtyard; directly opposite it is the lovely Postman's Park, and close by is the Post Office Museum, very likely on the same site as the Post Office where Burgess worked.

If we turn right and go down St Martin's Le Grand we come to St Paul's Cathedral, not listed as a Market in the *London Journal* editorial, but nevertheless attended by the mollies for more than religious purposes. In the curious lottery of 1699 which mentioned Captain Rigby's fate, it was suggested that mollies picked up the handsome apprentices who fre-quented St Paul's on Sunday afternoons.[7] In view of the Christian Church's attitude toward homosexuality, we may be surprised that the Cathedral itself was the scene of such 'abominations'. A particularly sad outcome to such activities was once brought about by John Rowden, long-time tour guide for the upper part of the Cathedral. At noon on 12 November 1730, he heard some odd noises and footsteps while making his rounds: 'I look'd thro' the Light of the Newel Stairs, and discover'd [two men, named William Holiwell and William Huggins] in a very indecent Posture' about 30 or 40 steps away. 'Huggins was stooping very low, so that I could not see his Head, his Breeches were down, his Shirt was turned upon his Back, and his Backside was bare. Holiwell was standing close by, with his fore Parts to the others Posteriors, and his Body was in Motion.' The moment they saw the officious intruder, 'Huggins got up, and was very busy in putting up his Breeches. I seiz'd upon Holiwell, and he struggled to get loose.' Holiwell ran to the door but discovered it was locked. Rowden retreated, locked them both in the side-aisle, and hurried off to fetch the Clerk of the Works and the Dean. When all three gentlemen had returned, they discovered that Holiwell had somehow escaped, but they soon caught him hiding in a gallery next to the organ loft. Later at the trial, the main evidence against the two men was 'Tokens of Emission' on Holiwell's shirt. This also suggested, fortunately, that penetration might not have been effected, so the charge was reduced to attempted sodomy. More specifically, Huggins was charged with 'consenting and submitting to the same.' Holiwell brought forth no character witnesses, though neighbours of Huggins testified that the latter was an industrious waterman, a husband, a father, and an honest man. Both were found guilty; Holiwell was sentenced to stand in the pillory near St Paul's for one hour, to suffer six months' imprisonment, and to pay a £40 fine, while Huggins received one hour in the pillory, eight months' imprisonment, but no fine.[8] It is worth noting that the man specifically charged with consenting to sodomy received the more severe punishment.

Just off Cheapside, to the north of St Paul's Cathedral, is Gutter Lane, where the extortioners Goddard and Rustead attempted to blackmail Richard Wise. A bit further, again running off on the north, is Wood Street, where Banner began his pursuit of the postboy. And St Paul's Churchyard was where Charles Hitchin, tried in 1727, was once a cabinet-maker. If we continue down Cheapside, and then down Poultry, we arrive at the Royal Exchange, identified as a molly Market in the *London Journal*, which had not much changed its character since the Swarthy Buggerantoes used to cruise it in 1700. Robert Whale and York Horner once stood in the pillory at the 'Stocks Exchange' on 13 January 1727, after being convicted for keeping a molly house presumably in this area.[9] Nearly a century later, in 1810, a certain Lyon and Barlowe were caught in the act in Lombard Street off Bearbinder Lane southeast of the Exchange: Barlowe fled and was captured in St Paul's Churchyard.[10]

Pope's-Head Alley was the scene of a brief and unpleasant encounter in

September 1730. One John Brailsford was walking through the lane and stopped 'to make Water', whereupon Peter Vivian, a peruke maker from Holland, 'came up to me, set his foot upon mine, caught hold of my Privities, and clap'd my Hand to *his.*' Another man appeared to help Vivian make good his escape, but tripped on a step in the Post Office yard, and both were captured and carried to a nearby alehouse. But once there, this unknown accomplice jumped out of a window and escaped, leaving Vivian alone to face the charges, for which he was subsequently fined 5 marks, sent to prison for one month, and pilloried at the Royal Exchange. At his capture, Vivian 'desired us to let him go, for he said he had suffer'd enough in having his Shirt and Ruffles torn.'[11]

If we continue our survey to the southeast we will arrive at Tower Hill, an area which also seemed popular with the mollies, particularly if we may draw inferences from the extortion attempts in this area. For example, on 6 November 1730, John Battle was led to the Castle tavern in Mark Lane, where John Lewis and John Jones threatened to expose him as a sodomite. Similar attempts were probably made in this area by Goddard and Rustead, for they were stood in the pillory once at Tower Hill in 1724. In addition, Dalton, in 1728, said that there existed 'a noted Molly-House, near Billingsgate' — that is, Billingsgate Market, just off Thames Street, halfway between the Royal Exchange and Tower Hill. And just to the east was Swedeland Court (now Swedenborg Gardens), East Smithfield, where Banner lived and kept a school. The area to the north of the Tower, from the Minories to Aldgate, was the haunt of George Duffus (whose case will be detailed in Chapter 6). Duffus regularly made pick-ups at a meeting-house in Old Gravel Lane (now just Gravel Lane), and in 1721, took a partner to an alehouse in the Minories, then to another at the Hermitage (now Hermitage Wall), southeast of the Tower, where he raped him. He was pilloried in Old Gravel Lane.

(3) The Sodomites' Walk

Certain sexual phenomena have sometimes been labelled according to the geographical location with which they were popularly associated: sodomy is described in Christian mythology as 'the sins of the Cities of the Plain — Sodom and Gomorrah'; in the eighteenth century and later, (hetero)sexually transmitted diseases were known as 'The Covent Garden Ague'; and, depending upon which country one lived in and what country one had antipathies towards, homosexuality has been variously described as 'the English vice', 'the French vice', 'the Spanish vice', or 'the Italian vice'. In the early eighteenth century, in London, one area was so popular with the mollies that it became virtually synonymous with homosexuality: Moorfields.

Long ago, this bog-like moor north of the City Wall was created when the Roman City dammed up the Walbrook river, thereby reducing it from a navigable river to a small stream. Eventually the water was drained and Bunhill Fields and Moorfields were developed; the latter was divided into Upper, Middle, and Lower Moorfields. By the late sixteenth century its character was already emerging, though the ground remained too spongy for extensive building; Moorfields also has the distinction of being the focus of the earliest extant map of London, Anthonis van den Wyngaerde's copper engraving of 1558/9.[12]

When the gay dramatist Christopher Marlowe first came to London in 1589, he lived with Thomas Watson in nearby Norton Folgate, and was involved in a sword fight in Hog Lane (now Worship Street) a few blocks north of Christopher Street, opposite Moorfields. In Stow's *Survey of London* we learn that Hog Lane no longer consisted of pleasant fields, but 'filthy cottages, . . . inclosures, and laystalls', deteriorating in an 'unsavoury and unseemly' manner. And of course it became a red light district. Pepys in his *Diary* for 24 March 1668, recorded a 'Tumult near Moorfields', the 'prentices pulling down the brothels . . . which is one of the great grievances of the nation.'

But the mollies soon took over the area. By the early eighteenth century, a path in the Upper-Moorfields, by the side of the Wall that separated the Upper-field from the Middle-field, acquired the name 'The Sodomites' Walk'. This path survives today as the south side of Finsbury Square, the square itself being the only open area left from the original fields, though underneath it is a car park. It was along this path that William Brown in 1726 had his privates grabbed by Thomas Newton acting as an *agent provocateur*; Brown was subsequently pilloried in Moorfields. Moorfields was identified as a molly Market in the *London Journal* editorial, and was obviously well known to all — Richard Rustead, the extortioner, was recognised by a serving boy in 1724 as a frequent user of 'the Sodomites' Walk in Moorfields', and he and his accomplice Goddard were captured by Constable Richard Bailey at the Farthing Pye-House near Moorfields. At another alehouse in Moorfields — the Green Dragon — Henry Clayton caused an uproar in 1727 by publicly calling Thomas Rodin a molly and a sodomite; Rodin was acquitted due to lack of evidence and produced the counter-claim that Clayton was a pimp whose whore had once been abused by Rodin. In another ambiguous case, in 1722, he brought Rodin to court on charges of having raped a man (unknown) in October 1722 at the home of Peter Wright the shoemaker, at the Three Shoes next door to Harrow tavern in Long-Alley, Moorfields (now Appold Street). Whatever the facts of the matter, the incident indicates the flavour of the area.[13]

Molly houses can also be found on the east side of the fields. Thomas

Wright kept one at his home in Christopher Alley (now Christopher Street), where he employed Ned Courtney to entertain his guests in 1725; Wright later moved several blocks west of the fields to Beech Lane (now Beech Street). The area retained its homosexual and unsavoury reputation from the late seventeenth century right through the early nineteenth century. John Wilmot, Earl of Rochester, notorious as the author of *Sodom, or The Quintessence of Debauchery* (1684), was called 'the MoorFields Author, fit for Bawds to quote',[14] and many decades later it was in Moorfields that Thomas Siney made a sodomitical assault upon a youth named Nicholson on 29 April 1810.[15]

(4) Lincoln's Inn

Let us now investigate the molly districts in Westminster, beginning once more in the area nearest to Holborn, to the southwest, Lincoln's Inn Fields and Lincoln's Inn, whose 'Bog-Houses' or public toilets are cited as Markets in the *London Journal* editorial, notorious for what the modern gay subculture calls 'cottaging'. The cistern for them was dug in 1691 and the structures on the east side of New Square, Lincoln's Inn, were completed in 1692. By 1693 the open kitchen garden behind them was known as Bog House Court. In 1726 the occupants of the chambers around the square had to pay a yearly sum of £3 for cleaning them out regularly, and £26 for a porter and a watchman for the Square.[16] By the 1890s the area was called The Bogs, though no one quite remembered why.[17] The area has not been built over, and is a neat little garden today. Presumably this area, and especially its privy, was popular because of the law students who frequented it. In 1728 one John Bennet was found guilty of attempted sodomy 'in the Bog-House at Lincoln's-Inn'.[18] Thomas Siney, just mentioned, lived in Task Street, Grays Inn Lane, north of Lincoln's Inn. Princess Seraphina, the molly butcher mentioned in Dalton's 1728 *Narrative* (to be discussed in Chapter 5), worked in Butcher's Row, Temple Bar, south of Lincoln's Inn. And the Golden Ball alehouse in Bond's Stables, running between Chancery Lane and Fetter Lane to the east of Lincoln's Inn, was the place were John Dicks sodomised John Meeson in 1722 — to be discussed in more detail shortly. To the northwest of Lincoln's Inn is Bloomsbury Market, where Ned Courtney first plied his trade as a hustler at the Yorkshire Gray alehouse before 1725. And running north to south on the west of Lincoln's Inn is Drury Lane, famous for its Ladies but not therefore eschewed by homosexual men: it was here in the 1720s that a certain Mr Jones the candle-maker kept a molly house at his tavern the Three Tobacco Rolls.[19]

3. The low range buildings on the left (in front of the trees) are the bog-houses on the east side of New Square, Lincoln's Inn, which were a favourite molly cruising ground.

This brings us to Covent Garden Market, the Piazzas of which are cited as one of the molly Markets in the *London Journal*. It was here, for example, that Sukey Haws, the highway robber and pickpocket, was picked up by a molly tailor in 1728, whom he subsequently blackmailed;[20] that Ned Courtney disturbed the peace at an unnamed molly house in the early 1720s; that Richard Scuse and James Coltis, each given one year's imprisonment for unspecified sodomitical practices, were sentenced to stand in the pillory in February or March 1726/7.[21] The arcades would have provided useful cover for making assignations.

The area running along the Strand, south of Covent Garden, past Temple Bar, and up Chancery Lane or Fetter Lane, east of Lincoln's Inn, was probably a popular molly cruising ground, as indicated by the case of a merry pub-crawl which took place in 1721, an incident interesting enough to be recorded in more detail. On the day that the first stone was laid at the church of St Martin-in-the-Fields, John Meeson was loitering about the churchyard when John Dicks made his approach, and clapping Meeson on the shoulder heartily asked him 'Honest Dyer! How fares it?' They fell a-talking about the coffins that had been dug up and were strewn about the churchyard, to make way for the new foundation, and presently Dicks asked Meeson to come along with him to an alehouse to take a pot. Meeson declined, but Dicks kept repeating his kind offer until the lad assented. Meeson drank cheers with him at the pub, 'and when he had made me almost fuddled', said Dicks, 'he buss'd me, put his Hand into my Breeches, and took my Hand and put it into his Breeches.' Meeson was not particularly displeased by this manner of behaviour, and from there they crawled on to a smaller tavern located in a cellar in the Strand, where they had another pint of beer. Meeson, being a delivery-boy, had some goods to carry to White Hart Yard in Flint Street, and departing from his new-found friend he promised to return shortly after his delivery was completed. Upon his return, they had another pint, but finding that place not quite private enough for their purposes, they crawled on to another alehouse in Chancery Lane, where they drank hot ale and gin. Finding this place still not private enough, they proceeded on their merry way to the Golden Ball in Bond's Stables near Fetter Lane, where they drank more ale and Geneva in a stall separated from the saloon by a thin partition. Meeson by this time was so drunk that he had to vomit, after which he lay down to go to sleep — or so he thought.

On the other side of this very thin partition were William Rogers and his girlfriend, whose sociable chat was rudely interrupted by the sounds of loud blustering kisses and sweet nothings such as 'My Dear', 'My Jewel', and 'My precious little Rogue' issuing from the next stall. Greatly disturbed by these noises — since they had seen but two men go into the stall — they called for the alehouse boy to see what was about. The alehouse boy went in, and saw Meeson lying upon the bench and Dicks slobbering over him. Dicks then asked the alehouse boy to sit and have a drink, which he did, and presently Dicks thrust his hand into the boy's breeches. The boy got up in a huff, stalked out of the room and reported the incident to Rogers and his girl who set about peeping through a hole in the partition. They watched in amazement as Dicks unbuttoned Meeson's breeches, turned him upon his face, and began his tender ministrations. In Rogers' words, 'I saw him in the very Act of Sodomy, making several motions with his body, and then I saw him withdraw his Yard from the Boy's Fundament.' Dicks spent his seed, then renewed his delights, whereupon the woman cried out 'I can look no longer – I am ready to Swoon – He'll Ruin the Boy!' Thereupon they all rushed indignantly into the room and seized upon Dicks as he lay panting upon Meeson's backside. In spite of being thus apprehended in so indecent a posture, Dicks looked up at the intruders and loudly protested his innocence. Having properly adjusted his attire, he was hauled off to the nearest magistrate, leaving Meeson in a drunken stupor upon the bench. For all the concern which Rogers and the woman had expressed for the fate of the delivery boy, they simply abandoned him in their fervour to bring a criminal to justice. Meeson reports: 'I fell asleep, and when I wak'd I found my Breeches were down, and I was almost starved with Cold.'

Dicks was brought to trial in April, but, since Meeson had to admit that 'I was not sensible enough to be certain' whether or not penetration actually occurred, Dicks was indicted for only an attempt to commit sodomy, a misdemeanour. During the trial proceedings, Dicks kept turning up the whites of his eyes in a very devout manner, and then testified in his defence that 'I was overtaken with Drink, and if I ever offer'd any such thing to Meeson, it was more than I knew of.' Dicks was found guilty, and sentenced to pay a fine of 20 marks, to be imprisoned for two years, and to stand in the pillory near Temple Bar.[22] Meeson returned to his delivery route near St Martin's Church, apparently none the worse for wear.

In some ways the church of St Martin-in-the-Fields in Trafalgar Square is a lasting memorial of the molly subculture. Its foundation stone was laid in 1721, on the day of the incident recounted above, and it was fully completed in 1726, at the time of the hangings as the result of the raid upon Mother Clap's in that year. Criminals hanged at Tyburn — for example, Jack Shepherd in 1724 — were sometimes buried in its church-yard and the vaults of its crypt, so it may have been the resting place for the bones of those mollies whose bodies were not unfortunate enough to be taken to Surgeon's Hall.

4. West London in 1731: Lincoln's Inn Fields and Clare
Market (centre left), Covent Garden (lower left), Drury
Lane (left), Fetter Lane (right), Field Lane and Saffron Hill
(upper right).

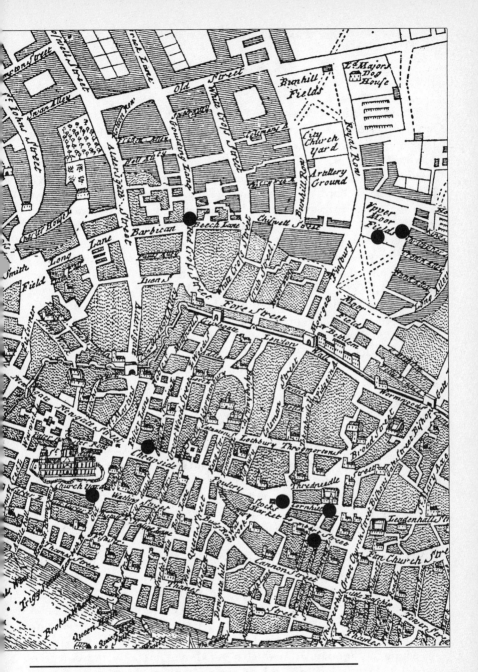

5. East London in 1731: Smithfield (centre left), Newgate and
St Paul's (lower left), Moorfields (upper right), Stocks Market
(lower right).

(5) Charles Hitchin

We now find ourselves upon the Strand, along which the alehouses were not unaccustomed to catering for a molly clientele, though no tavern may have been exclusively gay. Another not untypical molly pub-crawl is that followed by Charles Hitchin (or Hitchen), the Under City Marshal, formerly a cabinet maker in St Paul's Churchyard. On 29 March 1727, Hitchin met Richard Williamson at the Savoy gate and asked him to have a drink. They went to the Royal Oak in the Strand 'where, after we had two Pints of Beer', according to Williamson, Hitchin 'began to make use of some sodomitical indecencies.' Apparently Williamson was not particularly offended, for although he had to leave to carry out some business elsewhere, he left his hat as a pledge to return, and indeed did so. They then went to the Rummer Tavern where, while imbibing two pints of wine, Hitchin 'hugg'd me, and kiss'd me, and put his Hand —.' Then on to the Talbot Inn, and another pint of wine. The Chamberlain made a bed ready for them, and brought two nightcaps. In bed, Hitchin '— and — and —' (our court recorder is strangely reticent, but we get the gist of it).

Hitchin was well known at this inn; according to Christopher French, a servant there, Hitchin came frequently with soldiers and 'other scandalous Fellows' and was often seen with them in his room. The day after this incident, Williamson had misgivings, and confessed all to his relative Joseph Cockcroft; together they went to the inn and spied through the keyhole upon Hitchin in bed with one of his menfriends. Cockcroft says 'I took him by the Collar, and told him I had some Business with him. He laid his Hand upon his Sword, *Sir*, says I, *if you offer to draw, I'll whip ye thro' the Gills.*' Hitchin submitted, and in April was acquitted of sodomy but convicted of the attempt, and sentenced to a £20 fine, six months' imprisonment, and to stand in the pillory near the end of Catherine Street, just off the Strand.[23]

When Hitchin was brought to the pillory on Tuesday, 2 May, his many 'Friends and Brethren' had wisely barricaded the side avenues with coaches and carts so as to impede the angry mob. But such precautions proved futile, for the throng nevertheless broke down these barriers, and blood was spilled in the ensuing battle between them and the attending peace officers. This was the first act of gay resistance in modern times, predating the Stonewall Riot which began the gay liberation movement by almost 250 years. For half an hour, according to a newspaper report, a steady 'battery of artillery' was aimed at Hitchin by 'the Drury Lane Ladies', the rocks breaking windows when they missed the object of their hatred. One might expect other 'sexual minorities' to sympathise with the mollies, but the current of anti-homosexual prejudice flowed deeply through all social groupings, and some of the most virulent molly-haters were the female prostitutes. They always turned out in force when a molly was pilloried, vocally and physically expressing their indignation at the mollies depriving these 'more honest whores' of their rightful custom. As seems to be the way of the world, one outcast group tries to salvage some status at the expense of another outcast group, not recognising their common oppressor.

Hitchin, thoroughly pelted with filth, his nightgown and breeches literally torn away from his body by the force of the missiles, was finally let down, fainting from exhaustion.[24] Little wonder that he never recovered from this gruelling ordeal, and died shortly after his release from prison six months later.[25] He died in extreme poverty, and his wife petitioned the courts for relief.

Hitchin's 'friends and brethren' were probably a mixture of mollies and semi-professional criminals, for Hitchin was a prominent 'thief-taker', and his biography provides our surest clues about the overlapping of the molly subculture with the criminal underworld. That notorious criminal Jonathan Wild — who was virtually the director of a crime syndicate which thrived upon robbing people and then returning their goods for a reward, or smuggling them to Holland — began his career as an assistant to Hitchin. 'These celebrated co-partners in villainy, under the pretext of reforming the manners of the dissolute part of the public, paraded the streets from Temple-bar to the Minories, searching houses of ill-fame, and apprehending disorderly and suspected persons: but such as compliment these *public* performers with *private* douceurs were allowed to practice every species of wickedness with impunity.'[26] Hitchin's membership of the Society for Reformation of Manners,[27] and access to its network of information, would have added immeasurably to his power in the underworld, but it is nevertheless ironic that he pretended to be an active supporter of the very Society which was responsible for the purge of the molly houses which indirectly led to his downfall.

Hitchin was born about 1675; in 1703 he married Elizabeth, daughter of John Wells of King's Waldon, Hertfordshire, and may have had one or more children by her. They lived on the north side of St Paul's Churchyard, where he practised his trade as a cabinet maker. Elizabeth's father died in 1711, and Hitchin persuaded her to sell her inheritance to enable him to buy the office of Under City Marshal, in January 1712, for £700. This valuable post enabled him to regulate some 2,000 thieves, to blackmail them and others, to receive stolen goods and extract enormous sums of money from their owners for returning them.[28]

The major criminal areas at that time — survivors of the old 'Sanctuaries' of the medieval monasteries, even after their closure by Henry VIII — were The Mint, Southwark; Whitefriars; Shoe and Fetter Lanes; Holborn, especially Saffron Hill leading into Field Lane; Cripplegate; Smithfield; Whitechapel; Bankside; Thieving Lane around Westminster Abbey; The Savoy and Covent Garden up to St Giles in Westminster. These areas held a quarter of the entire population of London, and consisted mainly of paupers. Soon Hitchin was a familiar figure in every tavern, brothel and eating house between Temple Bar and Aldgate; he is known to have kept rendezvous in the following coffee houses and alehouses: Masey's Coffee House, Old Change; Mear's Coffee House, St Paul's House Court, near his own home; Hatton's, Basinghall Street, where he read the morning newspapers for advertisements offering rewards for stolen property; Woolpack alehouse, Foster Lane, where he wrote his blackmail letters; Cross Keys, Holborn; King's Head, Ivy Lane, where he lunched with thieves; Queen's Head, Paternoster Row; The Blue Boar, Barbican, where he made plans with thieves; the Clerkenwell Workhouse, where he had a gang of young pickpocket boys; and the Three Tuns and the Black Horse, both in Moorfields, where he distributed the booty to his men. He was frequently seen crossing Moorfields in the evenings, with a troop of ragged pickpocket boys in attendance.

In 1713 Hitchin was temporarily suspended because of complaints that he was abusing his office; however, he was reinstated on promise of good behaviour. He first made contact with Wild in that year, probably through two of his boys, Christopher Plummer and William Field, who were both in the Compter at the same time as Wild; they began a partnership that was to last for only a year. They seem to have become jealous of one another, and soon were again pursuing their separate careers. In 1718 Hitchin attacked Wild in *A True Discovery of the Conduct of Receivers and Thief-Takers*, libelling Wild as 'the king of the gipsies, . . . King among the thieves, and Lying-master-general of England, Captain-general of the Army of plunderers'; he exposed his crimes and those of his conspirators, including Wild's pickpocket wife, Mary Milliner, 'a common night-walker', and generally lamented that London had 'become a receptacle for a den of thieves and robbers, and all sorts of villainous persons and practices.'[29]

Wild immediately published a counter-attack, *An Answer To A Late Insolent Libel . . . With a Diverting Scene of a Sodomitish Academy* (1718), in which he weakly denied some of the charges, but fulminated against the Marshal 'and his Man the Buckle-Maker', calling Hitchin 'my old master in iniquity' and listing some of the Marshal's crimes: that he objected to those who would transfer whores from bawdy houses to houses of correction, 'for those persons very much lessen his interest in suppressing houses of lewdness, the keepers whereof have been generally pensioners to him. I can produce persons who will make it appear, that several houses of ill fame are supported by quarterly payments to him'; that he has extorted money from both the guilty and the innocent to protect their reputation against imputations of libertinism; that he has tried to get annual payments even from taverns of the best reputation; that he — 'in the silverbuttoned coat, and knotted wig, with sword by his side' — rendezvoused daily with his 'hell-cat' crew at 'an alehouse between Moorfields and Islington' to receive accounts of their doings, and to issue further instructions. This concludes with a caricature of 'the gigantic city marshal, [who] wants nothing but a cloven foot to personate, in all respects, his father Beelzebub.'[30]

The diatribe is rounded out with an account of an incident at a molly club. One night the Marshal took his man the bucklemaker to a molly house 'near the end of the Old Bayly' to introduce him to 'a Company of He-Whores'. When they entered, the Marshal was greeted with the titles of 'Madam, and Ladyship', which he explained to his companion 'was a familiar Language peculiar to that House.' Inside, the mollies hugged, kissed and tickled one another, assumed feminine airs and voices, and told others 'that they ought to be Whipp'd for not coming to School more frequently.' The Marshal was very merry at this assembly, 'and Dallied with the young Sparks with a great deal of Pleasure.' But then some men came in 'that he little expected to meet with in that place.' He lost the lads to them, and left, threatening to spoil their diversions. Going out, he told his companion that the others would probably have the impudence to make 'a Ball' such as those which regularly occurred at 'a noted House in Holborn' where such men dressed themselves as women to entertain others 'of the same Inclinations', with whom they would dance 'Etc'.

True to his promise to 'be reveng'd on these Smock fac'd young Dogs', the Marshal, 'knowing their usual Hours and customary Walks', placed himself and some constables in Fleet Street 'to Apprehend them in their return Home.' In due course several men in women's clothing were captured and sent to the Compter. Next morning they were taken before the Lord Mayor, still in their dresses: 'Some were compleatly Rigg'd in Gowns, Head cloths, fine lac'd Shoes, Furbelow Scarves, and Masks; some had Riding-hoods; some were dressed like Shepherdesses; others like Milk-Maids with fine Green Hatts, Wastcoats and Petticoats, and others had their Faces patched and painted, and wore very extensive Hoop-petticoats, which were then very lately introduced.' These mollies were committed to the Workhouse, being conveyed through the streets hither in their gowns. After 'a considerable Time', one of them 'threaten'd the Marshal with the same Punishment for former Adventures'; Hitchin accordingly applied to the Lord Mayor and they were released; one young gentleman died of mortification soon after his release.[31] (Is it possible that the 'noted House in Holborn' was Mother Clap's, or was her establishment not flourishing as early as 1717?)

No public action resulted from the mutual slanders in this pamphlet war, but at the trials which finally led to Wild's hanging on 24 May 1725, charges were again made which substantially supported the accusations from both sides. After Wild was cut down from the gallows, the mob received five shillings per man to convey his body to the Curdigan's Head, Charing Cross (where Ned Courtney had worked as an alehouse boy), from whence it was supposed to be carried to Surgeon's Hall to be anatomised. In the event, the coachmen were paid by Wild's wife to take the body from the alehouse to St Pancras Churchyard, where it was decently interred on 25 May.

Evidence was given against Wild by William Field, who once was one of Hitchin's men; Field himself was eventually hanged, and he is the person upon whom 'Fitch' in John Gay's The Beggar's Opera (1728) was modelled (Wild of course is 'Peachum'). Field's own sub-gang included James Dalton, whose Genuine Narrative (1728) is an invaluable record of information concerning the mollies, and is often referred to throughout this study; Dalton led a very heterosexual life and was hanged for robberies in 1730.[32]

In an illustration of Wild on his procession to the gallows, passing by St Sepulchre's, in Captain Charles Johnson's Lives of the Highwaymen (1734), the portly figure immediately behind the cart is Charles Hitchin, who of course remained as Under City Marshal until his own fall. Hitchin was not actually dismissed from office until after finishing his six months in prison — on the grounds of not having attended to his duties for the past six months.

It is of course ironic that a homosexual should have earned part of his living by overseeing or 'regulating' heterosexual bawdy houses; the Drury Lane Ladies certainly got their revenge upon him at last. He and his accomplices must have moved easily between the criminal underworld and the molly subculture. It is also likely that Hitchin protected the molly houses. No doubt those investigations which led to Wild's apprehension and conviction also led, via a subsidiary investigation of Hitchin, to the raids upon the molly houses, and played themselves out in the conviction of Hitchin. It is more than just a remarkable coincidence that the two major purges of the early eighteenth century — against Jonathan Wild's gang and against the molly houses — were both directed by Mr Jones, High Constable of the Holborn division, in 1725/26.

6. Jonathan Wild being taken in a cart to be hanged at Tyburn. Behind him rides the Under City Marshal Charles Hitchin who will supervise the hanging. Less than a year later Hitchin himself would be pilloried and imprisoned for attempted sodomy.

Jonathan Wild going to the Place of Execution.

(6) St James's

But to return to our survey of molly London. Just west of Charing Cross (where a molly named Tolson kept a brandy shop in the late 1720s,[33] and where Whale and Horner were pilloried for keeping a molly house), we come to St James's Square and Pall Mall, site of the Royal Oak molly house kept by George Whittle. Further south, on the walk between the Mall and the Roan, near Whitehall, Joseph Stone was robbed and beaten and threatened with being accused of sodomy. At the end of the Mall next to Buckingham House, John Casey robbed Francis Godelard on 5 November 1721, then accused him of sodomy in an attempt to evade capture (to be discussed in Chapter 8). The south side of the Park is cited as a molly Market in the *London Journal*, and several molly incidents are recorded as happening in St James's Park, much frequented by obliging soldiers. For example, on the morning of Sunday 20 August 1727, a foot-soldier and a chairman were caught in the act on the grass — one was carried to the Savoy, the other to the Gatehouse;[34] in January 1727/8 a certain Arrowsmith accosted a sentinel and offered to give him 'a Green Gown upon the Grass', that is, to have sex with him, leaving grass stains upon his clothing (from the heterosexual slang phrase which forms the basis of the song 'Greensleeves');[35] and Parliament Street, according to the extortionist William Cane, was still a known cruising ground as late as the early nineteenth century.[36] William Gent, alias Mademoiselle Gent, was a tradesman 'in Westminster' in 1726, along with his boyfriend John Whale, alias Peggy Whale.[37] John Croucher, a coachman to 'a gentleman in Westminster', was convicted of sodomitical practices and stood in the pillory in New Palace Yard in October 1727.[38] The notoriety of the area, even much later, is well attested to by the chapter on 'the unnaturalists' in *The Fruit Shop*, 1766, tellingly subtitled 'A Companion to St. James's Street'.

Some areas well beyond central London had their molly districts as well. In July 1727, police were given information 'that a Party of Sodomites had their Tail Quarters at an empty House near the Bowling Green at Marylebone', to the northwest, beyond Tyburn. A group of constables investigated on the evening of Sunday, 30 July, 'and found 8 of them, one of whom made his Escape, but the other 7 were taken and carried before a Justice of Peace, who committed 5 of them to New-Prison, discharged one, and admitted the other to Bail.'[39] This curious incident was widely reported in the journals of the following week — *The Weekly Journal, The British Journal, The London Journal*, and *The Country Journal*. Two men known as Dip-Candle Mary, a tallow chandler, and Aunt May, an upholsterer, worked in The Borough, i.e. Southwark, just south across the

Thames. Sukey Bevell's molly house was in The Mint, Southwark.[40] Sukey Haws sometime before 1728 was picked up by 'H[o]n the lat[e] C—y M—l', probably a titled gentleman, carried to 'a Bowling-Green House at Islington', to the northeast, where the latter tried 'to commit filthy Actions.'[41] And to the east, John Painter and John Green, convicted of having engaged in sodomitical practices on Stepney Church Porch, were pilloried in nearby Ratcliffe Gardens in September 1727.[42]

By the early nineteenth century Moorfields seems no longer to have been a molly area, though many of the other districts remained unchanged. Holloway in the *Phoenix of Sodom* (1813) notes that 'there are many [molly houses] about town', specifically 'one in the Strand', one in Blackman Street in The Borough, one near the Obelisk, St George's Fields, one in the neighbourhood of Bishopsgate Street, and of course the most infamous one, The Swan in Vere Street. He adds further that 'breeches-clad bawds' are to be found strolling in the Inns of Court, 'the Temple not excepted'.[43] Holloway, a lawyer himself, was quite surprised, for the Temple was noted for heterosexual prostitution. Joke Number 153 in Joe Miller's *Jestbook* (1739) makes this clear: 'A gentleman said of a young wench, who constantly ply'd about the Temple, that if she had as much law in her head, as she had in her tail, she would be one of the ablest counsel in all England.'[44]

Chapter 5

Maiden Names and Little Sports

(1) The Female Dialect

The molly subculture as a *unified subculture*, rather than simply a disparate collection of people and their behaviour, was reinforced by the communal use of a specialised dialect, a private lexicon whose terms were relatively unknown to the culture-at-large, just as in the twentieth century heterosexuals have been generally unfamiliar with the meaning of the terms that gays often use to make themselves known only to one another, or which they habitually acquire through constant use in the gay subculture. Modern gay slang is abundant — there are more than 20,000 such terms,[1] a number which we cannot hope to match in the early stages of the gay subculture in the eighteenth century.

Gay men within the molly subculture developed their own molly slang, called the Female Dialect, consisting largely of Maiden Names with which they affectionately christened one another.[2] Such sobriquets were usually preceded by a form of Madam or Miss: for example, there were Madam Blackwell,[3] Miss Kitten, alias Mr Oviat,[4] Miss Fanny Knight, Miss Irons, Mrs (i.e. Mistress) Anne Page, the clerk at Sukey Bevell's,[5] and Mrs Girl of Redriff.[6] Molly, Mary, and Margaret, etymologically related, provide the most frequent Maiden Names: Moll Irons, Flying Horse Moll, Pomegranate Molly, Black Moll, perhaps Moll King (a street robber convicted and transported sometime before 1721), China Mary, Primrose Mary (a butcher in Butcher Row), Orange Mary (an orange merchant), Garter Mary, Pippin Mary (alias Queen Irons), Dip-Candle Mary (a tallow chandler), Small Coal Mary.[7] There are occasional aunties: Aunt Greer, Aunt May (an upholsterer), and Aunt England (a soap-boiler).[8] Perhaps the auntie role — the older, more experienced homosexual to whom younger entrants into the subculture look for commiseration and advice on how to survive in a hostile society and how to behave within the subculture — was already beginning to develop. There were some prestigious names (which the modern gay subculture would call piss-elegant): Princess Seraphina the butcher, Queen Irons, probably a blacksmith,[9] the Countess of Camomile, Lady Godiva, a waiter, and the Duchess of Gloucester, a butcher.[10]

The Maiden Names were suggested by a wide range of physiognomic characteristics, occupational status, geographical origins, and personality traits. Flying Horse Moll must have been a serving man at a tavern named The Flying Horse; Orange Deb, alias Martin Macintosh, was an orange seller;[11] Mr Powell was called St Dunstan's Kate because he lived near St Dunstan's Church or even worked within the church, Kate Hutton was 'an old Man that never wears a Shirt', Hanover Kate probably was from Germany, Nurse Mitchell was a barber, Tub Nan and Hardware Nan possibly sold such utensils, Old Fish Hannah and Young Fish Hannah were probably fish mongers, Susan Guzzle was a gentleman's manservant who presumably was a hearty drinker, Johannah the Ox-Cheek Woman presumably had either big jowls or a big bottom, and Thumbs and Waist Jenny must have been sylph-like.[12] Sukey, though a genuine name, was frequent: Sukey Pisquill, Sukey Hawes, Sukey Bevell, which support Dunton's 1707 claim that pick-ups were addressed as Sukey. Other more obviously feminine names were Ellinor Roden and Rose Gudger.[13] (Nurse Mitchell the barber, incidentally, may have been John Mitchell, who was scheduled to appear on behalf of James Dalton at the latter's trial for assault and robbery in 1730, but it was noted that Mitchell had once stood in the pillory for falsely charging a man with sodomy, so he was not admitted for evidence.)[14]

The Maiden Names which the mollies assumed bore no relation to any specific male-female role-playing in terms of sexual behaviour. For example, Fanny Murray was 'an athletic Bargeman', Lucy Cooper was 'an Herculean Coal-heaver', and Kitty Fisher was 'a deaf tyre Smith'. Nor was there always a direct correspondence between their feigned names and their calling in life: 'Kitty Cambric is a Coal Merchant; Miss Selina, a Runner at a Police office; Black-eyed Leonora, a Drummer [of the Guards]; Pretty Harriet, a Butcher; . . . and Miss Sweet Lips, a Country Grocer.'[15]

Princess Seraphina, briefly mentioned in Dalton's *Narrative* of 1728, made a quite unexpected appearance in court in 1732. John Cooper, a butcher, prosecuted Thomas Gordon, an unemployed servant, for assaulting him in Chelsea Fields and stealing his clothes and money on 30 May 1732. This was the night of the Whit Monday holiday, when many people were out drinking and making merry. Cooper claimed that they met at a night cellar and drank three hot pints of beer together, then went for a morning walk as the weather was nice, and when they reached a secluded stand of trees Gordon took out a knife and forced Cooper to strip off his clothes, and exchange them with Gordon's clothes. Gordon said that if Cooper charged him with robbery, he would swear Cooper was a sodomite and had given him the clothes to let him bugger Gordon. Cooper was furious at losing his fine clothes, and obtained a warrant for Gordon's arrest at a brandy shop in Drury Lane. He brought the prosecution against him, which was a mistake, for not only did Gordon make the counter-charge that he had threatened to make, but a host of witnesses came forward to reveal that Cooper was what we now call a 'drag queen'.

Mrs Holder the landlady of the night cellar where they had drank their Huckle and Buff (that's gin and ale made hot), said that Cooper frequently came to her cellar with Christopher (Kitt) Sandford, a tailor, and other mollies, and was a runner who carried messages between such gentlemen: 'he's one of them as you call Molly Culls, he gets his Bread that way; to my certain Knowledge he has got many a Crown under some Gentlemen, for going of sodomiting Errands.'

Jane Jones a washerwoman revealed that she had overheard Cooper and Gordon arguing in a pub, Cooper demanding his clothes back and threatening to accuse Gordon of robbery, Gordon saying he was entitled to the clothes and threatening to accuse Cooper of sodomy. She ended her testimony with the startling revelation that John Cooper was commonly known in the district as the Princess Seraphina. The judge was so taken aback that she had to repeat what she had just said, and one can imagine the jury suddenly becoming very attentive at this interesting turn of events. Her story was confirmed by Mary Poplet, the keeper of the Two Sugar Loaves public house in Drury Lane, who astonished the court with her testimony:

> I have known her Highness a pretty while, she us'd to come to my House from Mr. Tull, to enquire after some Gentlemen of no very good Character; I have seen her several times in Women's Cloaths, she commonly us'd to wear a white Gown, and a scarlet Cloak, with her Hair frizzled and curl'd all round her Forehead; and then she would so flutter her Fan, and make such fine Curt'sies, that you would not have known her from a Woman: She takes great Delight in Balls and Masquerades, and always chuses to appear at them in a Female Dress, that she may have the Satisfaction of dancing with fine Gentlemen.... I never heard that she had any other Name than the Princess Seraphina.

Mary Ryley, one of the serving girls at the pub, said she knew the Princess very well, that he sometimes worked as a nurse, and that he dressed as a woman at the last masquerade, the *Ridotto al Fresco* at Vauxhall. Mary Robinson, a respectable lady, said that she and Cooper shared the same Mantua-makers in the Strand. He once asked to borrow her suit of red damask because it 'looked mighty pretty'; he wanted it to go to Mrs Green's in Nottingham Court by the Seven Dials where he was to meet some fine gentlemen. Mrs Green occasionally lent him a velvet scarf and gold watch. He wanted to borrow her laced pinners for the Vauxhall *Ridotto*, but settled for Madam Nuttal's mob cap and one of her smocks.

After the masquerade Mrs Robinson said 'And did you make a good Hand of it, Princess?' 'No, Madam', said Cooper, 'I pick'd up two Men, who had no Money, but however they proved to be my old Acquaintance, and very good Gentlewomen they were.' One of these gentlemen 'went to the Masquerade in a Velvet *Domine*, and pick'd up an old Gentlemen, and went to Bed with him, but as soon as the old Fellow found that he had got a Man by his Side, he cry'd out, Murder.' The other gentleman, alas, had since been transported for counterfeiting masquerade tickets.

Cooper lived at No. 11, Eagle Court, in the Strand, with Mr and Mrs Tull, whom he nursed through a salivation. He was their friend rather than a domestic servant; other lodgers were Mr Levit and Mr Sydney. The Princess was liked by all the women of her neighbourhood, and we can easily imagine her sitting down with them for a quiet cup of tea and a good gossip. The only person who disliked her was her cousin, a distiller in Warder Street (modern Wardour Street), who once gave her a shilling and told her to go about her business and not to scandalise the neighbours. Cooper's prosecution of Gordon was really no more than a quarrel that had got out of control and could not be stopped once the wheels had been set in motion. He was egged on by two men who expected a reward for capturing the supposed thief. But it had no disastrous consequences for either defendant or plaintiff; Gordon was acquitted as an honest working man, and no charges were brought against the Princess.[16]

Masquerades flourished in London from the 1720s onward, and took place in assembly rooms, theatres, brothels, public gardens, and molly houses. The commercial masquerades were quasi-carnivals first organised by the impresario John James Heidegger at the Haymarket Theatre from 1717 onwards. His 'Midnight Masquerades' were tremendously success-ful, and drew 800 people a week. They provided many people with the opportunity to explore fetishism and transvestism. Men disguised them-selves as witches, bawds, nursing maids and shepherdesses, while women dressed as hussars, sailors, cardinals and Mozartian boys. In the early days of the fashion, Richard Steele went to one where a parson called him a pretty fellow and tried to pick him up, and Horace Walpole passed for an

old woman at a masquerade in 1742. The opportunities for illicit assignations provoked a host of anti-masquerade satires, and many tracts were
mainly devoted to attacking the mollies who attended them, supposedly
imitating infamous homosexual cross-dressers such as Sporus, Caligula,
and Heliogabalus.[17]

(2) Masquerades

The molly houses emerged at the same time as London's coffee houses and
the first music halls, and bear some resemblance to the latter. Sadler's
Wells in Islington, London's first music hall, built by Thomas Sadler in
1683, began as little more than a room or two where apprentices and maids
drank ale and ate cheesecake while fiddlers were scraping and humming;
Ned Ward's descriptions of such places[18] does not much differ from his
descriptions of the molly houses, and a quick glance inside one of the latter
might have seemed to reveal only apprentices and maids, for on special
occasions some of the men dressed as women. This has led some modern
historians to claim that the molly clubs were frequented predominantly by
transvestites, but this is to seriously overstate the case.[19] Only a few
documents mention transvestism, and in nearly every instance it is clear
that female garb was reserved for the occasional masquerade ball or a very
special ceremony known as 'lying-in'. On 28 December 1725 a group of
25 men were apprehended in a molly house in Hart Street near Covent
Garden and were arrested for dancing and misbehaving themselves, 'and
obstructing and opposing the Peace Officers in the Execution of their
Duty.' They were dressed in 'Masquerade Habits' and were suspected of
being sodomites because several of them had previously stood in the
pillory on that account; but they were dressed in a range of costumes, not
all of which were female, and the date suggests a special holiday event
rather than a familiar practice. It is interesting to note that they did not
submit sheepishly to their arrest, but put up a show of resistance. Presently
20 of them were secured in various prisons, and granted their own
recognisances to the spring sessions, but no true bills of indictment were
found, perhaps because they all absconded.[20]

   Accounts of habitual male transvestism are extremely rare, and of
doubtful authenticity. A case in point is an episode recounted by the
anonymous author of *Hell upon Earth* in 1729. He claims to have been in
the company of a grave merchant, an ancient gentlewoman, a young
Irishman, and two young ladies on a stage-coach journey from Bristol. In
the morning the Irishman bragged to him how he had enjoyed the
embraces of both young women during the night. 'But how was he struck

with Shame and Confusion, when he found the two young Ladies metamorphos'd into two young Gentlemen, that for their diversion, and to pass the Time away, had purposely put on the Disguise to conceal their Sex, and had assum'd an Air suitable to their Appearance, to mortify some fond, conceited, passionate and whining Enamorado.'[21] This is patently a fabricated joke of the 'stupid Irishman' variety, and even then there is no suggestion that the young gentlemen's behaviour was habitual or that they were homosexual.

For slightly more trustworthy evidence we must turn to Ned Ward's pamphlet of 1709, in which he says that the mollies 'are so far degenerated from all Masculine Deportment that they rather fancy themselves Women, imitating all the little Vanities that Custom has reconcil'd to the Female Sex, affecting to speak, walk, talk, curtsy, cry, scold, & mimic all manner of Effeminacy.'[22] And in one of the 1727 trials we learn that 'they would . . . Dance and make Curtsies, and mimick the Voices of Women.'[23]

The student of human behaviour is justifiably curious about precisely what went on in a molly house, and it seems unkind to leave such things to the imagination, even though the anonymous writer of *Sodom and Onan* in 1776 felt that the mollies'

> *. . . Little Sports,*
> *Unrival'd in Chinese or Turkish Courts:*
> *Their Christ'nings, Lyings-in, Abortions;*
> *Their Caudle-makings, fifty foul Distortions,*
> *Unfit for public repetition,*
> *Shou'd be refer'd to Spanish Inquisition.*[24]

When these 'foul Distortions' are fully revealed, we discover that, though licentious and genial, they were not nearly so 'foul' as our author would have us believe, nor even so lost in hedonistic squalor as that pictured in William Hogarth's illustration 'The Orgy'. On the contrary, their entertainments were conducted with no little decorum, and were contained within a well-structured organisation such as that at Sukey Bevell's molly house in the Mint: 'The Stewards are Miss Fanny Knight, and Aunt England; and pretty Mrs. Anne Page officiates as Clark. One of the Beauties of this Place is Mrs. Girl of Redriff, and with her, (or rather him) dip Candle-Mary a Tallow Chandler in the Burrough, and Aunt May an Upholsterer in the same place, are deeply in Love: Nurse Mitchell is a Barber of this Society; but those which are call'd the topping Beauties of this Place, have no Occasion for Men of his Occupation.'[25] (This probably means that some of them wore their hair long so they could pile it up upon their heads on gala occasions.)

The most spectacular evidence for the mollies' occasional female identification was their performance in a highly formalised ritual during their 'Festival Nights' known as 'mock birth' or 'lying-in'. According to Ned Ward, 'Not long since[,] they cushioned up one of their Brethern, or rather Sisters, according to Female Dialect, disguising him in a Woman's Night-Gown, Sarsanet Hood, & Night-rail[,] who when the Company were men, was to mimick a woman, produce a jointed Baby they had provided, which wooden Offspring was to be afterwards Christened, whilst one in a High Crown'd Hat, I am [t]old old Bedlam's Pinner, representing a Country Midwife, & another dizen'd up in a Huswife's Coif for a Nurse & all the rest of an impertinent Decorum of a Christening.'[26] And according to James Dalton in 1728, 'they sometimes have a Lying-inn, when one of them is plac'd in a Chair, and the others attending with Napkins, a Bason of Water, &c. Susan Guzzle, a Gentleman's Servant, is the Midwife, and with a great Deal of Ceremony, a jointed Baby is brought from under the Chair he sits on. Mrs May was sometimes since brought to Bed of a Cheshire Cheese, Madam Blackwell and Aunt England, standing Gossips.'[27]

This ceremony may seem so grotesque as to impress itself vividly upon our imaginations, and prompt us to look at it more closely. I doubt very much that mock birth is simply an erotic game or merely an imitation or parody of an important event in a woman's life. Whatever meanings or values the ritual may have acquired by the eighteenth century, it almost certainly originated as an act of imitative magic designed to cast off sickness or evil spirits. Thus in a New Guinea tribe we hear of the Labuni, a disease- spirit in short petticoats, who is believed to enter humans by the rectum. Healing women would then perform a ritual by which the Labuni is ejected per rectum. So also among the Mohave Indians, when transvestite men mimic pregnancy and childbirth, and go to the fringes of the camp grounds where they are ceremonially delivered of stones. A host of other examples of the phenomenon — called *couvade* — can be gleaned from anthropological surveys .[28]

A more direct parallel can be found less than a century earlier — performed in the royal bedchamber where King James I lay on his deathbed. A grype — a young pig — was brought into the room dressed up as a baby. This infant — even more ludicrous than a pair of bellows — was duly delivered of the mother (one of the court ladies) by the Duchess of Buckingham, dressed as the midwife, and held while the baptismal service was read from a prayer-book by a courtier dressed as a bishop. When the christening concluded, the bewildered pig was chased squealing out of the room, much to the merriment of all and sundry. When the Duke of Buckingham — who had stood as the 'godfather' — was subsequently accused of blasphemy for organising this farce, he dismissed the charge by saying that it was merely to make the King laugh. And so it did. But also, suggests Margaret Murray in *God of the Witches*, 'The ceremony was obviously to transfer the pain from which the King was suffering, to an animal, and is the only complete account of the rite.'[29] It should be noted that the magical logic of transference would have been apparent had James himself 'given birth' to the pig-baby. The incident is not recorded in sufficient detail to indicate whether or not the King participated more directly than as a bemused spectator, or whether or not any of the laughter was stimulated by innuendos about the similarities of sickness and pregnancy, the sick-bed and the lying-in bed. Neither is the molly rite recorded in sufficient detail concerning the 'mother's' actions — for example, whether or not 'a great Deal of Ceremony' included such things as screams to imitate the pain of childbirth, bearing-down, and so forth — or how it was determined which molly would play the mother.

Of course the mollies would not have been consciously aware of the more primitive significance of mock birth, but their own rites may well have served the same function. But what was the suffering which the rite was to have mitigated? Geza Roheim suggests that the New Guinea rites 'symbolise disease as the consequence of repressed homosexual desire.' It might be more accurate to add 'and also oppressed homosexual desire'. The mollies were under daily pressures from a hostile society not to express their natural emotions, or run the risk of being hanged or publicly shamed in the pillory. Occasional 'lyings-in' could serve to relieve their collective anxiety through outrageous fun, and what today is called 'camp' behaviour. Theoretically it could also relieve the tension of guilt, but there is no evidence that the mollies felt guilty about their natures; that would come with the advent of psychology in the nineteenth century. During the eighteenth century, fear of being hanged was the more likely cause of anxiety.

Mock birth is not so much a case of aping heterosexuals or even mimicking women, as a means of blunting the end of heterosexual prejudice. The mollies were the scapegoats of society, and their own sub-society similarly needed a scapegoat, be it a wooden doll or a Cheshire cheese. A more learned molly might have been aware of Plutarch's *Life of Theseus*, in which we learn that at the annual feast of Gorpiaeus on the island of Cyprus, a boy dresses up as Ariadne, lies upon the altar in the sacred grove of Venus Ariadne, screams and struggles in imitation of childbirth, and ritually gives birth to an image representing the child of Theseus. As with the mock birth cited above, this also is a variation upon the scapegoat motif, wherein one person undergoes pain for the sake of the tribe, and his actions guarantee the renewal of another annual cycle of the seasons. The mother is impersonated by a boy because the world is believed to go topsy-turvy once a year in order to renew itself (just as an hour-glass is turned upside down to begin again each cycle), and hence the 'natural' order of procreation is appropriately inverted by a transvestite.

It is possible that 'lying-in' served the same mythical and tribal function for the molly clubs as they did in the primordial past. The ritual survived virtually unchanged well into the early nineteenth century. Sometime between 1810 and 1814 several people in Clements Lane 'near the new Church in the Strand were seized in the very act of giving caudle to their lying-in women, and the new-born infants personated by large dolls! and so well did they perform the characters they assumed, that one miscreant escaped the vigilance of the officers and the examining magistrates, and was discharged as a woman!'[30] I can find no references to similar rites in the later nineteenth-century subculture, nor any evidence that it was practised in the twentieth-century gay subculture, nor any suggestion as to why it has gone out of fashion.

(3) Molly Marriages

The much more commonplace practice among the mollies was that of 'Marrying', about which we have few specific details though the act itself is frequently referred to. Quite often the term is merely synonymous with 'fucking', and few can gainsay that this euphemism is superior to the other alternative, the lawyers' 'sodomitically assaulting'. Even if a molly house had its own Marrying Room, the nuptials celebrated therein generally involved only the most temporary bonds of intimacy and seldom lasted longer than the 'Wedding Night'. The men would 'go out by Couples into another Room on the same Floor, to be marry'd, as they call'd it', and 'when they came back they would tell what they had been doing, which in their Dialect they call'd Marrying';[31] this is somewhat analogous to publishing the banns, but unlikely to include any vows of fidelity. Indeed, at George Whittle's 'Chapel' at the Royal Oak, Ned Courtney was 'helped to two or three Husbands.'

Occasionally, however, Marrying went beyond a single Wedding Night — or even successive Wedding Nights — and was celebrated with at least some of the formality of the heterosexual equivalent. One Sukey Hawes, for example, informed James Dalton of a Wedding that took place around 1728, between Moll Irons, presumably a blacksmith, and another molly who was a butcher. The bridal pair were attended by two 'Bridesmaids', Princess Seraphina the butcher of Butcher-Row, and Miss Kitten (alias Mr Oviat, 'who sometime since stood in the pillory'). Two other members of the party were Powell, alias St Dunstan's Kate, and Madam Blackwell, men who themselves were 'deeply in Love' with one another. (Dalton reveals that John Potter, who was convicted in 1727 or 1728 for stealing rich hangings from the Duke of Montague, was testified against by none other than Madam Blackwell.[32])

Their functions at the nuptials are not specified, nor is there any mention of persons serving such roles as best man or priest. At Sukey Bevell's molly 'Club' in the Mint we have noticed the existence of Stewards, a Clerk and even a Barber; and some ceremonies there may have required a master of ceremonies, perhaps a figure such as Eccleston who guarded the door to the marrying room at Mother Clap's. Such functionaries no doubt served various matrimonial roles in some of the molly houses, though we find not the slightest allusion to a *bona fide* minister — or even mock-minister — officiating at such ceremonies until Rev. John Church performed those duties for the Vere Street Coterie in the early 1800s (the subject of Chapter 12). So despite a fair number of references to Chapels, Marrying Rooms, Wedding Nights, Husbands and Spouses, it seems likely that molly marriages seldom acquired the paraphernalia or significance of heterosexual marriages. Mating or pair-bonding is nevertheless documented in several instances, as previously noted: Moll Irons and the butcher were married to one another; St Dunstan's Kate and Madam Blackwell were 'deeply in Love', Robert Whale and York Horner who were jointly convicted for keeping a molly house lived together as a couple; Dip-Candle Mary and Aunt May were 'deeply in Love'.

In all these instances, and others, the terms of endearment were 'special Sweetheart', 'Husband' and 'Spouse'; curiously enough, there is no recorded use of the term 'wife'. Physically and verbally the molly marriage consisted of two husbands. At the very least this makes etymological sense, for the word 'marry' comes from the Latin *maritus*, meaning 'husband' (from *mas, maris,* 'man'): there is no linguistic reason why one husband should not take another husband. Nor is there any reason for us to assume that molly partners would adopt distinctive gender roles in their relationships; they both adopted female roles in so far as they both assumed Maiden Names at their festive gatherings, but sexually there is no indication of a strict dichotomy between inserter and receptor roles. In many molly houses all-round effeminate mimicry was the order of the day during times of merry-make, but we nowhere see the insistence upon butch-femme role-playing which plagued so many relationships in the mid-twentieth-century gay subculture, where partners all too often aped the stereotypes of heterosexual romance.

A number of the mollies were in fact legally married to women. The documents are too incomplete for us to be very certain about the ratio of married men to bachelors, but my general impression is that of those men who were sufficiently accepting of their own homosexuality to become active participants in the molly subculture and thus come to our attention, fewer than one-fifth simultaneously maintained a heterosexual marriage:

more than four-fifths were either bachelors, or widowers, or their wives were separated from them. Men who strictly speaking were bisexuals probably would not have become actively involved with the organised molly subculture for fear that their wives and family would hear of it; instead of contributing to the social life of the subculture, they sought same-sex partners in privies and cruising grounds or simply at haphazard. Today most men convicted for 'gross indecency' in toilets and saunas are either married or have an occupation especially vulnerable to scandal (teacher, clergyman and so forth), and a similar pattern emerges from the early eighteenth-century documents. It is not too surprising, for example, that William Brown, captured in the Moorfields cruising grounds, had been a married man for about 13 years, while the men convicted as a direct result of the raids upon the molly houses in 1726 were obviously more homosexual than heterosexual. Thomas Wright, George Kedger and Thomas Phillips were unmarried; Gabriel Lawrence had been married for 11 years, but his wife had died seven years earlier (he had one child, aged 13); George Whittle had been married, but his wife had been dead for two years (he had two children, one still living), though the court may have acquitted him partly because of his defence that 'I was going to marry another Woman, a Widow, just before this Misfortune broke out'; William Griffin was married and had several children, but did not live with his wife; of this group only Martin Mackintosh apparently lived with his wife.

It is doubtful that the documents have distorted the facts regarding heterosexual status, for a marriage alliance would have been brought forward whenever possible as good character testimony at a trial, and journalists would not have missed the opportunity to exploit such a scandalous version of adultery to liven up their satirical pamphlets. Those pamphleteers who clearly relied upon first-hand observation seldom mention such heterosexual marriages, and it is unwise to put any faith in the more sensational pamphlets which suggest, as does a poem in *The Fruit Shop* of 1766, that mollies' 'Women are kept for nothing but the breed.' In *Hell upon Earth* (1729) we find an anecdote which is very likely an updated version of Boccaccio's famous tale about the tables turned: one Tolson, a 'frequent buggerer, . . . once having caught a Foot-Soldier in Bed with his Wife, . . . insisted upon no other Satisfaction than to commit the detestable Sin of Sodomy with him, which the other comply'd with, and so the Affair was made easy.'[33] However, towards the end of the eighteenth century, when the molly subculture was being transmuted into the margery subculture, and certainly by the time of the mary-ann subculture of the early nineteenth century, we do find a higher number of marriages amongst the homosexual men, and some evidence that they may have abused their wives.

(4) Rogues' Lexicon

The dialect of the molly subculture may have had much in common with the Rogues' lexicon or canting dialect used by thieves, highway robbers, vagabonds and female prostitutes.[34] The mollies were certainly familiar with the Stews, or dens of heterosexual prostitution (derived from the medieval bathing houses used for such purposes), to which they are supposed to have offered innovations. That part of the molly subculture which is definitely known to have overlapped with the criminal underworld would have known such flash words as the Rumbo or the Whit for Newgate prison; the Spinning Ken, or Bridewell prison; a Flash Ken, or house frequented by thieves; the Nubbing Cheat, or gallows; to Shove the Tumbler, to be whipped at cart's tail; Buttock-and-File, pickpocket whore; Dudds, linen; Mish, shirt; Shap, hat; Stampers, shoes; Poll, wig; Margery-Prater, a hen; Queer Cuffin, justice of the peace; Queer-Ken, prison house; Queer Booze, bad drink; to Cut Queer Whids, to use foul language; and Queer-Bird, man lately released from prison.[35] We have no proof that homosexuals were called queers until some 200 years later, but a phrase such as Queer Cull, meaning 'a fop, a fool', might gradually have acquired this meaning.

The mollies adopted some terms current among thieves: they identified themselves as mollies, molly-culls, mollying-culls, and mollying-bitches.[36] A moll (as in the modern phrase gun moll) was a thief's or tramp's harlot; its ultimate derivation from the Latin *mollis*, meaning 'soft' (hence our term 'mollify') makes it a suitable description for an effeminate man. A cull, which dates from 1660, was a thief's mate or partner, but was generally used in the sense of bloke, fool, or just guy; in the cant used by highway robbers, a cull was the guy jostled by a pickpocket, while one of their most familiar enemies, the prison turn-key, was the quod cull. Culls, however, also meant testicles. It is not too difficult to make the transition from a thief and his mate to a pair of mates in the gay subculture, and on the whole 'molly cull' seems rather apt.[37]

Mollies were called sodomites, buggers, pathics, punks, and Jesuits. Amongst themselves, mollies in a moment of anger or playful banter might more likely use the epithets 'a Bold Face', 'little dear Toad', 'you bold Pullet',[38] bitch or queen. This term is derived from the Middle English *quean*, meaning whore. One of the mollies was named Queen Irons, but the term was far from being as commonplace as it is today, and I have located only a few examples. In the 1699 lottery which mentions Captain Rigby, a molly is caricatured as a ship named the *Queen of Sheba*. Alexander Pope in his *Heroic Epistle Bounce to Fop* heaps abuse upon 'The Motley Race of Hervey queenies / And Courtly Vices, Beastly Venyes.' (His allusion is to the bisexual Lord Hervey, to be discussed in Chapter 9.) And in a dialogue between two mollies in 1729 we overhear one enquiring of another, 'Where have you been you saucy Queen?'[39]

The use of Maiden Names has given rise to the view that the mollies were almost invariably effeminate. Effeminacy is not a simple phenomenon, and I am not going to attempt to account for its manifestations among the mollies. No one has been able to demonstrate more than an incidental link between homosexual behaviour and effeminate mannerisms, and a historical study such as this can only go a little way towards suggesting some of the social factors that tended to encourage certain kinds of behaviour. First and foremost, effeminacy is a form of self-advertisement. With the aid of exaggerated mannerisms and camp behaviour a man can deliberately call attention to himself and publicise his sexual availability, in exactly the same way that a coquette establishes contact. It is above all a tool of communication, a means of conveying an important message to like-minded men. A sense of identity arises from the reinforcement of that message, self-identification as a *molly* — not as a *woman*. It is an important distinction; as far as we can tell, gay men did not think of themselves as women trapped in men's bodies until the sexologists began popularising this theory in the 1860s.

Within the protective walls of a molly house, many men did adopt feminine mannerisms, names, and even clothing on special festive occasions, partly as a result of internalising society's view of them, but mainly as a way of enjoying themselves and letting off steam. Outside of the clubs, some continued to make use of maiden names as a kind of secret signal to members of a confraternity, and it was common even for non-effeminate men to use maiden names, irrespective of sexual role or mannerisms. But it will be seen that most of the men mentioned throughout this study were neither effeminate nor particularly conspicuous in appearance and manner. In fact we are left with an overriding impression of vigorous and lusty bonhomie, which ought to persuade even the most prejudiced observer that the mollies were more vulgar than aesthetic, and evinced more vitality than effeteness. Those men who took the risk of being visible members of the subculture tended to reinforce amongst themselves the marks of their differentness, of which effeminacy was the leading stigma to be internalised. The satirical and moralistic pamphleteers do of course present the mollies as effeminate 'he-whores' without exception, but this is mere invective rather than description, clearly based upon homophobic prejudice rather than honest observation, and in any study of homosexuality we have to exercise great care to distinguish self-image from satire.

Much of the molly lexicon, including the Maiden Name tradition, originates in the tendency of an oppressed subculture to adopt the abusive language with which a hostile supra-culture brands it, and then to modify it in such a way as to transform a contemptuous epithet into a humorous tag of affection — to take the sting out of the stigma. The early church fathers stigmatised homosexuals as *molles* or sissies, and secular society called effeminate men molly-coddles and homosexuals mollies; having no other self-referring terms except the even less appealing Sodomite or Bugger, gay men transformed Molly into a term of positive self-identification, in exactly the same way that the modern subculture has transformed Gay (which derived originally from 'gay girl', meaning a female prostitute) into a term of pride and self-liberation.

By the beginning of the nineteenth century the Molly subculture had become the Margery subculture, and young male prostitutes were known as Margeries, a term that remained in use through the 1920s. By the early nineteenth century a Margery was a boy who dressed as a woman and hung around such places as the Strand, picking up men. By the end of the nineteenth century Mary-Ann had become the accepted term for a male homosexual prostitute, derived from underworld slang for a pickpocket who merely pretends to be homosexual in order to pat a man about the hips and lift his wallet.[40]

The Maiden Name tradition is still with us, despite attempts to break away from self-derogatory labelling, and the most favoured name is still Mary, though simple inversions are also common, such as Michelle for Michael. Humorous sobriquets such as Miss Prude or Miss Thing were once very popular, and 'the Countess' is still commonplace, or just 'Herself'. By a curious twist of usage, Molly and Margery have virtually disappeared from the gay male subculture, only to reappear in the lesbian subculture, where a 'femme' gay woman is called a 'molly dyke' or even named 'Marge' to distinguish her from the 'butch' gay woman or 'bull dyke'.

Chapter 6

Caterwauling

(1) Little Sports

Not surprisingly, the molly dialect contains a fair number of terms referring to sexual activities, in addition to 'sodomy' and 'buggery'. Phrases such as 'riding a rump' were used, at least in satirical literature, but intercourse was most commonly referred to with the very same euphemism most widely used today: the mollies 'make Love to one another, as they call'd it.' Occasionally we find euphemisms such as 'the pleasant Deed'[1] and 'to do the Story'.[2] Swive was used indiscriminately to describe homosexual as well as heterosexual intercourse, and often the terms are more blunt, such as 'to indorse, as they call it, but in plain English to commit Sodomy', from contemporary boxing slang.[3] Another term for anal intercourse is 'caudle-making' or 'giving caudle', from the Latin *cauda*, a tail.[4] Towards the end of the century, sodomites were called 'backgammon players' and 'gentlemen of the back door'.[5]

Gay cruising grounds in the eighteenth century were called 'the markets',[6] where the mollies went 'strolling and caterwauling'[7] (from 'Caterwauling, Men and Women desirous of Copulation; a Term borrowed from Cats'[8]); if they were lucky, they 'picked up'[9] partners, or 'trade'[10] (both terms are still in common use among gay men today); if luckier still, they would 'make a bargain'[11] or agree to have sex. This may seem to be a rather commonplace monetary metaphor, but in fact it comes from the specific game known as 'selling a bargain', in which the seller had to name his or her hindquarters in answer to the question 'What?'. Example: 'It's white, and it follows me!' 'What?' 'Mine arse'.[12] Another variation is 'bit a blow', equivalent to the modern phrase 'score a trick'.[13] To 'put the bite'[14] on someone is to arrange for sex, possibly sex for money, derived from a contemporary phrase implying some sort of trickery, usually financial.

Our knowledge of the mollies' Little Sports would not be complete without some survey of the specific sexual practices in which they engaged. Unfortunately many of the trial records have been censored beyond recognition, and a passage such as the following is not very helpful: 'The Prisoner said — and —, and Jack said —, and the Prisoner said —, by which I concluded that they were committing Sodomy together.' All of the available evidence, however, suggests that oral intercourse, fellatio, was rarely practised by the mollies. The crime of sodomy or buggery was legally defined as *coitus per anum*, so naturally enough anal intercourse is the most frequently documented sexual practice in the trial records. But this is true of the pamphlet literature as well as the court records, and even the latter do not exclude circumstantial evidence of other non-prosecutable behaviour such as kissing, masturbation or interfemoral rubbing. Nor can one find any instances of slang which make puns upon licking or sucking or *soixante-neuf*. It is only towards the end of the century that one begins to find references to 'gamahuching' which can refer both to fellatio and cunnilingus in pornographic literature. The English have always regarded oral intercourse as especially unclean, and even in very recent times the British gay subculture regarded such activity as an American import.

Only a few instances of oral intercourse have come to light through the trial records. In 1704 John Norton took hold of the privates of John Coyney, 'putting them into his mouth and sucking them.'[15] In 1735 Henry Wolf met John Holloway on an errand for his master a brandy merchant, took him to several pubs where he fondled him, and then to Bishop's Gate Church Yard where he bought him a nosegay and a penny custard. Eventually he approached Bethlehem Hospital, which ran along the south side of Moorfields. 'Coming to Bedlam, he perfectly pull'd and haul'd me in to see the Mad-folks. There he took me into the House of Office, and pull'd down his own Breeches and mine, and — in his Mouth: Then he carried me into the Booth, to see the Wild Beasts. When we came out, he said, he hop'd he should see me often.' Wolf was apprehended at their next meeting, but no one appeared to support the errand boy's story, so he was acquitted.[16] This case is of course more interesting for what it reveals about daring (and crude) pick-up techniques, and the nature of the entertainments at Bethlehem Hospital, than for the fact that oral intercourse took place.

One case in Bath provides some interesting details: in 1802 the young James Reader applied for a job to Rev. George Donnisthorpe, who offered him liquor and money and said 'if he [Donnisthorpe] were a Lady and had ten thousand a year he would bestow it all on him [Reader].' Donnisthorpe took Reader's 'private Member in his hand, knelt down on one knee and put it into his Mouth', and then tried to lay him upon a sofa. Reader revealed his experience to a friend or guardian the following Sunday, but nevertheless saw Donnisthorpe four more times before warning him off. Donnisthorpe was indicted, but he claimed he had not received justice and the case was removed from the Quarter Sessions by a writ of *certiorari*, though he was not retried in a higher court.[17]

Anal intercourse was the preferred route, without refinements. One would infer that the mollies contented themselves with spit and persistence, for there are few references to the use of any lubricants other than saliva, and not even much indication that saliva was used to ease entry. Thus King Bolloxinion in the Earl of Rochester's play *Sodom, or The Quintessence of Debauchery* (1684) says:

> *Since I have bugger'd human arse, I find*
> *Pintle to Cunt is not so much inclin'd.*
> *What tho the letchery be dry, 't is smart;*
> *A Turkish arse I love with all my heart.*

The positions themselves were relatively unimaginative: the favourite style is clearly front-to-back, the inserter lying atop the receptor if they are in bed (or on the floor, or on a bench, or in the grass), or the receptor bending over to receive the inserter if they are in a public place and in a hurry. Foreplay such as rimming (oral-anal contact) is not recorded, though finger-fucking is occasionally noted (as in the Captain Rigby case); the knees-up position is not recorded, though often enough one man sits bare upon another's lap, which suggests that the lap position was not unknown. There are several cases of 'emitting between the thighs', *frottage*, though in nearly every instance this was because full penetration was somehow thwarted. The receptor or 'passive' role was not felt to be particularly humiliating or subordinate or even 'feminine' amongst the mollies themselves. Thomas Newton and Ned Courtney regularly adopted the receptor role, in contrast to modern hustlers who insist on assuming the inserter role. Foreplay regularly included kissing, 'kissing with open mouth', tongue sucking, embracing, caressing, and mutual masturbation, all accompanied by endearing sentiments. None of this is remarkable, and specialised interests such as whipping were resevered for heterosexual brothels.

The best description of the kind of straightforward sex in which eighteenth-century homosexual gentlemen engaged is provided by John Cleland in *Memoirs of a Woman of Pleasure*; the following passage, which is deleted from most editions, and does not even appear in the 1749 or 1784 editions, describes a scene witnessed by Fanny Hill on her trip to Hampton Court:

For presently the eldest unbuttoned the other's breeches, and removing the linen barrier, brought out to view a white shaft, middle sized, and scarce fledged, when after handling and playing with it a little, with other dalliance, all received by the boy without other opposition than certain wayward coynesses, ten times more alluring than repulsive, he got him to turn round, with his face from him, to a chair that stood hard by, when knowing, I suppose, his office, the Ganymede now obsequiously leaned his head against the back of it, and projecting his body, made a fair mark, still covered with his shirt, as he thus stood in a side view to me, but fronting his companion, who, presently unmasking his battery, produced an engine that certainly deserved to be put to a better use, and very fit to confirm me in my disbelief of the possibility of things being pushed to odious extremities, which I had built on the disproportion of parts; but this disbelief I was now to be cured of, as by my consent all young men should likewise be, that their innocence may not be betrayed into such snares, for want of knowing the extent of their danger, for nothing is more certain than that ignorance of a vice is by no means a guard against it.

Slipping, then, aside the young lad's shirt, and tucking it up under his cloaths behind, he shewed to the open air those globular fleshy eminences that compose the Mount Pleasants of Rome, and which now, with all the narrow vale that intersects them, stood displayed and exposed to his attack, nor could I without a shudder behold the dispositions he made for it. First, then, moistening well with spittle his instrument, obviously to make it glib; he pointed, he introduced it, as I could plainly discern, not only from its direction, and my losing sight of it, but by the writhing, twisting, and soft murmured complaints of the young sufferer; but at length, the first straits of entrance being pretty well got through, everything seemed to move and go pretty currently on, as on a carpet road, without much rub or resistance; and now, passing one hand round his minion's hips, he got hold of his red-topped ivory toy, that stood perfectly stiff, and shewed, that if he was like his mother behind, he was like his father before; this he diverted himself with, whilst with the other he wantoned with his hair, and leaning forward over his back, drew his face, from which the boy shook the loose curls that fell over it, in the posture he stood him in, and brought him towards his, so as to receive a long breathed kiss; after which, renewing his driving, and thus continuing to harass his rear, the height of the fit came on with its usual symptoms, and dismissed the action.[18]

As in the above passage, sex was usually a matter of mutual pleasure, rather than payment and profit. Undoubtedly there were amateurish attempts at prostitution — by alehouse boys, linkboys, post boys, and errand boys out to earn a little extra pocket money — but the practice was not widespread enough to provoke public comment, nor did it involve a network of pimps and male whorehouses. The case of William Curtis is typical. He was a country lad who came to London around the age of 17 in 1728, and lodged with a printer at the Old Bailey, acting as his servant. In due course he had to share his bed with a new servant, John Ashford, who one day 'began to kiss me, and call me his dear Billy, and to meddle with my Privy Parts, and gave me Money not to speak of it.' After three months of this, 'he over-persuaded me to let him bugger me. And after that, he did it frequently' for nearly two more years, as Curtis did not bring charges against Ashford until late 1732. When asked why it had taken so long for him to bring charges, Curtis claimed to be an ignorant country lad who did not realise the greatness of the crime, and because Ashford 'allow'd me 3s. a Week constantly, besides Presents that he made me at other Times.' Curtis eventually made the acquaintance of other mollies, whom he named as Bishop, Cadogan, and Catton, 'and used to lye out o'Nights', so he left his lodgings and became very slightly more professional as both a prostitute and a blackmailer. It was his attempts to blackmail these mollies that eventually led to several trials. Ashford was acquitted of the charge of sodomy, not so much because Curtis's story was untrue (he acknowledged sharing a bed with Curtis and giving him money and books), but because the alleged event had taken place so long ago and was impossible to prove.[19]

An organised system of prostitution such as that observed (or fabricated?) by Mirabeau in Paris in the 1770s would have been inconceivable in England. There, he claimed, the police allowed public meeting places for homosexual activity. Young people who joined the profession were inspected and subject to regulations. The handsomest obtained very good fees from bishops and financiers; those without testicles, but who never-theless were capable of giving and taking pleasure, received less; those who were impotent and entirely passive received the least, but their impotence was first confirmed by whipping their genitals with nettles, introducing a long red pepper into their anus, and putting mustard on the resulting blisters. Surely this is sheer invention; certainly the likes of Ned Courtney and William Curtis would never have submitted to such an ordeal. In the much more casual underground of London's gay world, sex generally occurred in private, between consenting adults of similar ages and similar social backgrounds, and pick-ups were made at the molly houses, bog houses, parks and public highways. Group sex was infrequent, though promiscuity rather than pair-bonding seems to have been most common.

(2) 'Nothing but Love'

Youthful good looks were of course valued, and there are occasional instances of what might accurately be termed paedophilia. Despite the identification of pederasty with homosexuality in the popular imagination, it must be emphasised that cases of paedophilia are extremely rare in the trial records, and more often heterosexual than homosexual. The following account is given merely to illuminate an extremely infrequent aspect of gay life in England at this time.

In 1730 Isaac Broderick, Master of the Free School of the Coopers Company, in St Dunstan's, Stepney, was charged with assaulting Edward Caley, aged 10, and William Ham, Jr, aged 11. William Ham claimed that Broderick 'bid me go up Stairs to move some Chairs out of a Room into a Closet. I did so, and as I was coming down he met me on the Stairs, and bid me go up into his Room, which I did, and he follow'd and asked for a Cane. Then he bid me down with my Breeches, after which he felt all over my naked Body.' On another instance, 'one Day as I was in the Kitchen, he bid me go up into the Garret, and look for a marble-cover'd Pocket-Book, and said he would give me a Half-penny if I found it. He presently follow'd me, and asked me what I ow'd him. I said I did not know what he meant. Then he bid me pull down my Breeches, and sat down in a Chair, and put a Handkerchief before my Face, and said he wonder'd if I could see any Thing. And then he put — between my Thighs, and—.'

Ham claimed that Broderick had done the same to other boys, including Rue Lewis, Edward Lewis, John Wright and John Meer. Henry Henneker, between 10 and 11 years old, said Broderick had 'stroked [me] all over'. And Edward Casey reported that one day the Master 'sent me up to look for some Buttons. He presently followed and locked me into the Room, and took a bit of Rod and bid me down with my Breeches. Then he felt all about me, and gave me a gentle Stroke or two, and bid me not cry out, for he would not hurt me, and then he put — between — and —.' Casey told his bedfellow William Allen what had happened, and showed him 'a Blister between his Thighs'. The incidents came to the attention of the boys' parents, and Broderick was brought to trial in May. Several witnesses appeared on his behalf, one of whom said 'I believe that all Trinity College would give him a good Character.' Broderick himself did not deny the charges, and made no excuses for his behaviour except to say that he used one of the boys so, 'to improve him in his Studies'. Broderick was found guilty and sentenced to stand in the pillory, once at Ratcliff Gardens and once in Charing Cross, to pay a fine of two nobles, and to go to prison for three months.[20]

The other case involves Gilbert Lawrence, a 34-year-old French gilder in St Brides, who sodomised his 14-year-old apprentice Paul Oliver in July 1730. One day, after Oliver had been with Lawrence for six months, the latter made offers, and they slept together. At two o'clock in the morning Lawrence 'jump'd upon me, and held me down so that I was ready to be stifled, my Breath being almost gone.' Oliver tried to get free, and cried out for help that never came. Lawrence 'hurt me so much, that I thought it would have killed me. . . . He put — a great way into — , . . . there was Wet and Nastiness, which he afterwards wiped away with a Sheet. He tore me so, that I could not tell what to do; for I could not do my Needs.' Oliver told his mother the next day, and a surgeon who examined him 'found his — quite open; it had been penetrated above an Inch; there was a hole in which a finger and thumb might be put; and the — was black all a-round, and appear'd like that of a Hen after laying an Egg.' Lawrence made no defence, except to say that he had been married, though his wife was now dead. He was hanged at Tyburn on Wednesday 7 October 1730.[21] Paedophiles of course were not part of the gay subculture, and they would not have found partners in the molly houses. We can only speculate on the frequency of paedophile contact in schools, but very few instances came to the attention of the courts.

Cases of homosexual rape are equally infrequent (though heterosexual rape is prominent in the trial records). The legal phrase 'sodomitical assault' does not, in fact, literally refer to assault, or sex accompanied by violence or the threat of violence. It is simply a catchall phrase indicating the abhorrence with which the law viewed every sort of homosexual intercourse, however entered into, and an unwillingness to recognise the fact that both parties could actually consent to such an act, with pleasure. I have found only a few clear instances of homosexual rape during the early eighteenth century, and here give an account of two cases, one of which is more humorous than horrible, and one of which may involve a false accusation.

On a Sunday in early September, 1721, Nicholas Leader met George Duffus at a meeting-house in Old Gravel Lane, London. When the service was ended, George came up to Nicholas and began to discourse in commendation of the minister. By this means, for three or four Sundays in succession, George insinuated himself into Nicholas' good opinion. In early October, George, quite a religious young chap, invited Nicholas to share a pot of ale with him at Mr Powell's alehouse in the Minories. Enjoying each other's company, they arranged to meet again a few days hence at the Three Merry Potters at the Hermitage. There, on 9 October, they sat together drinking and talking till it got rather late, when George said that since he lived a great way off he would be most grateful if he could share Nicholas' quarters for the night. Nicholas, being a trustful soul, made no objection, but as soon as they were got into bed together George began to kiss Nicholas and hug him and call him 'My Dear'. When Nicholas asked George what he meant by that, George answered, 'No Harm, nothing but Love', and thereupon he lay atop him and thrust his tongue into his mouth. Nicholas threw him off, but he climbed on again, and was again thrown off, three or four times, until Nicholas threatened to kick him out of bed if he would not lie still. At that, George seized Nicholas by the throat like as if to strangle him, flipped him over upon his belly, and, in Nicholas' inimitable words later at the trial, 'forcibly enter'd my Body about an Inch, as near as I can guess.' Nicholas continued to struggle in his awkward position, forcing George to withdraw at the last minute and to emit in his own hand. But clapping his cum on the tail of Nicholas' ruffled nightshirt, George shouted 'Now you have it!' Nicholas would no doubt have turned him out of doors, but for fear of disturbing his ancient grandmother who lay sick in the next room.

The next morning George told Nicholas that he really should not be so distraught at the previous night's experience, for he had often done the same to others, in particular to a cute young cabin boy, and they suffered no worse for it. Nicholas was not convinced, and a few days later acquainted some of his friends with what had happened, and they advised him to prosecute. So Nicholas obtained a warrant of arrest from Justice Tiller, and the following day went with a constable to the meeting-hall to apprehend George. George was devoutly seated in a pew, and Nicholas and the constable sat down on either side of him. Suspecting — because of whispers and pointed fingers between the two — that some design was being made upon his liberty, George calmly took up his hat and proceeded towards the exit with all due speed. Perceiving that he was being followed, as he walked down the street, George broke into a run, with Nicholas and the constable in hot pursuit. He led them a merry chase, but they overtook him, and refused to heed his pleas not to expose him to public shame, even though he protested the classic argument, 'We are all Sinners, and it is hard for a Man to suffer for the first fault.'

They hauled off poor George to the nearest magistrate, and when the case went to court in December it came out that his love assignations had a common pattern. Some months previously, he had met Mr Powell — owner of the pub where he first drank with Nicholas — at a lecture, had followed him out afterwards, and began to discourse with Powell on the excellence of the lecturer, and to tell him what a comfort and refreshment of soul such religious teachings provided him. This occasioned a good deal of converse between the two devout men, after which George arranged to meet Powell at his public house in the Minories. So a few days hence, on 12 October, they spent the evening together in pleasing religious discourse, and when it grew late George said he lived a far way off, and could he spend the night with Powell? Powell readily consented, but no sooner were they abed than George began to kiss him and take hold of his Privities. 'How lean ye be!' says he, 'Do but feel how fat I am!', therewith endeavouring to convey Powell's hand to his own Privities. Powell thought to ward off such advances simply by turning his back upon George, who thereupon thrust his Yard betwixt Powell's thighs and emitted. Powell declined George's request to do the same to him, for 'I was a Stranger to such Things', but he made no row about the matter. George left next morning, advising him to be not troubled, for such things were very common, and Powell let the matter rest.

But Nicholas, perhaps more upset at nearly being strangled than at losing his virginity by an inch, brought the matter to court, and in December George Duffus was indicted for attempted sodomy. He was found guilty in March, and sentenced to pay a fine of 20 marks, to be imprisoned for two months, and to stand in the pillory near Old Gravel Lane. It is not known whether or not he took up his old habits upon release. One of the more interesting aspects of this case is that Mr Powell, under very nearly the same circumstances, did not choose to prosecute, and to some degree even remained friendly with George; it is uncertain whether his reticence was due to naivety or to worldly wisdom.[22]

A more doubtful instance of sex-with-violence is the case of Thomas Rodin (or Reading). Henry Clayton, who slept in the same room with Rodin at the home of Peter Wright the shoemaker, at the Three Shoes next door to Harrow in Long-Alley in Moorfields, told the court that one night in March 1722 he saw Rodin attack a man unknown. 'The Prisoner bid him pull his Breeches off, which the Stranger not doing readily, the Prisoner struck him several times. — I believe he might give him fifteen Blows, — and then the Stranger let down his Breeches, and the Prisoner turn'd him on his Face, and fell on him.' The court said 'It's very surprising that a Man should make such an abominable attempt upon a Stranger; and that a Stranger should so soon comply; and that they both should do this before Witness.'

Rodin claimed that he sold fruit and that his wife sold greens, and that once he had quarrelled with Clayton at the Green Dragon alehouse in Moorfields and Clayton called him a molly and sodomite, whereupon Rodin indicted him at Hicks-Hall. Peter Wright testified that Clayton was both a 'scandalous Villain' and a pimp, and that one of his whores, Angelica Latham, had abused Rodin as a pickpocket and a 'Sodomite Dog'. It seemed reasonable to the jury to infer that Clayton had brought false charges out of spite. The judge's observations were persuasive, and since no victim ever appeared to give testimony, Rodin was acquitted of attempted sodomy in October 1722.[23] But the facts remain doubtful, and Rodin could have been a molly even if this specific charge were false. He may well have been the molly mentioned in Dalton's *Narrative* of 1728 who went by the maiden name of 'Ellinor Rodin'.

Homosexual rape may have occurred in prisons, as it does today, though I know of only one case. The prisons were overcrowded, and it is not surprising that the standard practice of sleeping two to a bed sometimes led to homosexual love-making. In 1732 P[atrick?] Kirk, a prisoner in the Fleet Prison, complained to the Chamberlain that his 'chum', Thomas Sylvester, for the past six or seven weeks had been attempting to sodomise him, and he begged to be allowed to share his bed with some other prisoner or to be sent to another prison. Kirk and Sylvester quarrelled with one another in the public room of the prison, and accused one another of being sodomites. Kirk forced the matter to be brought to court, where he claimed that Sylvester 'went to Bed before me, and as soon as I came to Bed to him, he caught me in his Arms and kiss'd me. I desired him to desist, for I did not like such Behaviour. I turn'd about, and went to sleep, and by-and-by he thrust his Y[ar]d so hard against my Fun[damen]t, that it waked me.' The Chamberlain denied his request for relocation, for 'the House was then so full that I could not be chum'd elsewhere.' The jury acquitted Sylvester, and obviously felt that both plaintiff and defendant were convicts too scandalous to merit consideration. Presumably Kirk was forced to continue to chum with Sylvester.[24] The problem may have steadily worsened, for by 1810 the London House of Correction was providing separate galleries for sodomites, apprentices, and soldiers.[25]

It was very common practice for men to chum together, or sleep together, throughout the eighteenth century and well into the nineteenth century. Servants always shared their beds, as did lodgers at public houses, inns, and lodging houses. An early Victorian pornographic weekly magazine cautions young men against sharing a bed with strangers, and illustrates the moral with an exquisite tale about a merchant's lad who shared a bed with a stranger at a public house in St Giles, and fell instantly into a deep sleep, 'from which he was awaked in the night, by a most acute smarting pain, and a horrible commotion in his guts. In fact, he found the enemy in full possession of his close quarters, who would not retire until he had completed his errand.'[26]

Chapter 7

Popular Rage

(1) Defences of Homosexuality

The mollies pursued their lifestyles with a bawdy insouciance, in marked contrast to the guilt-ridden behaviour of so many homosexuals from the 1860s through the 1950s. A surprisingly large number of the mollies admitted the 'crimes' with which they were charged, but did so readily, unblushingly, and without shame. We recall how William Brown 'was not ashamed to answer . . . *I think there is no Crime in making what use I please of my own Body.*'[1] On the one hand we have seen mollies whose tremendous presence of mind — call it bluff if you will — can enable them to deny the facts in the face of the most obvious evidence, as when John Dicks, caught in the very act, and lying panting on a youth's backside, nevertheless protested his innocence even while adjusting his attire.[2] On the other hand we have seen mollies who seem to be quite insensible to the notion that homosexual behaviour should be regarded with abhorrence by the multitude, as when Isaac Broderick defended himself against the very serious charge of molesting his pupil by claiming 'to improve him in his Studies.'[3] Some mollies positively glowed with pride over their natures, such as one of the members of the Vere Street Coterie in the 1810s, 'a deaf tyre Smith', who 'has two sons, both very handsome young men, whom he boasts are as full as depraved as himself',[4] or Tolson, who 'was not ashamed to confess' to buggery. It is true that some of the very first mollies to be arrested, in 1707, hanged themselves or cut their throats while awaiting trial, but such suicides are not again recorded for more than a hundred years.

Rarely do we find any expression of self-disgust, though naturally men would plead not to be exposed to public shame, for there was every reason to fear severe physical abuse during exposure in the pillory. Internalised guilt is absent not because the mollies were libertines or rakes, but simply because they enjoyed themselves, and seemed genuinely surprised when others called their pleasure sinful. Most of the mollies' *participes crimens* were quite willing partners who shared the same desire. Those few heterosexual men occasionally approached by a molly did not always react with the spontaneous revulsion which we might expect from them. Even the law-abiding citizens who lived in the neighbourhood of a known molly house seldom heaped abuse upon its customers or brought the tavern to the attention of the police. Generally they contented themselves with neighbourhood gossip until goaded into action by an interfering member of the Societies for Reformation of Manners.

The molly subculture was fairly open rather than furtive, sometimes so much so that their 'flaunting it' aroused the indignation of the self-appointed guardians of public morality. According to the author of 'Œconomy of Love':

> *Go where we will, at ev'ry time and place,*
> *Sodom confronts and stares us in the face;*
> *They ply in public, at our very doors,*
> *And take the bread from much more honest whores.*
>
> *Those who are mean, high paramours secure;*
> *And the rich guilty screen the guilty poor:*
> *The sin, too proud to feel from reason awe,*
> *And those who practice it too great for law.*[5]

As early as 1703 the mollies seem to have overrun the city, at least according to the author of *A New Dialogue between The Horse at Charing-Cross, and The Horse at Stocks-Market*: 'Such cursed Lewdness does infect the Town, / 'Tis a mere Sodom, or Gommorrah grown.' Apparently homosexuality in London was regarded with the same fashion as it was supposed to have been in Italy, where, according to the author of *Satan's Harvest Home*, sodomy is 'esteemed so trivial, and withal so modish a Sin, that not a Cardinal or Churchman of Note but has his Ganymede.'[6] In some satires we find the term 'Gany-boy'.[7] But of course the mollies were conscious that among the prejudiced populace they were generally regarded with disapprobation, sufficient evidence being their all-too-frequent fate on the pillory or gallows. The resulting stance of self-justification provoked such artifacts of molly culture as the following song once sung by 'that charming Warbler, Miss Irons' (presumably a blacksmith):[8]

Let the Fops of the Town upbraid
Us, for an unnatural Trade,
We value not Man nor Maid;
*   But among our own selves we'll be free,*
*   But among, &c.*

We'll kiss and we'll Sw[iv]e,
Behind we will drive,
And we will contrive
*   New Ways for Lechery,*
*   New Ways, &c.*

How sweet is the pleasant Sin?
With a Boy about Sixteen,
That has got no Hair on his Chin,
*   And a Countenance like a Rose,*
*   And a Countenance, &c.*

Here we will enjoy
The simpering Boy,
And with him we'll toy;
*   The Devil may take the Froes,*
*   The Devil &c.*

Confusion on the Stews,
And those that Whores do chuse,
We'll praise the Turks and Jews,
*   Since they with us do agree,*
*   Since they &c.*

They're not confin'd
To Water or Wind,
Before or behind,
*   But take all Liberty,*
*   But take &c.*

Achilles that Hero great,
Had Patroclus for a Mate;
Nay, Jove he would have a Lad,
*   The beautiful Ganymede,*
*   The Beautiful &c.*

Why should we then
Be daunted, when
Both Gods and Men
    Approve the pleasant Deed,
        Approve the &c.

This song may have been composed by a heterosexual satirist, but I tend to regard it as an authentic record of a molly oral tradition, similar to the bawdy songs such as 'Come, let us [bugger] finely' mentioned in the trial records as having been sung at Mother Clap's house. The lyrics are by no means beyond the capabilities of a non-professional poet, and one need not be a classical scholar to be familiar with its mythological allusions. Various bawdy ballads and lewd limericks still circulate in the modern gay subculture, though for the most part they remain unrecorded.

There were in fact several more serious defences of homosexuality, all from the rationalist and non-Christian standpoint. In *Gulliver's Travels* Swift ridiculed cultural relativism by the satiric suggestion that although the rudiments of lewdness are instinctive to women, the 'politer pleasures' of homosexuality in both sexes were 'entirely the production of art and reason' (Book IV, Chapter 7, last paragraph, which might have been added as a result of the raid on Mother Clap's molly house in the year of publication, 1726). Voltaire took a liberal attitude toward what he termed the *péché philosophique*. While at the court of Frederick the Great, Voltaire slept with an English gentleman as a 'scientific experiment'; he found it not to his taste. A few days later the Englishman informed him that he had repeated the experiment with another. Voltaire replied: 'Once, a philosopher; twice, a sodomite!'

Perhaps the earliest extended defence of homosexuality in literature occurs in Smollett's novel *Roderick Random* (1748), though it is uttered by the rascally Earl Strutwell and not meant to be taken seriously. In order to seduce Roderick, the Earl gives him a copy of Petronius' *Satyricon* and pretends to defend its lewdness (Chapter 51):

I own that his taste in love is generally decried, and indeed condemned by our laws; but perhaps that may be more owing to prejudice and misapprehension, than to true reason and deliberation. The best man among the ancients is said to have entertained that passion; one of the wisest of their legislators has permitted the indulgence of it in his commonwealth; the most celebrated poets have not scrupled to avow it. At this day it prevails not only over all the East, but in most parts of Europe; in our own country it gains ground apace, and in all probability will become in a short time a more fashionable vice than simple fornication. Indeed, there is something to be said in vindication of it; for, notwithstanding the severity of the law against offenders in this way, it must be confessed that the practice of this passion is unattended with that curse and burden upon society, which proceeds from a race of miserable and deserted bastards, who are either murdered by their parents, deserted to the utmost want and wretchedness, or bred up to prey upon the commonwealth. And it likewise prevents the debauchery of many a young maiden . . . not to mention the consideration of health, which is much less liable to be impaired in the gratification of this appetite . . . Nay, I have been told, that there is another motive, perhaps more powerful than all these, that induced people to cultivate this inclination, namely, the exquisite pleasure attending its success.

The sole advocate for the total decriminalisation of homosexuality was Jeremy Bentham, the Utilitarian philosopher and law reformer. In 1774–1775, and again in 1814–1816, he wrote some 300 manuscript pages reviewing the place of homosexuality in history and analyzing how it should be regarded from the Utilitarian standpoint. He could find 'no reason for punishing it at all: much less for punishing it with the degree of severity with which it has been commonly punished.' In ancient Greece 'everybody practised it: nobody was ashamed of it'; at the very worst, men such as Xenophon consider it 'as a weakness unbecoming to a philosopher, not as a turpitude or a crime unbecoming to a man.' The problem over interpretations of platonic Love with which the Victorians would wrestle, is easily resolved:

The Greeks knew the difference between love and friendship as well as we — they had distinct terms to signify them by: it seems reasonable therefore to suppose that when they say love they mean love, and when they say friendship only they mean friendship only. And with regard to Xenophon and his master, Socrates, and his fellow-scholar Plato, it seems more reasonable to believe them to have been addicted to this taste when they or any of them tell us so in express terms than to trust to the interpretations, however ingenious and however well-intended, of any men who write at this time of day, when they tell us it was no such thing.

Bentham did not believe that there was a fixed division between active and passive roles between persons of the same age who shared this taste, nor did he believe that those who preferred the passive role were in any way debilitated or effeminate. He emphasised that it could have no appreciable effect upon the growth of population except in the unlikely event of everyone becoming exclusively homosexual. 'If then merely out of regard to population it were right that paederasts should be burnt alive, monks ought to be roasted alive by a slow fire.'

The only charge against homosexuality that Bentham thinks merits serious consideration is that the indifference of the male toward the female would thereby defraud the latter of her rights. But he points out that the reality is just the opposite: women are already seriously denied their rights to freedom and happiness by the terms of monogamous marriage and by the censure heaped upon them if they partake of any of the pleasures freely allowed to the male sex. 'If a woman has a husband she is permitted to receive [sex] only from her husband: if she has no husband she is not permitted to receive it from any man without being degraded into the class of prostitutes. . . . As long as things are upon that footing there are many cases in which the women can be no sufferers for the want of sollicitation on the part of the men.'

And as for the charge that homosexuality is 'unnatural': 'If the mere circumstance of its not being necessary [to procreation] were sufficient to warrant the terming it unnatural it might as well be said that the taste a man has for music is unnatural.' Bentham noted that in ancient history paederasts usually had mistresses as well as boys, and exclusive homosexuality was comparatively rare. But in modern times he felt that the persecution of homosexuals tended to encourage exclusive homosexuality, and the rigour with which the laws against homosexuality were applied actually contributed to the growth of the gay subculture:

> the persecution they meet with from all quarters, whether deservedly or not, has the effect in this instance which persecution has and must have more or less in all instances, the effect of rendering those persons who are the objects of it more attached than they would otherwise be to the practise it proscribes. It renders them the more attached to one another, sympathy of itself having a powerful tendency, independent of all other motives, to attach a man to his own companions in misfortune.

Written in 1785, Bentham's cool, calm, clear-headed defence of homosexuality is a breath of fresh air in the otherwise stifling atmosphere of prejudice and ignorance that would prevail well into the twentieth century. But his comments had no effect upon public opinion or the law, and were never published during his lifetime, for reasons that are not difficult to understand. One page of jottings reveals his personal anxieties:

'To other subjects it is expected that you sit down cool: but on this subject if you let it be seen that you have not sat down in a rage you have betrayed yourself at once.'[9]

(2) Homophobia

Despite occasional eccentricities and odd patterns of behaviour, most of the mollies were quite ordinary men, sober, honest, and indistinguishable from their neighbours. But in the following paragraphs we shall examine in more detail the stereotype rather than the reality. Our information comes mostly from people who are strongly prejudiced against homosexuals, moralists castigating the abominable practices of beastly wretches; distortions, blind spots and lies are the necessary result. We find in the accounts few of those anecdotes that are commonly used to reveal the human side of even the worst criminals, whom the populace often secretly admires. We find instead the nonhuman monsters of the popular imagination, and they are exhibited as being quite irrevocably foul. This section deals not with the homosexual subculture as such, but with homophobia, the antihomosexual prejudice that runs throughout the heterosexual culture-at-large.

During the Age of Enlightenment, the most abusive epithet that could be thrown upon a man was 'Sodomite Dog!' To begin with, our deeply biased 'observers' regard homosexuality as a 'Contagion', an infectious disease that will spread through society like wildfire in the absence of legal restraints and punishments and preventatives. When the Camberwell labourer Richard Branson was tried in 1760 for an attempt to commit sodomy with James Fassett, one of the scholars of Dulwich College, the prosecutor argued, quite seriously, that if homosexual intercourse had taken place it would have infected the whole fabric of British society. A huge crowd in court nodded approvingly as the jury was asked for an exemplary punishment, 'for had he prevailed with this Lad, now Sixteen Years old, to commit this horrid and most detestable Crime, he would have infected all the others; and, as in course of Years they grew big enough, they would leave the College to go into the World and spread this cursed Poison, while those left behind would be training the Children to the same vitious Practises.'[10]

We may find this notion amusing, for it suggests that homosexuality is natural to man, that heterosexuality is merely an acquired social habit that will be cast aside at the first temptation. This belief probably originates in the basic sexist assumption that men are naturally superior to women. It follows that men would seek out other men were it not for the laws which prohibit such intercourse or the customs which prescribe heterosexual intercourse. I am not exaggerating this perverse logic, for this is precisely the belief of at least one anonymous writer to the *London Journal* for 14 May 1726:

> If the Legislature had not taken prudent Measures to suppress such base and irregular Actions, Women would have been a Piece of useless Work in the Creation, since Man, superior Man, has found out one of his own Likeness and Nature to supply his lascivious Necessities.

Such a sentiment is rarely put into print — and perhaps never so explicitly — for it embarrassingly reveals many men's subconscious fear of being homosexual. The author of these words not surprisingly bolsters his self-image and establishes his credentials by assuming the pseudonym of 'Philogynus', i.e. 'Woman-lover'. With such self-revelations so perilously near to the surface, we can understand why the satirists and moralists found it necessary to establish a distance between themselves and the mollies by means of gross exaggeration and distortion of the latter's vicious natures. No enemy is so monstrous as that which one fears lurking within oneself.

Homophobia is highly specific to the Christian tradition, which is one reason why sodomy is often ascribed to the Jews and Turks. The very terms 'sodomy' and 'sodomite' of course derive from the biblical tale of Sodom and Gomorrah, while 'buggery' derives from *bougre* or *Bulgarian*, from the heretical sect believed to have imported the practice into France in the eleventh century. Every tirade against a Sodomite Dog contains some allusion, however slight, to the sinfulness with which the Christian deity is supposed to have regarded the inhabitants of the Cities of the Plain. It is common for such religious terminology to be used more for political than for religious purposes, but a belief in the biblical myth sometimes seems quite genuine: 'However the Government having undertaken the Prosecution of them, 'tis not doubted, but strict Care will be taken to detect them, in order to avert from these Cities those just Judgments, which fell from Heaven upon Sodom and Gomorrah' (*London Journal*, 7 May 1726). Repeatedly we find threats of 'heavenly vengeance' if London's magistrates do not bring the sodomites under control. The mollies are referred to as 'that diabolical fraternity', and we are given to understand that the origins of homosexuality are not to be found upon this common earth, but in the very bowels of hell.

In the event, our writers are at pains to prove that this vice is not endemic to Great Britain. The lawyer Robert Holloway in *The Phoenix of Sodom* (1813) cites the very place and time of its appearance: 'From the best authority that can be gathered, this crime was first introduced into England about the year 1315, by a sect of heretics called Lollards . . . for from a note on the Parliamentary Rolls it is said, "A Lollard has committed the sin not to be named among Christians"' (pp. 26–27). But however heretical its supposed origins, British Christians frequently linked homosexuality with Roman Catholicism, as in *The Frauds of Romish Monks and Priests* (1691): 'I found at last, that they had secret Commerce with Women, or, what is worse, and that I would not willingly name viz. That they were addicted to the abominable sin of Sodomy.'[11] For similar charges see *The First Century of Scandalous, Malignant Priests* (1643), *The Master Key to Popery* (1742), *The Cloisters Laid Open* (late 1700s), and many more.

In the popular imagination these 'New Ways of Lechery' were believed to have been imported from Italy, France and Turkey. 'But of all the Customs Effeminacy has produc'd, none more hateful, predominant, and pernicious, than that of the men's *Kissing* each other. This *Fashion* was brought over from Italy, (the *Mother* and *Nurse* of *Sodomy*); where the Master is oftner *Intriguing* with his *Page*, than a *fair Lady*. And not only in that *Country*, but in *France*, which copies from them, the *Contagion* is diversify'd, and the Ladies (in the *Nunneries*) are criminally *amorous* of each other, in a *Method* too gross for Expression.'[12] We have previously noted that the Turks and Jews were believed to have a special fondness for sodomy; here is another example, from *Sodom and Onan*:[13]

> *Their Turkish Crimes, shou'd feel the Turkish Law.*
> *. . . But here the Laws have Avenues,*
> *Which pow'rful Sod'mites frequently abuse;*
> *Tamper with God, and terrify with Threats,*
> *'Till the astonish'd Ignorant forgets*
> *His injuries. Alarm'd at all he hears,*
> *Amaz'd, distracted with a thousand Fears,*
> *He sells his Country, quits his virtuous shield,*
> *And artful B[ugger]s Glory in the Field.*

Regardless of its supposed place of origin, sodomy was abhorred as a distinctly non-British luxury: '*Britons*, for shame! be *male* and *female* still. / Banish this foreign vice.'[14] Here again homophobia reveals the powerful alliance between sexism and national chauvinism. Xenophobia probably contributed to the first wave of persecution of homosexuality as part and parcel of the foreign ways brought to England by William and Mary.

One Christian feature of the xenophobia common to antihomosexual prejudice is the belief that homosexuality is bestial and unnatural. Within the most detailed Judaeo-Christian exegesis upon the myth of Sodom and Gomorrah, sodomy was held to be unnatural because of the cross-species mating of the Sons of Heaven with the Daughters of Earth, that is, angels with mortal women. Such an interpretation was not widely known outside the erudite circle of biblical scholars, though we do occasionally find it expressed in popular literature, as in this passage from *The Hell-Fire-Club* (1721): 'the filthy Sodomites did strive to join / With Substances Ethereal and Divine; / As if it was their Thoughts to get a Race / Of Demi-Gods to guard that cursed Place' (p. 14). But most people considered sodomy to be unnatural simply because it was not procreative. Thus in *The Fruit Shop* both mollies and masturbators are discussed in the chapter titled 'The Unnaturalists, or Deserters of the Fruit-shop': 'A still greater degree of criminality (than even what misguided and erroneous groping after chymerical but destructive self-sufficiency [i.e. masturbation] implieth) is chargeable to unnaturalism; which horrid form of sin stigmatizeth with public infamy, and calls aloud for heavenly vengeance on its followers.'[15]

Despite all the satires against the Jesuits, anti-homosexual prejudice itself is nourished by the Roman Catholic attitude professing the sanctity of procreation, as in this superb example of heterosexual bias: 'An old Proverb says *There is no Harm done where a good Child's got*. Faults of this Nature must be confess'd to proceed from a Richness in Constitution, and therefore, are more excusable than base and unmanly Practices. It is the Action of a Man to beget a Child, but it is the Act of a Beast, nay worse, to — I scorn to stain my Paper with the Mention.'[16] A similar broadside claims that the 'Roman Catholick Church . . . upon politick Reasons tolerates Whores and Stews, as knowing, if mens Lusts be damm'd up in their ordinary Course, they'll find a more filthy Channel: She allows *Simple Fornication*, to prevent *Adulteries* and *Sodomies*.'[17]

By means of a curious turn of logic which equates impotence with any form of non-procreative sexuality, the mollies were called eunuchs, though how they were supposed to be able to perform with men when they could not perform with women is never made clear: 'unable to please the Women, [they] chuse rather to run into unnatural Vices one with another, than to attempt what they are but too sensible they cannot perform.'[18] Prejudice of course needs no logic to support it, and operates primarily upon the principle 'heads I win, tails you lose.' Thus we learn that the mollies are 'like Eunuchs' and 'loath the dear Sex they have no Power to please': 'This must be the Case, if we consider the Majority of Persons suspected of this Vice, are antiquated Leachers'[19] — though trial records demonstrate that this is decidedly untrue. Bentham's closely reasoned argument against equating non-procreative acts with unnatural acts would have had little impact in combating such prejudice.

What we are really seeing here is the basic sexist assumption that 'each Sex should maintain its peculiar Character.'[20] Within this world view, men are hard and women are soft, men are active and women are passive, men are functional whereas women are decorative. The mollies were believed to be soft (the Latin term *mollis* means 'soft'), hence they were described as impotent or effeminate — these amount to much the same thing in the eyes of prejudice. We have already noted that the charge of effeminacy laid against the mollies was at least partly true, if we can rely on the accounts of the more objective observers. The more prejudiced moralists, however, disregard the particular circumstances and traditions of such things as mock births and maiden names, and would have us believe that all homosexual men universally imitated the ways of women — and this despite the paradox that arises when they are simultaneously supposed to 'despise the Fair Sex'. Effeminacy and male homosexuality are virtually indistinguishable; 'they would appear as soft as possible to each other, any Thing of *Manliness* being diametrically opposite to such unnatural Practices.'[21]

It is refreshing to find a pretended defence of effeminacy in *The Pretty Gentleman: or, Softness of Manners Vindicated* (1747), even though it quickly becomes apparent that this an equally vicious satire on homosexuality. But the satire starts well enough in praise of elegance, refinement and cultivation, and the author's historical survey seems to me to be pretty accurate: the first Pretty Gentleman he finds in history is James I, noted for his refined delight in a beautiful person and fine clothes; 'this Refinement sunk in Reputation' under Charles I, and harder still was its fate under the Republic and the Protector, when 'not a Man of any Elegance durst even show his Head'; taste was restored with the Monarchy, though 'the Prince was somewhat inelegant in Himself'; but in the current century the Pretty Gentleman has been 'an Object of general Contempt, and barbarous Raillery.' In defence, a 'Fraternity of Pretty Gentlemen' have organised themselves on the principle of mutual love, not inferior to the Sacred Band of Thebes, and their motto is *Magna est inter Molles concordia!* This is of course an attack upon the mollies, and soon we are introduced to a band of shrieking, camping, hysterical queens named Timidulus, Lord Molliculo (tender arse), Sir Roley Tenellus, Cottilus, Fannius, and Narcissus Shadow, Esq — all of whom tellingly prefer Leg of Lamb to Old English Roast Beef.

According to the author of *Plain Reasons for the Growth of Sodomy* (a separate section of five chapters appended to *Satan's Harvest Home*, 1749, probably by a different author), such effeminacy/homosexuality begins in early childhood with a sentimental or 'soft' education. Young men are brought up as 'Milksops'; they get up late in the morning, eat milk-porridge instead of a hearty English breakfast, go 'to a Girls'-School, to learn Dancing and Reading', then to a Master to learn Latin Grammar; in other words, mollies were supposed to be cultivated, refined, civilised, probably aristocratic — all of which is exactly the opposite of the way the ordinary gay tradesman behaved. 'Besides, his whole Animal Fabrick is enervated for want of due Exercise.' (Molly blacksmiths and butchers are not envisaged.) Modern education has become so decadent that a boy is 'brought up in all respects like a *Girl* (Needle-works excepted) for his Mamma had charg'd him not to play with rude Boys, for fear of spoiling his Cloaths.' It will be appreciated that these arguments reflect class antagonisms, specifically the lower-class prejudice against the 'soft' aristocracy. This prejudice against the upper classes becomes even more pronounced in the chapter titled 'The Italian Opera's [*sic*], and Corruption of the English Stage, and other Public Diversions', wherein the author laments that whereas men 'used to go from a good *Comedy* warm'd with the Fire of Love; and from a good *Tragedy*, fir'd with a Spirit of Glory; they [now] sit indolently and supine at an OPERA.'

Our author seems to have conflated the mollies with fops, dandies and beaux – probably ones seen on the stage, for theatrical stereotypes of effeminate men were as popular then as they are today. The mollies with whom we are familiar never seemed to dress so stylishly as those he paints for us. 'Party colour'd Silk Coats' and 'new-fashion'd Joke Hats' were probably seen less often in a molly house than a blacksmith's leather apron, and fancy hair-dos, if ever worn, were probably reserved for only the very special festival nights and masquerade balls. 'But what renders all more intolerable, is the Hair strok'd over before and cock'd up behind, with a Comb sticking in it, as if it were just ready to receive a Head Dress: Nay, I am told, some of our Tip Top Beaus dress their Heads on quilted Hair Caps, to make 'em look more Womanish; so that Master Molly has nothing to do but slip on his Head Cloths and he is an errant Woman, his rueful Face excepted; but even that can be amended with Paint.'

Doggerel about molly-eunuchs was commonplace, though such creatures existed only on the printed page, as in *The Petit Maitre*, 'A Poem. By a Lady': 'Tell me, gentle hob'dehoy! / Art thou Girl, or art thou Boy? / . . . / Man, or Woman, thou are neither; / But a blot, a shame to either.'[22] Not even Lord Hervey, the archetypal man-woman, could quite live up to such portraits, and it is with some relief that we occasionally hear other views to the contrary: 'It is a generally received opinion, and a very natural one, that the prevalency of this passion has for its object effeminate delicate beings only: but this seems to be . . . a mistaken notion; and the reverse is so palpable in many instances, that the Fanny Murry, Lucy Cooper, and Kitty Fisher, are now personified by an athletic Bargeman, an Herculean Coal-heaver, and a deaf tyre Smith.'[23]

(3) Mob Hysteria

Given the intransigence of the firmly-rooted Christian (and English) prejudice against homosexuals, we cannot be too shocked by the preventative remedies put forward to quash the contagion. It is best to nip it in the bud, according to a journalist in 1726, for 'If Vice in our juvenile Years becomes habitual, you will find it an hard Task to shake it off when you come to Years of Maturity.'[24] But, in lieu of an early preventative, the best way to stop its growth may be to outlaw men's kissing each other in public, no matter what the cost in self-control: 'I am of a Society of Gentlemen, and with Pride I declare it; who have made a solemn Vow, never to give, or take from any Man a Kiss, on any account whatever; and so punctual have we been in Observation of this Injunction, that many times at the Expence of a Quarrel, this Rule has been most inviolably kept among us.'[25] By the beginning of the next century, homophobia had effectively eliminated such public tokens of affection between men, as reported by a German traveller to England in 1818: 'The kiss of friendship between men is strictly avoided as inclining towards the sin regarded in England as more abominable than any other.'[26]

But for the man who has already become a molly, no hope is to be held out: 'Instead of the Pillory, I would have the *Stake* be the Punishment.'[27] Even the just lawyer Holloway recommends 'restraining this vice, either by castration, or some other cogent preventative.'[28] It is as though our moralists have been reading *Reasons Humbly Offer'd For a Law to Enact the Castration of Popish Ecclesiastics. As the Best Way to prevent the Growth of Popery in England* (1700). Indeed we must never forget the historical links between the condemnations of heresy, homosexuality and foreignness. Usually such proposals as castration are couched in the most outrageous invective whose fury tends to cancel itself out and become ludicrous. The author of *Sodom and Onan*, for example, had very strong feelings on the subject:[29]

> *Oh! that with legal pow'r I were endued*
> *To punish sodomite turpitude;*
> *Spaniards and Portuguese shou'd both resign,*
> *And Dutch the Inquisition at Amboyn!,*
> *When they but hear the tortures I'd invent,*
> *Unnatural transgressions to prevent.*
> *Let rank corruption, mining all within,*
> *Consume his vitals, . . .*
> *And may he one tormenting B[ul]boe feel,*
> *From the Corona veneris to the heel;*
> *While shankers, perforate his mouth and nose . . .*

and so on, for many more lines of damnable doggerel.

The mollies were regarded as the lowest of the low by many of the decent upper-middle-class citizens of eighteenth-century Britain. They were reviled as monstrous sinners and beastly wretches, creatures so like dogs that even the most inhumane treatment of them could be tolerated. Any student of the history of the laws against homosexuality will recognise that sodomy was a crime set apart, wholly different in nature from all other crimes, a crime committed by a different race from mere mortals, a crime which merited a severer form of punishment than even the most violent murder or rape. This ruthless and hardhearted attitude was not simply the official stance of the moralists, but was felt throughout many levels of society. It finds some of its worst manifestations — by deed rather than word — in the summary proceedings of the mob. For example, in July 1810 we hear of a certain Mr Chalk, a shoemaker and small shopkeeper in Balford, near Salisbury, who apparently misconducted himself toward his apprentice boy. The case was not brought to the attention of a sober court, but immediately dealt with by the mob. When his neighbours heard of it they angrily marched his effigy around town and consigned it to the gallows. In great despair at such a ruinous demonstration, Chalk hanged himself.[30]

Nor was it any safer to be found out in the metropolis. In October 1810 a man was set upon by a mob in Dowgate Hill, London, accusing him of an abominable crime. He was nearly killed by them until half an hour later a police officer arrived and took him to the Compter for his own safety. No one had come forward to charge him with a specific crime, so the next day the Lord Mayor sought out people to appear against him and he was committed to trial. The news correspondent who reported the incident deplored such mob action and cited the possibly malicious nature of the accusations, but hoped too that 'such miscreants should be punished with the utmost rigour of the law, and that the law against such crimes should be more severe.'[31]

The populace were wont to take their vengeance before as well as after a conviction. Earlier that same month a certain Carter had been confined to St James's watch-house for an unnatural crime against a young man in St James's Park. When he was brought to Marlborough Street station to be charged a few days later, the avenues were choked with 5,000 spectators. During the journey the mud and filth flew so thickly about him that the constables abandoned their posts and 'escorted' him from a safe distance behind. But Carter was not alone in his misery, for he was handcuffed to another man who had committed theft. When the crowd discovered that half their pelting had been mistakenly directed towards a mere run-of-the-mill criminal they redoubled their fury upon the sodomite and took up a subscription for the remuneration of the thief. Most of the mob waited outside during Carter's trial, and then accompanied him back to prison, hurling mud and imprecations all the way.[32]

Mollies unfortunate enough to be convicted of sodomy were hanged at Tyburn, while those found guilty of attempted sodomy were sent to the pillory (often twice), fined (usually £10–£30) and imprisoned (from six months to three years). Imprisonment often led indirectly to death because of gaol fever, which was widespread throughout most eighteenth-century prisons. Prisons were wholly lacking in sanitation and ventilation, and this variety of typhus sometimes raged so fiercely that gaols had to be closed to clergymen and prison officers and the inmates were simply locked up and left to their own devices until the fear of contagion abated.

The lesser punishment — to be stood in the pillory — was by no means a lenient one, for the victims often had to fear for their lives at the hands of an enraged multitude armed with brickbats as well as filth and curses. Modern anthropologists will point out that placing one in a pillory, including the dread procession from the prison to the pillory and back again, is founded upon a primitive rite of degradation or humiliation, whereby the victim becomes a scapegoat for the sins of society, and quite literally has heaped upon him the offal of civilisation. In the eighteenth century, when the mob was never very well kept under control, the victims in the pillory, male or female, found themselves at the centre of an orgy of brutality and mass hysteria, especially if the victim were a molly.

We have already mentioned how Charles Hitchin had his clothes literally torn from his body by the force of the missiles thrown at him while he stood in the pillory in April 1727.[33] In September of the same year, an unnamed gentleman and his coachman, John Croucher, were committed to Newgate for having made love to one another. I cannot trace what happened to the gentleman, but the coachman was sentenced to six months in prison and to stand in the pillory in New Palace Yard on 25 October, where he was subjected to treatment nearly as severe as that which fell upon Hitchin.[34] For the period from 1720 to 1740 gay men were stood in the pillory nearly every week. In many cases the reactions of the mob are not recorded; in others, little purpose would be served by citing them, as it becomes a matter of noting which ones attracted the greater attentions of the Drury Lane Ladies, or which ones were celebrated with more mud than brickbats, more dead cats than turnips, more rocks than offal.

Occasionally the event occurred which every convicted molly feared most: on 3 April 1763, an unidentified man who stood in the pillory at Bow, for sodomy, was killed by the mob. The coroner's jury brought in a verdict of wilful murder, and some persons were taken into custody for this outrage.[35] A pillory broadside was distributed just prior to his death, called *This is not the Thing: Or Molly Exalted*. It shows the poor sod in the pillory being jeered at by the populace: he laments 'I am now in the Hole indeed come all in my Friends', and the women in the mob shout 'Flogg him', 'Here's a fair Mark', 'Shave him close', and 'Cut it off'. The broadside ballad begins with the following quatrains:

> *Ye Reversers of Nature, each dear little Creature,*
> *Of soft and effeminate sight,*
> *See above what your fate is, and 'ere it too late is,*
> *Oh, learn to be all in the Right.*
> *Tol de rol.*
>
> *On the Fair of our Isle see the graces all smile,*
> *All our Cares in this Life to requite;*
> *But such Wretches as You, Nature's Laws wou'd undo,*
> *For you're backward and not in the Right.*
> *Tol de rol.*[36]

The peak of mob hysteria was reached in 1810, a year when it was very dangerous for gay men to be visible in London, and many in fact fled the country. In August of that year a certain Dickinson was convicted of attempted sodomy with a Drum Boy of the Guards. When he stood in the pillory at Charing Cross he 'received the most pitiless pelting from the indignant multitude, with mud, eggs, turnips and other missiles. He is a well-looking young man, about 22, and was a waiter at Hatchett's hotel, Piccadilly. In the course of the first ten minutes he was so completely enveloped with mud and filth, that it was scarcely possible to distinguish his back from his front; and it was with the utmost difficulty that the peace officers could prevent him from being torn to pieces by the mob, on his return from the pillory to the prison.'[37] In September five members of the Vere Street Coterie were stood in the pillory in Haymarket. On this occasion the mob hysteria (described in full in Chapter 12) was so staggeringly brutal that the incident seems to have made the authorities realise that such public proceedings were catering to the worst tribal instincts of the mob. In the event, the pillory was abolished in 1816 except as punishment for subornation and perjury, and totally abolished in 1837.

Only rarely do we hear the suggestion that the punishment meted out to homosexuals may be too great for their crimes. The lawyer Holloway felt that the crime of Cook, convicted of keeping a sodomitical house (but not of sodomy itself), 'is no justification of the brutality with which he was treated.'[38] And he noted that the authorities were beginning to realise that sodomy 'is an offence, like that of rape, easily charged, but very difficult to be disproved; the accusation should therefore, be clearly and incontestibly made out.'[39] Convictions for sodomy, a felony, were relatively rare, for they required incontrovertible proof of penetration (although a man could be convicted and hanged solely on the uncorroborated evidence of his own partner in the act). Convictions for attempted sodomy, a misdemeanour, were easier to obtain, for the criminal act could consist of anything ranging from an unsuccessful attempt at anal intercourse to a man's merely groping another about the front of his breeches; only one witness was required, either as observer or participant. The facts that one's partner was a consenting adult and the act took place in private were wholly irrelevant in the eyes of the law.

We might feel that the mollies were no worse off than many other 'criminals', for the law was universally harsh in its broad definition of what constituted criminal acts, in the weak nature of the evidence required for convictions, and in the general severity of its sentences. But such a conclusion would be wrong. The law and its application were very clearly biased against the mollies. This bias is obvious when we compare the homosexual cases mentioned throughout this study (most of them involving consenting partners, usually adults, often in private, and mostly resulting in convictions and harsh sentences) to the heterosexual cases in the same trial records — usually involving rape of a young girl, and usually resulting in an acquittal. Of 24 men prosecuted for rape from 1720 to 1731 (sometimes involving girls 10 to 12 years old, in one instance 5 years old), only three were sentenced to death (one of whom was pardoned), one was fined and imprisoned, one was imprisoned, one was fined, and 18 were acquitted.[40] Even Adam White, charged with having sodomised his 11-year-old daughter, was acquitted.[41] From 1730 to 1830 there were 294 prosecutions for (heterosexual) rape in the Old Bailey; a guilty verdict was given in only 51 of these cases (17 per cent), and 28 of the offenders were executed; 57 of the cases involved girls under the age of 10 years, and 10 of these offenders were found guilty; 10 years was legally regarded as the age of consent or age of sexual discretion for females, two years below the age at which a girl could marry.[42] Criminal statistics were not scientifically compiled by the Home Office until 1811, very near the end of the period of my survey in this book: in the returns for that year, 'four out of five convicted sodomists were executed, as against only 63 out of 471 other capital offenders.'[43] According to a House of Commons report published in 1819, there were 28 executions for sodomy from 1805 through 1818.[44] According to Home Office statistics published in 1837, 31 more men were executed for sodomy from 1819 through 1836; the peak years for executions were 1806 (six), 1810 (four), 1814 (five), 1819–25 (fifteen), 1826–32 (seven), and 1834 (four).[45]

And as for the Drury Lane Ladies — the law regarded them with bemused tolerance. Let us conclude this chapter with an incident which highlights the contrasting legal attitudes towards whores and mollies: on the same day in September 1810 that James Walker and Shudy Macnamara were committed to trial for having committed (consensual) sodomy, a felony punishable by death, at the Sun & Apple Tree, White Hart Yard, Drury Lane, 24 female prostitutes who were charged with behaving in a disorderly fashion in St James's Street, were dismissed on promise to conduct themselves with more propriety in future.[46]

Chapter 8

Blackmail

(1) Blackmailers' Charter

One of the more serious effects of social prejudice against homosexuals is that it makes them highly vulnerable to blackmail, particularly when the law itself supports such prejudice. Indeed, even the very existence of a subculture, however supportive in many ways, brought with it a disadvantageous visibility, at least to the eyes of another subculture, the criminal underworld. Before the nineteenth century, blackmail usually denoted extortion, that is, theft or robbery accompanied by a threat of physical harm. The phrase 'blackmail' or 'black money' in the Middle Ages referred to payments coerced by threat to life, limb or property. Criminals, bandits, and highway robbers often banded together to practise this kind of extortion, taking advantage of the disruptions within medieval society, and even government officials and justices of the peace often blackmailed people by threatening to arrest them.[1]

The Elizabethan Act of 1601 defined the offence as a form of robbery, reinforced in 1722 by the Waltham Black Act, notorious for enlarging the number of crimes punishable by death, which described 'several ill-designing and disorderly persons [who] have of late associated themselves under the name of "Blacks" . . . and have sent letters in fictitious names, to several persons, demanding venison and money, and threatening some great violence, if such, their unlawful demands, should be refused.' Prior to the Waltham Black Act, various statutes throughout the reigns of George I and George II had punished blackmailers with seven years' transportation; if the victim was threatened with murder, the blackmailer was to be sentenced to death.[2] In all of the cases I have discovered during the period covered by this study, the extortions and punishments followed this pattern.

Before the passing of the 1967 Sexual Offenses Act, the law prohibiting homosexual intercourse was aptly described as a 'Blackmailers' Charter', for very many — perhaps even most — blackmail attempts involved a threat to expose a man as a homosexual, whether or not he were in fact gay. This was equally true in the early eighteenth century. In 1735 an undoubtedly well-informed court recorder noted that 'This charging of Men with Sodomy is grown a common Practice with such Villains [i.e. highway robbers], in order to keep the Person they design to rob, from crying out for help when they attack him, or from prosecuting him afterwards, for fear of being suspects of so detestable a Crime, or perhaps having it sworn against them.' One of the reasons Jeremy Bentham gave for decriminalising homosexuality was to disarm blackmailers of one of their most powerful weapons, though Bentham never published his views for fear of being accused of the vice which he wished to defend. There is no way to estimate precisely how commonly this sodomitical ruse was practised by the blackmailers, but there are certainly enough recorded instances to indicate that it was a very serious problem — both for society at large and especially for the molly subculture. The following cases illustrate in more detail the extortioners' techniques, ranging from the very crude to the fairly ingenious; they also give some idea of the emotional turmoil experienced by the victims in the face of strong social norms regarding the necessity of maintaining a good reputation, and they throw some light on the interrelationship between the molly subculture and the criminal underworld.

In September or late August 1721, William Casey and Martin MacOwen assaulted Joseph Stone on the walk between the Mall and the Roan, near Whitehall. They knocked him down, and relieved him of his hat, wig, neckerchief and money. According to Stone, Casey 'almost choak'd me with my Neckcloth, and told me, if I cry'd out, they'd swear Buggery against me.' Stone was badly beaten. As his assailants fled, Casey bumped into a man named Mr Longueville and was thus caught. As a constable came rushing up, Casey swore that Longueville had buggered a man and killed him (i.e. Stone, whom he left for dead). The court justly ignored this transparent lie, and Casey was found guilty, although MacOwen was acquitted. Casey was 20 years old and had been for four years a soldier, partly in Spain. He was hanged at Tyburn on 21 September 1721, but in his dying speech he maintained his innocence, and expressed his hopes 'that the great Number of Sodomites, in and about this City and Suburbs, may not bring down the same Judgement from Heaven, as fell on Sodom and Gomorrah.' He may very well have had a genuine hatred of homosexuals, and may have chosen them as victims for this reason as well as for their easy vulnerability — the walk where he assaulted Stone was a known gay cruising ground.[3]

Fewer than two months later, on 5 November, his 18-year-old brother, John Casey, assaulted Francis Godelard near the end of the Mall in St James's Park next to Buckingham House, and stole one shilling. In his attempt to steal Godelard's watch (though the latter had none), Casey dragged him towards the canal, beat him up, stuffed a handkerchief in his mouth, and began searching. He 'ask'd me where my Watch was, I said, I had none. He swore I lyed, and with that he broke the Wastband of my Breeches to search me farther. I cry'd out Murder, and two Soldiers coming up, he told them I was a *Sodomite*. They ask'd him, *How he knew that?* and he answer'd, *Why don't you see my Hand in his breeches?*' One of the soldiers, Richard Allen, said that Casey actually 'had hold of the Prosecutor's Privities', which was taken as some proof, however slight, for his defence that Godelard '*wants to Bugger me; take him Prisoner.*' If Allen's observation was accurate, Godelard may have narrowly escaped some particularly sadistic act at Casey's hands. Casey's absurd defence was not believed, and he was brought to the gatehouse as an apprehended robber. But he was nevertheless acquitted at his trial in April for lack of specific evidence that a robbery had taken place.

Casey, however, did not learn to be more cautious, and on 24 April 1722, he and Arthur Hughes and John Levee, alias Junks, assaulted and robbed Michael Honeybourne in the Pimlico area. There is no evidence that he used the sodomy ruse this time. He was found guilty and hanged at Tyburn on 24 September 1722. The prison guard recorded that John Casey was a typical rogue, that he often quarrelled with his master and his father and kept loose company, and that he had been a highway robber for the past year, following in the footsteps of his brother Will.[4]

In addition to the St James's Park area used by the Casey brothers, another of the gay cruising grounds frequented equally by robbers and extortionists was Moorfields Gardens. There on 8 November 1724, Richard Wise was 'standing to make Water' near Bear-Key, when John Bollan came up to him and thrust his hand into his breeches — whereupon Benjamin Goddard and Samuel Axtell appeared from behind some hogsheads and started shouting 'Now by God we have got him! A Sodomite! A Sodomite!' They threatened to carry Wise before a justice and swear that he was readying himself to commit sodomy with Bollan. Wise was 'terrified at the Thoughts of coming under such a Scandal' and asked what he could do to placate them. He gave Goddard his two crystal buttons and promised to get them some money. They followed him home, but all he could give them was two lottery tickets each worth 30 shillings. They returned twice and got 15 shillings more. On 17 December they caught up with him in Gutter-Lane and demanded more; he gave them ten shillings. On 19 December they went again to his home and demanded yet more, and he gave them a diamond ring off his finger.

But Wise was exasperated with himself for giving them the ring, and he rushed after them to retrieve it. He caught up with them at an alehouse, where Goddard was having a drink with Richard Rustead, alias Rusty. When he began arguing to get his ring back, an alehouse boy came into the room and asked what was the matter. The boy recognised one of them: 'I know one of these Fellows, his Name is Rustead, he uses the Sodomite's Walk in Moorfields', whereupon Rustead and Goddard fled the scene. They were later captured when one of their accomplices attempted to pawn the ring at the same goldsmith's where it was originally purchased. The man, to save himself, led the constables to the Farthing Pye-House near Moorfields, where Rustead and Goddard were captured by Constable Richard Bailey. Eventually Axtell and Bollan were also apprehended. At the January trial of the entire gang, Goddard and Rustead insisted that Wise had confessed to them to having twice committed sodomy with Bollan. Whether or not that was true, all of the extortioners were found guilty, and sentenced to pay fines of £20 each, to suffer six months' imprisonment, and to stand twice in the pillory, once on Tower Hill and once at Cheapside Conduit.[5]

It is not unknown for one homosexual to blackmail another (indeed, that was commonplace until quite recent times). Although the blatant extortion is self-evident in the cases above, it is possible that some of the victims were gay: none of them protested that they were married. Some of the extortioners may also have been gay: Richard Rustead, for example, may well have used the Sodomites' Walk in Moorfields for pleasure as well as profit. In any case there are some instances in which it is certain that the extortioner was himself homosexual. We have earlier noted how, in July 1725, George Kedger was solicited by the 18-year-old hustler Ned Courtney, and how Ned threatened to swear George's life away if he would not give him money, and how he followed up that threat in court.[6]

One of the better-planned extortion attempts occurred on 7 November 1730, when John Jones took John Battle to the Castle in Mark Lane. There they met John Lewis, 'a Bridewell-Boy', leaning on a broomstick in a state of misery or at least discomfort. Jones said to Battle that 'The poor Fellow is very ill, he has got a Fistula: I have carried him to a Friend of mine, a Surgeon, who says it came by Buggery; and Lewis tells me that you have been concern'd with him. The Surgeon will have Ten Guineas for curing him, and insists upon Six Guineas loan; and if you don't pay the Money directly, we'll expose you.' Direct and to the point and probably untrue, but Battle, 'being in great Confusion, at having such a Crime charged upon me, for fear it should come to the Ears of my Neighbours, and blast my Reputation', gave them half a guinea and promised more. On 7 November they promised to go to Holland and trouble him no more if he would give them an additional 20 guineas. Battle agreed, but arranged for their capture when they came to collect. They begged for mercy and confessed, but were sentenced to stand in the pillory, once at the Exchange and once at Crutchet Friars, to suffer one year's imprisonment, and to give security for their good behaviour for three years following their release.[7]

One of the sillier blackmail attempts also took place that same year. Henry Thompson was walking along Chancery Lane and stopped to ask Williamson Goodman for directions; Goodman invited him to his quarters in St Mary le Strand, and once there, he began talking to Thompson about sodomitical practices. He 'told me of great Persons that us'd that way, and offer'd it to me so far as to undo his Breeches.' But Thompson was not interested in the proffered bum, so Goodman shifted to a new tack and said 'if I did not give him my Money, he would swear Sodomy against me.' Thompson was not going to allow himself to be blackmailed either, so as a last resort Goodman 'then seiz'd me by the Collar, and told me, 'twas in vain to resist, and took my Money from me by Force.' A few days later Goodman appeared at Thompson's lodgings with a pretended constable, threatening to take him up for sodomy, but his accomplice lost courage and ran away. The incompetent would-be sodomite-cum-black-mailer was arrested and taken to the Round House; he broke out of prison, but was recaptured, and subsequently found guilty of assaulting Thompson, putting him in fear and stealing money from him, and was sentenced to death.[8]

Some of the early blackmailers may have been inspired by the publicity attendant upon the raids on the molly houses. In 1727 William March was fined ten guineas for extorting his master by threatening to swear sodomy against him.[9] Also in 1727 Joseph Lee was fined 20 marks, pilloried, and imprisoned for so extorting an unnamed person.[10] In 1734 Nicholas Cales, alias Thomas Rogers, sent a malicious letter to John Reby, a servant to Mr Waldo who kept The Fountain in Bartholomew Lane, threatening to charge Reby with sodomitical practices if he did not supply him with one guinea. At his trial for the misdemeanour of sending a malicious letter, Cales claimed that he was merely trying to help Reby, as he knew several members of a blackmail gang who were going to swear sodomy against Reby, and he just wanted to warn him to save his reputation by showing him a letter written by one of this gang. The jury acquitted Cales because he could not be proven as the author of the letter.[11]

Joseph Powis, an experienced criminal and professional locksmith who was convicted of breaking and entering, and who was hanged at Tyburn on 9 October 1732, may also have been a blackmailer. In his confession and dying words which were published by the Ordinary of Newgate, he said that he once broke into the Chancery Office in Chancery Lane, where he picked open the locked drawer of the great table in the Masters' office, and discovered, among some silver and gold coins, three letters of an extraordinary nature, belonging to the Clerk of the Masters, in a leather letter case garnished with silver and bearing his name. Two were written in a hand he recognised, signed Molly Soft-buttocks, and one was anonymous. One was addressed to Dear Miss Sukey Tooke, and appointed an assignation under the Piazza in Covent Garden.[12] We do know from other evidence throughout the century that the mollies frequently wrote to one another, and even used messenger boys for the purpose. If such letters came into Powis's hands, I do not doubt that he attempted to make some money out of this discovery. On the other hand, his story may be a complete fabrication, though on the eve of his execution Powis would have little to gain by such an accusation except revenge. He may have had private reasons for blackening the character of the Clerk of the Masters of Chancery. Even if false, it is still interesting evidence that criminals knew about the habits of mollies, their cruising grounds and use of pick-up names.

(2) Blackmail Rings

Well-organised blackmail rings were not uncommon, and one of the more famous victims of such a conspiracy was the Hon. Edward Walpole, brother of Horace Walpole. Walpole refused to give in to their demands, and the blackmailers carried out their threat of exposure to the extent that in 1751 Walpole was in fact indicted for buggering John Cather, an unemployed servant, after beating him up. But the bill of indictment was removed by writ of *certiorari* into the Court of King's Bench, where a verdict of not guilty was reached. Walpole then prosecuted three of the men for conspiring to extort money from him by falsely charging him with sodomy; a fourth member of the ring absconded and was not tried. Walpole had been trying to find a place for Cather for some time, and was frequently seen together with him, but the charge against Walpole seems to have been completely groundless. One of the conspirators said that previous similar extortions practised by him had been successful, and another said they were planning similar conspiracies specifically focusing upon doctors, surgeons, and men-midwives. Three men were found guilty of extortion and sentenced to stand in the pillory and to suffer imprisonment for two to four years. Two more men were found guilty of forging a bond in Walpole's name; one man was whipped and imprisoned, while the other was hanged.[13] It may have been the notoriety of the Walpole case which prompted Tobias Smollett in his novel *Peregrine Pickle* (1751) to observed that a group of adventurers in London employed agents throughout England and particularly in the vicinity of Bath to cheat people of money by various kinds of gambling and fraud, one class of whom would 'extort money, by prostituting themselves to the embraces of their own sex, and then threatening their admirers with prosecution.'[14]

On 25 June 1759 Samuel Scrimshaw and James Ross stood in the pillory at Cheapside after being convicted — on evidence of their accomplice Peter Parry — of attempting to extort money from Humphrey Morrice of Dover Street by threatening to accuse him of buggery. They, with one Richardson, now absconded, had kept an intelligence office in Fleet Market. Perry was a friend of one Gosling, groom to Mr Morrice, and heard Gosling's wife call her husband a Buggerer. Parry related this to Scrimshaw. 'Scrimshaw no sooner heard the word Buggerer, but his fertile brain suggested a scheme to get money, and putting his finger to his nose, he said, *Something may come of this.*' Thus the conspiracy began. They were sentenced to three years in Newgate, but also to stand a second time in the pillory in Fleet Street, where they were severely pelted by the populace. One of the Sheriff's officers set upon the crowd with drawn sword, whereupon the mob diverted their fury upon him and forced him to retreat into an alley, where he made his escape.[15]

And so the cases continue unabated throughout the century. Actual trials for extortion are not particularly frequent, but threat of exposure as a sodomite is the basis of more than half of them (another common threat was to burn someone's house down unless they pay up). A careful reading of the fully detailed accounts of trials for highway robbery in the *Proceedings at the Old Bailey* will reveal that in one out of every seven or eight incidents, the robber 'puts his victim in fear' by threatening to accuse him of sodomy if he prosecutes. Nevertheless, the cases we can cite are probably only the tip of an iceberg, for most extortion attempts never came to the attention of the courts because they were successful, and many victims of highway robbery probably did not prosecute for fear of blasting their reputation.

This pattern continued with little change for the next half century. W.H.D. Winder notes that near the end of the eighteenth century 'the definition of robbery was relaxed to make it include the obtaining of a chattel as an immediate consequence of a present threat to accuse of unnatural crime.'[16] In the case of 'R Vs Jones' in 1776, the judges determined that a threatened accusation of sodomy constituted robbery in itself because it also involved a threat to use physical force.[17] But a slightly different definition of extortion emerged in the case of James Donally. On 16 February 1779 the Irishman was brought before the magistrate, Sir John Fielding, by Lord Fielding, eldest son of the Earl of Denbigh, and charged with twice attempting to extort money by threatening to accuse Lord Fielding of unnatural crimes, and once attempting the same with the Hon. Mr Fielding, younger son of Lord Denbigh.

Mr Fielding gave Donally half a guinea, then again another half a guinea later.

Donally was found guilty of 'highway robbery' at the Old Bailey on 19 February, and was capitally convicted, but the sentence was postponed while the judges tried to determine the legal points. On 29 March they met and decided that his threat was equivalent to, though not identical with, robbery with violence. 'Lord Mansfield with great energy observed, that it was a specious mode of robbery of late grown very common, invented by fraud to evade the law.'[18] One cannot help but feel that the curious twisting of definitions in this case was influenced both by the rank of the blackmail victim and by the fact that he was related to the magistrate. The lawyer Robert Holloway, writing 30 years later, claimed that Donally, an attorney's clerk, was importuned by the 18-year-old son of Lord Denbigh ('the son of a noble earl'), and regularly received money for his friendship; the event came to light because Donally mistook him for his younger brother one dark night in Berkeley Square; according to Holloway, Denbigh made an enquiry into both of his sons' conduct, and wrote to King George III, who granted Donally a pardon less than a week before his proposed execution.[19] The younger son soon went to live abroad, and died unmarried.[20]

The punishment for this redefined crime was the same as that for robbery; thus on 6 December 1779, John Staples, found guilty of extorting money from Thomas Harris Crosby by threatening to charge him with an 'abominable crime', was hanged at Tyburn.[21] In 1784, in the case of 'R Vs Hickman', Justice Ashurst gave the opinion that 'a threat to accuse a man of having committed the greatest of all crimes' was 'sufficient force to constitute the crime of robbery by putting in fear.' He added: 'To most men, the idea of losing their fame and reputation is equally, if not more terrific than the dread of personal injury.' And in the case of 'R Vs Knewland' in 1796 Justice Ashurst further refined this opinion: 'Terror is of two kinds; namely, a terror which leads the minds of the party to apprehend an injury to his person, or a terror which leads him to apprehend an injury to his character.'[22] Thus it was specifically the homosexual accusations that led to the development of more adequate laws against blackmail.

More cases were now brought under this new idea that blackmail need not be a form of robbery involving the threat of physical harm, though we still find blackmail rings, as when four men Ramsey, Clarke, Goff, and Hill at the Clerkenwell Sessions of 17 July 1810 were found guilty of extorting money from T. Fitzhugh by threatening to charge him with sodomy.[23] And the old pattern involving actual robbery would never entirely disappear. For example, on Friday, 6 July 1810, William Cane, a 36-year-old Sergeant of the Guards, accosted William Price, an Assistant Purveyor of Medicines to the Medicinal Board, York Hospital, Chelsea, in Upper Eaton Street, opposite Lower Grosvenor Place, hit him, grabbed his watch, then looked him very hard in the face and said 'I have seen you somewhere before in Parliament-street [a known cruising area], and I know you to be a b[ugge]r, if you do not promise to behave to me as a gentleman I will have you in the pillory in less than a week for sodomy.'[24] He demanded to be given £5 the next morning, but Price did not keep the meeting. Cane went to the York Hospital, Chelsea, where Price's brother worked, and arranged another meeting with Price. When they met on 11 July Cane said 'Sir, have you seen the newspapers in which there is an account of several persons having been taken up for a certain crime?' He was clearly inspired by the raid on the White Swan at Vere Street, the subject of Chapter 12.[25] There followed a series of meetings, in which Cane demanded another £5, then £50 (so he could procure his discharge from the Guards), then £100 (so he would never trouble Price again). Price realised this blackmail would never end, and he finally told his brother about it, and arrangements were made for two police officers to be present at the next meeting, when Cane was arrested.

At the trial, Cane said Price regularly walked with him, and took him into the Five Fields, near the Chapel, Chelsea, where 'he asked me if I was large, as Irishmen were in general; . . . he unbuttoned my small clothes and took my penis out in his hand; . . . he said, say nothing about it, now my life is in your hands, now I will ever be a friend to you as long as I live.' Cane, aged 36, was found guilty of extortion, and sentenced to death. At his last meeting just before his capture, he asked Price 'if he had heard of a certain nobleman who had paid £1,000 for concealment.' Almost certainly this will have been one of the noblemen who had visited Vere Street; Cane revealed the name in court, but it is omitted from the records. (It may not be relevant, but the Rector of the wealthy Chapel, Five Fields, was Rev. Parson Sandelands, a notorious drunkard and villain. He solicited alms for the poor and appropriated them for his own use; as head of a philanthropic annuity office, he swindled hundreds out of their money. A frequenter of brothels and gin shops, he was 'found committing a nameless offence' around 1822–1823, and decamped to France at the moment a warrant was issued for his arrest.[26])

The crime of blackmail is inseparably linked with the legal and social attitudes specifically against homosexuality. The largest percentage of all blackmail crimes involved the 'sodomitical accusation'. For the past two and a half centuries the ideal blackmail victim has been the homosexual, and the second best candidate is the heterosexual man who fears being accused of homosexuality; since this encompasses a good many men, such an accusation is the ideal ruse. There are several obvious reasons: homosexuality is viewed by society and the law as the greatest of all possible crimes, though in later years blackmail itself nearly usurped its place as the worst public nuisance; and once made public, the charge is virtually impossible to refute, and one is never really able to remove the stain, though this is now somewhat alleviated by the guaranteed anonymity of the victim in court proceedings; finally, homosexuality is the very antithesis of that which the typical blackmail victim treasures most: his reputation.

There is also a deeper psychological reason, arising from the nearly atavistic identification of a man's reputation, the public mask which he presents to the world, with his virility, his penis. 'A man's reputation was . . . the tenderest, most vulnerable part of his anatomy', observed John Mortimer QC in 1972, with reference to the Victorians,[27] but the observation is equally applicable to gentlemen in all ages. To have that reputation destroyed is tantamount to castration. There is no more effective way to destroy a man's reputation than to call him a queer, or a molly, or a pouf: a creature who, in the view of society at large, has been unmanned, a eunuch. In English culture, be it in the early eighteenth century or the mid-twentieth century, virility and effeminacy are at the opposite poles of the hierarchy along which one's reputation either rises or falls.

There may be another side to this coin, the possibility that a gay man will do whatever is necessary to protect his reputation, including falsely accusing someone of blackmailing him. This at least is the theory presented by the lawyer Holloway, who claims that many blackmailers of homosexuals have been convicted of extortion, and even deported or sentenced to death, because homosexuals will go to any length to clear their names. There are several known instances of this practice, which would support Holloway's own experience. For example, around 1824 Thomas Allison, a butler, was arrested for soliciting the favours of a young man in Hyde Park; the youth was so far implicated that he was also charged. Allison tried to cut his own throat with a piece of window glass, but failed in the attempt, and recovered sufficiently to face trial. At his trial it came out that he had prosecuted a man named Arnold four years earlier for extorting him by means of a false charge of buggery, and Arnold had been executed for this crime. The Magistrate at the examination said to Allison 'that he hoped he felt some compunction for having been the cause of a man's being executed some years ago. The prisoner said, that he had nothing to regret on that head.'[28]

But Holloway goes too far when he claims that homosexuals will use blackmail in reverse in order to achieve their desires: 'It seems to have come to this, that if a young man will not submit to Sodomy and hold his tongue, he must be hanged.'[29] I think this view is nonsense: it was far too risky a technique of seduction, nor is it supported by any real evidence. The reality is that extortioners often worked in gangs and they were by no means the helpless and innocent victims of wicked sodomites. Holloway himself cites cases in which the blackmailer was successful precisely because his charge was true. He was informed by his client Sir Francis Vincent of Stoke, for example, that 'about the year 1781 the late Felix Macarty, of no slender notoriety, was attacked by the son of a noble Lord of the County of Surrey, on the staircase leading to the great room at the Royal Academy. Macarty, Irishman-like, did not much approve of any caresses connected with breeches; and was no way solicitous of keeping the affair secret: of course, the transaction made some noise. The prejudice against an Irish adventurer, as Macarty was termed, gave the transaction an interpretation that conveyed an idea that his intention was to extort money from the nobleman.' However, after some serious investigation with Sir Francis and the father of the nobleman, 'the young gentleman confessed the truth of Macarty's charge, and was thereupon sent abroad.' Macarty was given 500 guineas to let the matter rest.[30]

Though no one was safe from blackmail, men who were in fact gay were much more vulnerable, and not very likely to bring charges against their blackmailers unless their demands became utterly impossible to bear. The most typical practice was that of Sukey Hawes, a highway robber-cum-pickpocket who in 1728 became an intimate member of the molly subculture, 'and where he found one that he could bully, he frequently made an Advantage of them.' In particular, he was once picked up by a tailor in the Covent Garden Piazzas, and, 'in the Way of his Trade, made the Taylor give him a broad Piece, and Three-Half-Crowns, otherwise he threatened to expose him.'

Such practices were not limited to London. In Bedminster, in April 1795 William Tyler, a yeoman, claimed that William Mason, a 21-year-old labourer from Bristol, had falsely charged him with attempting to bugger him so as to extort money; Mason and his accomplice Samuel Davis were prosecuted for extortion, but Tyler was nevertheless convicted of attempted buggery (blackmail is properly a criminal offense even if the blackmailer's allegations are true). It will be noted that the gay blackmail victims were more often tradesmen than aristocrats, though they valued their honour as much as anyone. An exhaustive search[31] of sessions records and defamation of honour suits in the ecclesiastical courts of Bath and Wells from 1740 to 1850 brings to light the predominantly lower and lower-middle class occupations of those whose activities were brought to public attention. A total of 42 sodomites are named in the indictments and informations, including only one gentleman (Sir Thomas Swymmer Champneys, who successfully brought a case against his blackmailer in 1821, but who was indicted himself in 1826, though no true bill was found), six clergymen, six yeomen, one apothecary, four tradesmen (a victualler, a brewer, a corndealer, and a clothier), one tailor, and 12 labourers. There were fewer than six indictments per decade except during 1800 to 1829, when there were 21 indictments, though only six or seven convictions.[32] But there was no real subculture in Somerset, either in Bath or its surrounding rural hinterland. All of the homosexual cases are isolated incidents, which came to light because of ill-judged sexual advances.

Chapter 9

The Third Sex

(1) 'Sporus'

The childhood of John, Lord Hervey was more vigorous than that of most noblemen. He heartily engaged in dice-playing and horseracing, and supped on mutton and plum-cake before retiring to bed with his doting father. At Westminster School, and then at Cambridge, Hervey's career very probably resembled that of the typical scholar he would later satirise: 'He went vigorously through a Course of Academical Learning, drank with his Tutor, lay with his Laundress, broke the Chapel Windows, and then took a Degree of Master of Arts.' On the other side of the coin, however, Hervey early acquired in Paris the habit of wearing white make-up to give his features a fashionable pallor, and in later life he would wear a set of false teeth carved out of brown mottled jasper. For a time he wore a silk eye patch for chronic watering of the eye, and his health steadily worsened until his frailty became proverbial. The modern opinion, now unverifiable, is that he suffered from periodic epilepsy. His generally highstrung nature and frequent fainting spells made his 'effeminacy' a subject for cruel satire. In 1735 Alexander Pope caricatured Hervey as 'Sporus', the youth whom the Emperor Nero had castrated and then married as his bride:

> Let Sporus tremble – what? that Thing of silk,
> Sporus, that mere white Curd of Ass's milk?
> Satire or Sense alas! can Sporus feel?
> Who breaks a Butterfly upon a Wheel?
> Yet let me flap this Bug with gilded Wings,
> This painted Child of Dirt that stinks and stings.

. . . Eternal Smiles his Emptiness betray,
As shallow streams run dimpling all the way.
. . . Now high, now low, now Master up, now Miss,
And he himself one vile Antithesis.
Amphibious Thing! that acting either Part,
The trifling Head, or the corrupting Heart!
Fop at the Toilet, Flatt'rer at the Board,
Now trips a Lady, and now struts a Lord.[1]

This masterpiece of malevolence (in which 'Butterfly' may be a pun upon 'catamite', and 'Bug' may be a pun upon 'bugger') possibly has had more influence in creating the stereotype of the Effeminate Pouf than any other document in English literary history, and even today it is seriously believed by some that these malicious lines accurately portray the modern homosexual male. Unfortunately the real Lord Hervey is relatively unknown to most students of English literature. He was certainly effeminate, but contrary to Pope's vindictive portrait of him as a eunuch, he was a reasonably robust bisexual. A biography of this man is not out of place in this study, for it simultaneously gives us some insight into the life of a molly who did not participate in the gay subculture, and illustrates how the archetype of the Pansy came about.[2]

***

Though Hervey could often be seen at the race tracks of Bartholomew Fair, and occasionally he would even take his seat in Parliament, his more usual social round was either at the spa in Bath, 'taking the waters', or in the London circle of aristocrats where, observed Lady Mary Wortley Montagu, 'writing verse was as common as taking snuff.' Another of Lady Mary's *morceaux choisis* has branded Hervey as the archetype of the so-called 'Third Sex': 'The world', she observed, 'consists of men, women, and Herveys'.

Hervey's ill health and effeminacy did not hinder his amorous pursuits. In 1720, at the age of 23, he secretly courted and then married Mary Lepell, a Maid of Honour whom Pope is believed also to have fancied. Indeed, Pope's foiled aspirations in the affair probably contributed to the vehemence with which he later attacked Hervey. In due course Mary Lepell gave birth to the first of the eight children she was to bear Hervey during their lifetime marriage — sufficient proof of the compatibility of effeminacy and virility.

But Hervey's attentions were not directed toward only one of the sexes. While recovering his health at Bath in 1726 (the year, incidentally, when Mother Clap's molly house was raided), he met and began wooing a 21-year-old country squire named Henry Fox. After Henry returned to his estate in Redlinch, Somerset, he and Hervey regularly courted one another through a fond epistolary intercourse. But when they met again in London the following year, Henry brought along his brother Stephen, aged 23, and Hervey, aged 31, promptly redirected his affection toward the older brother. And this time distance proved no barrier.

The friendship between Stephen Fox and Lord Hervey progressed rapidly, first with Hervey visiting Stephen at Redlinch, where they strolled in a garden playfully dubbed 'Hervey-Grove', then together for a two-month health treatment at Bath — while Lady Hervey remained at her husband's estate at Ickworth, which she sadly described as 'My Hermitage'. After taking the waters, Hervey and Stephen travelled together for 15 months on a Grand Tour: first to Ostend, in search of a more medicinal spa for Hervey's sake; then to Paris; then to Rome, where Stephen fell ill; then to Naples, where Stephen nursed Hervey through severe fevers and dizzy spells; then to Florence, where a surgeon so badly removed a large protuberance from beneath Hervey's chin that it left a noticeable scar. Lady Hervey, meanwhile, still at Ickworth, signed her letters 'your melancholy wife'.

During this period Hervey may have first discovered his capacity for loving a man, but the experience was not so simple as discarding a heterosexual facade for a homosexual core. Hervey was genuinely bisexual, and nine months to the day after he returned to greet his wife at Ickworth, Lady Hervey gave birth to their fifth child. Nor did Hervey abandon his travelling companion in favour of his wife. He persuaded Lord Bateman (who had been forced to separate from Sunderland's daughter because of his homosexual tastes) to open his house at Windsor so that Stephen could be near him. The three of them grew steadily closer, and Lady Hervey and Stephen were to remain lifelong friends even after Hervey's death.

Historical documents being what they usually are in such cases, we cannot be absolutely certain that Hervey copulated with Stephen. There is an awkward gap in the information regarding Hervey's early friendships: the first 26 pages of his volume of letters were torn out and destroyed by his grandson the first Marquess of Bristol. One cannot help but believe that Victorian prudery prompted this suppression. And all of the remaining letters, including those to Stephen, were preserved by copyists after Hervey himself had had the opportunity to excise any indelicate passages from the originals. There nevertheless is one letter to Stephen in which Hervey explicitly refers, with fond remembrance, to bruises left upon his frail limbs by Stephen's rough caresses. Common sense would suggest that such marks were the result of their vigorous lovemaking, although one scholar has been cautious enough to dismiss them as evidence merely of 'innocent horseplay'. Modern psychologists would recognise that even horseplay is seldom innocent, but I think the letter speaks for itself, and with passion, however playfully:

> You have left some such remembrance behind you that I assure you (if 'tis any satisfaction to you to know it) you are not in the least Danger of being forgotten. The favours I have received at Your Honour's Hands are of such a Nature that tho' the impression might wear out of my Mind, yet they are written in such lasting characters upon every Limb, that 'tis impossible for me to look on a Leg or an Arm without having my Memory refresh'd. I have some thoughts of exposing the marks of your pollisonerie [*sic*] to move Compassion, as the Beggers that have been Slaves at Jerusalem doe the burnt Crucifix upon their Arms; they have remain'd so long that I begin to think they are equally indelible.

Polissonnerie is the French word for 'lewdness'. There is also some second-hand evidence in a somewhat cryptic letter written by Charles Hanbury Williams to Henry Fox shortly after Hervey's death: 'Upon my word Lord Hervey has left Winnington a very *handsome legacy* & I suppose he'll *enter* into possession immediately — I suppose Lord Lincoln won't *push* at him any more. If he does, Hervey will certainly appear *backward* to him. Poor Fitzwilliams!' Lord Lincoln was famed among his friends for possessing a large penis, and using it well. The Earl Fitzwilliam was so frightened at his marriage that it had to be postponed for a day. Thomas Winnington MP, great friend of the Fox brothers, inherited a legacy from Hervey. Williams' own underlinings provide the clue for the following interpretation: Winnington now has an inheritance of his own and need not submit to the large penis ('handsome legacy') of Lord Lincoln; but if Lincoln persists in trying to bugger ('push at') Winnington, Hervey (as symbol of the inheritance he left Winnington) will appear to bend over and present his arse ('backwards') for Lincoln's desires. Or something along those lines; there are too many clever nudges and winks here for us to quite make sense of it all, but we can see easily enough that Williams is suggesting that Hervey liked to be buggered.

In the mind of the public, Hervey was a homosexual, not merely an effeminate fop but a hermaphrodite, as he is portrayed in the satire levelled against him by William Pulteney: 'pretty Mr. *Fainlove* . . . is a *Lady* himself; or at least such a nice Composition of the two Sexes, that it is difficult to distinguish which is more praedominant. . . . it would be barbarous to handle such a delicate *Hermophrodite*, such a pretty, little, *Master Miss*, in too rough a Manner; yet you must give me Leave, my Dear, to give you a little, gentle Correction, for your own good.'[3] In another libellous work Pulteney is even more explicit:

> But you seem, *pretty Sir*, to take the Word Corruption in a limited Sense and confine it to the *Corrupter* — Give me Leave to illustrate This by a parallel Case — There is a certain, unnatural, reigning Vice (indecent and almost shocking to mention) which hath of late, been severely punished in a neighbouring Nation. It is well known that there must be two *Parties* in the Crime; the *Pathick* and the *Agent*; both equally guilty. I need not explain These any farther. The Proof of the Crime hath been generally made by the *Pathick*; but I believe that Evidence will not be obtained quite so easily in the case of Corruption when a Man enjoys every Moment and Fruits of his Guilt.[4]

In other words, the proof of sodomy is provided by a medical examination of the receptor's anus in order to discover the evidence of semen or unusual dilation, caused by the inserter. The neighbouring nation to which Pulteney refers is Holland, where, in 1730/31, at least 60 men and boys were hanged, burned, beheaded, garrotted and drowned for the offence of sodomy, a notorious persecution which I shall discuss in more detail in Chapter 16.

The insinuations of Williams and Pulteney of course are not conclusive, though perhaps as near as we can expect at this distance in time. The fact nevertheless remains that Hervey's letters to Stephen are obviously love letters, interspersed with ejaculations such as these: 'Every Body has some Madness in their Composition, & I freely acknowledge you are mine'; 'I have often thought if any very idle Body had Curiosity enough to intercept & examine my Letters, they would certainly conclude they came rather from a Mistress than a Friend'; and 'Adieu, que je vous aime, que je vous adore; & si vous m'aime, de meme venez me le dire.' ('Farewell, how I love you, how I adore you; and if you love me too, come and tell me so.') Their friendship was rather more passionate than platonic, and it certainly became domestic when they set up housekeeping together in a house near St James's Palace (which still stands as No. 31 Old Burlington Street) — while Lady Hervey tended the children at their own town house in St James's Square, or in the country at Ickworth.

(2) Master-Miss

Hervey was a professional politician and courtier. A Member of Parliament in 1725, he carefully sought preferment through royal favour, though he was not immoderately ambitious. In 1730 he was appointed Vice-Chamberlain, a post he retained until 1740; his duties were the supervision of court functions: ambassadorial receptions, royal birthdays and marriages and funerals, court balls, and the seasonal removal of the Court from St James to Windsor, to Richmond and to Kew. His role as the master of ceremonies contributed even more material to his satirical persona as a fop of the highest order, as a creature of mere decorum.

But he also served Walpole's Whig ministry as a political propagandist, and his pamphlets provoked the opposition, whose leader William Pulteney descended to nasty innuendo about Hervey's sex life. Hervey may have been 'pathic', but he was by no means passive. He responded to this gross libel by challenging Pulteney to a duel, and he instructed Henry Fox to inform Pulteney of the time and place of combat: the New Walk (now Green Park) in St James's Park, at 4 o'clock, 26 January 1731. On that afternoon Hervey drank his chocolate as usual, gave his wife some verses to copy, and told her he would dine with some members of the House of Commons. He then proceeded to St James's, attended by Henry Fox as his second, where he met Pulteney and his second, Sir John Rushout. The duellists stripped to their shirts, though it was a frosty morning and snow covered the ground, and they crossed swords. It was a somewhat foolish act of valour, ending in Hervey being led fainting from the field with a slight wound in his side and four or five nicks on the hand, while Pulteney, with only one cut on his hand, strutted away victorious. The duel ended a 12-year friendship between Lady Hervey and Mrs Pulteney.

Hervey recovered quickly, and a few days later attended the Drawing-Room at St James's — where the duel 'made a great noise'. The Grub Street satirists seized their pens, and within days they had parodied the clash in numerous lampoons, limericks, broadsheets, ballads, and even a full-length opera. It was a disastrous occasion for Hervey's persona, for Pulteney's caricature of him as an hermaphrodite was lifted from his pamphlet, embellished and polished until it was eventually refined and sharpened by Pope's pen. Such was the line of coincidences which led to the literary stereotype which still continues to foster prejudice against homosexuals. One pamphlet calls itself *An Epistle from Little Captain Brazen to the Worthy Captain Plume* [i.e. from Hervey to Pulteney]. In another, Hervey is cast as Roderigo, Pulteney as Cassio, and Walpole as Iago. In the ballad opera *The Intriguing Courtier*, Hervey becomes Lord Whiftler, a coward who is relieved when the duel is forbidden (a very unfair perversion of the facts). In the broadside ballad *The Duel* we read:

> *It matters not how this Quarrel did rise,*
> *With Miss and with Master, and Master and Miss;*
> *Or whether a Coward he should not be stil'd,*
> *Sets his Sword to a Woman, and Wit to a Child.*

In another ballad, *The Court Garland,* we read this vilification:

> *Full hard I hold it right to tell,*
> *Which Sex may justly claim thee,*
> *For those scarce know, who know thee well*
> *What kind of thing to name thee.*

> *Thou powder-puff, thou painted toy,*
> *Thou talking trifle, H[erve]y;*
> *Thou doubtful he, she, je ne scais quoy,*
> *By G[o]d, the K[in]g shall starve ye.*

The anonymous squib titled *The Lord H[e]r[ve]y's First Speech in the House of Lords,* a direct source for Pope's own satire, has Hervey say:

> *So I, the softest, prettiest thing,*
> *This honourable House of Lords,*
> *Come here by order of the King,*
> *Created Lady of the Lords.*

Hervey was amused by this particular satire, and even sent a copy of it to Henry Fox. He expressed no offence in public, and remained strangely silent during the scurry of the scribblers, though he must have been aware that his transformation into the archetype of the effeminate pouf would effectively destroy his political reputation. Prime Minister Walpole may have advised Hervey – his political agent – to remain silent for fear of himself being drawn in as fuel for the fire. The Sunderland faction had been disgraced only recently by homosexual accusations against its members, and Hervey and Walpole would have known the dangers of stirring the waters. We must not forget that only a few years previously, widespread public attention had been given to the raid upon Mother Clap's molly house and the subsequent hanging of three sodomites, and in the same period, several homosexuals had been pilloried and hanged (e.g. Gilbert Lawrence was hanged at Tyburn on 7 October 1730). Only a few weeks prior to the farcical duel, one John Bambridge had been exhibited in the pillory for attempted sodomy. It would not have been wise for Hervey to have risked the scandal that might have been caused had he attempted to sue Pulteney for libel. Hervey did the most that he reasonably could be expected to do. Having failed to kill his most dangerous opponent, it was wiser for him to retire from the field altogether, than to pursue the matter and provoke a fate far worse than a nick in the wrist.

Frederick Prince of Wales, son of George II, may have given just such advice to Hervey, for fear that he himself would be accused of being the 'agent' to Hervey's 'pathick'. Hervey and the Prince were publicly intimate, though we know little about their private intercourse, for the two-year segment torn out of Hervey's *Memoirs* also covered the period when their relationship flowered. At the Prince's request, Hervey often wrote to him, sometimes likening their relationship to that of Alexander and Hephaestion. They were frequently together — once when ill, the Prince sent for Hervey to soothe him with conversation until he fell asleep — and the Prince carried with him a gold snuff box bearing Hervey's portrait. Indeed, they grew close enough for Stephen to become jealous, and Hervey wrote to reassure the latter of his abiding love: 'Adio, sempre amiable, & sempre amato.' Stephen wrote: 'Why did you not come to my Lodgings for a Minute after the Opera?' Hervey replied, seemingly careful to explain away all doubts: 'I did not stay a quarter of an Hour with the Prince; he went immediately to bed & I came home.' The Prince was doubtlessly a womaniser, though not necessarily exclusively so, and he confided his amours to Hervey, who replied: 'What Game you po[a]ch, Sir, what you hunt, what you catch, or what runs into your Mouth, I don't pretend to guess.'

The Prince and Hervey had a falling-out, however, when both became rivals for the affections of Anne Vane, a Maid of Honour. For a time she was mistress to the Prince, then to Hervey, or perhaps to both of them concurrently, or perhaps the affair was a bisexual ménage à trois, until she camped with Hervey after Frederick tired of her in 1734. A ballad opera called *Humours of the Court* exposed the triangle of Adonis (Frederick), Vanessa (Anne), and Aldemar (Hervey), the latter being a 'gay young Rover of Quality'. The identity of the father of the child which Anne bore in 1733 is still a matter for some dispute, with even a third candidate for the honours, Lord Harrington. Frederick's eldest sister settled the matter by decreeing that 'it was a child of a triumvirate'. In 1734 (the year, incidentally, that Lady Hervey bore another girl), Miss Vane finally left her various houses in Soho Square, Kew Green and St James's Street, where she was installed at the pleasure of the Prince, for a house in Wimbledon, where she and Hervey met until her death of convulsive fits in 1736. A sexual object and a political pawn, she was mourned by neither Hervey nor Frederick, who by now had patched up their friendship and often passed entire evenings together in the Prince's private apartments.

Hervey's steadily increasing duties often prevented him from living with or visiting Stephen at Redlinch; the less-busy summer season at Kew which allowed him two nights a week (Sunday and Monday) in London with Stephen became a luxury. He rigorously set aside these two days, he says, for 'pleasure'; the fact that Sunday was also the favourite day of rendezvous in the London molly houses has led to some speculation that Hervey went into town for this reason — but there really is no evidence to support the view that Lord Hervey ever would have entered a molly house. On the face of it, this was simply an opportunity for him and Stephen to be together. Robert Halsband in his definitive biography of Hervey suggests that the love between the two men gradually cooled, because of the sharp difference between their two natures. Stephen was a country squire, practically a rustic, while Hervey was a polished courtier; perhaps they had not enough intellectual interests in common to sustain a relationship whose physical basis would naturally mellow with time.

But, on the other hand, this marked contrast between city and country pleasures might have been one of the chief delights of their love throughout its duration, and not likely to be undermined as it might had they been in continual contact with one another. Hervey said he preferred Stephen 'rusty better than any other body polish'd.' Hervey's visits to Redlinch became shorter in duration, but this may well be due more to Hervey's increasing attendance at court than to any deliberate evasion or gradual attempt to break away. A lessening of their emotional attachment is refuted by the fact that their frequent separations and reunions continued to provoke in Hervey vehement fevers and faintings, extreme ecstasies and deep depressions. Hervey in 1736 arranged for Stephen's marriage to the child-heiress Miss Horner, which was merely a formal bond until they lived together in 1739, after which Hervey and Stephen continued to be close friends. As we have seen throughout the court of King James earlier, homosexuality was never sufficient reason for a man not to marry; it would have been unthinkable for a man of any public consequence to play a role in society without a hostess, or at any rate without a wife back at the country seat.

(3) Swan of Padua

One friendship need not exclude another, and in 1736 (the year, incidentally, that Lady Hervey bore her eighth and last child) there ensued an additional romance when Hervey, like most of the London aristocracy, was awestruck by the arrival of 24-year-old Francesco Algarotti. In tribute to the grace with which Algarotti glided through the courts of Europe, the ordinarily philosophical Voltaire had dubbed him 'the Swan of Padua'. In somewhat more gossipy vein, Voltaire later called Algarotti 'the Venetian Socrates', and once quipped of the Swan's relationship to the young male secretary of the French ambassador to Berlin: 'When I see the tender Algarotti crush with passionate embrace the handsome Lugeac, his young friend, I imagine I see Socrates fastened onto the rump of Alcibiades.'

Algarotti was a paragon of beauty, with the full lips of the Italian sensualist. His genius lay in his ability to charm the *cognoscenti*, and his immediate election to the Royal Society was one step higher on the ladder of his achievements. His verse resembled Ariosto's, his prose resembled Locke's, and he had translated Newton's *Optics* into a set of graceful dialogues. Hervey fell passionately in love with him. Unfortunately Hervey's very good friend Lady Mary Wortley Montagu proved to be his rival for the affections of the Socratic Swan, for Algarotti was also bisexual. Thus began one of the silliest love-triangles in the eighteenth century.

After a brief summer in London, during which Hervey was repeatedly detained at Kensington with Queen Caroline, Algarotti returned to Venice to prepare his Newton for publication. Soon he received an avalanche of *billets doux* from both of his devoted English admirers. Lord Hervey wrote, *'je vous aime de tout mon coeur'*; Lady Mary wrote, *'je vous aimerai toute ma vie.'* Hervey and Lady Mary boasted to one another how frequently they were receiving letters from Algarotti. In one pair of letters that must have been a source of great amusement to the young Italian, Hervey invited Algarotti to come to him in England while Lady Mary invited herself to go to him in Italy. Algarotti returned polite encouragements to both, but had his own affairs to attend to. At this precise moment he had taken up with a young man named Firmaon in Milan, with whom he made a leisurely tour of southern France. Lord Hervey playfully scolded Algarotti for not writing more often; Lady Mary sent agonizing pleas for more missives. Lord Hervey wisely controlled his hurt; Lady Mary foolishly kept posting *cris du coeur*. Lord Hervey grew jealous; Lady Mary became distraught. Lord Hervey cynically acknowledged the ways of the world; Lady Mary wept like Dido upon losing Aeneas.

Algarotti finally returned to London in March 1739, staying briefly with the young lawyer Andrew Mitchell in his chambers in the Middle Temple; then moving into Hervey's apartment in St James's Palace; then moving on to Lord Burlington's villa at Chiswick; then, in May, accompanying Lord Baltimore on a voyage to St Petersburg, during which he wrote to Hervey: 'Vouchsafe, my Lord, not to forget a poor traveller, who, sailing to the North-east, casts his eyes from time to time upon the rhumb of the compass that is to guide him back to you. . . . continue to love me, and sometimes think of me.' Lady Mary resolved upon abandoning her friends, home, family, and dull husband Wortley for Algarotti's sake. In

July she set off on a pilgrimage of love to Venice, hoping someday to be reunited with her wayward Swan.

While Lady Mary, like Hannibal, was crossing the Alps with elephant loads of baggage and an enormous snuff box, Algarotti was heading back towards England — but with an eight-day stopover at the court of Berlin. Crown Prince Frederick of Prussia was immediately infatuated with his guest, and Algarotti returned his affection, though he also wrote to Hervey that he hoped soon they would be able to sup together in London, 'where you will certainly be the tastiest dish for me [*le meilleur plat pour moi*].' But hardly had Algarotti stepped foot upon English soil eight months later — and into the welcoming embrace of Lord Hervey — than he received word that Frederick's first royal act upon the death of his father was to recall Algarotti to Berlin. After the reunited lovers had spent a sufficient number of months walking in St James's Park and 'dining' together, Lady Hervey kindly lent Algarotti the money for the return trip. In short order Algarotti was to replace the Crown Prince's former favourite Baron Keyserling.

It will not be out of place to digress briefly upon the loves of Frederick the Great (1712–1786), King of Prussia (1740–1786) and Prince of the Enlightenment. His friends as a youth included two young lieutenants, the Scottish Jacobite Keith and Hans von Katte, eight years older than Frederick and believed to be the 'active' partner. Frederick's father had been suspicious about their relationship for some time, and had tried to interrupt this pattern by providing Frederick with a military tutor, Count von Keyserling. But Keyserling had the same tastes as his pupil, and was soon to become the sole favourite. Frederick had conspired with Keith and Katte to flee to England; the plot was revealed, and on 6 November 1730, Frederick's father had Katte executed in public, outside his son's window.

Frederick was temporarily a broken man, and henceforth obedient, though he retained other intimates such as his valet the young solder Fredersdort. He dutifully married, but seldom saw his wife. Eventually his father died, and, as we have just noted, Algarotti became his Chamberlain, while Voltaire became his writer-in-residence. The latter described Frederick as 'a likeable whore'. Frederick, for his part, told Voltaire: 'We've got here a cardinal and several bishops, some of whom make love before and others behind — good fellows who persecute nobody.' Frederick's younger brother was especially notorious for his homosexual liaisons. Mirabeau, special envoy at the Prussian court, claimed that 'An old servant of Prince Henry, apt in serving his master's passion for pederasty, became his favourite at first and was then made canon of Magdenburg where the prince was bishop. . . . The aristocracy of the army knows that with Prince Henry the Ganymedes have always made and shall always make the decisions.'[5] Prince Henry was actually put forward as a candidate to head the proposed constitutional monarchy of the United States, though eventually the plan was dropped.

The period 1740–1741 was a time for titles: Algarotti became a Count in the court of Berlin; Lord Hervey was appointed Keeper of the Privy Seal; and Stephen became Lord Ilchester, Baron of Woodford Strangways. Meanwhile, in the world where Don Quixote still quests after Dulcinea, Lady Mary had begun her trek across Europe: from Venice to Rome, then Genoa, then Naples, then Turin where she 'almost accidentally' met Algarotti at last, who was on a diplomatic mission from Frederick. Their meeting ended in disaster. Though they spent the greater part of two months together, there was a definite rift, with Lady Mary finally realising that her pursuit was futile. In May they went their separate ways, he back to Berlin and she in the opposite direction.

Back in England there was another disastrous rift. Prime Minister Walpole was defeated in 1742, and Lord Hervey dismissed from office. In a bold yet petty gesture of defiance against the King, Hervey went into opposition. He tried to persuade Stephen — now Lord Ilchester, and therefore a Peer — to join him, but Stephen wisely refused. Their consequent argument finally brought to an end their 15 years of friendship. Hervey was a broken man, politically, emotionally, and physically. He retired in very ill health, and his last words to Lady Mary — in her bored retirement at Avignon — were hardly the sugar plums from a Thing of Silk: 'The last stages of an infirm life are filthy roads, & like all other roads, I find the farther one goes from the capital the more tedious the miles grow. May all your ways be ways of pleasantness and all your paths peace. Adieu.' Hervey died in 1743, at the age of 46; Alexander Pope, whose *Epistle to Dr Arbuthnot* with its vicious portrait of Sporus was now in its sixth edition, remarked, *'requiescat in pace!'*

Regrettably Lord Hervey's last act was to humiliate his wife by leaving her only the minimum required by the terms of the marriage contract, which necessitated the disposal of even her personal jewels. This provided gossip for Grub Street, despite there being no evidence that their marriage was ever anything less than amicable. A granddaughter of Lady Mary suggested that Lord and Lady Hervey 'lived together . . . without any strong sympathies, and more like a French couple than an English one', yet nowhere can we find any reason for his apparent vindictiveness at the final hour. Perhaps there was a recent domestic quarrel, ordinarily of little consequence but now compounded by the bitterness of political disgrace and by the pains of his severe illness — the last flourish of rebellion from a sick man on his deathbed.

As for the other characters in this drama: Count Algarotti moved to the court of Poland in 1742 but returned to Frederick in 1747, until ill health forced him to seek the warmer climate of Italy, where he remained until his death in 1764. Lady Mary retired to Brescia, and then to Venice from which she and Algarotti corresponded with restrained flattery and kind remembrances of Hervey; she returned to London in 1762, and died six months later. Lady Hervey lived on in modest but not severely restricted circumstances until her death in 1768. Stephen, who often visited her, had settled into a happy marriage, produced numerous offspring, became an Earl, and died in 1776.

Hervey's correspondence and his *Memoirs*, though seriously truncated by his heirs, remain the only enduring monuments of their circle. Lady Mary's reams of letters were similarly excised by her descendants, and very few of Algarotti's personal letters survive; his translations and travel essays are largely forgotten. But all of these lives and works have been eclipsed by Alexander Pope's abusive portrait of Sporus, the 'Illustrious Nothing'. In the year of Hervey's death, Pope revised his *Dunciad*, and portrayed Hervey, in a kind of begrudging epitaph, as 'a Fool of Quality'.

Chapter 10

The Warden of Wadham

(1) Robert Thistlethwayte

Although the molly subculture as such seems to have been confined to metropolitan London, undoubtedly there were some quasi-subcultures in the academic communities of Oxford and Cambridge from time to time. The early diarist Dudley Rider in 1715/16 had advised that 'among the chief men in some of the colleges sodomy is very usual and the master of one college has ruined several young handsome men that way, . . . it is dangerous sending a young man that is beautiful to Oxford.'[1] A particularly revealing incident is that involving Robert Thistlethwayte, Doctor of Divinity, the 52-year-old Warden of Wadham College, Oxford, which gave rise to some very popular limericks:

> There once was a warden of Wadham
> Who approved of the folkways of Sodom,
> > For a man might, he said,
> > Have a very poor head
> But be a fine fellow, at bottom.

or:

> When they said to a Fellow of Wadham
> Who had asked for a ticket to Sodom,
> > 'Oh, sir, we don't care
> > To send people there',
> He said, 'Don't call me Sir, call me Modom'.

and a quatrain, upon the College being insured against fire:

> *Well did the amorous sons of Wadham*
> *Their house secure from future flame;*
> *They knew their crime, the crime of Sodom*
> *And judg'd their punishment the same.*

On Saturday, 3 February 1739, Robert Thistlethwayte sent his manciple to fetch Master William French, a commoner of the College for the past two years. Immediately after Divine Service early that afternoon, Mr French went to Thistlethwayte's lodgings, and did not return until supper time at 6 o'clock that evening. When he sat down to sup with his fellow commoners, they observed that his demeanour was 'very much disorder'd, and uneasy'. When asked what was the matter, he vouchsafed no reply, but went to the Gentleman's Room, where he remained, vomiting for some time. When he returned to the table, he began muttering that the Warden of Wadham was a Scoundrel and a Villain, and he asserted that it was within his power to have him expelled. Thus was precipitated a series of events that would shake Wadham College to its foundations.[2]

On Monday, 5 February, French breakfasted with several of his friends, including George Baker, who advised him to either hold his tongue or to take the matter to a magistrate if it be so terrible. When the others left, Charles D'Oyly dined with Baker, and revealed that French told him that 'the Warden did not love Women.' From this cryptic remark they concluded that Thistlethwayte must have made 'a Sodomitical Attempt' upon Mr French. They decided to consult with Mr French in his rooms, and tried to persuade him to prosecute. Mr French replied that he was afraid of offending the Warden and being expelled before he received his Bachelor's Degree, but that he would do so 'if he could do it with Safety to himself.' He added that he was afraid that his tutor, Rev. Mr John Swinton, might try to quash the matter. The three decided to seek further advice from the Fellow the Rev. Mr Stone, to whom they despatched a message.

On Tuesday the Rev. Mr Stone arrived. They conferred, and decided to ask the advice of the Rev. Mr Watkins, to whom they despatched a message. On Wednesday the Rev. Mr Watkins arrived and conferred. He advised them to get the advice of a solicitor in London, to whom they despatched another message. On Thursday, while awaiting a reply from the solicitor, Mr French composed and signed a Declaration laying out what had happened in Thistlethwayte's lodgings. Unfortunately that document has been lost. One Fellow who saw it reports that it contained an account 'of which the Particulars are judged too gross and obscene to be repeated, and such as amounted to the most notorious sodomitical Attempt conceivable.' So we are prevented from conceiving the Attempt.

On Friday the conferring fivesome received by post, advice from counsel, to wit: that French should give an affidavit to a justice of the peace and to the Vice-Chancellor, but that chances of prosecution were slim in so far as there was only French's word for it, and that it would be best to get the opinion of French's father before proceeding further. So on Saturday French set out to see his father, with a letter from Baker describing the inconceivable Particulars. On Thursday, 15 February, Mr French returned to Oxford with his father, the older gentleman in a great rage and 'inexorably determined upon Justice'. On Friday George Wyndham, Barrister, arrived upon the scene and began preparing his case. On Saturday morning they brought the matter to the attention of the Vice-Chancellor, who prudently requested a Testimonium concerning Mr French's character.

Mr French prepared the Testimonium, and — as was customary procedure — gave it to Thistlethwayte, who, as Warden, had the duty of passing it around to all the Fellows for their signatures. The Warden smelled out the proceedings against him, and after it was returned with the signatures, he found fault with the form, and requested that it be rewritten and circulated once more. Mr French did so, and then brought it back for the signature of the Warden himself, who replied:

> 'Mr French, I am sorry to find the firm Friendship, which has subsisted so long between you and me, is about to be broken off.'
>
> 'In what manner?' says Mr French.
>
> 'Why, I hear', says the Warden, 'that you are going to make known to the World my Behaviour to you some time ago in my Parlour.'
>
> 'Yes, Sir', says Mr French, 'I have been with the Vice-Chancellor already, and am come to you with this Testimonium to know whether you will sign it. Tell me whether you will or will not. Have you any Objections to my Character or Behaviour in the College?'
>
> 'No indeed, Sir', says the Warden, 'I always thought you the most regular Man in my College.'

Thistlethwayte pleaded with French to conceal the matter, as it would be the ruin of them both, but French was relentless, and the Warden finally signed the Testimonium. Wherewith Mr French, clutching the Testimonium in his fist, rushed forth from the Warden's lodgings, into the Quadrangle where were gathered a group of ten or twelve Scholars, shouting 'Bribery! Bribery!' He revealed to them the inconceivable Particulars aforementioned, whereupon the Testimonium was immediately after signed by all the Fellows in the College.

At 6.00pm on Saturday there assembled in Warden Thistlethwayte's lodgings Mr French and his father, George and Nicholas Baker, the Vice-Chancellor, the Warden, J. Birt, Dr Prado (Principal of Jesus College), Counsellor Wright, and several Justices of the Peace. Dr Prado lectured Mr French for an hour about the difficulties he faced if he could not prove his charges. Several witnesses testified to Mr French's disorder at the dinner-table after returning from the Warden's lodgings, and Mr French gave a deposition to the Magistrates. The meeting ended at 10.30pm.

At 11.00am on Sunday Mr French and his father met with his tutor Mr Swinton, and asked Swinton to testify to the fact of his having gone to Thistlethwayte's rooms on the Saturday in question, there finding the door bolted, and waiting for some time before it was opened and he saw that French was in the room with Thistlethwayte. He agreed to so testify. Later that evening Swinton privately met with Mr French and tried to persuade him to put off the prosecution for a few days, but Mr French was set upon his course.

At five o'clock in the morning on Monday, old Mr French was rudely awakened by loud knocks at his chamber door. It was William Boxley, Swinton's bed-maker for the past two years, bearing a message from his master requesting old Mr French's company in Thistlethwayte's parlour. After some persuasions, old Mr French got out of bed and put on his periwig, and was led across the Quadrangle under cover of darkness. Thistlethwayte, Swinton, and old Mr French sat in the Warden's parlour before a warm fire, drinking burnt wine and eating chocolates. Thisthle-thwayte and Swinton entreated old Mr French to take his son into the country, and promised to provide handsomely for him. They also asked him to sign a paper of which he was not permitted to see the contents. Old Mr French rejected both requests, and went off in a huff, leaving his burnt wine behind him.

At six o'clock that morning the Vice-Chancellor was rudely awakened by William Boxley, and informed that Mr French the younger had decided to put off the formal College enquiry. At seven o'clock the Vice-Chancellor sent for Mr French, who arrived and denied having decided upon such a postponement, and they scheduled the formal proceedings to begin at nine o'clock that morning. When the proceedings began, Swinton could nowhere be found in order to give his testimony. Baker and Birt testified that they had overheard William Boxley bragging to his fellow servants that Thistlethwayte had sodomised him. The Vice-Chancellor replied that he could not force Boxley to so testify. The justices of the peace arrived, and determined that the case should go to court at the next Assizes. Thistlethwayte arrived and was ordered to post £200 bail. He did so, then promptly departed from Oxford, never to return.

So in due course the case went to court without the presence of the accused. Mr Swinton was subpoenaed, and he testified about Thistlethwayte and Mr French being together behind bolted doors. Robert Langford, the Butler of the College, was subpoenaed, and gave some damaging testimony: five or six years previously, Thistlethwayte had invited Langford to supper, and while drinking a bottle of wine Thistlethwayte had tried 'to kiss and tongue me, and to put his Hand into my Breeches.' Langford told Thistlethwayte to cease and desist, but, heated by the wine, he became even more forceful and nearly violent, 'upon which I expressed great Resentment, and quitted the Room.' Langford avoided the Warden henceforth, though the latter frequently sent his servant to fetch him. Then, about two years previous, while Langford was leaving the Buttery and heading for home through the Quadrangle, Thistlethwayte caught sight of him from his study window in one of the 12 garrets facing the Quadrangle, and called him in. Seeing some other Fellows about, and knowing it would not be proper for the Butler to ignore the Warden, he went in, whereupon he was promptly pounced upon as before. Langford entreated the Warden to get himself a woman or a wife, but the Warden laughed and replied, 'I would not give a Farthing for the finest Woman in the World, for I love a Man as I do my Soul.' Langford expressed great resentment, and again quitted the room. He avoided crossing the Quadrangle thereafter.

William Hodges, the Barber of the College, was subpoenaed, and had an interesting story to tell: 'About a Year and a half ago I went to shave the Warden, about Eleven in the Forenoon. The Warden being dressed in his Gown and Cassock, I put his Nightgown over him, to avoid daubing him. Whilst I was shaving him, I found something tickling about my Breeches, but thought at first that it might be the effect of the Gown's not sitting right upon the Warden, wherefore I altered the Position of it, and went on. Immediately after I found the Warden trying to introduce his Hand into my Breeches. Whereupon I asked him what he meant. The Warden answered, "There is no Harm in this, my Dear", and talked to the same effect so long, that I swore I would never shave him again, for I knew what he wanted, and that I was the wrong Person for his Purpose.' Hodges expressed great resentment, and quitted the room. A few days later, the Warden again sent for the Barber, and as soon as he appeared, the Warden said, 'How dost do, my dear Barber? It's fine Weather my dear Barber. How does thy Cock do, my dear Barber? Let me feel it.' The Warden tried to kiss the Barber, but the latter shouted 'Damn you, you Son of a Bitch! What do you mean?' and knocked him backwards into his chair. The Warden leaped up and tried to kiss him again, whereupon the Barber knocked him flat upon the floor, and quitted the room, expressing great resentment.

The court case concluded *Nemine Contradicente* — 'no one to contradict'. The Rev. Dr Thistlethwayte, who had been a Fellow of Wadham since 1715, sent a letter to the College on 22 February 1739, resigning all his offices, including the Prebendary of Westminster and the Rectorship of Winterslow in Wiltshire. He forfeited his bail by not appearing in court, and fled across the Channel where he set up house in Boulogne. He died there five years later, and his remains were shipped to Dover, where on 4 February 1744 he was laid to rest in the churchyard of St Mary the Virgin.[3]

(2) John Swinton

But this case had hardly closed when a new case seemed to be opening up — this time against Rev. Mr Swinton. George Baker knew that John Swinton and Thistlethwayte had been close friends ever since Swinton's return from a trip to Italy several years back; and that William Boxley, who had jokingly bragged about being sodomised by Thistlethwayte, was now a servant to Swinton. He likewise recalled some gossip about Swinton having once slept with a servant boy named Robert Trustin, so he began to investigate these links. First he paid a visit to Francis Smith and his wife, who waited upon Swinton and other fellows of the College, and whose servant Bob Trustin was. According to Smith, Bob some years ago had been gone for two or three nights, and, being questioned by Smith upon his return, Bob said he had been waiting upon Mr Swinton. Smith, knowing that Swinton already had a bed-maker, believed the boy was lying and beat him. But Bob persisted with his story, and told Mrs Smith that 'while waiting upon Mr Swinton sometimes I sat up in a great Chair, sometimes lay down before the Fire, and Mr Swinton sometimes bid me lie down on the Bed, which I accordingly did.' Smith threatened to break the boy's bones if ever again he went near Swinton's bed, as he would 'fill him [i.e. Swinton] full of Lice.' Swinton heard about the matter, and sent for Smith to tell him that he should not have beaten the boy, that Bob was giving him medicines and that he would like him to continue doing so.

After hearing this story from Smith, Baker arranged to meet Bob Trustin at the King's Head Tavern in Oxford. The boy came, and repeated the story to Smith and Baker, adding that 'I used to lie in the Bed with Mr Swinton. Mr Swinton used to tickle and play with me in the Morning, and I used to play with Mr Swinton's Cock, which used to stand. Mr Swinton used to kiss me.' Baker asked Bob 'whether Mr Swinton used to put his Tongue into your Mouth?' to which the boy answered 'No'. But on being asked 'Whether Mr Swinton did not use to get upon your Back?' he answered, 'No, but that he used to put his Cock into my Arse Hole, and that I felt something warm came from him, and he sometimes made me wet between my Thighs.'

Armed with these particulars, Baker assembled the Fellows of Wadham once more and revealed his fresh discoveries. Swinton, learning what was afoot, sent his new bed-maker John Himber (poor Boxley in the meantime had been dismissed by the new Warden, Mr Lisle) to fetch Bob Trustin. Bob agreed to say that he was lying to Baker, and Himber gave him some money to seal the pact. The Vice-Chancellor meanwhile also sent for the boy, and Bob told him that Baker had given him money to lie about Swinton. Swinton, who had more mettle in him than Thistlethwayte, then brought a complaint against Baker for malicious slander. The parties concerned, along with Dr Prado and the Fellows of the College, on 20 March assembled before the Vice-Chancellor, Theophilus Leigh. Smith, who was now acting as the Under Porter at New College, affirmed the boy's story to him and Baker at the tavern, and when asked by the Vice-Chancellor 'Did Mr Swinton ever put his Cock into your Arse Hole?' the boy said, 'Yes, sometimes.' Not being a very bright lad, Bob both affirmed and denied all of the questions subsequently asked of him, while Swinton denied the charges and Himber denied the bribery.

Under harassment the boy became 'confounded', and the Vice-Chancellor rebuked Baker for believing 'an ideot boy and ragamuffin'. He offered Baker the options of recanting, being imprisoned, or being expelled. Baker agreed to request Swinton's pardon. Leigh let Swinton draw up the recantation document, which made it appear that the charges were derived solely from malicious motives. Baker prepared a milder form, but Swinton insisted upon the first. Baker protested that signing such a document 'would make me seem so great a Wretch in the eyes of the World, who knew nothing of the circumstances', but Leigh advised him it was a mere formality, and threatened to either imprison or expel him, so he signed it. Then the Rev. Dr Conybeare (Dean of Christ-Church) moved that Baker be required to deliver unto Swinton a £100 bond as guarantee of his good behaviour toward Swinton, and he did so.

The next day, 21 March 1739, the recantation document, without Baker's knowledge, was published in the *Daily Advertiser* and the *London Evening Post*: 'I George Baker, Bachelor of Arts, and Scholar of Wadham College in Oxford, do acknowledge, that I have made a very unjust and inhuman Attempt to ruin the Character of the Rev. Mr Swinton, Fellow of the said College, by reporting that he hath been guilty of a Sodomitical Attempt and that I had no Foundation or Authority for any such Story; and I heartily ask his Pardon, and the Pardon of the University, for it, being sensible of the Folly and Injustice I have been guilty of.' It is difficult to determine to what degree Baker's reputation may have been injured by this document. We only know, from the Register of Wadham College, that

Baker remained there until 1741, when he vacated his scholarship, and he failed to proceed to the degree. Mr French received the Bachelor of Arts in 1740, but having failed to show up for three successive examinations, he was deprived of giving his exhibition in Greek six weeks later.[4]

Baker's recantation probably prompted a satire on the corrupt age which appeared in 1739, in which his masters were barely disguised, and even Lord Hervey was hauled before the public once again: What is the world coming to, laments our author,

> When T[histlethway]te both Sexes acts, before
> A vile Indorser, and behind a Whore;
> And 'twixt the Males of O[na]n, Scenes are past
> Which make old D–'s leud Nocturnals chaste.
>   Say Dear Swintonius what detested Clime,
> Taught Latium's learned Sons so dire a Crime?
>   ... Here Sporus live and once more feel my Rage,
> Once and again I drag thee on the Stage,
> Male-female Thing, without one Virtue made,
> Fit only for the Pathick's loathsome Trade.[5]

This is the end of the story that can be gleaned from the extant historical documents, and perhaps there is no moral to the tale other than to point up a mood that somewhat prevails even in twentieth-century Oxford. The scandal does merit being dredged up from the obscurity in which it has lain these many years, if only for the sake of demonstrating that curious mixture of naivety and earnestness that was so typical of the early eighteenth century. On the one hand we see the solicitors and school administrators engaging in their cautious and solemn deliberations, and on the other hand we see the innocence of the working class and servants — Boxley joking about being buggered by Thistlethwayte, Smith worrying that Bob will give Mr Swinton lice by sleeping with him — and one feels that many of the fellows must have regarded these scandals with more amusement than abhorrence. In the midst of these conflicting parties, Thistlethwayte and Swinton behaved in ways both foolish and cunning, trying to brazen out the situation. One point worth emphasising is the lack of guilt or shame in the gay protagonists, though of course they feared losing their reputations.

---

7. Mary Blandy ascending the scaffold, attended by Rev. John Swinton (in his surplice), the gay chaplain of Oxford Castle and Fellow of Wadham Collage.

MISS BLANDY *at the place of Execution near Oxford, attended by the Rev. Mr. Swinton.*

It is not easy to identify what motivated some of the parties involved. Mr French was repulsed enough to vomit, but we do not know the 'inconceivable Particulars' of what took place; the length of his stay in Thistlethwayte's parlour suggests that he was persuaded to participate in some form of homosexual intercourse. The fact that he did not cry out for help, even when Swinton knocked on the door, suggests that he had not been violently attacked. His revulsion came somewhat after the event, probably due to an inner turmoil at having consented to something which people of his middle-class background believed to be quite wrong.

The authorities conducted their enquiry with the greatest possible care, wishing to avoid a full-scale investigation into homosexual activities at Wadham. The servants such as Boxley and Hodges were wise to the fact that such things were not uncommon. Swinton stayed on at his post, unharmed by the publicity of the case, performing such duties as giving spiritual aid to prisoners in Oxford gaol. He again came to prominence with the trial and conviction of the infamous Mary Blandy in 1752, for poisoning her father. Swinton was the Ordinary of Oxford Castle, where she was imprisoned, and he received her dictation *Miss Mary Blandy's Own Account of the Affair between Her and Mr Cranstoun*, which achieved wide popularity. In that work she describes Swinton as 'the worthy clergyman who attended me in prison.' She took an interest in another case – that of Elizabeth Jeffries, tried in Chelmsford for helping her lover murder her uncle – resulting in *Genuine Letters between Miss Blandy and Miss Jeffries*, where she says 'It was barbarous, but I am sorry for her and hope she will have a good divine to attend her in her last moments, if possible a second Swinton, for, poor unhappy girl, I pity her.' Swinton gave her the sacrament on 5 April, and attended her to the place of execution on 6 April, where she was hanged.[6]

Swinton became absent-minded in his old age, which was the subject of a humorous anecdote related by Thomas Warton concerning Samuel Johnson's visit to Oxford in 1754: 'About this time there had been an execution of two or three criminals at Oxford on a Monday. Soon afterwards, one day at dinner, I was saying that Mr Swinton, the chaplain of the gaol and also a frequent preacher before the University, a learned man but often thoughtless and absent, preached the condemnation-sermon on repentance, before the convicts, on the preceding day, Sunday; and that in the close he told his audience that he should give them the remainder of what he had to say on the subject the next Lord's Day. Upon which one of our company, a Doctor of Divinity and a plain matter-of-fact man, by way of offering an apology for Mr Swinton, gravely remarked that he had probably preached the same sermon before the University. "Yes, sir, (says Johnson) but the University were not to be hanged the next morning."'[7]

Chapter 11

The Age of Scandal

(1) Disgrace

The various Societies for Reformation of Manners had become inactive by 1740; the organised crusade of the 1720s was over, and the gay subculture was no longer so systematically purged. Prosecutions still occurred with some regularity, but they were mostly unconnected to one another, and form a history of isolated incidents. I have the impression that the heyday of the molly houses was also over, that they were going out of fashion, slowly declining in popularity and steadily being superseded by more organised prostitution and even male brothels on the one hand, and by public cruising grounds on the other.

In 1757 a well-organised molly was apprehended, who 'got his Livelihood by prostituting himself' by means of sending letters to wealthy men, offering them his services. The Rt. Hon. the Earl of Tankerville did not appreciate the letter of assignation that had been sent to him, and arranged for his capture by pretending to meet him. The prostitute was found to have many such letters in his pocketbook, with blank spaces for names to be filled in, and he had a list of names and addresses of men of various degrees of social standing. He revealed that mollies cruised Kensington Gardens and 'the obscure Places in Hyde-Park', and some of his papers indicated that there were 'many Clubs' of such men about town. But he preferred his independent way of doing business: 'it appeared that he lay in Bed every Day till after Twelve; that he constantly breakfasted in Bed, wore a Bed Gown, and a Woman's Cap and Knot: His Paint and Patch-Boxes were found on his Toilet. In a Word, he is the completest Gomorrean that has been met with for some Time.'[1]

The more fashionable West End of London had by no means

completely replaced the original site of the gay subculture in the East End. On 18 April 1761 Thomas Andrews, who kept the Fortune of War public house at Pye-Corner near Smithfield, offered to share his bed with John Finnimore. They supped, drank freely, and went to bed. 'As soon as Finnimore was in bed he fell asleep, but about four o'clock he awaked, with a violent pain and agony, and found Andrews' yard in his body. . . . in getting away from him he felt something warm, but what it was, he could not say.' He got out of bed and sat on a chair, but after 15 minutes was persuaded to return to bed, where, after ten minutes, the same thing occurred again, whereupon he got up and was let out of the house. Andrews denied the charge, and claimed it was an attempt at extortion. The jury found him guilty and sentenced him to death, but the King gave him respite and afterwards a full pardon.[2] A publisher of a collection of trials in 1779 personally knew two of the members of the jury that convicted Andrews, and was assured by them that there was no doubt whatsoever about his guilt. 'What sort of interest it was that procured a pardon for this man, it may be improper, because it could hardly be decent, to say.'[3]

Another pardon that provoked a great deal of public comment was that given to Robert Jones, a lieutenant in the army, called Captain Jones. In July 1772 he was convicted at the Old Bailey for sodomy upon Francis Henry Hay, aged 13. The newspapers were full of the case, and there was much debate over his guilt or innocence. He was a well-known figure, much celebrated for personating the character of Punch at a recent masquerade,[4] and the author of popular treatises on artificial fireworks and ice-skating that went through numerous editions.[5] Jones was sentenced to death, but on the very day he was to be hanged (11 August), this was respited to imprisonment, and one month later he was granted His Majesty's pardon.[6] He was clearly guilty, but 'the utmost interest was exerted in his favour; and such representations were made to the King, that his Majesty was pleased to grant him his pardon, on the condition of his transporting himself for the term of his natural life.'[7] The case provoked a 'Latin Epitaph on Bob Jones':

> Underneath this stone there lies
> A face turn'd downward to the skies;
> A captain who employ'd his parts
> Upon male b[um]s, not female hearts:
> Who turn'd his arms not against foes,
> But against friends, whence Sodom rose,
> . . . He was repriev'd from gallows death,
> At Tyburn had resign'd his breath;
> But George, in vengeance, let him live,
> Like Cain, till conscience should forgive.[8]

Jones had little conscience about transporting himself no further than the Continent, and the newspapers reported with chagrin that 'the famous Capt. Jones lives now in grandeur with a *lovely Ganymede* (his footboy) at Lyons, in the South of France.'[9]

Another career also ended abruptly in 1772, that of Isaac Bickerstaffe, the dramatist who was responsible for establishing comic opera on the English stage.[10] Bickerstaffe grew up in Dublin as one of Lord Chesterfield's pages in the 1730s, and through his efforts obtained a commission in the Fifth Regiment of Foot, the Northumberland Fusiliers, at the age of 12. He resigned his lieutenancy in 1755 (some said under scandalous circumstances, but this was not proven), and went on ensign's half-pay, and moved to London to begin his writing career. There he produced a series of comic operas, including the very popular *Love in a Village*, and during the 1760s he was dining out with Dr Johnson, Sir Joshua Reynolds, Boswell, Goldsmith, and most of the leading London artists of the day; Garrick and Bickerstaffe were the reigning king and queen of the stage. A modern study of his accounts has shown that he earned a very great deal of money and spent it on purposes unknown, chiefly on frequent trips to the Continent.

His last trip abroad was prompted by a notice which appeared in *The Daily Advertiser* on 30 April 1772 :

> *Whereas* on Tuesday Night last, between the hours of Eight and Ten, A Gentleman left with a Centinel belonging to Whitehall Guard, a Guinea and a half, and a Metal Watch with two Seals, the one a Cypher, the other a Coat of Arms, a Locket, and a Pistol Hook. The Owner may have it again by applying to the Adjutant of the first Battalion of the first Regiment of foot-Guards at the Savoy Barracks, and paying for this Advertisement.

In the fateful days that followed, the ad was explained in the *St James Chronicle* and other London newspapers:

> The History of this Watch, &c. is this: A *Gentleman* grew enamoured, the other Night at Whitehall, with one of the Centinels, and made Love to him; the Soldier being of that rough cast, who would rather act in the Character of *Mars* than *Venus*, not only rejected the Lover's Suit, but seizing him, threatened to take him immediately to the Guard-Room. The Affrighted Enamorato, to avoid the consequences of Exposure, with the greatest Precipitation gave the Soldier his Watch, Rings, and other Valuables, for his Liberty.

The paper went on to explain that the sentinel bragged about his good fortune to the corporal, the corporal told the sergeant, the sergant the adjutant, and soon the whole corps of officers knew about it, as did the press.

Some of the articles, such as a mourning ring, easily established the identity of the owner as 'a Man of some Fame in the Literary World'. On 18 May the *Northampton Mercury* reported that the Literary Character had absconded, and the day after that everyone knew this was Garrick's good friend Isaac Bickerstaffe. Mr Thrale told Dr Johnson that Bickerstaffe had long been a suspected molly. Dr Johnson was shocked, and replied, 'By those who look close to the ground, dirt will be seen, Sir. I hope I see things from a greater distance.'

Rather than attempt to reclaim watch and rings, Bickerstaffe sailed to St Malo, where he assumed the name Burrows and took lodgings in a bookshop near the cathedral. He wrote to Garrick on 24 June:

> *Ayant perdu mes amis, mes espérances, tombé, exilé et livré au désespoir comme je suis, la vie est un fardeau presque insupportable; j'étois loin de soupçonner que la derniére fois que j'entrais dans votre librairie, serait la derniére fois que j'y entrerais da ma vie, et que je ne reverrais plus le maitre.* (Having lost my friends, my hope, fallen, exiled and delivered into despair as I am, life is a burden almost unbearable; little did I suspect that the last time I entered your study would be the last time in my life that I would enter it, and that never again would I see its master.)

Garrick wrote on the letter: 'From that poor wretch Bickerstaffe. I could not answer it.' Garrick desperately felt the need to dissociate himself from his former friend, in order to defend his own reputation. He was attacked by his fellow dramatist William Kenrick, who accused him of being Bickerstaffe's lover in *Love in the Suds*.[11] This eclogue is spoken by Roscius (Garrick), lamenting the loss of his Nyky (a diminutive of Isaac):

> *Whom fliest thou, frantic youth, and whence thy fear?*
> *Blest had there never been a grenadier!*
> *Unhappy Nyky, by what frenzy seiz'd,*
> *Coulds't thou with such a martial thing be pleas'd?*
> *What, tho' thyself a gentle horse-marine*,*
> *Couldst thou with foot-soldiers at land be seen?*

(*Nyky is an half-pay officer of marines. The term horse-marine is well known to some kind of sailors. *Modò vir modò foemina.*)

Roscius defends his lover's taste:

> *And yet, ah why should Nyky thus be blam'd?*
> *Of manly love ah! why are men asham'd?*
> *A new red-coat, fierce cock and killing air*
> *Will captivate the most obdurate fair;*
> *   Yet slight the cause of Nyky's late mishap;*
> *Nyk but mistook the colour of the cap:*
> *A common errour, frequent in the Park,*
> *Where love is apt to stumble in the dark.*

This *apologia* praises homosexual love as being more refined than and superior to vulgar heterosexuality, though the Italian *gusto* and *bon ton* of France make but slow advance among the lowbred English. Precedents for such love can be found in classical Rome and ancient Greece, where it was practised by men such as Virgil, Socrates, and others: 'The gay Petronius, sophists, wits and bards, / Of old, bestow'd on youth their soft regards.' Kenrick finds it necessary to disclaim these 'Southern modes' and 'Platonic love' in a footnote in which he describes himself as 'A Briton blunt, bred to plain mathematics, / Who hates French b[ou]gres, and Italian pathics.'

Kenrick's satire went through five editions in 1772, and Garrick began a prosecution for libel. Kenrick had to publicly apologise to Garrick and disclaim the libel, but the war of libels and counter-libels raged in the newspapers for several years, until by 1777 several newspapers also had to make apologies. Kenrick privately admitted that he never believed Garrick to be a molly, but that he thought it was a good opportunity to attack a competitor. But he did believe that Garrick knew about, and tolerated, an earlier affair between Bickerstaffe and 'a masculine dancer', presumably a ballet dancer.

In 1777 Bickerstaffe wrote once more to Garrick, this time from Vienne, to complain that Garrick in the libel controversy was destroying his reputation even more than it had already been destroyed. He concluded by begging Garrick for £10, as he was impoverished. Garrick never replied. The *Biographica Dramatica* of 1782 noted that Bickerstaffe 'is said to be still living at some place abroad, to which a deed without a name has banished him, and where he exists poor and despised by all orders of people.' In the years that followed, there were newspaper reports that Bickerstaffe was drinking two pints of spirits a day, that he died in Sussex in 1783, that he had drowned himself, that he had hanged himself, that he was writing for the Marseilles stage, that he was living in Milan, that he was sighted in Charing Cross in 1811. He sent a play to Mrs Jordan for one of her benefits in 1790, but no other plays from these last sad years of his life have been traced. He probably died at the age of 75 in 1808, the last year in which he drew his half-pay pension.

(2) Samuel Foote

Several years after the 1772 scandals involving Captain Jones and Bicker-staffe, society was regaled by the scandalous dispute between another dramatist, Samuel Foote (sodomite), and the Duchess of Kingston (biga-mist). Rev. Richard Polwhele, historian of Devonshire, called Foote 'a libertine, in *every sense* of the word', but some people would contend that the word 'libertine' meant more in Cornwall than it did in London. Although we certainly know that Foote was accused of being homosexual, with disastrous consequences for him, there is little evidence to prove this beyond reasonable doubt. But a brief look at the life of the playwright whom contemporaries called 'the English Aristophanes' is nevertheless in order, if only to chart the progress of homophobia in the late eighteenth century.

Samuel Foote, a native of Cornwall, was baptised on 27 January 1720, and in due course sent to study law in the Temple, one of the Inns of Court, thus becoming a 'Templar'. As a scholar he was more elegant than erudite, and law did not appeal. 'He was remembered, by many Templars in my time', recalls his first biographer, 'as one of the greatest beaux of the year *forty*, living in handsome chambers, with all the paraphernalia of study around him, but without the gift of application. His greatest delight consisted in making a figure at the coffeehouses whither resorted the *beaux-esprits* of the day.'[12] He commonly began the day at the Grecian in the Temple, and by evening had moved on to the Bedford Coffee House, Covent Garden, where he enjoyed the wit of the drama critics and acquired his taste for the theatre. One of the taverns which he frequented was the Royal Oak, 'standing by itself, near the *path* that led from Finsbury to Sir Thomas Boleyn's Grange, . . . the midnight walk of numerous footpads, and many murderers, as the annals of Newgate attest'[13] — this would be the infamous Sodomites' Walk in Moorfields.

Foote continued at law for three or four years, living 'fashionably and ostentatiously', even more so after receiving an inheritance at the death of his father in 1754. But his real vocation began in 1743, when he and his friend Macklin entered on an enterprise in a little wooden theatre in the Haymarket, and soon he was on the path to fame as both actor and playwright. In our own time Samuel Foote is regarded as the Father of Farce, for those who came after him certainly plundered his works for their plots, characters and jokes; and in his own time he received his cognomen 'the English Aristophanes' because of his introduction of characters based upon real people, unlike the stereotyped figures common to the sentimental comedy that was so popular at the time.

Foote 'possessed a rich talent for ridicule'; his satire was illiberal and his characters were recognisable: inevitably his early plays aroused much resentment among those whom he satirised, and those who feared that their turn would be next. Today it is difficult to appreciate what all the fuss was about, since those whom he satirised are even less well known to us than either Foote or his plays. But constables were prompted to close his plays, using a law which allowed only two playhouses to operate in Westminster. Foote evaded this by the technical ploy of re-opening 'Tea-parties' at the Little Theatre in the Haymarket; instead of offering performances of plays, he pretended to be 'training' his actors while the audience sat drinking their tea — and his wit was more scathing than ever.

Around 1748 some undocumented scandal prompted Foote to depart for France, where he remained until 1752, maintaining no contact with his friends and losing his fortune. In 1754 his former friend Macklin, now penurious, left the theatre, and opened both a school of oratory and a coffee house, in the Piazza in Covent Garden. Foote caricatured him in *An Inquisitor* (also known by its more famous title as *Tiddydoll*), and Macklin, in foolish revenge, charged Foote with robbing a friend of a portmanteau. In 1758 he visited Dublin with his friend Tate Wilkinson; his pieces were well received at Sheridan's Theatre. The pair returned to London for the following season, then went on to Edinburgh, and then back to Dublin, where in 1760 one of his finest plays, *The Minor*, was first produced and soon became a hit at the Haymarket Theatre. *The Minor* is essentially an attack on Methodism, and as a result there were several attacks upon him in the press; he responded with a desultory libel suit.

While on a visit to John Savile, Lord Mexborough in 1766, on a chase with the Duke of York, Lord Delaval, and Sir Francis B. Delaval, 'his earliest friend', Foote fell and broke his leg; this had to be amputated and replaced by a cork leg — which gave rise to 'foot and leg' jokes amongst his detractors. But the untoward accident was a kind of stepping stone in his rise to fame. On 25 June of that year the Duke of York helped him to secure the royal patent for a summer theatre; he purchased the Haymarket Theatre, pulled down the old premises, rebuilt it more substantially, and opened next year with *An Occasional Prelude*. In 1768 he cleared several thousand pounds with the immensely successful *Devil upon Two Sticks*, but lost it all gambling in Bath. The play was also taken to Dublin, where Foote became friends with Lord Townshend. *Dr Last in His Chariot* was co-authored with Isaac Bickerstaffe in 1769, and other successful plays followed on its heels through the early 1770s.

Then came his sudden downfall, this time more serious than a fall from a horse. In 1775 Foote was preparing his play *The Trip to Calais*, in which he satirised the Duchess of Kingston in the character of Kitty Crocodile. Elizabeth Chudleigh, Duchess Dowager of Kingston, fearing that its presentation would have a damaging effect upon her forthcoming trial for bigamy, understandably registered a protest. In the ensuing correspondence in the newspapers, Foote publicly apologised and denied the allegation that Kitty Crocodile was intended to portray the Duchess, but he did so in such a way as to leave little doubt that it was indeed a caricature of her. This made her furious; she replied virulently against his slander, and he replied with scathing contempt, alluding to her bigamy: 'Pray, madam, is not J—n the name of your female confidential secretary? and is not she generally cloathed in black petticoats made out of your weeds? "So mourn'd the dame of Ephesus her love."' This was a reference to her male secretary, Rev. William Jackson, who would get his full revenge in the following year. The Chamberlain at the instigation of the Duchess refused to license the performance of *Calais*.

Foote re-wrote the play as *The Capuchin*, in which he satirised Jackson as Dr Viper. Sarcastic and abusive letters between Foote and the Duchess appeared in the press, which did not help her cause. She was convicted of bigamy in April 1776. She claimed privilege of peerage to escape corporal punishment, and was therefore discharged upon payment of her court costs.[14] A bigamist would ordinarily be flogged or at least burnt in the hand. In any case, she had already gone abroad, and continued to lead an irregular life on the Continent.

In May, Jackson in his own newspaper *The Public Ledger* accused Foote of being homosexual. Foote took out a libel suit, which he won, but Jackson renewed the attack in late June and published, under the pseudonym of Humphrey Nettle, *Sodom and Onan: A Satire Inscrib'd to [Foote] Esq. alias, the Devil upon two Sticks* (a reference to Foote's popular play); at the appropriate place in the title was inserted a recognisable portrait of Foote, together with an illustration of a large naked foot.[15] In this satire Foote was portrayed as the archetypal sodomite. The mock-heroic preface is full of appalling puns, such as 'Your last capital *Man-oeuvre* cannot be sufficiently applauded.' There are obvious allusions to anal intercourse as the author heralds Foote as a Genius 'whose *extensive* Abilities are calculated for the *Deepest* Penetration', and as a 'Master of *Fundamental* Knowledge'. The long poem which follows is exceedingly nasty, quite explicit about the sodomitical lust of 'Aristoph', and a rich source of information about celebrated sodomites.

One such was 'his Compeer Drybutter', who was able to 'evade the Law' and 'to defy / The Hand of Equity.' Samuel Drybutter was the bookseller who was pilloried in 1757 for selling copies of *Fanny Hill*. On 30 December 1770 he was probably the 'man of genteel appearance' who was arrested for an attempt to commit sodomy with someone in Lombard Street, and who gave bail the day afterwards.[16] But he seems to have escaped justice, to judge from a contemporary satirical illustration showing him in fetters standing beside the hangman, titled 'Ganymede & Jack-Catch'. 'Jack-Catch' (or 'Ketch') holds up a noose to put around his neck and says 'Dammee Sammy you'r a sweet pretty Creature & I long to have you at the end of my String.' He is tweaking the chin of 'Ganymede', who replies 'You don't love me Jacky.'[17] By curious coincidence, on 19 January 1771, a bit more than a fortnight after Drybutter's arrest, Michael Welch was convicted for stealing a silver candlestick, a French plate candlestick, several watches, snuff boxes, and a large parcel of silver buckles from Drybutter's shop in Westminster Hall in November.[18] Perhaps Welch was a bit of rough trade who saw an opportunity for getting more from the man who picked him up. Drybutter appeared in court to testify that he was now a jeweller, and to identify the stolen property, including a silver nutmeg grater, silver thimbles, and silver-plated candle snuffers. Welch was convicted and sentenced to transportation.[19] Some modern sources say that Drybutter was convicted of an unnatural offense in 1771, but in fact neither he nor anyone else was tried for attempted sodomy in 1771. Perhaps no bill of indictment was granted at the magistrate's examination which would have preceded a trial, or perhaps he stayed around long enough to testify against Welch, and then absconded before his own trial.

In *Sodom and Onan* Foote is likened to 'his compeer Drybutter', the implication being that both men had escaped justice. Drybutter was nicknamed Ganymede because of his amours, though both men would more properly be personified as Zeus rather than Ganymede:

> . . . *In [Foote's] soul*
> *Ingratitude had firmly fix'd her seat,*
> *And troops of crimes march in without defeat:*
> *Sodomy old, see at the van appear,*
> *Polluting Onan sly, brings up the rear.*
> . . . *and his inverted Eye disdains*
> *Objects of Female softness. – with pleasure*
> *He beholds, (like Ganeymede) that* Treasure
> *Exquisite, a lovely Youth, whose Innocence*
> *'Gainst his prevailing Arts, prove weak defence;*
> *E'en age attractions has; but Youths a Prize!*
> *An handsome Boy's a* Jewel *in his Eyes.*

In a satire such as this, emphasised words always have a double meaning. Both 'Jewel' and 'Treasure' may be allusions not only to Drybutter's new occupation, but also references to William Jewell, the treasurer of the

Haymarket Theatre, Foote's very close friend who would eventually put up a monument to his memory after his death.

Jackson claimed that Foote was protected by a host of 'pow'rful Sod'mites':

> *As heaven's Viceregents Kings of Earth are plac'd,*
> *But G[eorg]e the seal majestic hath disgrac'd;*
> *Inveigled by Scotch Institution*
> *To pardon Sodomites and damn the Nation.*
> *S[ackvill]e, both Coward, and Catamite, commands*
> *Department hon'rable, – and kisses hands,*
> *With lips that oft' in blandishment obscene*
> *Have been employ'd, yet now, (oh shame!) he's seen*
> *An haughty headstrong Minister of State,*
> *Controuling Men of minds immaculate.*
> *View straddling B[e]rt[ie], that Bedchamber Lord,*
> *(Felon in Gyves as well might grace a sword,)*
> *Leering he eyes when, M[exborough]'s undrest,*
> *And on a **** cou'd make a princely feast:*
> *Yet such divinity doth hedge a King,*
> *That Catamites their off'rings dare not bring:*
> *But as I'm less than King, I shall take care*
> *E'er I undress, that B[ugge]r B[er]t[i]e is not there.*
> *Ne'er in my house a welcome Guest he'll be,*
> *Ent'ring my doors, he'll want to enter me.*
> *. . . Where is the Author of the village Love?*
> *Sweet Isaac Bickerstaff, who never strove*
> *To wipe away the ignominious stain,*
> *Convinc'd that kicking 'gainst the Pricks was vain.*
> *For safety flown to soft Italia's shore,*
> *Where Tilney, B–l, Jones and many more*
> *Of Britain's cast outs, revel uncontroul'd,*
> *Who for their Beastial lust their Country sold,*
> *Who dissipate Estates in Foreign Climes*
> *To buy indulgence, for their darling Crimes.*

Jackson says that the chief mourner at Foote's tomb will be Drybutter, while 'Bick[ersta]ff, B[er]t[i]e, B–l, Bu[gge]rs all, Jones, S[ackvill]e, D–v–is shall support the pall', and that the audience of his plays will be comprised of '*Male Whores of Quality*'.

Who are these men? In 1760 Lord George Sackville (later Germain) was court-martialled for refusing to obey orders and advance into combat at the Battle of Minden, to which Jackson explicitly refers. He was about 60 years old, and was Lord Commissioner of Trade and Plantation, and Secretary of State for the American Colonies. Though twice married, he was called 'the pederastical American Secretary' and lived with his wife and protégé.[20] His homosexuality is alluded to in some verse by Churchill: 'Trust not to Marriage, in Mankind unread;/ S[ackville]'s a married man, and S[troud] new wed.'[21] Peregrine Bertie, Duke of Ancaster and Kesteven, Earl of Lindsey, Lord Great Chamberlain and Master of the Horse, died in 1779 age 64. I cannot find other sources to substantiate the homosexuality of John Savile, Earl of Mexborough. Lord Tilney and Lord Cowper both lived in Italy; after Cowper's death, his family tried unsuccessfully to prosecute a journalist who accused him of unmanly vices;[22] John Tilney (or Tylney), Earl Tylney of Castlemaine, died unmarried in 1784. Bickerstaffe, as noted above, was probably living in France rather than Italy. Captain Jones lived in Lyons with his Ganymede. I have not identified D—v—is. B—l may be Frederick, Earl of Bristol, the mitred earl who spent most of his life in Italy, whose brother was Elizabeth Chudleigh's first (and only legal) husband, whom she had abandoned in favour of the Duke of Kingston.

The publication of *Sodom and Onan* was followed up in July by the Duchess instituting legal proceedings against Foote — for sodomy — and a warrant was issued for his arrest. He appeared on stage to tell his audience that he had been falsely accused and was endeavouring to redress his reputation, and then proceeded to play his part.[23] The criminal prosecution before Earl Mansfield at the King's Bench on 9 December 1776 was paid for by the Duchess of Kingston, and organised behind the scenes by Rev. Jackson. Foote's former footman John Sangster stood up to charge Foote with an attempt to commit an unnatural crime upon his person twice in May 1775. Sangster had been hired by Foote in November of that year, and had accompanied him to Dublin that winter, and back to England in February. According to Sangster, on the days in question Foote had tried to seduce him at his town house in Suffolk Street; Sangster had resisted, then resigned. Foote promised to pay his wages next day, but in order to receive them Sangster was required to go up to Foote's country house at North End, Hampstead. There Foote asked him to follow him into the stable to see a new horse, where he again made unwelcome advances. Sangster struck a blow, and rushed forth from the stable hurling abusive names after his master.

Several other servants, such as the gardener and coachman, testified that the name-calling incident did indeed occur, and a friend of Sangster testified that the footman had confided to him the nature of the advances. On cross-examination Sangster admitted that Foote had also 'indecently treated' him much earlier, in Dublin, though he had not quit at that time. Several witnesses asserted that Foote was not in town on 1 May, though others were unsure of his whereabouts. Lord Mansfield summed up his belief that the whole thing was a conspiracy to blacken Foote's character, and Foote was acquitted.[24] This was a just verdict, for obviously there was not enough evidence for a conviction; it is also clear, however, that the charge was not a fabrication concocted by the Duchess and her chaplain: they merely exploited rumours and dug up the year-old accusation by a disgruntled servant.

We cannot fail to note some similarities to the Oscar Wilde debacle more than a century later: the trial would not have occurred but for Foote's unnecessarily arrogant treatment of the Duchess, much as Wilde treated the Marquess of Queensbury, and both playwrights underestimated the malicious influence and pertinacity of their aristocratic opponents. Foote occupied the same rank as Wilde at the time: he was at the height of his career, and both admired and mistrusted for his unkind wit and disregard for conventional propriety. And the trial, despite the verdict of Not Guilty, had socially disastrous consequences. Henceforth, Foote would never be above suspicion, and Rev. Jackson would do his best to ensure his ostracism by society.

Foote's plays, such as *The Minor*, were always felt to have been licentious,[25] but he no longer had the strength to resist the attacks upon his personal reputation. Foote's health broke under the strain of the trial and its publicity. He bravely reappeared on the stage in *The Devil* in 1777, but he was lank and emaciated, and had a paralytic stroke. He had to dispose of his patent to George Colman for £400 quarterly, and he went into retirement at Brighton for the summer. Physicians advised him to go to France for a change of air. I suspect he was also well advised to leave England in order to avoid further prosecution. He reached Dover on 22 October, but the winds were unfavourable for a crossing. The next morning he had a shivering fit, and he died in the afternoon, age 57. His contemporary Hester Lynch Piozzi (Thrale) in a note written in the margin of a printed volume of letters observed that 'Doctor Johnson was not aware that Foote broke his heart because of a hideous detection; he was trying to run away from England, and from infamy, but death stopped him.'[26] His funeral was held on Monday, 27 October 1777. Jewell arranged for his body to be removed to his house in Suffolk Street at the back of the Haymarket Theatre, and that night the body was attended to Westminster Abbey by three mourning coaches, where Foote was secretly buried by

---

8. Samuel Drybutter ('Ganymede') escapes being hanged for sodomy in 1771. The hangman ('Jack-Catch') says 'Dammee Sammy you'r a sweet pretty creature & I long to have you at the end of my string', and Drybutter replies 'You don't love me Jacky.'

GANYMEDE & JACK-CATCH

Pub 39 Strand by Darly.

torchlight somewhere in the cloisters, without a carved stone or any other mark. Jewell set up a monument to him in St Martin's Church, Cannon Street, Dover, on which he signed himself 'his affectionate friend'.

In Foote's will, among bequests to agents, printers, and his treasurer Jewell, we find reference to two sons, Francis and George, one of whom had died earlier, though as his biographer notes, 'To the day of his decease, we have no positive proof of Samuel Foote's having embraced the rites of wedlock.' A story has arisen that Foote kept 'his washerwoman for wife, or, more properly, the daughter of one. I believe she lived to an advanced age as Mrs. Jane Nuthall.'[27] We must note, however, that there is no mention of such a person in his will, nor any record of her preparations to leave the country with him, nor her presence at his funeral, nor in any marriage records. The 'revelation', if such it be, first occurred when Sir Francis Blake Delaval married Lady Harriet Paulet, for the sake of her £80,000–£90,000 (she died soon after), and asked Foote why *he* did not take the lady; after some hesitation Foote is supposed to have replied that he was already married to his washerwoman, and he then introduced Delaval to Jane. This sounds very much like a pleasantry of the moment; it is certain that no 'Mrs Foote' ever presided at his table in Suffolk Street or at North End, nor is there any other gossip that he had any female paramours or even flirtations.

On the other hand, it is clear that the main object of Foote's affections was Sir Francis himself: 'his very intimate acquaintance and inseparable companion, whenever they were both in town together, and to whom he dedicated *Taste*.'[28] Delaval was a remarkably handsome man until just before his death in 1772, from corpulence and drink. He and Foote invariably dined together, at each other's houses, at taverns, at friends' houses. Together they visited all the exhibitions from the Tower to Hyde Park Corner, and were often seen at masquerades, and more often at the Turk's Head Tavern in Gerard Street. They even arranged sack races at Sir Francis' country house in Seaton Delaval. 'Pleasure, through its infinite ramifications, was the great object of their lives; and both having fortunes . . . to support this object, they pursued it in all its sources; from books to the lowest species of buffoonery.'[29] Foote secluded himself for three days of grief at Delaval's death.

Elizabeth Chudleigh died in 1788, and William Jackson went on to become an Irish revolutionary. He established another newspaper in 1776, the *Morning Post*, in which he provocatively published the American Declaration of Independence. In 1794 he was arrested in Dublin on charges of being a spy trying to ascertain the chances of a successful French invasion of England. He was found guilty of high treason in April 1795; while his counsel were disputing the conviction, he dropped down dead in the dock, having poisoned himself to foil his enemies.

SODOM and ONAN,

A SATIRE,

INSCRIB'D to

Esqr.

alias, the *DEVIL* upon two Sticks.

9. Title page of *Sodom and Onan*, 1776, the satirical attack upon Samuel Foote, represented by an engraving of a portrait by Rowlandson, and a naked foot.

The Duchess and her chaplain had done their work well. Despite Samuel Foote's paramount position in late eighteenth-century theatre, the English Aristophanes is hardly remembered today, and his biography was felt to be not quite proper for subsequent histories of the theatre. Of course we must also admit that the taste for his kind of farcical satire is quite dead, and even his *bon mots* — for which he was famed as much as was Oscar Wilde — seldom bear repeating; they depend almost entirely upon puns, often at the expense of his own lack of one leg, and many are anti-Irish. For example, after returning from a visit to Ireland, Foote was asked if he had ever been in Cork — 'No, sir, but I have seen a great many drawings of it.' Only occasionally did he indulge in Wildean paradox: to a Lady, he defined 'a good man' as 'one who preserves all the exterior decencies of ignorance.'

Like Oscar Wilde, Foote is supposed to have excelled in the art of conversation, a talent notoriously difficult to convey to posterity before the invention of recording. But Samuel Johnson, whose judgement can be trusted, appreciated this humorist: 'The first time I was in company with Foote was at Fitzherbert's. Having no good opinion of the fellow, I was resolved not to be pleased; and it is very difficult to please a man against his will. I went on eating my dinner, pretty sullenly, affecting not to mind him; but the dog was so very comical, that I was obliged to lay down my knife and fork, throw myself back in my chair, and fairly laugh it out. Sir, he was irresistible.'

(3) Madge Culls

By the last quarter of the eighteenth century the gay subculture in London was pretty well established, though its members were now being called 'Madge Culls' as well as mollies, from a slang term for the female pudenda. In the satirical literature they are derided as effeminates, as usual:

> See womanhood despised, and manhood shamed
> With infamy too nauseous to be named,
> Fops at all corners, lady-like in mien,
> Civeted fellows, smelt ere they are seen.[30]

Prostitution was probably increasing. When the Theatre Royal, Drury Lane, was remodeled in 1783, the backs of the front boxes were enclosed, and 'became a nest for prostitutes of both sexes.'[31] The madge culls were becoming increasingly visible, and they met more frequently in public places. They even developed a repertoire of secret signs and dress codes by which they could recognise one another:

> These wretches have many ways and means of conveying intelligence, and many signals by which they discover themselves to each other; they have likewise several houses of rendezvous, whither they resort: but their chief place of meeting is the Bird-cage Walk, in St. James's Park, whither they resort about twilight.
>
> They are easily discovered by their signals, which are pretty nearly as follow: If one of them sits on a bench, he pats the backs of his hands; if you follow them, they put a white handkerchief thro' the skirts of their coat, and wave it to and fro; but if they are met by you, their thumbs are stuck in the arm-pits of their waistcoats, and they play their fingers upon their breasts.
>
> By means of these signals they retire to satisfy a passion too horrible for description, too detestable for language.[32]

The population of the entire country was steadily increasing, and it is possible that centres such as Bath, Bristol, and York were developing their own gay subcultures. There is recurrent evidence of organised rings of madge culls in the provinces. At the Lammas Assizes in York in 1775, David Mirsey (or Mercer) was convicted of attempted sodomy with James Doe, John Palmer, Thomas Pickersgill, and George Crawford, and fined and sentenced to two years' imprisonment; the full details are not known, but some kind of confederacy was involved.[33] Around 1789 in Exeter 15 mollies were tried but acquitted, whereupon the enraged multitude were so convinced of their guilt that they burnt them in effigy.[34] At the Lancaster Assizes in August 1806 five men were convicted of sodomy; James Stockton, Thomas Fox, John Powell, and Joseph Holland had regularly assembled at the home of Isaac Hitchen on Monday and Friday evenings, where they engaged in homosexual pleasures and called one another 'brother'; Hitchen was 62 years old, and Holland, a gentleman of some property, was also advanced in years. Two of the men had relations with John Knight, one of the most affluent men in Warrington, who was not tried; the details are not clear, for the Judge ordered that no notes should be taken at the trials. All of them were sentenced to death; Hitchen and Fox were respited, but Stockton, Powell and Holland were executed, on the new drop erected at the back of the castle.[35]

In London itself, molly houses still existed, but some of them were more secret places than they had been at the beginning of the century, almost hideouts. A club of mollies used to meet on Monday nights at a tavern near Clare Market. There are conflicting accounts as to its location; one account says they met in the Bunch of Grapes public house, but another account says they were packed together in a small room behind a barber's shop. In November 1794 the police, having been informed of the club, infiltrated it for three consecutive Mondays and then raided it: 18 men were arrested; two of them were dancing together, dressed in women's muffs, shawls, turban-like bonnets, and silken pinafores, with their faces painted and powdered. Each member of the molly house had a Maiden Name, such as Lady Golding, Countess Papillon, and Miss Fanny. They were handcuffed in pairs and taken to prison with a strong escort of soldiers, but mud and stones were thrown by a huge mob which had gathered, threatening to lynch them. But none of them were tried, either because there was no evidence of sodomy, or because they absconded.[36]

Chapter 12

The Vere Street Coterie

(1) The White Swan

At the beginning of the nineteenth century another moral clampdown was impending. In February 1804 Mathusalah Spalding was hanged at the Old Bailey for having 'a venereal affair' with James Hankinson.[1] In October 1808 Richard Neighbour was convicted for buggery with Joshua Archer, and sentenced to be hanged.[2] In 1809 Richard Thomas Dudman and Edward Wood were convicted of a 'conspiracy' to commit sodomy, and sentenced to two years' imprisonment and to stand for one hour in the pillory, where they were pelted with offal supplied by the butchers of Newgate and Fleet Markets.[3] By the end of the first decade of the new century there were probably 50,000 female prostitutes in London,[4] — and some male prostitutes as well. Society wanted to clean things up, to have another reformation of manners. One house of homosexual ill-fame in Charles Street, Covent Garden, was kept by David Robertson, formerly master of the Hand and Arms in Leicester Fields. In May 1806 he was indicted at the Old Bailey for an unnatural crime with a lad, and sentenced to be hanged. He was 66 years old, a grey-bearded man of sallow complexion and low stature. On Wednesday, 13 August he appeared before the debtors' door of Newgate, dressed in black clothes and turn-down boots. 'When turned off [the platform], he suffered much, his body being very light: he pulled up his legs repeatedly with great violence.'[5]

But some people ignored the signs of a backlash and decided to set up shop. Early in the year 1810 a man named Yardley met James Cook at the King's Arms, Bund Court, in the Strand, and proposed that they jointly set up a public house and male brothel. By degrees he revealed his plans to Cook, 'and told him he was acquainted with a great number of gentlemen, some hundreds, who would frequent a house that he kept.' Yardley pressed forward his point by speaking of a man he knew who kept a house of this sort, 'who, in three years, got money enough to live upon and retired.'

Indeed it seems likely that the demand exceeded the supply, and they did not fear their competition; according to the lawyer Robert Holloway, in his remarkable but trustworthy account *The Phoenix of Sodom*,[6] 'there are many [such houses] about town', for example one in the vicinity of the Strand, one in Blackman Street in the Borough, one near the Obelisk, St George's Fields, and one in the neighbourhood of Bishopsgate Street 'kept by a fellow known by the title of the Countess of Camomile; perhaps the title was derived from his ancient place of residence! — This wretch was sent to the cold bath of Newgate for two years, by way of quenching a flame that had been raised by the charms of an uncomplying boy.' Hustling or male prostitution apparently had become a brisk trade by the early years of the nineteenth century, and 'breeches-clad bawds' were to come even from the ranks of lawyers in the City, especially the Inns of Court, 'the Temple not excepted'.

Yardley and Cook soon took the White Swan in Vere Street, Clare Market (not to be confused with Vere Street off Oxford Street), and furnished 'the fatal house' most appropriately for its purposes. 'Four beds were provided in one room: another was fitted up for a ladies' dressing-room, with a toilette, and every appendage of rouge, &c &c: a third room was called the Chapel, where marriages took place, sometimes between a *female grenadier* [i.e. a soldier dressed as a woman], six feet high, and a petit maitre not more than half the altitude of his beloved wife! These marriages were solemnized with all the mockery of *bride maids* and *bride men*; and the nuptials were frequently consummated by two, three, or four couple, in the same room, and in the sight of each other!'

As in the molly houses of the preceding century, many of the customers mated with one another free of charge; but the frequenters of this house could also purchase the favours of young companions, primarily 'servants out of place, and other distressed characters' who had been lured there by offers of money from 'old worn-out catamites . . . stationed in different lodgings' for this purpose. 'The upper part of the house was appropriated to wretches who were constantly in waiting for casual customers; who practised all the allurements that are found in a brothel, by the more natural description of prostitutes.' It does not seem that they catered for any unusual special interests such as whipping — so popular in heterosexual brothels — but otherwise there were few pleasures Cook's clients could not obtain provided they had sufficient funds. One man, for example, 'generally amused himself with eight, ten, and sometimes a dozen different boys and men' simultaneously.

A wide class division was now common to most of the transactions: 'Men of rank, and respectable situations in life, might be seen wallowing either in or on the beds with wretches of the lowest description.' There seems no doubt that the wealth of some of the customers was quite substantial. 'This vice is a great expense': one man is said to have wasted £30,000 in a short time. A certain 'Miss' Fox, who had been homosexual since the age of 12 and who was sent to Newgate for three years after his third conviction at about the age of 24, had been 'the darling of a young man of rank' who introduced him to his family as a fellow student and 'in one year, squandered seventeen hundred pounds' on him.

Of course not all of the customers were wealthy, nor were all of their relationships baldly mercenary. One man who worked as a chimney sweeper and nightman once 'married' a certain 'Miss' Read in the homosexual nuptials, and then brought him home — where already lived the chimney sweeper's wife — to live with them as a young boarder: the rent was given by the chimney sweeper to his mate, who then paid the sweeper's wife for the lodgings.

The majority of the customers probably came not from high society, but from nearby Clare Market, where on Sundays people gathered from as far as 30 miles away. Their occupations were represented by Kitty Cambric, a coal merchant; Miss Selina, a runner at a police office; Black-Eyed Leonora, a Drummer of the Guards; Pretty Harriet, a butcher; Lady Godiva, a waiter; the Duchess of Devonshire, a blacksmith; and Miss Sweet Lips, a country grocer.

There is no convincing evidence that many of the customers were married, though Holloway thinks that this was generally the case: 'It seems that many of these wretches are married; and frequently, when they are together, make their wives, who they call *Tommies*, topics of ridicule; and boast of having compelled them to act parts too shocking to think of' (e.g. perhaps compelled them to submit to anal intercourse). (A Tommy was a masculine woman about town, and the term was also used to describe lesbians.) Holloway cites the case of a man called 'Venus' who at one time raped his wife and sodomised his lover, as did Lord Audley, to whom he refers in an historical aside. Holloway further claims that homosexuals tend to marry women for money (a motive not unknown to heterosexual men!); he sympathises with the wives' resulting misery, and regrets that such situations are not sufficient to constitute grounds for divorce. Holloway may be drawing upon his experience as a lawyer, but his allegations are largely unsupported. Cook, the proprietor of the brothel, was himself married, and his wife ran a more straightforward public house in Long Acre. In his written statement to Holloway, Cook claimed to be exclusively heterosexual: 'I own I participated in all the guilt except the final completion of it, which is abhorrent to my nature. I am, therefore, the more criminal, because I had no unnatural inclinations to gratify: I was prompted by *Avarice* only.' Conceivably this is an attempt to whitewash himself, to ensure that he would be sent to the pillory instead of to the gallows, but his later actions do indeed suggest that his sole motivation was greed.

The White Swan had been open for fewer than six months when it was raided by the constables on Sunday, 8 July 1810. Three separate patrols were despatched from Bow Street: 'such was the secrecy observed, that the object of their pursuit was unknown, even at that moment, to all but the confidential agents of Mr Read, who headed the respective parties.' As many as 27 of the most habitual frequenters of the house — including Cook the landlord and the waiter Philip Hot[7] — were rounded up and taken to the watch-house of St Clement Danes, whence they were 'conveyed in hackney-coaches, between ten and eleven on Monday, to Bow Street for examination', amidst an 'enraged multitude, the majority of whom were females', acting so violently that 'it was with the utmost difficulty the prisoners could be saved from destruction.'

Examination by the magistrates established their guilt in greater or lesser degrees. They were not treated well by their lawyers. Holloway criticises the attorney Wooley for going around to all the accused in different prisons, and, 'under pretence of assisting the offenders in obtaining their liberty, and enabling them to escape justice, stripped them of every guinea they possessed, and, indeed, of every article that would produce one at a pawnbroker's.' Wooley had obtained £30 from Cook's wife and wanted still more, and 'after he had exhausted every stratagem that his colleagues and the devil and himself could devise to get money, and finding no more could be extracted from nakedness, he became wholly negligent of his client; and in order to get rid of Cook's importunities, told him he must have fifty pounds more, or he could not get him liberated.' In the event, Cook was left without a lawyer at his trial, and sentenced to the pillory; Holloway suggested that his attorney ought to have been sentenced to the gibbet.

Most of the men were eventually set free due to lack of sufficient evidence for a successful prosecution (or maybe through bribery). Whatever may have been the class of men who frequented the White Swan, all of the men who were convicted belonged to the lower middle class. On Saturday, 22 September, at the Middlesex Sessions, Clerkenwell, seven men were tried. James Cook the landlord, whom Holloway is at pains to emphasise was not charged with sodomy, was convicted for running a disorderly house. The other six were found guilty of attempted sodomy: William Amos, alias 'Sally Fox', who had twice before been convicted for similar offences, was sentenced to three years' imprisonment and to stand once in the pillory; Robert Aspinal, who, not appearing to be so active as the others, received only one year's imprisonment; Philip Kett; William Thomson; Richard Francis; and James Done. These latter four men, along with Cook, were sentenced to two years' imprisonment, and to stand in the pillory.

The pillorying of six of the convicted men (excluding Aspinal) took place in the Haymarket, opposite Panton Street, on 27 September.[8] Holloway refers to the 'ruffianly scene of human degradation' as 'a scene that never could have disgraced the streets of London but in the Sheriffalty of Mr Matthew Wood' who was noted for his fondness for pillories. As amply indicated by several newspaper accounts, it was the most astonishing public punishment of the century.[9]

Early in the morning the Old Bailey was completely blockaded by thousands of spectators; by noon the size of the mob put a stop to the business of the Sessions, the shops from Ludgate Hill to the Haymarket were shut, and the streets were lined with people waiting to witness the procession. 'Such was the degree of popular indignation excited against these wretches, and such the general eagerness to witness their punishment', that the streets in the vicinity of the Haymarket were rendered impassable. 'All the windows and even the very roofs of the houses were crowded with persons of both sexes; and every coach, waggon, hay-cart, dray, and other vehicles which blocked up great part of the street, were crowded with spectators.' Shortly after noon, butchers' boys from the neighbouring markets appeared with the 'ammunition waggons', carts filled with offal, dung and so forth, from their slaughter-houses. Hucksters 'carried on their heads baskets of apples, potatoes, turnips, cabbage-stalks, and other vegetables, together with the remains of divers dogs and cats. The whole of these were sold to the populace at a high price, who spared no expence to provide themselves with the necessary articles of assault.'

A number of fishwomen attended with stinking flounders and the entrails of other fish which had been in preparation for several days. These articles, however, were not to be sold, as their proprietors, hearty in the cause, declared they wanted them 'for their own use'.

About half-past 12 the Sheriffs and City Marshals arrived with more than 100 Constables mounted and armed with pistols, and 100 on foot. This force was ordered to rendezvous in the Old Bailey Yard, where a caravan, used occasionally for conveying prisoners from the gaols of London to the Hulks, waited to receive the culprits. The caravan was drawn by two shaft horses, and led by two men, armed with a brace of pistols. The gates of the Old Bailey Yard were shut, and all strangers turned out. [The six offenders (four had been removed from the House of

Correction to Newgate on the Wednesday evening, to join Cook and Amos)] were then brought out and all placed in the caravan. Amos began a laugh, which induced his vile companions to reprove him, and they all sat upright, apparently in a composed state, but having cast their eyes upwards, the sight of the spectators on the tops of the houses operated strongly on their fears, and they soon appeared to feel terror and dismay.

Their terror was to be more than justified.

At the instant the church clock struck half-past twelve, the gates were thrown open. The mob at the same time attempted to force their way in, but were repulsed. A grand sortie of the police was then made. About 60 officers, armed and mounted as before described, went forward with the City Marshals. The caravan went next, followed by about 40 officers and the Sheriffs. The first salute received by the offenders was a volley of mud, and a serenade of hisses, hooting, and execration, which compelled them to fall flat on their faces in the caravan. The mob, and particularly the women, had piled up balls of mud to afford the objects of their indignation a warm reception. The depots in many places appeared like pyramids of shot in a gun wharf. These were soon exhausted, and when the caravan passed the old house which once belonged to the notorious Jonathan Wild [in Cock Alley], the prisoners resembled bears dipped in a stagnant pool.

A shower of mud accompanied the men on their passage through Fleet Street and the Strand, and 'Before they reached half way to the scene of their exposure, they were not discernible as human beings. If they had had much further to go, the cart would have been absolutely filled over them.' They could not lie entirely at the bottom of the cart because of the way they were chained to their seats; they could only shelter their heads by stooping — despite which, several were struck by brickbats and bled profusely — but perhaps that was just as well, otherwise they would have been suffocated by the mud. The stout and bulky figure of Cook could be seen sitting aloof from the others, who were of slighter build; he was recognised by the crowd who renewed their attack with redoubled vigour. 'Dead cats and dogs, offal, potatoes, turnips, &c rebounded from him on every side; while his apparently manly appearance drew down peculiar execrations on him, and nothing but the motion of the cart prevented his being killed on the spot.'

At one o'clock four of the men were placed simultaneously in the pillory, which had been specially built for the occasion, with two additional wings, all moveable. For one hour they walked round in a hellish circle while being pelted with dead cats, addled eggs, muck from the tubs of blood supplied by the butchers of St James's market, hurled chiefly by a crowd of about 50 women who were permitted to stand in a ring in front of the pillory. They were completely encrusted with filth despite the little shelter afforded by the four wings of the machine. At the end of their hour they were taken from the stand and conveyed to Cold Baths Fields Prison, through St Martin's Lane, Compton Street, and Holborn. At this intermission 'the butchers' men, and the women, who had been so active, were plentifully regaled with gin and beer, procured from a subscription made upon the spot.'

The remaining two men, Cook and Amos, who in the meantime had been removed to St Martin's watch-house, were then brought back to stand in the pillory by themselves, their faces already disfigured by mud and blows. Two wings of the machine were removed; while preparations were being made, 'Cook held his hand to his head, and complained of the blows he had already received; and Amos . . . shewed a large brick bat which had struck him in the face. The Under Sheriff told them that the sentence must be executed, and they reluctantly mounted.' Within the space of a single minute they appeared a single heap of mud, and they received a battering more severe than that meted out to the previous four.

Cook was hit several times in the face, and 'had a lump raised upon his eyebrow as large as an egg', while Amos's two eyes were completely closed up from swelling. When they were finally untied, Cook was nearly insensible, and it was necessary to help both of them down and into the cart, whence they were conveyed to Newgate, subject to a renewal of the same torment they had received during the procession earlier that day. Cook lay upon the seat in the cart, while Amos lay as flat in the vehicle as he could manage, both of them covered with ordure, 'till their entrance into Newgate sheltered the wretches from the further indignation of the most enraged populace we ever saw.' For good measure, as they passed the end of Catherine Street, a coachman stood upon his box and gave Cook five or six cuts with his whip.

The journalists who reported the scene agreed that 'it is impossible for language to convey an adequate idea of the universal expressions of execration, which accompanied these monsters on their journey', and that the police officers were quite unable to restrain 'the popular rage' of the immense multitude, though no one seems to have questioned the view that the wretched miscreants got what they deserved. Next day, the *Times* reported that during the pillorying the Bow Street officers and patrol apprehended many pickpockets in the crowd, including Samuel Brooke,

William Hall, George Cohen, and John Fregeur, a porter at the Saracen's Head, Snow Hill. So some at least profited by the event.[10]

(2) Hepburn and White

However severe the punishment dealt out to Cook and his five companions in misery, this was not yet the worst that would befall some of the men captured in the raid upon the Swan. On 26 July 1810 Thomas White, a Drummer of the Guards in a Portugal Regiment, aged 16, and John Newbolt (or Newball) Hepburn, an Ensign in a West India Regiment, aged 42 (or 46 or 49 according to other accounts), had been committed to Newgate.[11] On 19 September they were arraigned for buggery, but their trial was postponed to 21 October due to the absence of two material witnesses.[12] But by that date one material witness, a drummer in a regiment in Portugal, had not yet appeared. Lord Ellenborough said the court could not direct the War Office to recall this man to give testimony, but he agreed to postpone it again to give Hepburn's lawyers time to get this witness, which they never succeeded in doing.[13]

The trial finally began on 3 December.[14] There was only one witness for the prosecution, James Mann, Drummer of the Third Regiment of the Guards. He said that Hepburn had accosted him one day on the parade ground in St James's Park, and said 'he was very anxious to speak to the boy who was then beating the big drum, meaning White, and said he would reward him if he would bring the lad to his lodgings, at No. 5, St. Martin's Church-Yard', and gave him half a crown. Mann and White went to Hepburn's that evening, where they were cordially received, and invited to dine with him the following Sunday. But White proposed that it would be better for them to meet at the White Swan in Vere Street. On the day appointed, 27 May 1810, they met at the Swan, had dinner, then were shown into a private room, where Hepburn and White enjoyed sex. The trial has no mention of the exchange of money; obviously there were financial transactions, but we cannot determine if Cook got any share from White, or if he merely earned his money for providing the dinner and private room.

It was not until two weeks later, as a result of the publicity given to the raid on the White Swan, that Mann informed his drum-major of these facts. White was immediately confined, and an officer was sent to capture Hepburn on the Isle of Wight where he was now stationed. Hepburn was brought to Bow Street magistrates court and committed for trial. Hepburn and White were both capitally indicted on Wednesday, 5 December, and sentenced to be hanged.[15] White was convicted of buggery, and Hepburn was convicted of, first, 'consenting & permitting Thomas White to Commite the crime of Buggery with him', and, second, 'for committing the crime of Buggery with each other.'[16] White, 'being an universal favourite, was very deep in the secrets of the fashionable part of the coterie' according to Holloway. He wished to make a confession in writing, but the transcriber was so sickened by the details that he was unable to proceed. The evidence against them was given by a person who was himself *particeps crimines*, though Mann was not prosecuted. When Hepburn was put to the bar on 11 December and given the opportunity to say why sentence of death should not be passed, he replied, from a written paper, that he was convicted 'upon the false testimony of a single and perjured witness.' Holloway notes that had the evidence been stripped of circumstantial details, particularly that concerning their earlier reputation, they would have been acquitted – the real evidence in his view being insubstantial.

They were hanged before the debtors' door at Newgate on the morning of Thursday, 7 March 1811. 'White came out first; he seemed perfectly indifferent to his awful fate, and continued adjusting the frill of his shirt while he was viewing the surrounding populace.' Hepburn came out two minutes later, accompanied by the clergyman, his servant, the hangman, the ordinary, and other functionaries. The executioner put a cap over his face. White fixed his eyes upon Hepburn. 'After a few minutes prayer, the miserable wretches were launched into eternity. A vast concourse of people attended to witness the awful scene. The Duke of Cumberland, Lord Sefton, Lord Yarmouth, and several other noblemen were in the press-yard.'[17] Holloway notes this aristocratic presence, implying that these noblemen had availed themselves of White's friendship in the Swan. It is said that White's ghost 'pays his nocturnal visits to old Moggy, the rumprider, Park-street, exclaiming,

> *"Monster! Amidst the din of infernal howl*
> *"The fiends in hell will scramble for thy soul."'*

A rumour was widely circulated concerning the Duke of Cumberland, future King of Hanover. It was said that he had been detected 'in an improper and unnatural situation with [his valet] Neale by the other servant Sellis, and exposure was expected.' In the early hours of 1 June 1810, Sellis was discovered in bed in his room in St James's Palace with his throat cut – apparently murdered by the Duke to prevent him from talking. A coroner's jury concluded that Sellis had committed suicide after trying to assassinate the Duke in a fit of madness. 'A journalist who published this rumour in 1813 was sentenced to 15 months in prison'[18] and the case was still controversial 20 years later. In 1832 one Phillips republished the rumour in the book *Authentic Records of the Royal Family during the last 70 Years;* he was brought to trial for libel on 25 June 1833, and found guilty and sentenced to six months.[19] (It may not be irrelevant to mention another curious case, that of a certain Tranter, a footman in the service of the Prince of Wales for six or seven years, and previously in the service of the Duke of Queensbury. For reasons unknown – or suppressed – he shot himself on 25 July 1810, in Carlton House, and died in the arms of his master.[20] This was a few weeks after the raid on the White Swan; had he used its services?)

Cook was later to attempt to blackmail some of his patrons whom he had refused to implicate. We cannot doubt that important men were implicated in the Vere Street affair. This seems likely from Cook's attempts to escape justice; in order to avoid the pillory, he threatened to make known a list of names, and even met to negotiate with officials at the Office of the Secretary of State. When he returned to Newgate, the head turnkey Suter said 'it was not intended that you should have come back alive!' So he nearly avoided assassination on the orders of someone important. Alderman Plomer – successor to sheriffs Atkins and Wood – heard of this meeting, and visited Cook several times in prison. Holloway says that Plomer received the list from Cook, and promised to befriend him after his sentence was served; he said he could not reduce the sentence because Cook had offended high officials. In the event, Plomer died before Cook finished his sentence.

The *Times* (28 September 1810) reported that 11 men were convicted. As far as I can tell there were seven convictions in September (Cook, Amos, Aspinal, Kett, Thomson, Francis and Done), plus two indictments (White and Hepburn). Two other men were committed to Newgate around this time, though we are not certain this was as a direct result of the raid on the Swan. Thomas Hammet was committed to Newgate on 31 July,[21] and on 19 September he was charged with assault with attempt to commit buggery upon Charles Pendrell; he was bound over to the next sessions but was found not guilty.[22] On 3 September, George Rowell was committed to Newgate, and on Friday, 21 September he was indicted for buggery with a person unknown; he was ordered to be transported for 14 years, but on 25 September his sentence was respited, and he was sentenced to pay one shilling, and to be imprisoned at hard labour in Clerkenwell for six months.[23]

Several other cases were prosecuted at this time, but were probably unrelated: in July a certain Dickinson was convicted at the Westminster Sessions and sentenced to one year's imprisonment and to stand in the pillory at Charing Cross;[24] in August John Carey Cole was sentenced to death for having sodomised three boys in an academy where he was an usher.[25] Numerous incidents can be found in the Old Bailey Sessions Roll for 19 September 1810, which were never prosecuted: on August 25

Thomas Scott paid a bond of recognisance, promising to appear to testify that William Billingham had assaulted him with intent to commit buggery, in the Parish of Paddington; on 18 August George Friestman paid a bond of recognisance, promising to appear to testify that Thomas Innis had attempted to commit an unnatural crime with him in the New Road, Parish of St Marylebone; on 22 August Thomas Innis paid a bond of recognisance, promising to appear to testify that George Friestman had assaulted him with intent to commit an unnatural crime; on 28 August John Kench and Robert Thompson (a private in the First Regiment of Guards) were charged with taking indecent liberties with one another; on 12 September, James Walker and Shudy Macnamara paid bonds of recognisance, charged with 'unlawfully and wickedly committing and perpetrating with each other divers filthy lewd nasty and Sodomitical acts and practices.'

Cook served his sentence and was finally released from prison on 21 September 1812. 'In the course of a few days after', writes Holloway, 'he accidentally met John Church, and recognised him as the *gay parson*, whom he had formerly seen at a certain house in the London Road, and at his own house in Vere Street. A friendly correspondence' ensued. This was the Rev. John Church (the subject of the following chapter), whom Cook had met in May 1810, in company with Mr Yardley and Mr Ponder, a Drummer of the Guards, and whom Kitty Cambric soon persuaded to act as the chaplain at the White Swan, officiating at the homosexual marriage ceremonies. Church was one of the members of the Vere Street Coterie lucky enough to escape detection, and Cook evidently thought he was ripe game for blackmail. There is extant a facsimile of a letter to Cook from about 13 October, in which Church wishes him success in 'getting a house fit for the Business in the public Line' and giving him £1/1s, 'As I am By no means Rich.' This was addressed to Cook 'at mr. halladays Richmond Budgs Dean St.' This letter suggests nothing immoral, but there is the suggestion that Holloway was acting as Cook's agent in requesting money, tantamount to extortion. In another letter, postmarked 20 October, Church says 'I am very much grieved i have not been able to comply with the request concerning Mr C But I shall certainly keep my eye upon him and Do him all the Good it lays in my power where ever he is he knows my disposition too well to impute any remissness to my conduct But I cannot Do impossibilities'; this is addressed to 'Mr Oliver, or (Holloway) at No 6 Richmond, Dean, Soho.' These attempts at blackmail failed when Cook and his wife went to Church's home, but were chased away by Church's current boyfriend Roland Hill, with dagger drawn. Perhaps Cook, in revenge, was the person who gave information to the editor of *The Weekly Dispatch*, which began a slur campaign against Church in April 1813.

Cook also attempted to blackmail another Reverend, a former customer (Church was not the one in question, for this unnamed minister

'had been unfrocked while in Newgate'). Both he and his wife approached
this man, received no satisfaction, and left; upon their departure they were
chased by J. Shenstone, who caught up with them, seized Mrs Cook by the
arm and knocked her down. Cook hit him in the nose and mouth. Bleeding
profusely, Shenstone ran back to a certain Moggy Stewart's, where he
recovered after a fainting fit. Shenstone then obtained a warrant against
Cook and his wife for assault; they were ordered to find bail. The papers
reported that Cook had assaulted Shenstone after failing to extort money
from him; Holloway argues that this was absurd, for Shenstone was a mere
servant in rags.

Mrs Cook acted as an accomplice to her husband's blackmail, for she
herself had been ruined at the time of the raid on the White Swan. Her own
public house the White Horse, Long Acre, had been seized by the brewery
firm of Starkey and Jennings for lack of payment for beer and other items.
This included six butts of porter belonging to Henry Meux, who had
placed a £60 levy against her on 18 July 1810. Mrs Cook was turned out of
her own lodgings in 1813. Both of the Cooks were indicted for the assault
upon Shenstone and held in Fleet prison. Holloway bailed her out, but she
was seized within a week and imprisoned in the Poultry Compter (where
prostitutes and ruffians were usually detained) despite the bail. The
seizure was made by a constable Creswell, whom Holloway says was paid
for this outrage. She was again discharged, but again arrested, questioned
and even beaten for two or three hours, and then discharged again. This
is the last we hear of Mrs Cook, but the pattern of persecution against her
lends some support to Holloway's charge that influential sodomites were
determined to eliminate Cook's threatening presence at any cost. Even
Cook's brother, a bedstead maker, was degraded and ruined. He was
evicted from his house by his landlord, and forfeited £10 which he
deposited to cover court expenses and a debt of £23 for which Cook was
detained immediately upon his first release.

This was the state of things at the close of Holloway's pamphlet, which
was published in early 1814 in an effort to raise money to relieve Cook's
situation. The notoriety of the Vere Street affair had a traumatising effect
upon the gay subculture, and the magical power which a scandal possessed
to sell massive quantities of newspapers, even prompted journalists to dig
up old stories about Captain Jones and Isaac Bickerstaffe and to report on
their current whereabouts. Holloway's pamphlet, sensational enough in
itself, was clearly intended to attract buyers, as it was advertised in a
handbill, claiming that it contained 'an exhibition of the gambols practised
by the ancient lechers of Sodom and Gomorrah; embellished and improved with the modern refinements.'

Chapter 13

A Child of Peculiar Providence

(1) The Foundling

In the early eighteenth century in London we have already noted the existence of Marrying Rooms and Chapels in the molly houses, and of Weddings and semi-formal bonding patterns between gay men. But as far as I can discover, no duly ordained minister officiated at these ceremonies until the early nineteenth century, when the Reverend John Church appeared upon the molly circuit and began celebrating the first gay rites of Holy Matrimony.[1]

John Church's origins are obscure. He was found, sometime between 1782 and 1784, when but an infant who could barely toddle, on the steps of the Church of St John's in Clerkenwell (or, by another account, the Church of St Andrew in Holborn). Unable to locate his parents, the elders of the parish church sent him to the Foundling Hospital, where the nurses took him in hand and gave him the appropriate name 'John Church'. Johnnie came out at an early age. When he was only nine years old, the good nurses became alarmed at discovering that he was playing forbidden games with the other orphan boys. The governors of this worthy institution thought 'that it was prudent to apprentice him out at that early age, to obviate the possibility of the contagioun [sic] spreading among the rest of the boys who partook of that charity.' He was accordingly apprenticed to a gilder in Blackfriar's Road (or, by another account, to a gilder in Great Portland Street) for an 11-year indenture, during which time he served as virtually a domestic servant.

When he was about 15 he fell in love with a younger girl who came to serve the same family. When they found out that he was having relations with her, he was punished by being locked in a coal bin — which he later recalled in his autobiography as a frightening and traumatic experience. Eventually he appealed to a magistrate for the successful release from his legal bondage. For a while he worked for a composition ornament maker in Tottenham Court Road, and during his spare time he began practising how to preach the gospel. In short order he became a Sunday School teacher in Tottenham Court Chapel, and for several years he was a member of various groups of itinerant dissenting ministers — the Baptist Society, the Expounding Society, the Westminster Itinerant Society. He even founded the Fitzroy Sabbath School on Cleveland Street (a street that would become notorious for its gay brothel in the late nineteenth century). In 1801 he married the daughter of a Mr Elliott from Hampshire, and in due course she would bear him six children — though the time he spent at home with his wife was limited by his duties as a wandering preacher.

At Tottenham Court Chapel he met a devout young chap named William Webster — and promptly fell in love with him. He and Webster and another candidate for the priesthood (whose name is not recorded) hired out a garret in the Soho district, in a whorehouse on Orange Street run by Old Mother Barr. There, using a chair as a pulpit, the three men practised their oral delivery. Old Mother Barr and the ladies of the house often varied their routine by going upstairs to sit and listen, for it was a marvellously convenient way of edifying their souls. Sometimes a hearty blacksmith or lusty grocer's boy would mistakenly enter the wrong room, only to receive a sermon instead of certain other pleasures that had been anticipated.

Eventually Church became friendly with Rev. J. L. Garrett, a Professor of Natural Philosophy, whom contemporaries referred to as 'a notorious Sodomite'. This generous-souled sodomite obtained for Church a living as the minister of the parish church of Banbury, north of Oxford. This lasted for several years until August 1808, when the Banbury elders heard rumours that Church had been 'sodomitically assaulting' several of the devout young men in his congregation. The particulars of this case — said to be 'of a very scandalous nature' — are only vaguely recorded. Though Church seemed to have had a regular boyfriend at Banbury, who acted as a porter during his travels, he also had made friends with 'several buckish young men', whom he enjoyed watching while they bathed naked in the river, and in whose company he passed his time into the unseasonable hours of the night. Church was very popular in the Banbury area, particularly at Kingham, where he once took liberties with the two sons of the host who regularly sheltered him on his journey. And he took indecent liberties with his young hairdresser and a young grocer.

---

10. Rev. John Church, the handsome and popular Obelisk Preacher who became chaplain to the Vere Street Coterie.

Robinson Pinxt.

Freeman Sculpt.

REVD. J. CHURCH.

The report quickly spread, and such was the popular indignation, that it was found necessary to keep the Meeting-house shut
up as both that and the persons who had attended it were in
danger, from the insults of the enraged people of the town; the
people were hooted and shouted at in the streets, and branded
with the opprobrious name of S[odo]m[ite]s; the same was
written upon the doors, walls, and window-shutters of the place
of worship, and fears were entertained that the Chapel would
have been burnt or pulled down.

Church immediately fled to Birmingham when the story broke, and
wrote an apology to his former host: 'I have done most foolishly — I have
acted most imprudently . . . the boys tell a simple plain story, and you do
right to believe them in what they say; and I own that I have been too
imprudent, but I am not conscious of having done the actual crime; if any
thing of that nature has been of which they speak, it must have been
without my knowledge, when I was asleep, and supposing I was in my own
bed with my wife.' He further promised 'to forsake the company of the
young' in favour of the company of 'the aged and grave', if only they would
let him return. But the Managers of the Chapel, as reported by Samuel Hall
in a letter dated 7 March 1810, made a thorough enquiry into the affair,
with the result that Church was sent a missive containing 'positive orders
never, on any account, to return to Banbury again.' Although a full report
against Church was drawn up, the deacon Mr Lambert refused to sign it
for fear he would lose £17 Church owed him. But a letter was nevertheless
sent to the constabulary, and Church hurriedly sent a letter to Banbury
giving instructions for sending his wife and children (a girl had been born
that year) and belongings 'by the first coach to London; she knows where
to find me in town.' He and his family then secluded themselves in the
country until things passed over.

Church eventually returned from this ignominious solitude, but no
sooner had he settled down at Chapel Court in The Borough, Southwark,
than his former friend Garrett publicly accused him of sodomy, perhaps
for reasons of petty spite. Church was again forced to flee the scene. But
the matter was again forgotten, and he returned to settle finally as the
regular conventicle preacher at the Obelisk Chapel, St George's Fields.
The chapel derived its name from the presence nearby of an obelisk in the
centre of St George's Circus. The obelisk survives, though it was removed
to the corner of the grounds of the National War Museum in August 1905,
and bears on its four sides these inscriptions: 'Erected in XI. Year of The
Reign of King George the Third MD CCL XXI / The Right Honourable
Brass Crosby Esquire Lord Mayor / One Mile from Palace Yard Westminster Hall / One Mile XXXX Feet from London Bridge / One Mile CCCL

Feet from Fleet Street.' Church lived in Great Dover Street nearby.

The Rev. John Church's would-be boyfriend at this time was the young attendant at the Obelisk, a certain Edward B— (his last name has been expunged from the court records) who lived at 3 Rodney Street in The Borough. All we know about their relationship — which lasted exactly four months — is contained in two letters from Church to his 'Ned' (dated 3 March and 13 March, 1809). From these we may infer that Ned rejected Church's advances, possibly because of more legal troubles which seemed likely to involve Ned. These two documents are rather astonishing testimonials affirming the power of love, and since Church has never made his way into the history books, I would like to quote them at some length (despite the difficulties of his unpunctuated style):

> I can only say I wish you was as much captivated with sincere friendship as I am but we all know our own feelings best — Friendship those best of names, affection those sweetest power like some powerful charm that overcomes the mind — I could write much on this subject but I dare not trust you with what I could say much as I esteem you — You would consider it as unmanly and quite effeminate, and having already proved what human nature is I must conceal even those emotions of love which I feel[.] I wish I had the honor of being loved by you as much and in as great a degree as I do you . . . Sometimes the painful thought of a separation overpowers me, many are now trying it but last night I told the persons that called on me that let them insinuate what they would I would never sacrifice my dear Ned to the shrine of any other friend upon earth . . . I find dear Ned many are using all their power to part us but I hope it will prove in vain on your side . . . Stand fast my dearest Ned to me I shall to you whether you do to me or no, and may we be pardoned, justified, and brought more to the knowledge of Christ.

A number of people were attempting to blackmail Church, or simply to discredit him, and in a few days following this letter they persuaded Ned to turn informer. The secret was let out because Church refused to pay the money, and this prompted his reply *de profundis* to Ned:

> I never, never thought you would deceive me — O what an unhappy man am I; the thing that I most feared is come upon me, no excuse can justify such apparent duplicity; O my distress is great indeed. O my God! what shall I do? O Christ! O God! support me in this trying hour, what a night am I passing

through, I cannot sleep, tis near three o'clock;. . . . I have lost my
only bosom friend, nearest dearest friend, bosom from bosom
torn, how horrid. . . . How the Philistine will triumph,. . . all will
rejoice, and I have lost my friend, my all in this world, except the
other part of myself, my wife and poor babes . . . what shall I do
for matter [i.e. a sermon] for Sunday; O that I could get
someone to preach for me; how can I lift up my head. . . .
Miserable as I am, I wish you well for ever, for ever. I write in the
bitterness of my soul which I feel. May you never be cursed with
the feelings I possess as long as you live. What a day I have before
me; I cannot go out of my house till Sunday morning. How can
I conceal my grief from my dear wife? how shall I hide it? what
shall I say? I am miserable, nor can I surmount the shock of it all.

The primary grief Church expresses in this letter is over the loss of a friend.
There is no record of any arrest or prosecution. There is a faint suggestion
of blackmail, which he perhaps paid to Ned, for he retained his position
at the Obelisk for nearly ten more years. In the event, he certainly sur-
mounted the shock, for by November he was an active member of a gay
coterie. On 16 November he performed the funeral services for Richard
Oakden, a bank clerk who the day before had been hanged for sodomy at
Tyburn (on 20 September, Oakden had been convicted of buggery with
Thomas Leager). After the funeral, the hearse and coach returned to the
Hat and Feathers public house kept by Mr Richardson in Gravel Lane,
where Church and company partook of a jovial feast in honour of the
dead.

(2) Molly Chaplain

In the summer of 1810 James Cook and Yardley set up the molly house at
The Swan in Vere Street, as discussed in the previous chapter. One
member of the party, the coal merchant who went by the maiden name of
Kitty Cambric, persuaded Rev. Church to officiate as the chaplain of their
Marrying Room, which they called The Chapel. Except for the presence of
several beds, this room resembled a Christian chapel, and was fitted out
with accoutrements suitable for marriage ceremonies.

On a number of occasions Rev. Church married three or four male
couples simultaneously, and the nuptials were consummated by the
'bridesmaids' as well as by the marriage partners. If these madge culls ever
engaged in mock birth ceremonies such as those performed in the early
eighteenth-century molly houses, the Obelisk Preacher no doubt would

have administered the baptisms. The White Swan was of course a brothel, and undoubtedly a great deal of lighthearted fun figured largely in the proceedings of the marriage ceremonies in its chapel. However, in view of the strong and positive views Church held about homosexual love, it would be unwise to dismiss his participation as merely humorous or mischievous. Homosexuality had been justified before by reference to ancient pagan times, but Rev. Church's letters to Ned reveal the first stirring of a specifically Christian gay pride in the early gay subculture, and I have no doubt that he felt he was making the correct Christian response to two men in love.

He may or may not have had reservations about the lascivious side of the coin. The Swan was undoubtedly more bawdy than the average gay pub or club, as noted in the previous chapter. Church was relatively indifferent to the charms of the regulars such as Miss Selina the police constable, Black-Eyed Leonora the Drummer of the Guards, or Pretty Harriet the butcher, and unwisely fell in love with the landlord himself. James Cook, like Church, was married, but unlike Church he was not bisexual. In May, Church asked Cook to take a pleasant walk with him; Cook said he had to wash first, and instead left Church in the parlour with Kitty Cambric, the Queen of Bohemia, and Mr Ponder (another Drummer in the Guards), while he went to bed, as his tastes did not lie in that direction. After a two-hour wait, Church knocked at his chamber door and said, according to Cook:

> if I would but speak to him, he should go away happy, I found I could not get rid of him, so I went down stairs[.] he said well, Sir, I hope your nap has done you good, I said I dont know, dont bother me, he said I was very cross to him, I told him there was other men without me, if he wanted to preach, not to preach to me about crossness. He said well if that was the case he was very sorry he had offended me, I told him he had not offended me nor pleased me, but as I was not well and the less any one talked to me the better I liked it. He said if I was but friends with him, and shake hands with him, he should go away happy. Mr Yardley said I never see such a fellow as I was, for I had affronted every body that came to the house.

Soon after this, The Swan was raided, and Church would not see Cook for the next two years, while the latter served his prison sentence. As noted in the preceding chapter, Cook attempted to blackmail Church soon after his release, but failed. He nevertheless told his horrid little tales, and in April 1813 Rev. Church, who had not been implicated in the Vere Street Coterie until now, found himself the subject of a smear campaign waged by the editor of *The Weekly Dispatch*. This newspaper began by publishing several accounts of Church's activities in Banbury many years ago, and went so far as to interview Mr and Mrs George and Frances Gee, the keepers of the cake shop in the New Cut, above which Church and his wife had lived for one and a half years. According to the Gee's, Church 'would be frequently out almost all hours of the night, and would lie in bed till ten o'clock in the morning. Several times he and his wife would have skirmishings and fighting between themselves, while their children would be left to run about the streets out of school hours, and allowed to keep company with children that would swear in our hearing most shockingly.' The Gee's observed that 'fawning on young men, that was his chief delight', but even these pious shopkeepers had to admit that Church 'always paid the rent'.

The Sunday after this item appeared in the paper, a number of people gathered outside the Obelisk to argue Church's virtues. He was so stoutly defended by many of his parishioners that a riot ensued. One of the troublemakers was jailed for inciting the riot by urging the mob to set the Chapel afire. Editor Robert Bell of the *Dispatch* bailed out the prisoner, a certain Webster, who next day went to the magistrates to accuse Church of having sodomised his younger brother William ten or eleven years ago! The younger brother was fetched, and a deposition was taken to the effect that Church had indeed sodomised him with his consent. Consent was irrelevant in the eyes of the law, and a warrant was issued for Church's arrest. Church appeared in court to post bail, remained to begin a libel suit against the *Dispatch*, and returned to preach that evening as usual. The *Dispatch* pursued its investigations, and in due course made it known that Church had made an advance to William Clark of Ipswich only last year. Clark was sent for, and produced the following deposition:

> Having been called by providence to Colchester, I went to hear John Church preach in a barn, was invited to Mr Abbott's; was prevailed upon to sleep with John Church; I did sleep with him three nights; after being enticed to many imprudences, I was under the necessity to resist certain attempts, which, if I had complied with, I am fearful must have ruined both soul and body; the crime is too horrid to relate. P.S. This took place in March last, 1812. [Signed by Clark in the presence of Richard Patmore, J. Ellisdom, C. Wire and H.T. Wire as witnesses.]

But Clark of course did not bring forward this charge until six months after the alleged incident, and in the meantime he had accepted a one pound gift from Church. Two barristers examined the document and wisely advised that it could not be prosecuted after such a long interval of silence; the case was dropped. Not to be rebuffed by this legal setback, Clark's aged father came to London filled with indignation and fury, intent upon revenge. Immediately upon his arrival, he rushed into the Obelisk chapel as a meeting was taking place, with two loaded pistols, one in each pocket, intent upon murdering the minister preaching from the pulpit. But in the excess of his agitation he fainted away, and was carried out and deposited in the street.

Church finally won his suit against the *Dispatch*, which was ordered to cease publishing its libellous reports. The editor's last words on the issue were that 'The chief duty of a Journalist is to check the progress of any public evil, by giving activity and force to the LAW OF OPINION, when the municipal law cannot reach the same.' The *Dispatch* had already accomplished much of its real purpose, to boost its own circulation over its competitors: 'The statement published in the two last numbers of the *Dispatch* respecting this person have excited a degree of public attention unexampled in the history of newspapers . . . it serves to shew, how large a mass of virtuous feeling prevails among the people of England.'

During the period from 1 January to 12 July, 1813, Church was subjected to much public abuse. He became accustomed to seeing large placards on the street corners bearing such notices as 'JOHN CHURCH, INCARNATE DEVIL', followed by detailed descriptions of his 'Filthy Frolics in the Temple of Sodom.' The following wretched verses are typical of the many broadside ballads which circulated at the time, titled 'An Epistle From the Devil to his Friend and Follower John Church':

> *We are hypocrites both,*
> *To deceive nothing loth,*
> > *In short we're just form'd for each other;*
> *Then come Johnny, do,*
> *Or I must come for you, –*
> > *Oh, come to Old Nick, your dear brother.*

> *You shall be treated well,*
> *Dearest Johnny, in h[ell],*
> > *You on sulpher and brimstone shall feast;*
> *We'll with fires keep you warm,*
> *And do all things to charm,*
> > *As befits so illustrious a guest.*

In h[ell], John, you'll meet
Many friends from Vere-Street,
  Which quite cosey and handy will be;
For their chaplain in h[ell]
You may be, John, as well
  As on earth you us'd one time, be.

Even after Church won his case against the *Dispatch*, the editor of that sensation-mongering newspaper industriously had published accounts of his 'infamous' life in the newspapers across the Channel. A vast amount of pamphlet literature against Church was turned out by Grub Street printers — such as Hay and Turner and Fairburn — in chapbooks that commonly went through as many as five editions. Church may have overestimated, but not by much, that as many as 20,000 pamphlets and broadsheets were distributed to the detriment of his character. His notoriety grew apace, and in his own words, 'Vast crowds assembled round the chapel on Sunday nights, so that the congregation had to pass through them as the Israelites through the Red Sea.' The scandals damaged his wife's health; ever since she first heard of the charges, she 'was in a continual state of intoxication', and she died in 1813. Church soon afterwards married a woman who kept a seminary for ladies at Hammersmith.

With his notoriety grew his fame, and soon Church's flock had doubled in size, bringing in more money. During a ten-week period in 1813 he founded and built a new chapel nearby, leaving himself £1,000 in debt, which he eventually paid off. The Surrey Tabernacle, known locally as the Obelisk Tabernacle, was opened in 1814, with Rev. John Church as its first minister, and enlarged in 1838. In 1865 the building was sold to the Vestry of St George the Martyr, and the chapel was continued in a new building in Wansey Street, known as the New Surrey Tabernacle. (The site of the old chapel is now occupied by the Hunter Buildings, 1899; opposite the Borough Polytechnic.) The foundation stone of the Tabernacle in Wansey Street was laid on 17 October 1864; it became the Baptist Chapel in 1920, then the Borough Synagogue in 1927. Pictures of the building with its beautiful classical facades are in the Newington Library archives, which also hold some of Church's sermons. The building was demolished in 1970. The only building left from Church's time is a former dairy at the corner of Borough Road and New London Road, bearing the just-visible sign painted over the bricks on its side wall: 'Est 1810 fresh milk from the country.'

In a letter dated 6 October 1816, Church wrote to Mrs Hunter, a member of his congregation, and described himself as 'a Child of Peculiar Providence'. If ever man was fated to bear the cross, it was he. The trials and tribulations of his life were far from over. In 1816 new rumours had begun to spread, and he was indicted at the Surrey Assizes in Croydon, this time on charges of attempted sodomy upon the person of Adam Foreman. Foreman was a 19-year-old servant at a house where Church was staying briefly, who accused him of coming to his bed during the night, placing his hand upon his privates, and pretending to be his mistress (feigning a woman's voice) in order to sleep with him. The weak defence of Church's attorneys was that Foreman could not have identified the molester as Church due to the darkness, and the court testimony consists mostly of arguments about the proximity of a street lamp outside the window. The trial and subsequent appeal — for Church was never a man to give up — lasted for one year and three months, which took its toll. 'My mind was borne down with trouble, company was a burden, and I longed to retire from observation and all society.'

On 17 August, Church was found guilty as charged, and a huge mob assembled outside his door carrying marrow-bones and cleavers. They threw mud and filth upon him, and burnt him in effigy with a straw figure dressed in a black silk gown with pictures of a 'church' on either side. He was to be sentenced on 6 November, but this had to be postponed due to the recent death of Princess Charlotte, whose funeral was publicly cele-brated on 18 November. On Sunday, 23 November Rev. John Church delivered his last sermon, on the text 'Rejoice not against me, Oh mine enemy; though I fall, I shall rise.' On 24 November he was sentenced in Westminster Hall to two years' imprisonment and £500 surety against his good behaviour upon eventual release.

Church served exactly 730 days of his term, in Newington gaol and then in Horsemonger Lane, pulling old rope to pieces. His female disciples considered him a martyr, and every day they came to his prison bars with delicious food, wine and spirits. He was well treated in prison, for he was daily attended by a young man who used to be an officer's servant. His quarters were reasonable, and he received all the books he requested. Although he was allowed visits from friends and family, it was a time of dull aching sorrow, and he tried to sustain himself by constantly comparing his situation to that of the Israelites during the Babylonian captivity. It was also a time for reflection, and he spent his time writing letters, sermons, and his memoirs, which were subsequently published in 1823 as *The Foundling: or, The Child of Providence*.

Finally he was freed, and on the night of his release he returned to the Obelisk to preach to an assembly of 1,000 persons, for he still retained the loyalty of numerous supporters. He had paid his debt and would not skulk away like a beaten dog. He held his head high and continued to preach at his church in Dover Street for at least the next five years, for even by mid-1822 'his Church is crammed whenever it is announced to be opened.'[2] But his preaching had grown sepulchral and guttural; his manner became feeble, as if he were a broken reed, and he was frequently overcome with drink.

Unfortunately the remaining course of his life is not documented. The last sermon he published appeared in 1824, and there are no more records of him being in the public eye, either as a preacher or as a defendant in further trials. I have not been able to locate a notice of his death; mortality records kept by dissenting churches are very incomplete. He would have been about 45 years old in 1824, and a natural death around this age would not have been entirely unusual, particularly for one subjected to such stresses of persecution and imprisonment. Had he actively continued his preaching career, it is likely that his sermons would have been published. Except for this anti-climactic disappearance from history, the documents of his life and writings are fairly abundant, and one must be grieved that Rev. John Church has never been granted even a footnote in any historical study. He is not mentioned even in H. Montgomery Hyde's *The Other Love*, despite the fact that the public controversy surrounding Church's life is as illustrative of the hypocrisy of his age as was the Oscar Wilde debacle more than half a century later.

'The greatest act of all is to set another before you', observed William Blake, the poet roughly contemporary with the preacher, and one hesitates to attempt a final assessment of Church's character. At the outset it must be granted that Church, as any person who is not a mere caricature of conformity, very likely was a man of contradictions and self-deception. If it is true that he once may have cynically remarked, 'My old women would believe the moon to be made of green cheese, if I was to tell them so, and I must tell them something' (and his observation is very likely correct), it is equally true that his numerous sermons, mostly on the redemptive meaning of Christ's sacrifice, are explicated with both logic and conviction, and informed by genuine Christian fervour.

More importantly, all the evidence indicates that John Church was a sincere, perhaps even pious, man who believed that gay love was congruent with the Christian way of life. Some of his sermons, his letters, and portions of his autobiography are devoted to a discussion of the meaning and worth of friendship, though the references to the erotic potential of friendship are ambiguous. But the real hypocrites, he observes, are his accusers: 'some degrade me to cover their own infamy; some from pharisaic principles; some to exalt themselves upon my ruin; some to please those above them, and some to gain money by it, which they have.' Indeed, the editor of *The Weekly Dispatch* bragged about 'the great increase of sale which this paper experienced on Sunday last and their continual demand for it ever since.'

It is worth considering whether John Church acted in a manner that was imprudent, or merely natural. J.T. Gardener, who travelled to Kingham to investigate the Banbury charges, discovered that Church was in the habit, when retiring for the evening, of clasping a man or boy around the shoulders and saying 'Come, now, you must be my bed-fellow to-night', for 'he was apt to be troubled with a lowness of spirits in the night after the fatigue of walking and preaching.' In response to the specific charges that he slept with two boys, Church wrote 'I have done most foolishly — I have acted most imprudently.' Yet one feels that this handsome preacher, just under six feet tall, branded on the back of one hand by a hot wire, as were all orphans, acted in a manner instinctively affectionate and unselfconsciously frank, as noted by a Rev. T— A— : 'Mr. Church kindly put his arms round my neck and kissed me twice, and asked me politely to sleep with him.'

I would not want to sentimentalise John Church's character, yet once we objectively examine the blatantly prejudiced attacks upon his virtue, we find little indication that he was ever 'vicious' in spite of his 'vice'. His convincing argument throughout his autobiography is that he was fundamentally an innocent person, a man who was no more a sinner than all other persons. In marked contrast to the malicious pamphlet literature issued against him, Church never castigated the sins of the Cities of the Plain; he never attempted to refute specifically any of the charges that he was homosexual, and he never confessed any guilt about being a Child of Peculiar Providence. If we seek out the archetypal Christian hypocrite in this tale, such is not to be found in the person of Rev. John Church, but in the person of Rev. T. Latham, who replaced him at Banbury in 1808, and who coldly observed: 'We commiserate "poor human nature", quite as deeply as the reverend Mr. Church, but, then, our pity is limited to natural sins.'

Chapter 14

Men of Rank and Fortune

(1) Lord Chartley

The trials of the Vere Street Coterie taught men an important lesson: far better to flee the country than to face trial. Public ignominy at home was a price worth paying for a life unmolested abroad, particularly now that Europe had adopted the more tolerant measures of the Code Napoléon. The enlightened French penal code of 1791 made no reference to homosexuality; it was allowed to remain absent (and thus be 'legalised') when the code was revised in 1801 and when it took its final form in early 1810. Many Englishmen had to ask themselves, Why be hanged at home for an act that was not a crime abroad? The pattern that most clearly emerges during the first quarter of the nineteenth century, is that men who were arrested for attempted sodomy would merely post their bail and abscond, and the authorities were quite happy to allow them time to make their escape.

A typical case is that involving George Ferrars, Earl of Leicester, known as Lord Chartley, about whom there were many rumours during the first decade of the nineteenth century. The *Morning Herald* on 3 December 1808 reported that 'a noble lord' had been accused by his lady of crimes similar to those laid by Lady Audley against her husband, Lord Castlehaven, many years before. On 5 December it added that: 'The wretched son of an English Marquis has absconded, on charges which Lady C. has exhibited against him.' Earlier that year the *Herald* had noted that Lord and Lady Chartley had separated, so readers could not fail to make the connection. Lord Chartley, or rather Lord Leicester now that his father the Marquis of Townshend had died recently, unwisely decided to prosecute the newspaper's proprietors for publishing false and malicious libels against him. The defendants appeared in court on 29 June 1809 and were able to demonstrate that the 'flying rumours' about Lord Leicester's character were not without foundation.

They began by claiming that he had had relations with his Italian secretary Neri, with whom he had travelled abroad, and whom after his return he 'had kept in a most expensive manner.' They named other men, Hayling and Playfair, who frequently dined and even slept at his Lordship's home in Westbourn Place, Paddington, while her Ladyship lived separately at their other house in Gloucester Place. Apparently the Lord and Lady shared the same house for only three nights after their marriage, and lived apart ever since. Neri had been a waiter at William Newton's Cocoa-nut Coffee-house in 1792 or 1798. While he had lodgings with Mr Ridgway for 18 months beginning in 1801, Lord Leicester visited him there once a week regularly.

John Newby, chapel clerk of Trinity College, Cambridge, testified that Lord Leicester kept Neri more as a companion than a servant whilst at college, and Neri slept in his Lordship's chambers; Neri played a guitar — both men were musical, and played duets together. Newby said that Leicester was considered to be an eccentric character at the college, because he often shut himself up in his rooms and saw no one, dressed his hair effeminately, and — especially shocking — generally wore a pink robe (rather than a purple one to which his nobility entitled him). Farington in his diary for 1807 noted that Leicester 'wore pink ribbons to his shoes.' His fellow students nicknamed him Miss Leicester, but the chapel clerk noted that many of the gentlemen were 'like ladies' themselves.

Leicester availed himself of the services of the military gay subculture of which Hepburn and White were a part (perhaps he was even one of the noblemen who witnessed their hanging). Colonel Rainsford, First Guards, said he had heard vile reports about Leicester, who used to walk arm in arm with the privates of his regiment in May and June of 1806. Leicester regularly met with private Frith, to whom he gave a gold watch; when Rainsford left the service he was surprised to discover that many of his former colleagues sported fine gold watches, and wore expensive clothes when not in uniform.

Leicester did in fact win his libel case, because the Judge said it was not proper for newspapers to freely publish rumours, but the Judge also instructed the jury to grant damages of only £1,000 instead of the £20,000 demanded by Leicester, because of the circumstances of the evidence.[1] Leicester was not present in court to hear the derisory judgement, for he had already fled abroad, first to Paris (where he was still residing in 1823). Eventually he settled down in the Villa Rostan at Pegli, near Genoa, where he assumed the name of Signor Giorgio Feres Compton (from his grandmother's maiden name), and lived in relative obscurity until his death at the age of 77 in 1855.[2] He had 'subscribed to every charity in London. It is odd that men whose hearts appeared warmed with manly feelings, should in one particular be worse than brutes.'[3]

(2) Crimes of the Clergy

Men of the cloth were similarly subjected to enquiries rather than full legal proceedings. So many clergymen were abusing their privileges that William Benbow launched an astonishing attack upon organised religion aptly called *The Crimes of the Clergy*, in which he catalogued the flights from justice of more than a dozen gay men, mostly clergymen and gentlemen, who resided happily abroad at the time of his writing. This was published in serial form from about 1820. Benbow was sent to prison in May 1821 for publishing the first instalments, and it is appropriate that while in prison he was surrounded by adulterers, drunkards, sensualists and men guilty of 'vices I dread to think of, and dare not name.'[4]

One of Benbow's criminal clergymen was Rev. John Fenwick, who had spent seven years at Wadham College, was a skilful musician, 'and his apartments were frequented by fiddlers and singers of the lowest class in Oxford.' One day he and his favourite companion, named Laurence, were discovered in bed together by the washerwoman. She spread the tale, and he was denied admission to the College Hall, though at a formal enquiry she retracted her claim. Fenwick left for a living in Byall, Northumberland, and when his brother and later his father died, he moved to the family mansion and lived the luxurious life of a country squire with a pack of hounds and horses to race at Newmarket. He was 'very active in procuring recruits for the army', and one day a raw countryman named Harpell had to jump out of the squire's library window to escape his embraces. The magistrate ridiculed Harpell's charges, and he was given a bounty and his discharge; soon afterwards he was seized by a press-gang and shipped off on board a man-of-war.

Fenwick was suspended from his living, and called a cheat and a sodomite at an argument at the races, and even horsewhipped. He promised to reform, and even married, but his reputation was ruined, and at a ball in Durham the master of ceremonies instructed him to leave quietly or be thrown out. He threw all caution to the winds, shut his wife out of the bedchamber, and slept with his curate Johnston. A warrant was issued for their arrest in 1797; Fenwick fled to France, but Johnston was captured, convicted, and confined to gaol for a year. By 1823 Johnston was living near Arbroath, in Scotland, on a pension of £100 per annum, which had been 'settled on him by his paramour many years ago.' Fenwick was now living on an estate at Ponte de Avernum, or in his town-house near the Castel de Nova in Naples. His companion was Captain Sawyer, who had been court-martialled for sodomy in 1796 but was merely discharged from the service because of his wealth. In Naples, 'such monsters are tolerated, and even esteemed', and far from being outcasts, both men were friends and frequent visitors to Lady Hamilton.[5]

Several clergymen, such as Rev. Parson Walker, of Chichester, were indulged with time to flee to America.[6] Also fled to America was Rev. V.P. Littlehales MP, Prebendary of Southwell. After receiving his M.A. from Cambridge, he obtained two livings in Lincolnshire, and resided at Burton, in Lord Monson's park. He was a man of great learning, and kept a small school for sons of the nobility. In 1812, while visiting Dr Woolaston, he accosted the footman in his room. The incident got around the country, and his activities were repeatedly looked into over a period of several years. Littlehales begged the gentlemen of Lincolnshire to desist from investigating these rumours, but finally he gave up: 'I foresee it will be useless, as I have long known that this is the rock on which I should split.'[7]

While commenting on the pillorying of the Vere Street Coterie, Henry Spencer Ashbee in 1877 thought fit to add some further particulars of this vice, especially as practised in Scotland during the first quarter of the nineteenth century. The Earl of Findlater and Seafield lived on the Continent for most of his life, so as to indulge his tastes more easily. Upon his death about 1820 he left nearly the whole of his property to a family of the name of Fischer, 'chiefly to a young man who had acted first as his page, and afterwards as private secretary.' The Earl's family disputed the legacy, but were eventually persuaded to stop proceedings because of the stigma which they were attaching to their name, and the Fischers were given an out-of-court settlement of £60,000.

Other Scotsmen who fled the country included John Wood, a high society advocate in Edinburgh, who went to America; and Dr Greenfield, a highly respected clergyman in Edinburgh, who 'augmented his means by taking as boarders young men who were studying at the University. He was observed indulging in unnatural lusts with some of these youths. From the respectability of the parties the matter was hushed up.' He resigned, and lived the rest of his life in retirement, while the family changed their name to Rutherfurd.[8] Dr Greenfield was not altogether forgotten, for in 1824 a broadside ballad called *Lion in Tears* lamented the stain which he had brought upon his profession:

Those who the Holy Craft despise,
*   And hold as mere humbugging,*
What can they think when Priests practize,
*   That blasted crime – Bumbugging.*

There was a certain grave Divine,
*   Esteem'd as wise as Mentor;*
Each Sunday did in Pulpit shine,
*   But B[u]gg[e]r'd his Precentor.*

He was the Church's prop and stay,
*   Penn'd a' her sage addresses,*
But yet forsook God's holy way,
*   And f[ucke]d in barber's a[rse]s.*[9]

The authorities often colluded with such offenders, because they felt that the scandal afforded by a public trial of men of the cloth was not in the best interests of society, as it would undermine the beneficial influence of those very people whose lives ought to serve in the edification of *hoi polloi.*

(3) Bishop of Clogher

The least edifying spectacle of the period was provided by Percy Jocelyn, Lord Bishop of Clogher, who was caught with his trousers down in the company of a mere common soldier.[10] The story really began in 1811, the year after the Vere Street raid. In that year James Byrne, coachman to the Bishop's brother John, also a distributor of Bibles and a member of the Society for the Suppression of Vice, accused the Bishop of committing an unnatural crime. But Clogher denied the facts, and prosecuted Byrne for bringing false charges against him. Byrne confessed to this under duress, and was tried and convicted, and sentenced to two years in prison, preceded by three floggings; he nearly died as he was severely whipped at cart's tail through the streets of Dublin. The truth of his accusation did not emerge until 11 years later.

On the evening of Friday, 19 July 1822 John Moverley (or Movelley), a 22-year-old soldier in the Foot Guards, of slightly effeminate appearance, went to the White Lion public house, St Alban's Place, Charles Street, Haymarket. He looked into the pub two or three times before entering, then went in and ordered a pint of porter and took it into the back parlour. Shortly afterwards a Bishop arrived, about 58 years old, six feet tall, stout, with powdered hair, sallow complexion and pointed nose, dressed in his clerical garb. He exhibited the same odd pattern of behaviour before ordering a drink and going into the back parlour. The landlord immediately suspected that an unnatural assignation was taking place on his premises. He and his son went around to the back yard, and observed the proceedings through a window across which the occupants had not quite succeeded in drawing the curtain. They were shocked by what they saw; they went back into the public rooms and fetched half a dozen witnesses to go round to the yard to see for themselves, while they went to call a watchman. In short order the entire assembly burst into the back parlour, where both offenders had their trousers down round their ankles.

The Bishop and the soldier were immediately dragged through the streets nearly naked, and as they passed the gates of Carlton Palace they were severely beaten and had their remaining clothes torn to pieces by the crowd which had gathered; bleeding from his nose, the Bishop pleaded for mercy, but both men were locked into cells in the St James's watch house in Vine Street. Next morning they were taken to Marlborough Street station, and both men were much distressed and shed tears at their examination. Crowds of people assembled outside while six or seven witnesses gave their evidence. Clogher refused to reveal his identity, and as a constable moved forward to search him, he took a paper from his pocket and tore it up and threw the fragments into the fireplace. He wrote a note which he asked the constable to deliver to John Waring of 21 Montague Street, Portman Square, with whom he had been staying: 'John; — Come to me directly, don't say who I am, but I am undone. Come instantly, and inquire for a gentleman below stairs, 12 o'clock — I am totally undone. P. C.' (for Percy, and Clogher). The officer refused to deliver this, and it was produced as evidence in court. Clogher prayed on his knees in his cell all night long, crying for mercy.

At the examination before the magistrate the following day, both men remained silent and were professionally represented. There had been no fire in the grate, and the torn letter was produced: it was addressed to the Bishop from his nephew the Earl of Roden. Clogher demanded the letter as his property; it was handed to him and he tore it into shreds so no fragments could be produced in evidence at any subsequent trial. But finally Clogher had to divulge his name and address in order to get bail. Mr Waring soon appeared, to give one of the two £500 sureties granted to the Bishop (the other surety was given by his grocer, who lived in Montague Street, Montague Square), and Clogher was granted bail of £1,000 and allowed to leave in safety by a back door. Moverley was committed for trial, where he was visited by Lord Sefton, who had attended the hanging of White and Hepburn in 1811. Within a few days, two respectable tradesman appeared to stand bail for the soldier and he was set free.

Tiny notices of the scandal appeared in the Sunday newspapers and during the following week, though the Bishop's name was suppressed. But by the end of the following week, everyone knew that the principal actor in the affair was the Lord Bishop of Clogher, uncle to the Earl of Roden, and the scandal became the talk of the town. Clogher was noted as a member of the Society for the Suppression of Vice, a revival of the earlier Societies for Reformation of Manners. His hypocrisy did not pass unnoticed by the authors of illustrated broadsides, pamphlets, and even epigrams:

> The Devil to prove the Church was a farce
> Went out to fish for a B[ugge]r.
> He baited his hook with a Frenchmans arse
> And pulled up the Bishop of Clogher.

(Moverley was probably of French origin; an alternative version of this epigram substituted 'Soldiers' for 'Frenchmans'.)

Clergymen who were seen on the streets of London were jeered at by the populace, and most of them fled indoors. The landlord of the White Lion showed the room where the horrid occurrence had taken place, for a small fee. The Marquis of Hertford contributed £20 towards a public collection for the wrongly accused James Byrne, whose reputation was cleared though he was never formally pardoned.[11] The scandal probably encouraged many mollies to leave the country, and it led to at least one suicide. Robert Stewart, Viscount Castlereagh, who was both the Foreign Secretary and Leader of the House of Commons at the time, was visibly overwrought throughout June and July. He forgot appointments and his handwriting became hardly legible. He had an audience with King George IV on 9 August to reveal the fact that he was being blackmailed, and to confess that 'I am accused of the same crime as the Bishop of Clogher.' The King advised him to consult a physician. He went to his country seat in Kent, and on 12 August cut his throat with a pen-knife.

Needless to say, neither Clogher nor Moverley showed up when the Clerkenwell sessions commenced on 9 September, and it was not long before the *Dublin Morning Post* reported that Clogher and Moverley had absconded and forfeited their bails. Moverley simply disappeared, while Clogher had sailed in a small boat from Ramsgate to Ostend on the very evening he was released from custody. The newspapers railed against the offering of bail to a man who earned at least £20,000 a year and could easily spare the trifling sum of £1,000, but at least the bailing of Moverley prevented the public disaffection which would have ensued had the Bishop escaped and the soldier been punished. The Bishop did not disguise his name while in Paris, nor did he change his mode of dress; he was often seen strolling the boulevards and dining at Very's the Restaurateurs in the Palais Royal. He was cordially received by French society, and lived in the cottage vacated by the Dublin poet Thomas Moore in 1822.

A true bill was found against both men in their absence in September. In October the Metropolitan Court of Armagh solemnly stripped the Bishop of his ecclesiastical dignities, but he had already managed to auction off the entire contents of the episcopal palace, leaving it 'as a naked ruin', and the revenues to the see had not been stopped in time to prevent him from selling his tithes for a reasonable profit.[12] The fate of his 'man-mistress', the only servant he had kept with him at the episcopal palace, is not known.

11. Confirmation or the Bishop and the Soldier. The Bishop of Clogher is discovered soliciting the favours of the soldier John Moverley in the back parlour of the White Lion public house.

Mr Parkins, a former Sheriff who saw an opportunity to make some money out of the affair, wrote to Byrne and offered his services as treasurer for handling his subscription and arranging collections for him. He paid for Byrne's passage to London, and offered to buy him a coach and horses. Placards were printed, public dinners were held in aid of the subscription, and money was collected in five dozen tin boxes. The celebrated coachman and his wife and daughter lived in the two rooms above Parkins's stables, and he had unwittingly become a low-paid keeper of Parkins's livery. Parkins gave Byrne small amounts of money from time to time, but never enough to provide the capital Byrne needed to fulfil his dream of opening a public house. Parkins was pocketing a hefty share of the proceeds for his own expenses, and when the day of reckoning came he refused to give Byrne the surplus of the subscription, and turned him out of the house. The unlucky Byrne finally had to prosecute him in 1824, and was awarded damages of £194. 4s. 4½d.[13]

On 19 December 1824 a notice was read aloud to the congregation of Marylebone Church and then posted by the Bailiff, calling upon the Bishop to surrender to the Sheriff of Middlesex to face charges 'or you will be outlawed.' Despite being a fugitive, an outlaw, Clogher eventually returned to Britain, for reasons unknown, and went to Scotland, where he took the name of Thomas Wilson and worked for a period as a butler. He died incognito in Edinburgh in 1843, age about 77. Benbow condemned Clogher as 'a deserving faggot' for the flames of hell, which may be an early instance of one of the odder terms of abuse applied to homosexuals.[14] Benbow observed that the Bishop's homosexuality was not a great surprise, for he never engaged in sports while at Trinity College, Dublin.

The author of one of the pamphlets about the Bishop of Clogher prefaced his attack with some recent history about London's gay subculture. He remarked that 'the Vere-street gang can never be forgotten . . . who can ever forget the sound pelting that the wretches received', and he lamented that the pillory had been done away with at the time of his writing, 1822.[15] 'The crime has considerably increased since its abolition, and it has of late been ascertained that there are various houses in the Metropolis used by such wretches for their nefarious purposes, especially in the neighbourhood of Mary-le-bone.' So the molly houses had been moving towards the more fashionable West End, but one gets the impression that they are small back rooms used for private purposes rather than the more sociable taverns of the previous century. Four men were arrested in such a 'den' very shortly before the Bishop's arrest, and another house 'was said to be visited and supported some time ago by a nobleman.' Apparently the avenues leading to theatres were thronged by gay men, and the galleries were full of well-dressed sodomites looking for simple minded youths to accost, boys from the country who would have neither the wits nor the rank to press charges.

Our pamphleteer observes the class distinctions relative to the prosecution of this offence: men of wealth or distinction are less likely to be charged with the felony; they are charged with the misdemeanour and granted bail; after being released, they either bribe the prosecutors not to press charges, or they forfeit their bail by absconding, and that is the end of it. According to our pamphleteer, reporters are allowed into court when 'poverty-struck wretches' are charged, but they are excluded from the court if persons of consequence go to trial.[16] However, I do not think this is true; William Jackson, commenting on a case involving a molly publican in 1806, says that 'in such cases the judge generally forbids notes to be made',[17] and no official notes were taken during the trial of the soldiers White and Hepburn in 1811 (or else they were totally suppressed). All sodomy trials were far more briefly recorded during the early nineteenth century than they had been throughout the eighteenth century, to the extent that the trial records cease to be useful sources of information about the gay subculture. The men who jumped bail prior to trial were predominantly tradesmen and middle-class shopkeepers. If upper-class men absconded or pulled rank to escape public notice, they did so before they were arrested and before any charges were made, for their names are missing from the Sessions Rolls as well as the trial records.

(4) Beckford of Fonthill

Few men attained greater celebrity during this period than William Beckford (1760–1844), the wealthiest man in England.[18] With enormous wealth as his Aladdin's lamp, he decided to make his Arabian dreams come true. By the time he died at the venerable age of 83, he had built the loftiest domestic residence in the world, had assembled a virtual harem of boys, had his own militia to protect his Fonthill estate of 6,000 acres, had written the first Oriental-Gothic horror novel in English literature, and had become the most scandalous connoisseur of hedonism in the modern world. His society bemusedly tolerated most eccentrics — even *nouveau riche* ones — but they chose to ostracise this remarkable personality, dubbing him 'The Fool of Fonthill'.

Beckford's father, twice Lord Mayor of London, was the richest man in England, with extensive holdings in the cloth industry, property, government bonds, and sugar plantations. As a result, Beckford received a brilliant education, and was widely learned in French, Latin, Greek, Italian, Spanish, Portuguese, philosophy, law, literature and physics by the age of 17. His private piano teacher was Wolfgang Amadeus Mozart — at least that is the legend, too romantic to be discouraged. He was being brought up as an empire builder, but his father died when Beckford was only ten, leaving him with no political ambition, and a millionaire's taste for pleasure.

But even money cannot stop the mouths of gossip-mongers. When this self-styled Caliph was 19, he fell in love with the Hon. William Courtenay, later 3rd Viscount and 9th Earl of Devon, then ten years old and regarded as one of the most beautiful boys in England, borne out by paintings of him. Beckford and Courtenay saw each other frequently either at Fonthill or at Powderham Castle in Devon, Courtenay's home, for nearly six peaceful years. But then, in 1784, a visitor to Powderham claimed to have heard some 'strange goings on' in Courtenay's bedroom, with Beckford apparently in bed with the lad. Soon the newspapers started circulating rumours about the country squire and his 'Kitty', as the beautiful Courtenay was effeminately dubbed.

Greville wrote to Sir William Hamilton in Naples to say that Beckford 'probably will be obliged to vacate his seat, and retire to Italy to make up the loss which Italy has sustained by Lord Tilney's death.' Most men would have fled immediately to the Continent, but for nearly a year Beckford braved out the storm of abuse and secluded himself at Fonthill. No criminal charges were filed, but King George III, who personally wished that Beckford could have been hanged, dismissed Beckford's application for a peerage. Beckford and Courtenay were forced to separate to avoid further reprisal. Beckford finally went abroad, where he remained for the next ten years, living mainly in Portugal, followed by an entourage so magnificent that during his travels he was often mistaken for the Emperor of Austria — and charged accordingly. Courtenay, now Lord Devon, secluded himself at Powderham, which he inherited after his father's death.

Beckford found solace in his exile by writing additional episodes for his thinly veiled fantasy-autobiography, *The History of the Caliph Vathek*, published in 1786. Beckford portrayed himself in his most wicked colours as the villainous Vathek, the caliph who is satiated with sensual pleasures and builds a tower so he can penetrate the forbidden secrets of heaven itself. Prince Gulchenrouz is modelled upon Courtenay, 'the most delicate and lovely creature in the world' who occasionally puts on the dresses of Princess Nouronihar (modelled upon Courtenay's aunt Lady Loughborough). Princess Carathis, based upon Beckford's mother, is a witch who is always mixing the powder of Egyptian mummies with frogs' warts, and running up and down the palace casting evil spells, much as she did in real life. Vathek becomes insanely jealous and murders both Nouronihar and Gulchenrouz, but Gulchenrouz ascends straight to heaven and lives in a perpetual childhood surrounded by a bevy of beautiful boy-houris. Vathek sacrifices 50 lovely lads, who 'stripped and presented to the admiration of the spectators the suppleness and grace of their delicate limbs. . . . At intervals they nimbly started from each other for the sake of being caught again and mutually imparting a thousand caresses.' They are thrown over a cliff one by one, but are rescued by a magic genie and taken to join Gulchenrouz in his merry sports. Vathek finally ends up in hell, 'wandering in an eternity of anguish' for his venture into eighteenth-century sadomasochism.

The scandal of 1784 was partly fabricated or at least exaggerated by Courtenay's vindictive uncle Lord Loughborough, and we cannot be sure that specific sexual acts took place; but the general charge was almost certainly true. Beckford, though he would marry and have two daughters (his wife died in childbirth), was primarily homosexual: by 1807 he was caricaturing himself as Barzaba, from *bar saba*, Syriac for 'voluptuary', but used in the specific sense of 'boy-fancier', in his letters to his agent and general factotum Gregorio Franchi, whom he brought back with him from Portugal. Upon his eventual return to England, Beckford shielded himself behind an eight-mile-long, twelve-foot-high wall topped by iron spikes, surrounding his estate (it was also built because he loved animals, and wanted to keep out hunters), and began to act out some of the dreams of Vathek. He imported a dwarf to be his doorkeeper (and with whom he shared the pornography occasionally sent by Franchi from London), an abbé from France as spiritual advisor (and also as tolerant confidant concerning boy-troubles), a physician from Italy, and a harem of boy-servants for diversion, some picked up in England.

His household of young male servants were all given revealing gay nicknames: 'there is pale Ambrose, infamous Poupee, horrid Ghoul, insipid Mme Bion, cadaverous Nicobuse, the portentous dwarf, frigid "Silence"', Miss Long, Miss Butterfly (slang for catamite), Countess Pox, Mr Prudent Well-Sealed-up, The Monkey, The Turk (Ali-dru, an Albanian with whom Beckford travelled and bathed), and others: 'we have enough ragamuffins here.' As for the stableboys, 'none of them are in the least promising.' Not all of them were willing partners: 'It's not worth talking about Bijou — he's not of the right kind and never will be; we'll need other angels if we go to another paradise.' There are some problems with Mademoiselle Bion, his valet Richardson, who seems to grant all favours except one, in which respect he is berated as frigid: 'What most confounds and disgusts me is a certain kind of frigidity and insipidity like Mme Bion's (the devil take you, you blond beast)'; and yet, 'Bion always counts for something.'

Very few people gained entrance to the cathedral Beckford called home, and naturally rumours arose concerning wild orgies of the caliph and his male harem. These rumours are exaggerated — as is everything connected with Beckford — but they cannot be dismissed altogether. Where there was so much smoke there were bound to be a few flames flickering. Beckford was a collector and builder on a mammoth scale, and he was probably more interested in acquiring *objets d'art* than fawn-youths. But the two manias were aligned: 'it's cruel to hear talk of fair boys and dark Jade vases and not to buy them.'

His exclusion from society was compensated for by the transformation of Fonthill Abbey into a Gothic cathedral to rival nearby Salisbury Cathedral. With the help of the leading architect of the day, James Wyatt, he raised a tower that was nearly 300 feet high. The main enfilade had an uninterrupted vista of 300 feet from the north through the south transepts, and four of the bedrooms were perched 120 feet above ground. (All that remains of Fonthill Abbey today is less than half of the north wing, containing the Lancaster Tower, Sanctuary, and Oratory, which used to house an alabaster statue of Beckford's patron saint, St Anthony, flanked by 36 lighted tapers in silvergilt candelabras, as the focal point of the vista.) A grand opening was arranged in 1800, though even the exterior was hardly near completion, and his guests of honour were Admiral Lord Nelson and his mistress, Emma Hamilton — the kind of people who dared to defy the conventions. But for the rest, his visitors were limited to painters such as Benjamin West, writers, artists, artisans and art dealers, and tradesmen, and his dinners were patched up from social odds and ends. Even in Portugal the English colony had refused to pay visits, and did all they could to prevent Beckford from being presented at court. Beckford had no hope of ever again moving in polite society, and we should not underestimate the pervasive ostracism to which he was subjected. The liberal Sir Richard Hoare of nearby Stourhead asked to see the famed Abbey, and was conducted around by Beckford in 1806. But when the Wiltshire neighbours heard of this, they demanded an explanation from Sir Richard, lest he be shunned by them as well; he made excuses for this gaffe, and never again saw Beckford.

During the completion and furnishing of the Abbey, Beckford was simultaneously engaged with Franchi in the pursuit of youths. For example, throughout September and October 1807, Beckford wrote directions to Franchi to do some pimping for him: 'If it is at all possible, go to see an angel called Saunders who is a tight-rope walker at the Circus Royal and the certain captivator of every bugger's soul. Ah!' Saunders and his troupe disappear but are caught sight of again: 'find out what you can about the site of the Earthly Paradise. Many have sought it in vain: some in Syria or Mesopotamia, some in Abyssinia, others in Ceylon, but I (according to the latest information) in Bristol.' His home was discovered to be in Duke Street, London, and Franchi was advised to visit his father, and to make 'a proposition for a journey to foreign parts, and even a life-annuity—all this is possible.' Letters urging Franchi to make arrangements flowed furiously throughout October. By the end of that month Beckford himself had been to 'the Leg household' (a pun upon tights), and was lodging in Brunets' Hotel, Leicester Square, an area frequented by theatrical people and foreigners, waiting to see Saunders in his room. Years later, in 1811, Beckford was still following the travels of Saunders, this time to York, as well as those of a young horseman who was part of the troupe: 'I would not fly from a nice York patapouf [catamite] if Providence sent him to me.'

Master Saunders was born in 1789, so he was 18 (though made up to look younger, as he was billed as 'the celebrated Equestrian Infant-Phenomenon') when Beckford saw him, and Beckford was not literally a pederast; it would be more accurate to read 'youths' or 'lads' whenever he writes of 'boys'. The Turk stayed with Beckford a good many years, and their relationship did not fade with the passing youth of the former. Beckford's interest was not limited to ephebes: 'I'd like to run away, Heaven knows where, with some great Jock' (18 September 1813). He was also attracted to a soldier in Bath, hoping to 'take some lessons in drilling from him' (12 October 1819).

Beckford never again mingled with high society, but he was not permanently sequestered at Fonthill, and his letters to Franchi suggest that he sometimes ventured into the homosexual subculture of London. From 1811 to 1817 he rented No. 6 Upper Harley Street (now 100 Harley Street), where Franchi often stayed. He also stayed at 'Brunets' bagnio', sometimes in company with The Turk. The apartments cost 11 or 12 guineas a week, which 'isn't very cheap'. And occasionally he stayed in Louis Jacquier's Clarendon Hotel, New Bond Street: 'late last night, coming out of Jacquier's, I went in search of a little amusement in an accustomed quarter. I knock. They've gone away' (19 January 1819). The Seven Dials neighbourhood in St Giles' Parish he called 'the Holy Land', his term for the gay cruising area, where he hoped to 'kiss the relics' (1 July 1812). And, further out, in August–September 1810 he found a 'little rogue' on Hounslow heath, a 'Paradise' where a barracks was conveniently sited; he may well have shared the pleasures of the Vere Street Coterie in that year.

As for the youth for whom Beckford's reputation had been ruined, William Courtenay seems to have been more actively and exclusively homosexual than his supposed seducer; he never married, and was not very cautious. According to the diarist Joseph Farington, by 1810 few of the gentlemen of Exeter would visit their scandalous neighbour, and the people of Torquay so reviled his servants that Lord Courtenay had to give up plans to build a summer residence there. By 1811 an Essex magistrate had gathered enough evidence to convict Courtenay of unnatural crimes; on hearing that a warrant had been issued for his arrest, he fled to France, where he lived in obscurity for the next 24 years. But the lower classes missed their benefactor, even as late as 1823, for Courtenay 'was so humane and charitable, that to this day all the poor in the neighbourhood of Exeter lament his absence.'[19] A distant cousin with a passion for genealogy in 1831 helped to revive the Earldom of Devon in his favour (a title which the cousin would inherit upon Courtenay's death), and the newspapers taunted the new Earl of Devon for not returning to England to claim his seat in the House of Lords. But the laws of England were not so tolerant as the Code Napoléon, and Courtenay preferred to spend his remaining years in his Paris house in the Place Vendôme to being imprisoned or hanged in his native country. And who can blame him?

(5) Beckford's Scrapbooks

Of particular interest to our examination of William Beckford's life is the interest he maintained in the molly subculture. He is forever gathering information sent by Franchi concerning the gay areas in such places as York or even Cornwall (he hoped that amongst the 'brothers' or Methodists there he could find 'one who was a bit of a mameluke', i.e. catamite, 26 July 1810), or gossip concerning a general and a batman in the barracks, nicknamed 'Mary Clarke' (22 October 1817). His immense library contained not merely rare and valuable books, but also a few works of homosexual interest, such as *The Penitent Death of . . . John Atherton* (he and his tithe proctor were hanged for buggery in 1640 in Dublin), the *Trial of Lord Audley* (Mervyn Touchet, Earl of Castlehaven, beheaded for rape and sodomy in 1631), and a specially bound copy of the trial of Colonel Robert Passingham and John Edwards, who had conspired to blackmail George Forrester by accusing him of unnatural crimes in 1805.

In addition to these volumes, for many hours he poured over a special scrapbook into which he pasted press reports of all the homosexual scandals of the day, and he sometimes recorded his reactions to such events in letters to Franchi. For example, here are his comments on the arrest of the Vere Street Coterie, which he read about in the *Morning Chronicle* of Tuesday, 10 July 1810: 'Poor sods — what a fine ordeal, what a procession, what a pilgrimage, what a song and dance, what a rosary [i.e. string of prisoners]! What a pity not to have a balcony in Bow Street to see them pass, and worse still not to have a magic wand to transform into a triumph the sorry sequence of events' (11 July 1810). According to the newspaper, one of the men arrested was Matthew Saunders of Duke Street, Aldgate, who may be identical with Saunders the tightrope walker pursued by Beckford. Beckford's anger at the persecution of the madge culls never took a more active form than vexatious rage and vain sighing, but at least he was not ashamed to be homosexual himself and he clearly recognised the prejudice of his society. Beckford was a friend of Lord Roden, nephew of the Bishop of Clogher, and in 1822 he referred briefly to 'the St Albans Street procession', that is, the arrest of the Bishop and the soldier Moverley who were dragged through the street and beaten by the mob along the way.

Beckford collected newspaper cuttings about homosexual scandals until the very year of his death, carefully wrapped in packets of gilt-edged paper together with cuttings of obituaries, coronations, sales of books and pictures, and curiosities. I think he shuffled and reshuffled them as he grew older, and even in March 1844, less than a month before his death at the age of 83, he was still labelling the contents of these packets in the shaky hand of an old man. Dozens of these gay cuttings are now scattered throughout the Beckford Papers at the Bodleian Library, University of Oxford, no longer in any particular order. They are as astonishing in their own way as the *Love-Letters* were 150 years earlier, and they have many interesting things to tell us about gay life at a time of high moral fervour.

Some of the cuttings refer to scandals about notable gentlemen, usually by means of innuendo. Beckford cut out a report concerning one of his neighbours in Wiltshire, Mr Seymour. In 1828 he and his servant Mr Macklin were discovered having sexual relations in the master's dressing room, and their trial was attended by great numbers of the Wiltshire gentry. Mr Seymour claimed that the servants were conspiring against him, and that 'he had been leaning over Macklin, with one hand upon his shoulder, looking at a book of accounts.' Both men were found guilty after a trial lasting 41 hours, but Mr Seymour absconded.[20] One cutting concerns 'a certain English Marquis' who left the country some years ago amidst 'strange circumstances connected with his early propensities', whose case involving large estates was now arriving at maturity in the Court of Chancery; this was probably the Earl of Leicester, previously mentioned.[21] Another cutting concerns Mr Heber, brother of the Bishop of Calcutta, who sued the *John Bull* newspaper in 1826 for insinuating that he had left the country to avoid a homosexual prosecution. The libel stated that 'The backwardness of the seasons renders the Continent more congenial to some constitutions', and that he had 'an over addiction to *Hartshorn*', presumably the name of his lover. (Beckford annotated this 'H.H.H. Heber and Hartshorn'.) This cutting is particularly sad, because it notes the similar flight of Beckford's boyfriend of many years previous: Heber 'is supposed (for after all it is but supposition) to have left England for much the same reason that my *Lord Courtenay* — the Bishop of Clogher, *cum multis aliis* [and many others], have deemed it expedient to emigrate to foreign climes.'[22]

Soldiers are not altogether absent from these cuttings. In 1826 a well-dressed lad of 16, said to be the second son of an Irish Peer, was charged with having made indecent proposals to a sentry on duty at Knightsbridge Barracks.[23] But usually the soldiers were more willing, sometimes notoriously willing. In 1827 a sergeant of a distinguished cavalry was drummed out of the barracks for having carried on a homosexual affair. The entire regiment was drawn out, mounted and in full costume, for the solemn ceremonies. The sergeant, a young and fine-looking man, guarded by four soldiers with sabres drawn, slowly walked across the yard, his neck encircled by a halter, while trumpets and kettle drums played the 'Rogue's March'. Then there was dead silence for several agonising minutes as he walked the last few yards out of the barracks gate, alone, carrying only a small bundle of clothes with him, the archetypal outcast.[24] A 'gang' of mollies who used to pick up soldiers at the Horse Guards Parade regularly frequented a room in the Bull public house in Bullen Court, the Strand, where they were apprehended in April 1830. Some escaped, but six were taken prisoner and conveyed to the police station while a mob of 500 people covered them and their guards with mud and filth. One soldier was dealt with under military law, and six civilians were ordered to find bail.[25]

A fair number of cuttings concern clergymen, who were deemed newsworthy because of the presumed hypocrisy of their gay affairs. One cutting refers to the Bishop of Clogher, and says that 'Other Clergymen of the Established Church, too, have of late years figured occasionally in Police Offices, and not for taking liberties with females.'[26] A typical headline is 'Flight and Disgraceful Conduct of Two Religious Hypocrites', accused of assaulting boys in Manchester in 1832.[27] In 1825 Rev. William Hayes, one of the Minor Canons of St Paul's, was 'found in a disgusting situation with a boy in a lane leading to a wharf in Upper Thames-street.' He was granted bail and absconded, but was recaptured in Reading, found guilty by default, and sent to Reading gaol for six months.[28] In 1833 in Suffolk a rector and a curate were charged with the capital crime of sodomy, but they did not come forth to defend themselves, and lost their recognizances.[29]

Although gentlemen figure largely in these cuttings, many of them are self-made middle-class gentlemen, rather than members of the gentry or aristocracy, and their relations are with men in the lower-middle classes. For example, in 1828 G. Harvey, proprietor of a mustard manufactory in Blackfriars Road, and Robert Nethercott, a footman belonging to Henry Seymour, Esq, of 39 Upper Grosvenor Street, were charged with having sex together. Mr Harvey's father stood bail for his son, and two tradesmen stood bail for the footman.[30]

A very interesting case involved a dirty old gentleman named John Grossett Muirhead of St George's, Hanover Square. In 1825 Muirhead met an apprentice outside a print shop in Sackville Street, off Piccadilly, where he showed him some indecent prints and books, and two 'skins' which he bet he could not fit into. One of these condoms was later produced in evidence in court, and its use had to be explained. He took the young man to a coffee house for a pint of cider and biscuits, where he showed him some more dirty pictures, held his hand and fondled him, gave him a crown, and arranged for another meeting to have sex. The lad thought Muirhead was 'a good-natured old gentleman' and was not averse to his attentions, but two other boys to whom he told this story said he had to be careful. The following Sunday Muirhead took all three boys, one aged 14 and one aged 21, to an oyster shop, where he showed them more pornography and fondled them and gave them a crown apiece. Before he could proceed any further, two officers, by previous arrangement, burst in and arrested him.

Muirhead's case was important for re-confirming that privacy and consent were no defence in law for homosexuals. He did not deny the events, but he argued that there were no legal grounds for a prosecution: 'first, that it was not an assault, because the prisoner had the consent of the party; and secondly, it was not an offence indictable in the present shape, because it was committed in private.' But the judge replied that 'In crimes of this atrocious description, consent or non-consent did not alter the offence, and it was an offence against public morals, not only because it was committed in a public coffee-room, but because it was an attempt to destroy the morals of youthful members of society.' His crime was exacerbated by the fact that he was a member of the Society for the Suppression of Vice and a Director of the Auxiliary Bible Society of St George's in the Fields. He was sentenced to nine months' imprisonment for the first offence and six months' for the second. He pleaded for clemency on the grounds that he was 72 years old and infirm, and not likely to survive prison. The judge said he would be treated humanely. He certainly did survive prison, for three years and nine months later Beckford took another newspaper cutting, reporting that he had been arrested in Dover for a similar offence.[31] Soon afterwards, according to Ashbee, he fled to the Continent, though he had been a wealthy property owner in Lanarkshire.

Beckford's newspaper cuttings provide a marvellous introduction to the gay history of this period. They may not reveal much specifically about the organised gay subculture, but they do at least reveal some of the gay cruising grounds, and they illustrate the changing patterns of contact between men of different social backgrounds. The cuttings are especially valuable when read in conjunction with Beckford's reactions to the reports, contained in his letters to Franchi. His most scornful, and most despairing, comments were expressed upon the hanging, in 1816, of John

Attwood Eglerton, a waiter with wife and children who was accused of
sodomy by a stable boy. It took the jury only ten minutes to return a verdict
of guilty and a sentence of death. Beckford wrote to Franchi on 22
September: 'Tomorrow (according to the papers) they are going to hang
a poor honest sodomite. I should like to know what kind of deity they fancy
they are placating with these shocking human sacrifices. In a numerous list
of thieves, assassins, housebreakers, violators ("a man for a rape") etc, he
was the only one to be sent to the gallows; all the others were "respited
during pleasure". The danger must be great indeed and everyone in the
country must be running the risk of having his arse exposed to fire and
slaughter.'

Beckford pasted into his scrapbook the report from the *News*, Sunday
29 September, and wrote to Franchi on 3 October concerning a document
about the mollies which Eglerton gave to the prison chaplain Rev. Horace
Salusbury Cotton on the night before his execution: 'You may or may not
know that this man of honour, before his end, put in the hands of his
Anglican confessor, the most Reverend Mister Cotton, Grand-Almoner of
Newgate, a tremendous list of the gentlemen affiliated or associated with
him! He wanted to inform the populace *viva voce*, but Father Cotton said
with evangelical sweetness, "My dear Sir, better not, better not." The
stupid, hypocritical, bloodthirsty vermin! The day will come when their
infamous vices and stinking hypocrisies will be revealed to the eyes of all
Europe. . . . The Portuguese did well to set sail in time before the Annals
of Father Cotton' — this is a reference to a Portuguese molly compatriot
of Franchi who had escaped arrest.

Beckford himself contemplated fleeing to Portugal as early as 1808,
with Saunders and a troupe of artists: 'If I were at my last gasp I would rise
for this one. *Gloria in excelsis* (full organ) *et in terra papale Pax, non Pox* —
I hope' (30 June 1808). Apparently Beckford during his previous travels to
Portugal had had an affair with Jacintho Fernandes Bandeira, elder
brother of the first Count of Porto Covo da Bandeira, and he believed the
atmosphere of that country to be much more tolerant. He also spent time
in Paris, where society and the law were even more tolerant; there he
hoped to find agreeable inexpensive lodgings where he could buy books
in the morning 'and have boys in the evening' (22 July 1814).

Arrogant and petulant, Beckford was deeply embittered at being
snubbed by his social equals and inferiors; he was obsessed with his
pedigree, and his aspirations were devastated when King George III
refused to grant him a peerage. The remarkable thing about William
Beckford — aside from the unique records of his letters and scrapbook —
is that he braved out his ostracism by society. Weaker men than he such
as Courtenay, Leicester and the Earl of Findlater, and a host of clergymen
and aristocrats would have permanently resided abroad in order to escape

notoriety. Ironically we have come full circle, for Beckford's estate at Fonthill Gifford once belonged to Mervyn Touchet, Earl of Castlehaven, the first homosexual to be prosecuted in the English courts. The frieze of St Michael's Gallery in Fonthill Abbey was lined by armorial shields delineating Beckford's descent from the family of Mervyn.

Chapter 15

Tommies and the Game of Flats

(1) Hidden from History

Lesbians in England are fortunate in that they have never been hanged, and very rarely imprisoned, fined or exhibited in the pillory for expressions of their love, but the absence of legislation against them does mean that they have been more effectively hidden from history than have gay men. In the eighteenth century, as today, society's fear and prejudice were directed not against homosexuals in general, but specifically against gay men rather than lesbians. The satirists, and even less moralistic members of society, blinded themselves to the possibility of lesbianism. One reason for this is the essentially antifeminist opinion that allowances must be made for 'the weaker sex', and anything that women did amongst themselves was beneath serious notice by men. Thus the author of *Satan's Harvest Home* (1749) condescendingly admits that 'Woman Kissing Woman, is more suitable to their natural Softness' (p. 54). The commonly held belief that women, like children, are naturally affectionate toward one another, meant that observation of their intimacies seldom gave rise to darker suspicions. Feminine waywardness was not felt to be a matter for grave concern amongst men, and homosexual acts between women have never been recognised by British law. Thus trial records, an otherwise rich source of material on the gay subculture, yield virtually nothing about lesbians, while diaries and memoirs and letters reveal only romantic friendship between literary ladies of the middle and upper-middle classes. Amongst the lower classes, where girl servants slept together, where women did not feel it so necessary to get married, and where women moved more easily along the rough fringes of the criminal classes, I do not doubt that there were a fair number of lesbians, but their lives have not been recorded.

Unfortunately in most of the sources we consult, the descriptions of lesbians are based almost entirely upon masculine fantasy rather than observed fact. Hundreds of documents can be sieved, to yield the bare minimum of facts, mostly obtained from records in countries where various kinds of lesbian acts were criminal offences, and most of the cases involved transvestism. Two nuns were burned for such behaviour in sixteenth-century Spain, and several women were flogged and sent to the galleys in Granada; in France one woman was burned alive in 1535 and another was hanged in 1580; one woman was executed in mid-sixteenth-century Geneva; in the early seventeenth century Sister Benedetta Carlini, Abbess of the Convent of the Mother of God in Pescia, was imprisoned for 35 years for having a two-year affair with Sister Bartolomia Crivelli; two lesbian transvestites were flogged and banished from seventeenth-century Leiden; in 1721 a lesbian transvestite was executed in Germany.[1] Also in 1721, in Hungary, Catharina Margaretha Lincken performed intercourse with another woman by means of a dildo, or artificial penis, an act adjudged 'sodomy', for which she was executed; at about the same time, Countess Sarolta Vay of Hungary dressed as a man and married another woman.[2] There is also a small body of curious medical evidence concerning tribades and fricatrices, viragos with prominent pudenda which they purportedly rubbed together in order to achieve clitoral friction.[3]

The evidence that I shall examine in this chapter concerns the two major types of lesbian experience in history, crossdressing and romantic friendship. Because of the paucity of material in English records, it is with some perverse satisfaction for us to note that the eighteenth century was possessed of at least a few prejudices concerning lesbians. In *Satan's Harvest Home* lesbianism is described as 'the Game of Flatts' (p. 61) — a reference to games with playing cards, called 'flats', and an allusion to the rubbing together of two 'flat' female pudenda. (By the nineteenth century, 'flatfuck' was a colloquial term for lesbian activity; curiously enough, a more recent term for women, 'broads', derives from another term for playing cards.) The author happily devotes the whole of one chapter to a history of lesbianism, beginning, of course, with a commentary upon the honoured poetess of Lesbos (p. 18):

> *Sappho*, as she was one of the wittiest Women that ever the World bred, so she thought with Reason, it would be expected she should make some Additions to a *Science* in which Woman-kind had been so successful: What does she do then? Not content with our Sex, begins *Amours* with her own and teaches the Female World a new Sort of Sin, call'd the *Flats*, that was follow'd not only in Lucian's Time, but is practis'd frequently in *Turkey*, as well as at *Twickenham* at this Day.

The allusion to Lucian is to that author's *Dialogues*, several of which are spoken by lesbians, and in defence of lesbianism. The reference to the Latin poet is not as learned as it might appear; his knowledge probably goes no further than *A Dialogue Concerning Women* published in 1691, which cites the description of Sappho's lesbianism in Lucian's dialogues *Cleonarium* and *Leoena*, and in Lilius Giraldus' *De Poetis*.[4] Such references only serve to underline the fact that the author can deduce few examples from his contemporary experience. His lack of knowledge concerning lesbians in London is further exposed by his quoting a tale from Busbequius' *Travels into Turkey* about Turkish women bathing together, which leads them to burn with love for one another.[5] This is followed by the more intriguing story about an old woman of Constantinople who falls in love with a girl, disguises herself as a man, successfully charms herself into the graces of the girl's father, marries her, is discovered, judged before the city Governor, and soundly chided for her 'bestiality'. She retorts: 'Away, Sir, says she! You do not know the Force of Love, and God graunt you never may.' She is sentenced to be executed, and drowned in the sea.

From Constantinople he turns his attention to the Continent, where he is shocked to discover that in France 'the Ladies (in the *Nunneries*) are criminally *amorous* of each other, in a *Method* too gross for Expression.' In his excess of phobia against foreigners he seems to forget that he has hinted at some scandals at Twickenham; all he will say about his homeland is that although English ladies also kiss one another in public, he seriously doubts that they are lesbians (p. 51). His information about gay men, quoted in earlier chapters, is not very trustworthy; his information about lesbians is worthless, except as evidence of prejudice.

During the Restoration there were female rakes as well as the more common male libertine, and the freethinking dramatist Aphra Behn and her husband were an archetypal gay couple. But despite the new freedom of expression and action taken by women in the court or on its fringes, factual details about lesbians is difficult to locate. The *Memoirs* of the Chevalier de Gramont is our primary source concerning Miss Hobart, Maid of Honour to the Duchess of York. Apparently she made advances to most of the young ladies in the household, but was repeatedly rebuffed. Her first signs of success were with Anne Temple, another Maid of Honour, who was also the beloved of the bisexual rake the Earl of Rochester. Miss Hobart and Rochester intrigued against one another for the favours of Anne, but Rochester eventually won the day and broke up the relationship by publicly accusing Miss Hobart of being a notorious lesbian and a dreadful creature. In the lampoons that circulated at court, Miss Hobart was satirised as a hermaphrodite.

During the eighteenth century, an object of occasional satire was Mrs Anne Seymour Damer, the cultivated sculptor who inherited Horace

Walpole's fortune. She was widowed at the age of 27 (her husband got into vast debt and blew out his brains); she never remarried, but developed a close friendship with Miss Mary Berry, who became Walpole's literary executor. After Walpole's death they travelled together on the Continent and in England, and Miss Berry performed in the amateur theatricals that Mrs Damer organised at Strawberry Hill when it became her property. The lesbian nature of her passion is said to be revealed in her manuscript journals in the W.S. Lewis collection in Farmington, Connecticut.

'Mrs D–r' was the object of *A Sapphick Epistle* by the pseudonymous 'Jack Cavendish', in which she is encouraged to grant his suit for her hand, although she has a horror of men and marriage.[6] He begins with some back-handed praise of Sappho: 'Miss Sappho, who was the first young classic maid that bestowed her affections on her own sex . . . when an old maid, and unfit for man's love, she pursued the young girls of Mytelene, and seduced many. She was the first Tommy the world has upon record; but to do her justice, though there hath been many Tommies since, yet we never had but one Sappho.' Fair enough.

> By Penny-post she sent her odes,
> To matrons, widows, whores and bawds,
>   And won them to her will:
> . . . Thus happy Sappho past her time,
> In making love, and making rhime,
>   To all the Lesbian maids:
> Who were more constant and more kind,
> More pure in soul, more firm of mind,
>   Than all the Lesbian blades.
> . . . Strawberry-hill at once doth prove,
> Taste, elegance, and Sapphic love,
>   In gentle Kitty —.

This line is meant to rhyme with 'thrive', and obviously refers to Kitty Clive the actress, a frequent visitor to Walpole and a friend of Mrs Damer and Miss Berry. In 1788 Mrs Damer read the epilogue to a play in which appeared another actress friend, Miss Elizabeth Farren, who was victim of another satire prior to her marriage to Lord Derby: 'superior to the influence of MEN, she is supposed to feel more exquisite delight from the touch of the cheek of Mrs D–r than the fancy of any *novelties* which the wedding night can promise with such a partner as his lordship.'[7] Mrs Damer was sometimes seen wearing a man's hat, jacket and shoes, and her attachments to other women were no great secret, but they were whispered about rather than fully documented.[8] The author of the satire may have chosen the name 'Jack Cavendish' in order to point a finger to

Mrs Elizabeth Cavendish, another lesbian member of the Twickenham set, to judge from an obscene pun in Walpole's correspondence: 'Lady Dysart is dead too, and Mrs Cavendish *in-cun-sole-able*.'[9]

(2) Lesbian Marriages

Much greater public attention has been given to 'breeches-clad bawds'. Women disguise themselves as men in order to exercise the privileges and freedom usually reserved for men — freedom of movement, freedom to engage in business, freedom to travel unmolested, freedom to express oneself in a frank manner, freedom to be assertive and outgoing — and there are enough cases on record to fill a full-length study. There is a large body of literature from the late seventeenth century concerning 'roaring girls', 'Amazonian maids' and 'female warriors'; these viragos were very often married to soldiers, and donned male clothing in the first instance in order to go in pursuit of their husbands, and then became soldiers themselves and discovered that they had a great taste for battle; in their military adventures they sometimes laid siege to young women, but their lives were predominantly heterosexual, and their identities were usually discovered when they had to avail themselves of the services of a midwife.[10] But however interesting may be the lives of such women as Courageous Betty of Chick Lane or Moll Cutpurse, in this study I must concentrate on those cases which seem to come closer to our modern understanding of lesbian experience.

Around 1695 in the borough of Southwark a mother advertised that whoever would marry her 18-year-old daughter would receive a gift of £200 on the wedding day. Among the flock of admirers who offered themselves, the young woman especially liked a young Irish lad Mr K—, and she accordingly married him. But on the wedding night she received only a kiss or two. Her mother confided to her that a man is not always capable of duty, and not to despair. The next night she boldly put forth her hand to claim what was her due, but to her surprise she discovered that her husband was a woman. She leaped out of bed with such violence as to awake her companion, but pretended to have a convulsion so as not to reveal her discovery. But the 'counterfeit bridegroom' suspected her discovery, and absconded with the dowry.[11]

It was in fact possible for two women to marry one another without any fuss being made, at least to judge by two inexplicable entries from the marriage register of the parish of Taxal, Cheshire:

Hannah Wright and Anne Gaskill,
   Parish of Prestbury. 4th September 1707.
Ane Norton and Alice Pickford,
   Parish of Prestbury. 3rd June 1708.

These are not clerical errors (except possibly the spelling Ane for Anne). 'Normally in this as in other registers the man's name comes first but there does not seem to be any room for manoeuvre at all here — these four names are feminine. And why go to Taxal? Was the incumbent there more lenient? There does not appear to be any attempt to cover up.'[12]

But counterfeiting was more common, and a surprisingly typical example is that of Mary East. In 1731 she donned masculine clothing, assumed the name of James How, and took a small public house at Epping for 'himself' and 'his' consort, another woman. Here, and subsequently at the White Horse public house at Poplar, the two women lived together as man and wife for 18 years — 'and raised a considerable sum of money.' Though relatively wealthy, with £3,000 to £4,000, they kept no servants, and entertained no friends at home, presumably to keep the husband's real sex a secret. As 'James How', Mary served on all the parish offices, and was occasionally a foreman on juries, establishing a very good reputation with 'his' neighbours.

But the secret of Mary East's real gender was discovered by a woman who had known her in her youth, and the couple became the victims of an escalating extortion. Ultimately the price for silence became too much to bear, and in 1766 East, now dressed as a woman, brought the matter to court. She boldly prosecuted her blackmailer, William Barwick, for extorting considerable sums of money from her for concealing her sex; he was convicted and sentenced to stand four times in the pillory and four years' imprisonment.[13] This public disclosure, however, made it necessary for the two women to abandon the White Horse, and the couple went into retirement. Mary boldly returned to the parish to settle her affairs and collect her property. 'She was dressed in a riding habit, with a black hat and feather: so that her acquaintance could hardly believe her to be the same person, she having generally appeared in an old man's coat, woollen cap, blue apron, &c.'[14] 'Mrs How' died after a total of 39 years of 'matrimony'; Mary East survived her partner for a long time, but never took another 'wife'. Our historian claims that both women adopted this arrangement as a result of both their husbands-to-be having been hanged for highway robbery. They probably fabricated this explanation in an effort to account for what would otherwise be inexplicable for the conventionally-minded; surely they were lesbians.[15]

Hannah Snell *in Her* Regimentals *as She performs the Manual Exercise of a Soldier at Goodmans Fields Wells 1750.*

Join ÿ right Hand to ÿ Firelock.   *Present and Fire.*

Charge ÿ Bayonet Breast High.   Rest your Bayonet on ÿ left Arm.

Goodmans Field Wells
1750.

A better-known case is that of Hannah Snell, who even at the age of ten had organised 'Young Amazon Snell's Company' of soldiers among her playfellows in Wapping, and who dressed herself as a man upon being deserted by her husband. She served as a soldier from 1745 to 1750 in the British Army under the name of James Gray. While in Carlisle for manoeuvres, she was asked to pimp for Sergeant Davis, but she turned the tables and became intimate with the lady in question; the Sergeant accused her of neglect of duty and 'a crime which Nature put it out of her power to perpetrate' and gave her 500 lashes. She fled to Portsmouth and later joined the British marines. She experienced many adventures as the ship's boy, and wrote her own account of the famous siege of Pondicherry; seriously wounded in the groin, she extracted the ball herself so as not to disclose her sex.

At Fort St Davids she found it difficult to explain why she did not share the homosexual appetites of her mates. Although her fellow sailors did not recognise her gender, they did take note of her lack of a beard, and dubbed 'him' 'Miss Molly Gray' — that is, they treated her as if she were an effeminate man, a molly. Hannah much resented this, and in order to prove her masculinity, when the ship put in to Lisbon, she made a number of conquests over the women of the port. Thus we have the paradox of a female transvestite establishing her 'manhood' by a series of lesbian adventures. Similar encounters occurred at Portsmouth when she heard that her husband had been hanged. Eventually she revealed her true gender to her fellow-sailors, in an unseemly manner that left no doubt in their minds, and then capitalised on the publicity by going on the stage.[16]

A less happy fate was meted out to cross-dressing women who had the audacity to marry other women. In 1746 Mary Hamilton, alias Charles, George, and William Hamilton, was tried for fraud at the Quarter Sessions at Taunton in Somersetshire, for posing as a man and marrying a woman.[17] Mary was born on the Isle of Man on 16 August 1721. During her childhood she never gave 'any cause of suspicion that she would one day disgrace her sex by the most abominable and unnatural pollutions', but sometime around the age of 14 she was seduced by her neighbour Anne Johnson, who converted her to Methodism as well as lesbianism. 'These two young women became now inseparable companions, and at length bedfellows', and she went to live with Mrs Johnson, who 'was, it seems, no novice in impurity, which, as she confess'd, she had learnt and often practiced at Bristol with her methodistical sisters.' Criminal transactions 'not fit to be mention'd past between them.' They moved to Bristol and took lodgings together, but soon their 'vile amours' were ended when Mrs

12. Hannah Snell, exhibiting her regimental drill on stage at
    Goodman's Fields Theatre in 1750.

Johnson fell in love with a Mr Rogers and married him. Mary was frantic with jealousy at this unhappy turn of events: 'she tore her hair, beat her breasts, and behaved in as outrageous a manner as the fondest husband could, who had unexpectedly discovered the infidelity of a beloved wife.'

Abandoned by her first lover, Mary dressed in men's clothes and embarked for Ireland, where she became a Methodist teacher. She first took lodgings in Dublin, in a back street near St Stephen's Green, in a house with a 40-year-old widow, whom she began to court as a man, but the widow shortly afterwards married a cadet in an Irish regiment. She was now about 18 years old, and the next object of her affection was Mrs Rushford, widow of a rich cheese monger, aged 68. Mary had intended to reveal her real sex after gaining her affection, 'hoping to have the same success which Mrs Johnson had found with her', but she proceeded to marry the widow as a man. There was a public wedding with the usual joking and merriments, and afterwards Mary continued to deceive her wife, 'by means which decency forbids me even to mention.'

The old lady eventually discovered the truth, and Mary fled, with as much money as she could stuff into her breeches' pockets. She sailed to Dartmouth, then went to Totnes, where she pretended to be a doctor. There she eloped with her first patient, the young daughter of Mr Ivythorn. They were married in Ashburton in Devonshire, and returned to Totness to the welcoming embrace of the father, relieved that his daughter had been made respectable by marriage. After a fortnight, a sudden violent storm in the night caused the doctor's nakedness to be exposed to her wife, who sadly declared 'you have not — what you ought to have.'

Mary fled once again, this time into Somersetshire, and arrived safely at Wells, where she took the name of Charles Hamilton. Shortly afterwards at a dance, she met the beautiful 18-year-old Mary Price, with whom she fell madly in love. 'With this girl, hath this wicked woman since her confinement declared, she was really as much in love, as it was possible for a man ever to be with one of her own sex.' The doctor wrote two letters to Mary Price:

> I assure you, my angel, all I write to you proceeds only from my heart, which you have so entirely conquered, and made your own, that nothing else has any share in it; ... do let me have once more an opportunity of seeing you, and that soon, that I may breathe forth my soul at those dear feet, where I would willingly die, if I am not suffer'd to lie there and live. My sweetest creature, give me leave to subscribe myself
> Your fond, doating,
> Undone SLAVE.

And Mary Price replied:

> Sur,
> I haf recevd boath your too litters, and sur I ham much surprise
> hat the loafe you priten [pretend] to haf for so pur a garl as mee.
> I kan nut beleef you wul desgrace yourself by marring sutch a
> yf [wife] as mee, and Sur I wool nut be thee hore of the gratest
> man in the kuntry. For thof [though] mi vartu his all I haf, yit hit
> is a potion I ham rissolv to kare [carry] to mi housband, soe noe
> moor at presant, from your umble savant to cummand.

Such innocence and purity captivated the doctor's heart, and there
followed a tender and delicate interview between the lovers. They were
married within two days, on 16 July 1746 at Wells, and continued happily
married for two months.

But during a trip to Glastonbury, Charles Hamilton was recognised as
Mary Hamilton by an acquaintance from Totnes, who reported the story
of her previous marriage. This quickly got back to Mary Price's mother,
who confronted her daughter with some searching questions, but Mary
insisted that the report must be false. In her eagerness to defend her
husband, she endeavoured to prove too much — 'she asserted some things
which staggered her mother's belief, and made her cry out, O child, there
is no such thing in human nature.' Soon everyone in Wells was talking
about the affair, and by the time Doctor Hamilton returned from Glastonbury, she was laughed at in the streets, and her neighbours threw dirt
at her and verbally abused her. Mary's mother had gone to a magistrate
and a warrant was granted for the arrest of the Doctor, who was seized on
18 September. Mary was resolved to stand by the side of her husband,
claiming that the information was malicious, but the truth was revealed to
her; she fell into a fit and recovered but with difficulty.

Appearing before the justice, Mary had to admit that she had been
tricked 'by the vilest and most deceitful practices', and she revealed her
plight to the authorities: 'After their marriage they lay together several
nights and that the said pretended Charles Hamilton who had married her
aforesaid entered her body several times, which made this woman believe
at first that the said Hamilton was a real man.'[18] And before the justice was
exhibited 'something of too vile, wicked and scandalous a nature, which
was found in the Doctor's trunk, having been produced in evidence against
her', presumably a dildo, whereupon Mary Hamilton was committed to
Bridewell to await trial.[19] As she was conveyed to the gaol, 'she was
attended by many insults from the mob', and even her deluded wife was
cruelly abused.

No one was quite able to define exactly what crime Mary Hamilton had committed, as no statute covered such an outrage; at the advice of a learned counsel, she was prosecuted under a clause of the vagrancy act, 'for having by false and deceitful practices endeavoured to impose on some of his Majesty's subjects.' Mary revelled in the notoriety given to her case by all the newspapers. As reported in the *Bath Journal*, 'There are great numbers of people flock to see her in Bridewell, to whom she sells a great deal of her quackery; and appears very bold and impudent. She seems very gay, with Periwig, Ruffles and Breeches; and it is publicly talked that she has deceived several of the fair sex by marrying them.'[20] In fact it was claimed at the trial that she had married 14 women.[21]

Mary Hamilton was duly convicted of fraud. During the winter of 1746, she was publicly whipped in the four market towns of Taunton, Glastonbury, Wells, and Shepton Mallet, and then sent to prison for six months. It will have taken a great deal to break her spirit:

> These whippings she has accordingly undergone, and very severely have they been inflicted, insomuch, that those persons who have more regard to beauty than to justice, could not refrain from exerting some pity toward her, when they saw so lovely a skin scarified with rods, in such a manner that her back was almost flead [flayed]: yet so little effect had the smart or shame of this punishment on the person who underwent it, that the very evening she had suffered the first whipping, she offered the gaoler money, to procure her a young girl to satisfy her most monstrous and unnatural desires.[22]

Similarly brutal treatment was meted out to Ann Marrow, who was also convicted of fraud. In July 1777 she was found guilty 'for going in man's cloaths, and personating a man in marriage, with three different women, . . . and defrauding them of their money and effects.' She was sentenced to three months in prison, and to stand in the pillory at Charing Cross on 22 July 1777: there she was pelted so severely, primarily by the female spectators, that she was blinded in both eyes.[23]

Discovery did not always have such severe consequences, but it invariably led to separation and ostracism. Around 1815 Helen Oliver, a maidservant, dated a ploughman from a neighbouring farm in West Kilbride, Scotland, who turned out to be a woman, and who persuaded Helen to abandon female dress and duties. Helen donned men's clothes and took the name of her brother John, and went to work for her cousin in Glasgow, who did not recognise her as a woman. Later she went to Paisley, then to Johnstone, where she married a young woman. Eventually she became an apprentice plasterer in Hutcheson, but after four years her real sex was discovered, and in 1821 she was forced to leave town, and disappeared from view.[24]

Women who had the necessary force of character to live like men were often desirous of publicity, and even wrote memoirs. Charlotte Charke (1710–1760) in her autobiography derived much pleasure from exhibiting the success of her disguises. She worked as a strolling actress playing the breeches parts, 'a grocer, a clerk, a pastry cook, a hog merchant'. After a marriage that lasted only one year (and produced a daughter), she left her husband and adopted men's clothing offstage. She played her various parts well: 'Making seeds and plants the general subject of my discourse, was the true characteristic of the Gardener; as, at other times, a Halter and horse-cloth brought into the house and awkwardly thrown down on a chair, were emblems of my stable profession.' At various times she worked as a small shopkeeper, a sausage maker, a pastry cook, and she gained penetrating insights into the symbols and roles of male dominance. Even at the age of four she confessed to having 'a passionate Fondness for a Perriwig', but she never fully revealed her private life; throughout all of her vagabond adventures she was accompanied by her companion Mrs Brown, a younger woman who repeatedly nagged her into settling down. But we are told little else about 'My Friend', and we are never given any explanation as to why she decided to pass as a gentleman — 'My going into Mens Cloaths, in which I continued many Years; the Reason of which I beg to be excused, as it concerns no Mortal *now living*, but myself.' She was not approved of by her daughter when she grew up, or by her father the famous dramatist Colley Cibber, though her brother Theophilus Cibber gave her financial help.[25] She wrote a novel, *The History of Henry Dumont* (1756), in which there is an effeminate male cross-dresser, a 'male-madam' who is ducked in a fish pond.[26]

(3) Lesbian Pirates

Women who dress as men are often viragos and swashbuckling adventurers, perhaps none more exotic than the lesbian pirates Anne Bonny and Mary Read.[27] We first hear of Anne Bonny, born Anne Cormac, in 1710 as a 13-year-old tomboy in the port of Charleston, South Carolina, in the pre-Independence New World. Although the daughter of a wealthy lawyer and plantation owner, her red hair was cut short, her face was dirty, and her habits were rowdy. As one historian notes, Anne 'grew up into a strapping, boisterous girl, of a "fierce and courageous temper" which more than once led her into sad scrapes, as when she slew her English servant-maid with a case knife. But apart from such occasional outbursts of temper she was a good and dutiful daughter.'

About five years later we again hear of her, seen frequenting the taverns of the port, on the arms of various buccaneers, and there are stories that a would-be suitor was hospitalised for a month after she beat him with a chair. She once used her sword to publicly undress her fencing master, button by button.

Her father disinherited her when she eloped with James Bonny; in revenge, she burnt down the family plantation, then fled to the British-controlled port of New Providence (on modern Nassau in the Bahamas), a haven for such pirates as Blackbeard and Captain Kidd. Upon her arrival, she quickly established herself by shooting off the remaining ear of an already one-eared drunken sailor who blocked her way when she disembarked. In a short while she discarded her husband and went to live with the pirate Captain Jennings and his mistress Meg. Advised to get some male protection, she became the mistress of Chidley Bayard, the wealthiest man on the island. But eventually she deserted him for the pirate John 'Calico Jack' Rackham, so named because of the loud striped patchwork trousers which he wore. Although they had one child (mysteriously disposed of), it has been suggested that Calico Jack may have come to New Providence as the paramour as well as quartermaster to a Captain Vane.

Another of Anne's menfriends was much more certainly gay: Pierre Bouspeut (sometimes called Pierre Delvin or Peter Bosket), who ran a coffee shop, hairdressing and dress-making shop, as he was a designer of fine velvet and silk clothing. Anne and Pierre got word that a French merchantman richly laden with costly materials would be sailing by, and together they organised their first 'privateering' raid. With the aid of some of Pierre's friends they stole a boat from the abandoned wrecks in the harbour, and liberally covered the topsail, deck and themselves with turtle blood. In the bow they placed one of Pierre's dress dummies, dressed in women's clothing and similarly splashed with blood. Anne stood over this nightmare figure with a blood-soaked axe, and they sailed out to the merchantman. When its crew caught sight of this demonic ship by the light of the full moon, they were so horrified by the impending mayhem that they turned over the cargo of their vessel without a fight.

Less theatrical acts of piracy were of course commonplace in the port, and Captain Woodes Rogers in due course attempted to secure the power and jurisdiction of the British government by offering the King's Pardon to all pirates who would turn themselves in and offer to reform. But Anne refused, knowing that she could not be pardoned for the attempted murder of her father. She and Calico Jack and Pierre broke through a blockade that Rogers had positioned in the harbour: for this incident, Anne was stripped to the waist like an Amazon, and dressed in black velvet trousers designed by Pierre; with one hand resting on the hilt of her sword, and the other waving a long silk scarf at the astonished Governor, she sailed past 'as daintily as any fine lady being seen off on a long ocean voyage.' Soon she established her position aboard this ship by shooting a sailor whose attentions were becoming obnoxious to her. Though officially she was second in command, after Calico, she had thrown him out of the Captain's quarters and resided there alone.

But eventually her crew decided to accept the pardon, which was made easier by Rogers' having obtained a special pardon for Anne, and they returned to New Providence peacefully. There it was that Anne met Mary Read alias 'Mark' Read. Mary's mother long ago, in England, had dressed her daughter as a boy and had pretended that she was her dead son Mark, in order to ensure an inheritance from Mary's grandmother, such inheritances, like so much else, being reserved for the male. Mary eventually came to prefer her masculine role so much that her mother disinherited her. She was apprenticed as a footboy, then ran away to join the army as a soldier. She married a soldier and together they opened the Three Horseshoes Inn; but after three years her husband died and the public house failed, so she again donned men's clothes and signed on a Dutch merchantman as Mark Read. This ship was captured by English pirates, whom she was persuaded to join, and thus it was that she eventually found herself finding pardon in New Providence and joining up with Anne.

At about this time — though Anne and Mary were already fast friends — Anne's husband, James Bonny, reappeared to reclaim his wife, i.e. his property. He kidnapped her and brought her bound and naked before the Governor, charged with the felony of deserting her husband. He suggested 'divorce by sale', a more 'lenient' punishment, hoping to profit by the proceeds of such an auction. But Anne refused to be, as she said, 'bought and sold like a hog or cattle'; in fact she expressed herself so vehemently that no buyer dared step forward to claim such a 'hellcat'. The Governor was forced to release her on condition that she return to her rightful master, but James, who only wanted the money, fled in terror from the storm she had raised. Mary had to persuade Anne not to shoot the Governor. Instead, together they set out in a sloop in pursuit of James; he escaped after a merry chase, but they burnt his turtle business to the ground.

In due course the pirate crew was re-formed, with Anne and 'Mark' constantly together aboard ship. This intimacy aroused the jealousy of Calico Jack, who threatened to slit Mark's throat, but bursting into the cabin one day with just this in mind, he discovered Mary stretched out on the bed before Anne, not entirely clothed and visibly a woman. Some (male) historians would have us believe that only minutes before, Anne had ripped off Mary's clothing, and herself had only just discovered Mark's true gender. This is highly unlikely. The two women had already been intimate far too long — and had shared such a rough lifestyle at that — not to have been fully acquainted with one another's gender. (Even if Mary had pretended to be a boy, surely Pierre would have discovered this long ago.) The bowdlerisation of this episode and attempts to explain it away are typical of how this pair of women have been treated by historians; Anne Bonny frequently appears in biographical collections for children (her story in a tiny booklet in a pack of Shredded Wheat cereal inspired Steve Gooch's play *The Women-Pirates* in 1969), where she is conventionalised as merely a pirate captain's mistress, rather than the leader she actually was.

In the event, Anne and Mary — no longer 'Mark' — remained inseparable, and both women alternately donned male and female clothing. In due course they took command of another ship, and men-of-war were sent out to capture 'those infamous women'. They abandoned all caution and raided numerous other ships. One of the victims of their piracy happened to be the *Royal Queen*, a vessel owned by Anne's former 'lover' Chidley Bayard, and commanded by one Captain Hudson. On this occasion Anne seduced Hudson into bringing her aboard, then drugged his wine instead of sleeping with him, and secretly doused the firing pins of the cannons with water. She left the next morning, then returned with her pirates. The *Royal Queen*'s gunmen were unable to open fire and they were easily captured. Only Captain Hudson was killed in this otherwise bloodless battle — by a jealous Mary.

13. The lesbian pirates Anne Bonny and Mary Read, inseparable and well-armed, before their capture near Jamaica.

Eventually Anne and Mary were captured by a Captain Barnet. In the heat of this final battle their crew deserted them, staying below deck and refusing to fight. So Mary shot two of their own men, and wounded Calico. But it took an hour for Barnet's entire crew to subdue the two women. They and their pirate crew were taken to trial in St Jaga de la Vega, Jamaica, convicted of piracy on 28 November 1720, and sentenced to be hanged. Anne and Mary promptly 'pleaded their bellies' and were pardoned. This was a common plea amongst women sentenced to death, the point being that no court would hang an innocent albeit unborn life — though neither of them in fact bore a child, and almost certainly neither was pregnant.

Anne visited Calico before he was hanged, and said 'I am sorry to see you in this predicament, but had you fought like a man you would not now have to die like a dog.' Mary herself died of a fever contracted in prison, and Anne just disappeared. One unlikely story is that she got married and returned to Charleston where she would still have been wanted for arson, attempted parricide, and conspiracy against the King's authority. An even more unlikely story is that she went into a nunnery.

Pirate literature is not noted for its accuracy, and there has never been any thoroughgoing research into the lives of Anne Bonny and Mary Read. Their story, like that of all pirates, has been treated as a peg upon which the bourgeois imagination can hang its thirst for mobility, ill-gotten gains and romantic independence. And like all tales of high adventure, their story comes in widely different versions, according to the whim of the historian or novelist or playwright. The story I have told above seems to be the most accurate we can cull from the very earliest documents. Evidence of their homosexuality is not so clear cut as we might wish, and at most they were bisexual, so 'lesbian' is a misnomer. Some less substantiated legends claim that both women were brought up in boy's clothing, and that there was a thriving gay subculture in New Providence; homosexual men certainly did flee persecution in places such as Amsterdam, and they may well have ended up at New Providence. In any case, we must take into account Anne and Mary's dismissive treatment of their temporary male paramours and even their children, their obvious enjoyment of their cross-dressing, and the fact that they acted together as a couple and obviously loved one another; so the evidence suggests that they must be relevant to any history of lesbian experience.

(4) Romantic Friends

During the last third of the eighteenth century we can find numerous accounts of passionate female friendship, part of the Age of Sentiment and the growing Romantic movement in life as well as literature. The *vade mecum* of romantic female friends was the novel *A Description of Millenium Hall* (1762), based fairly closely upon the life of its author Sarah Scott. She married in 1751, but left her husband after a year, and went to Bath to live with Barbara Montague, sister of Lord Halifax. They had been inseparable friends since 1748, and Lady 'Bab' had even accompanied Sarah on her honeymoon. In 1754 they took a house together at Bath Easton, where they lived and worked together on a charity project for poor girls until Lady Bab's death. Scott's novel tells the story of a pair of romantic friends who live and travel together, and who are eventually joined by three more women, a pair of whom are also romantic friends, and this 'establishment becomes a model of happy, generous living' without men.[28]

The love of Sarah Ponsonby and Eleanor Butler, the 'Ladies of Llangollen', is more famous, and does not need retelling here. Disguised as men, they eloped together in 1778 and shared their lives in Plas Newydd for 53 years. They were visited by all the notable people in society, the Duke of Wellington, Wordsworth, Wedgwood, Edmund Burke, Hester Thrale Piozzi, Sir Walter Scott, Lady Caroline Lamb, and they became a byword for pure romantic friendship. But as far as we can tell, they shared everything except sex: they were conservative, and easily shocked by immodesty and immorality (they dismissed their servant for being pregnant without being married).[29] George Elers in his *Memoirs* records falling in love with a girl who was quite unresponsive to him. 'After I went abroad she formed a most romantic attachment to a young lady by the name of Arabella Ross. At that time Lady E. Butler and the Hon. Miss Ponsonby lived in Wales together. Their affection, I presume was founded on similar principles . . . poor Sophie died at the early age of twenty five, leaving the whole of her fortune to her friend Miss Ross, for life.'[30]

Early death or eventual marriage usually resolved the dilemmas raised by love between women in the middle classes. Respectable women were pretty well trapped either into marriage or into caring for their aged parents and living at home if they remained unmarried. Many women formed romantic friendships with other women, engaged in flirtation and courting, and even dreamed of living together without men. In America, according to the observations of Saint Méry during his journeys of 1793 to 1798, there were many romantic women friends, and 'they are not at all strangers to being willing to seek unnatural pleasures with persons of their own sex',[31] but there is no evidence of this willingness in the more formal ambience of English society.

On the opposite side of the coin, our insight into the lives of eighteenth-century lesbians is helped no more by diatribes and gossip sheets than by the numerous poems, plays and pornography which mention lesbianism. These of course are not to be trusted at all — though they certainly indicate the attitudes of the public towards lesbianism. In Sylvain Marechal's *Almanach des sonnettes femmes de la Société Joyeuse* we learn that March is the month for *fellatrices*, November for *tribades*, and December for *voyeuses* — a seasonal survey which is pleasant enough entertainment, but little else. Diderot's major novel *La Religieuse (The Nun)*, begun in 1760, contains numerous love scenes between a nun and a mother superior, and is supposedly based upon a real *cause célèbre*, but its sensational admixture of sex, sadism, and anti-Catholicism is obviously devised for a certain readership. Casanova asserted that lesbianism was so common among nuns (and the women of Provence were especially inclined to it) that many confessors did not even bother to impose penalties. But the frequent theme of lesbian nuns merely emphasises that for most writers and historians the lesbian exists only between the pages of a novel catering to masculine lust and anticlerical prejudice.

The term 'lesbian pornography' is a misnomer, for it so patently exploits lesbians for the titillation of heterosexual men, that I cannot imagine it would give great pleasure to a lesbian readership. It reveals little about any genuine lesbian experience or subculture, but much about the popular stereotypes concerning lesbians. A typical example is an account of 'The Loves of Sappho' which was serialised in the weekly magazine *The Exquisite*, around 1842, beginning with a history of Sappho, who is supposed to have turned to women after being rejected by Phaon. The author acknowledges that Sapphic love exists in all countries including England, France, Italy, Turkey and the oriental climates, and to demonstrate this he presents an interminable and tedious tale of 'exquisite' soft porn which runs through many issues.[32] In such works as this, lesbians are acknowledged solely as sexual creatures, whose homosexual tastes are merely experiments on the path to full heterosexual pleasure. While male sex is portrayed in a fairly healthy manner, as rough and ready and ordinary, lesbian sex is portrayed as being exquisite, not part of everday life, but reserved for sumptuous and expensive brothels or strange and exotic secret societies and nunneries. Lesbian interludes are *de rigueur* in otherwise heterosexual pornography such as *Memoirs of a Man of Pleasure; or, The Amours, Intrigues, and Adventures of Sir Charles Manly* (1827), but the deeply prejudiced nature of such novels is revealed when the lesbian sex is described as causing great distress to the male baby in the heroine's womb! The more realistic flavour of eighteenth-century French semi-pornography would not be matched by the English until the later nineteenth century, but that is a subject that goes well beyond the limits of the present study.

There is no indication that homosexual women in England ever gathered together in a real subculture until quite modern times. In 1792 there is supposed to have existed in London, 'a female whipping club', which met every Thursday evening at its premises in Jermyn Street. Though its members 'are mainly married women', only women were admitted, and they enjoyed chastising one another at their meetings: 'the whipping starts on the calves and goes up to the posteriors.'[33] But this sounds suspiciously like titillating fiction rather than fact.

It is however possible that lesbian clubs existed in the late eighteenth century, at least upon the Continent, in sophisticated capitals such as Paris and Vienna. According to Baron K. von Reizenstein in his *Trip to Vienna* (1795), the most fashionable women 'are no longer so stupid as to seek the company of the other sex; they organise general gatherings in secluded places to which they would rather admit the Devil than a man. Various cabals and intrigues are set afoot to get novices. Young and charming girls are not safe, neither by day or night, from the ceaseless pursuit of the priestesses who officiate in this unclean temple.'[34] The absence of specific details in Reizenstein's account suggests that it is composed of a high degree of fantasy. The existence of erotic secret societies in Vienna is somewhat more definitely established for the mid-nineteenth century. Joseph Hormayr in his *Kaiser Franz und Metternich* (1848) claims that one lesbian club was comprised of the ladies Thun, Ruspolo, Lichnowsky, Khevenhüller and Thürheim, and the notorious Queen Caroline of Naples. Hormayr, however, was quite malicious, and we must be careful not to accept his evidence wholeheartedly.

However, there are so many accounts of a distinguished lesbian club which flourished in Paris in the 1780s that it seems genuine despite the colourful and elaborate descriptions of it. This was the Anandrynes, founded by Mme Furiel whose house was the meeting place. The president was the notorious actress Mlle Raucourt. Procuresses such as La Gourdan assisted in recruiting new candidates or 'Desirantes', who would be bathed, perfumed, and garbed in a *'chemise à la tribade'* with an open, slit front (from the girdle down) and decorated with ribbons, and then led to Mme Furiel, a brunette of about 30 with a manly appearance, who as the 'affectionate Mama' showed the candidate the club's symbol of two billing and cooing turtle-doves, gave her a kiss *'à la Florentine'*, and inspected her bosom to determine 'whether it possessed the firmness of marble.' Then followed two hours of instruction in lesbian love by another woman. On the second day of the initiation the candidate was led to the centre of the 'Temple of Venus', a circular room illuminated from above and from the sides, with a statue of Vesta hovering over a globe. The walls were decorated with representations of the female private parts. On two altars were statues of Sappho and a bust by Houdon of Mademoiselle/Chevalier D'Eon the male transvestite, strangely described as the 'most famous modern Tribade'. An elaborate ceremony concluded in a banquet and an orgy. Candidates who wished to ascend in the hierarchy, were locked into a room filled with a statue of Priapus, phallic objects, figurines of men and women in coitus, and a host of heterosexual stimulants, and required to tend the fire of Vesta, which, if it went out, was proof of their lack of lesbian determination.

Members of the Orders of Anandrynes supposedly included even married women such as the Marquise Terracenes, the wife of the Attorney General; likewise it appealed to actresses such as Mlle Arnould. The sources — which include *Hic et Haec ou l'Elève des RR.PP. Jesuites etc* (Berlin, 1798), *La Cauchoise, etc* (London, 1788), *Le Petit-Fils d'Hercule* (1788), *L'histoire de la secte anandryne*, and Mairobet's *L'apologie de la Secte Anandryne* and his more notorious *L'espion Anglais* (1779) — are overwhelmingly literary and imaginative and salacious, and quite difficult to integrate into a study of the gay subculture in England. The descriptions sound like pure fantasy, but we must remember that this was Paris, which was far in advance of London in the liberty it allowed its citizens.

Chapter 16

From Twickenham to Turkey

(1) The Old World

The molly houses of London were as nothing compared to their counterparts in less intolerant parts of the world. But it is difficult to document the existence of male prostitution or a gay subculture as such in more than a few of the most exotic countries. William Lithgow in *The Totall Discourse, Of the Rare Adventures, and painefull Peregrinations* (1632) reported that during his visit to Malta in 1616 he 'saw a Spanish soldier and a Maltese boy burnt in ashes, for the public profession of sodomy; and long or night there were above a hundred *bardassoes* — whorish boys — that fled away to Sicily in a galleot for fear of fire, but never one bugeron stirred, being few or none there free of it.'[1] Of Morocco, which is commonly believed to be the modern gay paradise, Lithgow also has a few words: 'There are some twelve thousand allowed brothel-houses in this town [Fez], the courtesans being neatly kept and weekly well looked to by physicians. But worst of all, in the summer time they openly licentiate three thousand common stews of sodomitical boys. Nay, I have seen at midday, in the very market places, the Moors buggaring these filthy carrions, and without shame or punishment go freely away.'[2] Turkey was regarded as the sink of lascivious luxury, and the Turks were said to be particularly addicted to sodomy, 'which they account as a dainty to digest all other libidinous pleasures.'[3] As late as 1822 the author of a pamphlet could advise the scandalously absconded Bishop of Clogher to 'take a trip to Turkey, where he can worship his god without the fear of being branded or hanged.'[4] The xenophobia of the typical Englishman goes a long way to explain the belief that homosexuality was prevalent *abroad*, be it in the exotic east or closer to home, particularly in papist Italy. Lithgow saw it celebrated throughout Italy, not only in the great cities, but even in 'the smallest village of Italy. A monstrous filthiness, and yet to them a pleasant pastime, making songs and singing sonnets of the beauty and pleasure of their bardassi, or buggared boys.'[5] A character in Robert Greene's *A Quip for an Upstart Courtier* (1592) has this to say to another: 'And whereas thou saiest thou wert borne in *Italy*, & caled hether by our courtiers, him may wee curse that brought thee first into *Englande*: for thou camest not alone, but accompanied with multitude of abhominable vices, hanging on thy bumbast nothing but infectious abuses, and vaine glory, selfe love, sodomie and strange poisonings, wherewith thou hast infected this glorious Iland.'

Homosexuality is as indigenous to England as to most other countries, but if it is possible for the *structures* of homosexuality, i.e. the gay *subculture*, to have been imported into England, then it was probably brought over from the rather more prosaic territory of the Netherlands by William III and his court. The gay subculture certainly flourished concurrently in both countries, and the major anti-gay purges of the eighteenth century occurred in Holland at the same time as the lesser purges in England. The astonishing purges of 1730 to 1731 probably sent men running for cover even in England, where it was publicised, and remarked upon in Lord Hervey's circle. In April 1730 some men were arrested in Utrecht; they incriminated others, and on 21 July the States of Holland issued a Placat, posted in every town, that set off wide-scale persecution. Sodomy was to be punished by death, and those who offered their homes for its commission were also to die, and their corpses to be burned to ashes and thrown into the sea 'or exposed as unworthy of burial', and the names of the convicted — including the fugitives — would be publicly posted.

Some 250 men were summoned before the authorities; 91 faced decrees of exile for not appearing. At least 60 men were sentenced to death. In Amsterdam, Pieter Marteyn Janes Sohn and Johannes Keep, decorator, were strangled and burnt; Maurits van Eeden, house servant, and Cornelis Boes, 18, Keep's servant, were each immersed alive in a barrel of water and drowned; Laurens Hospuijn, Chief of Detectives in the Navy, was strangled and thrown into the water with a 100-pound weight. At The Hague, Frans Verheyden, Cornelis Wassemaar, milkman, Pieter Styn, embroiderer of coats, Dirk van Royen, and Herman Mouil-liont, servant, were hanged and afterwards thrown into the sea at Scheven-ingen with 50-pound weights; Pieter van der Hal, grain carrier, Adriaen Kuyleman, glove launderer, David Muntslager, agent, and Willem la Feber, tavern keeper, were hanged and thrown into the sea with 100-pound weights. In Kampen, Jan Westhoff and Steven Klok, soldiers, were strangled on the scaffold and buried under the gallows. In Rotter-dam, Leendert de Haas, 60, candle maker, Casper Schroder, distiller,

Huibert v. Borselen, gentleman's servant, were strangled, burnt, and their ashes carried in an ash cart out of the city and then by ship to the sea and thrown overboard. And at Zuidhorn, at least 22 men were executed on 24 September 1731, including Gerrit Loer, 48, farmer, Hendrik Berents, 32, Jan Berents, 19 — all scorched while alive and then strangled and burnt to ashes; 12 others aged 20 to 45 were strangled and burnt; and eight aged 16 to 19 were strangled and burnt, including Jan Ides, 18, who said upon hearing his sentence: 'I forgive you for the sin which you have committed against me.'[6]

It seems as though most of the men were in fact 'guilty' of being homosexual, that is, this was neither a political reign of terror, nor a hysterical witch-hunt which rounded up 'innocent' people. Not enough research into the actual trial records has yet been done, and we cannot be certain how well the gay subculture was developed, or how Dutch immigrants such as Peter Vivian, the peruke maker, may have contributed to the formation of the English subculture. But we are certain that the subculture existed, and the Dutch evidence is surprisingly similar to the English evidence. As early as 1703 there were specific cruising grounds in The Hague where homosexuals recognised each other by special signs. In the 1730s, in the provinces of Frisia and Groningen, homosexual men gave each other female names. By the middle of the eighteenth century, in Amsterdam, gay men met not only in public toilets and under the arcades of the town hall, but in molly houses or taverns called *lolhuysen*. They developed a sense of gay identity supported by the use of special mimicry, love names, and a network of friends and contacts, and some men even sealed marriage contracts with blood.[7]

Research has been unable to reveal much evidence of gay subcultures in other countries during this period. Perhaps in response to the Dutch Placat, the Swedish penal code of 1734 required that convicted sodomites be beheaded, but there is no evidence of a Swedish gay subculture (although there were certain gay notables such as King Gustavus III). Similarly in Prussia we find gay members of the nobility such as Prince Henry, but little evidence of an organised gay subculture outside the court, at least not until the late 1800s. During the wars of independence at that time, a Freemason Lodge in Berlin was accused of being a club for pederasts. The entrance to this club was at the rear of the building, and over the door was the inscription 'Wise men shall find the entrance' — supposed to be an allusion to the superiority of anal intercourse. German homosexuals at that time were called 'warm brothers', a phrase still in use much later.[8]

In France, the gay subculture flourished primarily in the court. Philippe d'Orleans, 'Monsieur', was notorious for the public manner in which he displayed his boyfriends, and his wife, Elizabeth Charlotte, adopted a liberal attitude of necessity, as in her letter of 3 December 1705 to Ameliese: 'Where can you and Luise have been hiding, to know so little of the ways of the world? I should have thought it was quite impossible to spend any time at all at any Court without getting a good idea of it. If one were to detest every man who is fond of young fellows, it would be impossible to find even six people to like, or at least not to dislike.'[9] For the nobility, private life was relatively unhampered by petty moral conventions. In the closing years of the seventeenth century, for example, a homosexual club had been founded by the Duc de Grammont, the Maltese Knight de Fillodet, Manicamp and the Marquis de Bizan. All of the members submitted to the 'rigueurs de Noviciat, qui durerait jusqu'à ce que la barbe fut venue au menton.' But shortly after its founding, a royal prince joined it and the King, on discovering this, ordered its dissolution; the Prince was punished on the part of his body by which he had offended. Our source for this anecdote is a chapter in *La France galante* (1695) which is significantly titled 'La France devenue Italienne' — 'France, turned Italian'.

As early as 1702 an organised system of male homosexual prostitution was discovered in Paris; several prominent men were burned, while others cut their own throats to escape public punishment and avoid disgrace. As late as 1750, two pederasts were burned alive in Paris.[10] By the middle of the eighteenth century, France could boast of some thriving lesbian clubs and pederastic circles such as the Guebres and the Arracheurs de palissades. In Charles Gervais de Latouche's anti-clerical *Histoire de Dom Bougre* (c. 1745) — which was widely read, and treasured by the Marquise de Pompadour — there are miscellaneous criticisms of ecclesiastical buggery and tribadism; in a typical scene, while Susannah sleeps at the cloister Sister Monika slips into her bed and initiates her into lesbian pleasures, and continues to do so, interrupted by heterosexual bouts. But a clearly recognisable gay subculture does not seem to have emerged until the 1780s.

Restif de la Bretonne, who saw everything on the underside of Paris life, came across homosexual men primarily at the masked balls during Carnival time: 'Since coming to Paris I had heard talk of effeminates, but apparently these creatures either never went out, like queen bees, or else disguised themselves, for it was not until this dance that I first saw them in their full horror. Five or six gorgeous creatures appeared at Coulon's, ten times more womanish than women, and were instantly surrounded. They were absolutely determined to show themselves off, and a swarm of bold coquettes soon sought them out and began to make provocative remarks, even to pay court to them. The fops withdrew, not in a timid way, but with a kind of insolence that was more striking than if they had retaliated.'[11] Bretonne, though himself a foot and shoe fetishist, puritanically scorned fashionable sodomites, and was scandalised by their preference for men over women on the grounds of the gay proverb 'You don't serve leg of lamb without the bone.' He could not accept mere pleasure as a motive: 'in this class must be included schoolboys who do it for mischief, soldiers for lack of money, and monks of necessity. As for *mignons*, it is certain that they do so only from avarice.'

(2) The New World

Such a *laissez-faire* philosophy did not prevail in the New World. The Colony of Massachusetts Bay in its Body of Liberties (1641) welcomed refugees trying to escape 'the Tiranny or oppression of their persecutors', but it did not extend a similarly warm greeting to its homosexual immigrants. For example on 23 June 1629, aboard the ship *Talbot* sailing for the New World: 'This day we examined 5 beastly Sodomiticall boyes, which confessed their wickedness not to be named. The fact was so fowl we reserved them to be punished by the governor when we came to new England, who afterward sent them backe to the company to bee punished in ould England, as the crime deserved.'[12] It was not long, however, before the colonies could mete out their own punishments, and as late as 1776 male homosexuals were universally subject to the death penalty in the original thirteen colonies. Laws are notorious for being created in a vacuum of intellectual abstractions, but William Bradford in his *History of Plymouth Plantation* reported that in 1642 wickedness was 'much witnesed against, and . . . narrowly looked into, and severely punished when it was knowne. . . . Even sodomie and bugerie, (things fearful to name,) have broak forth in this land, oftener than once.' In some states such as Maryland and Virginia where no specific law applied, trials and at least one execution were carried out under the English statutes presumed to be in force. One of the tragedies of the New World was that it did not sufficiently question the validity of the laws of the Old World. After the Revolution, Pennsylvania was the first to reform its laws in a less sanguinary direction. In 1786 sodomy was no longer punished by death, but by forfeiture of all lands and goods, and servitude for a term not exceeding ten years. Reforms elsewhere took place slowly and in a bizarre fashion. Thomas Jefferson proposed that sodomites be castrated and that lesbians be punished 'by cutting thro' the cartilage of her nose a hole of one half inch diameter at the least.' His measures were not adopted, but in 1792 Virginia made sodomy a capital offence with a mandatory death sentence. Gradually the penalty was reduced to fines, whipping, and imprisonment (often for life), though death was still the penalty in North Carolina until 1869, and in South Carolina until 1873 – under the Buggery Act of Henry VIII.

These harsh laws would have supported a reign of terror in the colonies, but in fact few prosecutions have come to light. In 1624 Richard William Cornish, Master of the ship *Ambrose*, anchored in the James River, Virginia, was hanged for committing sodomy with the 29-year-old cabin-boy William Couse.[13] In 1646, in Massachusetts Bay Colony, William Plaine was executed for having committed sodomy with two persons in England, and because 'he had corrupted a great part of the youth of Guilford by masturbations, which he had committed, and provoked others to the like above a hundred times.'[14] Also in 1646, in Manhattan, New Netherland Colony, Jan Creoli, a negro, was sentenced to be choked to death and burned to ashes for a second offence of sodomy; his partner, ten-year-old Manuel Congo, was then carried to the place of Creoli's execution, tied to a stake, with faggots symbolically piled around him, and flogged.[15] In New Netherlands Colony there is a reference to attempted sodomy by N.G. Hillebrant or Hillebtantsen in 1658; and to alleged homosexual rape by J.Q. van der Linde (or Linden) in 1660 – he was tied in a sack and drowned in a river, while his victim was whipped and 'sent to some other place.'[16] In 1674, in Massachusetts, a young man named Benjamin Goad was castrated for a crime which seems to have involved masturbating himself in front of, or with, other boys.[17]

There are virtually no references to homosexuality in the United States for the next 100 years, an inexplicable gap which must be due to insufficient research. In 1775 the British Colonial Secretary, Lord George Germain, previously mentioned under his earlier title Lord George Sackville, is said to have desired a relationship with the American Benjamin Thompson.[18] In 1778 one of George Washington's soldiers, Lieutenant Frederick Gotthold Enslin, was court-martialled for attempted sodomy with another soldier.[19] In that same year, Governor Zespedes investigated the rising incidence of homosexuality among the Spanish army in Florida, some involving boys of English parents, and had the offenders arrested and sent to Havana for punishment.[20] The French lawyer Moreau de Saint Méry reported that many young women in Philadelphia, from 1793 to 1798, were lesbians.[21] In 1810 a man named Davis was indicted in Maryland for having sodomised a 19-year-old man, and sentenced to stand once in the pillory for 15 minutes and to pay a fine of $500.[22]

The lack of evidence seems to suggest that there was no gay subculture in America until well into the nineteenth century. The first glimpse we have into a possible American gay subculture is found in a broadside dated 25 April 1826. It was written by Louis Dwight, who stated that he had examined numerous prisons since 1824, between Massachusetts and Georgia, especially in New England and New York, where he found enough 'testimony to establish one general fact, viz. That boys are prostituted to the lust of old convicts' and that 'the Sin of Sodom is the vice of prisoners, and boys are the favorite prostitutes.' He asked several convicts if they ever knew of boys who retained their integrity in a Penitentiary, and was told 'Never'. The boys — called *kinshon* — frequently boasted of their behaviour, and received adequate rewards for being kept. The older convicts vied with one another to secure the favours of the fair ones, giving them presents, and eventually contriving to get them to occupy the same room. Then a strong attachment followed, in which they shared meals and presents, and the older ones took the blame and punishment in place of their mates.[23]

(3) Australia

The prison environment of course produces a highly circumscribed and specialised sort of gay subculture, one which was known (though not admitted) by prison superintendents since time immemorial, and it was this sort of milieu which produced the gay subculture of England's other great colony. Australia is unique in gay history for having had founded upon its shores an artificially created gay subculture, a subculture so visible and widespread that New South Wales was openly referred to in the newspapers as Sodom.[24]

England's colonisation of Australia began on 26 January 1788, with the arrival of the First Fleet in Sydney Cove, under the command of Captain Arthur Phillip. He had been appointed Governor-elect of New South Wales on 25 October 1786, and in a memo written shortly afterwards he advised the Minister that it would be impossible to keep apart the men and women prisoners on the transportation ship; indeed, 'I don't know but it is best if the abandoned [of the women] are permitted to receive the visits of the convicts [male] in the limits allotted to them at certain times, and under certain restrictions.' The reason for this unconventional suggestion is made clear in the next paragraph: 'The death penalty should be limited to two offences — those of murder and sodomy. But I doubt whether the fear of death ever prevented a man of no principle from committing a bad action. I would deliver a murderer or sodomist as a prisoner to the natives of New Zealand and let them eat him, for, the dread of this will operate much stronger than the fear of death.'

Captain Arthur Phillip (1738–1814), Australia's Founding Father, despite his public statement against homosexuals, and despite his two (childless) marriages, may have been homosexual himself. At any rate it is certain that he had a strong interest in young men, such as 13-year-old William Neate Chapman, whom Phillip wished to take with him on that first voyage to Botany Bay, but whose parents refused; and a certain Landmann, a young man who had been a midshipman 'without any duties' on Phillip's ship, and who recalled him in 1796 as 'my oldest and most intimate friend'; and young Henry Waterhouse, a midshipman aboard the *Sirius*, whom Daniel Southwell the Mate described as 'his minion, his young lieutenant, his favorite, his darling, at least six or seven years younger and three quarters here in camp at his full range!' When Waterhouse visited Phillip in retirement in Bath in 1806, Fanny Chapman commented in her diary: 'Their friendship is deep and the Admiral is always speaking of this young man in tones of warmth and endearment. The Captain is more than a son to the Admiral.'

Although the laws of Britain now governed the Australian colonies, there is no record of any sodomite being hanged (or sent to the cannibals) during Phillip's term as Governor, nor is there any indication that men convicted of sodomy or attempted sodomy were transported to the colonies. But there can be no doubt that homosexuality would have been rife by the time the prisoners arrived at the colonies. On the First Fleet, aboard the *Sirius*, were 568 men and 191 women convicts; between 1787 and 1800, 5,595 men and only 1,440 women arrived at New South Wales. This disparate proportion of men and women did not vary much over the years: by 1844 the population of Sydney consisted of 87,000 men and 43,000 women; in 1821 there were seven men for every woman in New South Wales. At the same time the marriage rate steadily decreased, from 181 in 1809, to 52 in 1813, to 47 in 1817. The results of close confinement on the ships and in the penal institutions and the imbalance of the sexes can be imagined. One person wrote of convict life: 'But though a man might be a light-weight criminal when convicted . . . a few depraved, defiant men could soon corrupt and harden the milder sort, and every vice from profanity and bullying to sodomy could be learned in such schools, along with the niceties of pocket-picking and burglary.'

In 1822 one James Hall reported that the Colonial Secretary, Gouldbourn, wished to reduce the amount of sodomy on the government farms by sending women convicts to the Emu Plains establishment; there was a public outcry. The Quaker missionaries James Blakhouse and George Washington Walker often wrote about sodomy among the convicts in Sydney and Van Dieman's Land during their visits of 1832 to 1838. In 1837 there were rumours in Sydney that Rev. Mr Yates was having relations with the Maori boys at Waimate, a mission station near the Bay of Islands, New Zealand; Rev. Samuel Marsden, senior chaplain in Australia, investigated the matter, with the result that Rev. Yates was sent back to England. In 1852 Henry Hallyer, architect and surveyor for the Van Dieman's Land Company, killed himself upon hearing the rumour that he was 'a dirty sodomite'.

In 1837 to 1838 the Select Committee on Transportation sat to gather evidence on the problems of transporting criminals, and spent much of its time discussing sodomy. Sir Francis Forbes, one-time Chief Justice of New South Wales, claimed to know nothing personally of such goings-on in his colony, though he admitted this was the common supposition. Major James Mudie testified that the convict boys of New South Wales called each other 'Nancy' and 'Kitty', and that the 'sods' were not even ashamed of their behaviour. Lieutenant-Colonel George Arthur, one-time Governor of Van Dieman's Land, claimed there were few 'unnatural crimes' among the settlers. But Catholic Archbishop William Bernard Ullathorne claimed that there was so much iniquity and moral pollution among the boys in the barracks that he would willingly give his life to remove the evil of 'unnatural crime' amongst them. In the late 1840s, Bishop Wiltson, Catholic Bishop of Van Dieman's Land, complained that 'men convicts actually boasted of being married to each other.'

Homosexuality was so widespread, and so openly and unabashedly enjoyed, in the early history of the Australian colonies, that it is not really accurate to refer to the gay *subculture*: it was heterosexual behaviour that was the subculture. This seems to be borne out by the steady decline in marriages even as the population grew. Even within the first few years after the arrival of the First Fleet, there was a gay 'ghetto' in old Sydney Town, with drag shows, gay bars and hotels, a high concentration of gay activities in Rowe Street and the Rocks, and the first two gay cruising grounds, known as Mrs Macquaries' Chair and the Domain. And the entire city of Moreton Bay (later named Brisbane) was established in 1822 specifically as the place to which were sent those 'who practised the sins of the Cities of the Plain.'

(4) Conclusion

This survey seems to have carried us rather far afield, but the modern gay subcultures of Australia, Britain and America have their roots in the molly subculture of early eighteenth-century England. I have ended this survey around 1830, which marks the death of George IV and the end of the 'Georgian' era. After a short interlude under William IV, the gay subculture of the succeeding 'Victorian' era deserves a study unto itself, as a great many new influences impacted upon the development of the subculture in the nineteenth century. The increasing wealth of the middle classes, for example, contributed to the development of prostitution, in which a newly emerging middle-class gay subculture fed itself upon the original working-class gay subculture. The cash nexus was much more obviously important during the nineteenth century than during the eighteenth century, and male prostitution has been the subject of several studies. The upper-class and upper-middle-class gay man's search for satisfaction amongst the working classes and rough trade — which Oscar Wilde called 'feasting with panthers' — is an immensely interesting subject, but not enough study has been given to how the panthers (be they post office boys, guardsmen, or gondoliers) interacted amongst themselves while they were not being feasted upon. For example, the major scandal of the 1870s, the trial of Boulton and Park, involved the son of a stockbroker and his drag-queen boyfriend, and their trial exposed a fair number of homosexuals in the world of amateur theatricals whose motives had very little to do with money, but who seemed to be carrying on the unbroken tradition of the mollies' Festival Nights. My own view is that the working-class molly subculture survived relatively unchanged at least through the 1860s–1870s, and that prostitution was grafted upon this pre-existing subculture, contrary to the commonly-held view that prostitution provided the base from which the subculture grew. But this is a subject for further research.

The position of gay men and women worsened throughout the nine-teenth century and the first half of the twentieth century. This may seem to be a surprising statement, because we naturally feel that it is at least better to be imprisoned or fined than to be hanged or pilloried. But disastrous consequences were to arise from the disease theory of homo-sexuality which steadily gained ground from the 1830s. Sir Alexander Morison in *The Physiognomy of Mental Diseases* (1838) called it 'monomania with unnatural propensity', and suggested it was sometimes curable by camphor in large doses. Thus the theory of sin was superseded by the theory of insanity, and prejudice was enforced by the tools of science as well as those of religion. The oppression which the Georgian molly faced was largely external: fear of capture, conviction, and execution. But the oppression experienced by the Victorian margery and the modern poof and queer became internalised as shame and guilt — repression from which there is no escape. For many, especially for the puritan middle classes, fear was replaced by self-loathing, and executions were replaced by suicides. The attempt by early reformers such as John Addington Symonds to liberalise the law were largely ineffectual, and the Freudian model eventually was used as a justification for such 'cures' as lobotomy and electric shock treatment (despite Freud's personal liberalism). By the 1950s the gay subculture was riddled with self-oppression, an issue that was addressed and challenged by the gay liberation movement of the 1960s, a movement which successfully revitalised the gay subculture and trans-formed it into the viable gay community of today.

Unfortunately, too often the modern gay community has rejected its own history because we have not looked far enough beyond the 1950s or the 1890s; we have rightly rejected the guilt of the former period and the exploitation of the latter, and have understandably felt rather foolish about always harking back to the ancient Greeks. But I hope I have shown throughout this study, that prior to the distorting effects of the intervening years of persecution, there existed a gay subculture characterised by camaraderie, solidarity, resistance to oppression, and positive self-identity. With the aid of historical research, we can look back through the veil of repression, and discover a gay heritage worth celebrating.

Notes

Chapter 1: Queen James and His Courtiers

1. H. Montgomery Hyde, *The Other Love* (London: Heinemann, 1976).
2. Robert Holloway, *The Phoenix of Sodom, or the Vere Street Coterie* (London, 1813), p. 26.
3. Alan Bray, *Homosexuality in Renaissance England* (London: Gay Men's Press, 1982), p. 71, in a summary of various researches.
4. William L. Edgerton, *Nicholas Udall* (New York, 1965); *Nicholas Udall's Roister Doister*, ed. G. Scheurweghs, in *Materials for the Study of Old English Drama*, vol. 16, ed. Henry De Vocht (Louvain, 1939; repr. Vaduz, 1963).
5. Bray, p. 48.
6. Bray, p. 43.
7. *The Poems of John Marston*, ed. Arnold Davenport (Liverpool, 1961).
8. Rev. William M. Cooper, *Flagellation and the Flagellants: A History of the Rod* (London, c.1885), pp. 156–157.
9. T[homas] M[iddleton], *Micro-cynicon. Sixe Snarling Satyres* (London, 1599).
10. Bray, p. 43.
11. E.J. Burford, *The Orrible Synne: A Look at London Lechery from Roman to Cromwellian Times* (London: Calder & Boyars, 1973), p. 218.
12. Cited by Burford, p. 167.
13. Bray, p. 70.
14. *The First Century of Scandalous, Malignant Priests* (London, 1643), cited in Pisanus Fraxi, *Bibliography of Prohibited Books* (London, 1879; New York, 1962), vol. 2, pp. 40–41.
15. E.S. Turner, *The Court of St. James's* (New York, 1959); Antonia Fraser, *King James* (London: Weidenfeld and Nicolson, 1974); see also A.L. Rowse, *Homosexuals in History* (London: Weidenfeld and Nicolson, 1977).
16. *The Works of Sir Francis Bacon*, ed. James Spedding *et al*, 14 vols. (London, 1857–1874); John Aubrey, *Brief Lives*, ed. Andrew Clark (Oxford, 1898); Daphne du Maurier, *The Winding Stair: Francis Bacon, His Rise and Fall* (London: Victor Gollancz, 1976); Sir Simonds D'Ewes, *Autobiography and Correspondence*, ed. James Orchard Halliwell, 2 vols. (London, 1845). The

263

pertinent passage omitted from Halliwell's edition (it should have appeared on page 192 of vol. 1, Ch. X) was printed separately as 'The Fall and Great Vices of Sir Francis Bacon', and bound up as an appendix to Thomas Hearne, *Historia Vitae et Regni Ricardi II; Prince Charles's Journey into Spain* (London, 1729), pp. 387–388 (for the original manuscript, see MS Harleyana 646).

17.   Daphne du Maurier, *Golden Lads: A Study of Anthony Bacon, Francis, and their friends* (London: Victor Gollancz, 1975).

18.   Anthony Weldon, *The Court and Character of King James* (London, 1651), vol. 1, p. 13 (repr. in Francis Osborne, *Secret History of the Court of James the First* [Edinburgh, 1811], vol. 1, p. 443).

19.   *The Tryal and Condemnation of Mervin, Lord Audley Earl of Castle-Haven* (London, 1699); *A Complete Collection of State Trials*, ed. T.B. Howell, vol. 3 (London, 1816), pp. 402–418, 419–426; see also H. Montgomery Hyde, *The Other Love*. Touchet's case was widely reported for many years to come, as in *The Exquisite* (London, 1842).

Chapter 2: The Birth of the Subculture

1.   John Florio's 1611 Italian/English dictionary defines 'Catamito, one hired to sin against nature, an ingle, a ganymede' (*Queen Anna's New World of Words*, p. 88; cited by Bray, p. 53).

2.   *Relations and Observations*, Book 2, Second Part, p. 257; cited by Bray, p. 53.

3.   John Wilmot, *Sodom, or The Quintessence of Debauchery*, introduced by Albert Ellis (North Hollywood, California: Brandon House, 1966).

4.   *A True Narrative of the Sentence of Titus Oats for Perjury*. London, 1685 (in a collection of Miscellaneous Sheets, British Library shelfmark 515.l.2.(101).

5.   *Analecta* (Maitland Club, 1842–1843), vol. III, p. 443.

6.   Narcissus Luttrell, *A Brief Historical Relation* (Oxford University Press, 1857), diary entry for 10 April 1694, vol. III, p. 291.

7.   *The Diary of John Evelyn*, ed. E.S. De Beer (Oxford: Clarendon Press, 1955), entry for 22 April 1694, vol. V, pp. 175–176.

8.   *The Plot Discover'd: Or Captain Wilson's Intrigues laid Open* (London, 1694).

9.   In a collection of Tracts, British Library shelfmark Cup.363.gg.31.(1). A cutting from a periodical of 1800 is pasted at the front, with details about Mrs Villiers and Mr Law's trial.

10.   *Trial of John Lawe*, Proceedings in the Old Bailey for 18–20 April 1694, in a collection of trials in the British Library, shelfmark 515.l.2.(154).

11.   A letter published as an appendix to the second edition of the English translation of Mme de La Mothe's (D'Aulnoy) *Memoirs of the Court of England in the Reign of Charles II*, entitled 'The Unknown Lady's Pacquet of Letters', cited in the *Dictionary of National Biography*, entry under Edward Wilson.

12.   For the two marriages, see Narcissus Luttrell, diary entries for 3 January 1694/5 (vol. III, p. 427) and 16 September 1699 (vol. IV, p. 561).

13. For the Parliamentary debates see Abel Boyer, *The Political State*, vols. 21–23, 1721–1722.
14. Britannicus [Thomas Gordon], *The Conspirators* (London, 1721), pp. 24–25.
15. From the follow-up pamphlet by Britannicus, *The Conspirators, Or, The Case of Catiline. Part II* (London, 1721), p. 44.
16. Boyer, *Political State* for June 1721, vol. 21, pp. 623–627, 633.
17. Boyer, *Political State* for November 1721, vol. 22, pp. 445–453.
18. Boyer, *Political State* for April 1722, vol. 23, pp. 452–453.
19. *The Yale Edition of Horace Walpole's Correspondence*, ed. W.S. Lewis, vol. 30 (London: Oxford University Press; New Haven: Yale University Press, 1961), p. 309.
20. *Jenny Cromwell's Complaint Against Sodomy*, reprinted by Dennis Rubini, 'Sexuality and Augustan England: Sodomy, Politics, Elite Circles and Society', in *The Pursuit of Sodomy: Male Homosexuality in Renaissance and Enlightenment Europe*, ed. Kent Gerard and Gert Hekma (New York and London: Harrington Park, 1989), p. 381.
21. *The London Spy*, January 1700, p. 13.
22. Dudley W.R. Bahlman, *The Moral Revolution of 1688* (New Haven: Yale University Press, 1957).
23. Rubini, p. 356.
24. The report of the trial is in a collection of Miscellaneous Sheets in the British Library, shelfmark 515.1.2.(168), *An Account of the Proceedings Against Capt. Edward Rigby*, Old Bailey Sessions for 7 December 1698.
25. *The Diary of John Evelyn*, ed. E.S. De Beer (Oxford: Clarendon Press, 1955), vol. V, p. 284.
26. [William Walsh], *A Dialogue Concerning Women, Being a Defence of the Sex*, with a Preface by John Dryden (London, 1691), esp. pp. 58–59, 103–104, 123–124.
27. *Characters of Gentlemen That have* put in *to The Ladies Invention*, no. 1, probably printed in February 1699, in a collection of broadside ballads in the British Library, shelfmark 816.m.19.18x).
28. According to *The Post Boy* for 24 March 1699, and *The Post Man* for 25–27 May 1699.
29. *An Account of the Proceedings Against Capt. Edward Rigby*, Sessions Paper for 7 December 1698, collection of Miscellaneous Sheets in the British Library, shelfmark 515.1.2.(168).
30. Reported in *The Post Man* for 27–29 July 1699.
31. John Charnock, *Biographia Navalis* (London, 1795), vol. III, pp. 50–51; and Wm. Laird Clowes, *The Royal Navy, A History* (London, 1898; repr. New York: AMS Press, 1966), vol. II, p. 531.
32. Narcissus Luttrell, *A Brief Historical Relation of State Affairs* (Oxford University Press, 1857), diary entry for 9 May 1699, vol. IV, pp. 513–514.
33. Rubini, pp. 349–381.
34. Cited by Gordon Rattray Taylor, 'Historical and Mythological Aspects of Homosexuality', in *Sexual Inversion*, ed. Judd Marmor (New York and London: Basic Books, 1965), p. 141.

35. Elisabeth Charlotte, Duchesse D'Orleans, *Letters from Liselotte*, trans. and ed. by Maria Kroll (New York: McCall, 1970), p. 70.

36. Nesca A. Robb, *William of Orange: A Personal Portrait, Volume Two: 1674–1702* (London, 1966), vol. 2, p. 399; cited by Randolph Trumbach, 'London's Sodomites: Homosexual Behavior and Western Culture in the 18th Century', *Journal of Social History*, vol. 11, no. 1 (1977), p. 20.

37. Rubini, pp. 371–372.

38. Referred to in the preface to *The Tryal and Condemnation of Mervin, Lord Audley Earl of Castle-Haven* (London, 1699).

39. Luttrell, diary entry for 1 August 1699, vol. IV, p. 543.

40. Reported in *The Post Man* for 9–12 September, *The Post-Master* for 9–12 September, and *The London Post* for 8–11 September, 1699.

41. Rumour reported in *The London Post* for 13–15 September 1699, *The Post-Master* for 9–12 September, and *The London Post* for 8–11 September, 1699.

42. Bahlman, p. 10.

43. *Account of the Progress of the Reformation of Manners in England, Scotland and Ireland* (1703), pp. 26–28; cited by Rubini, p. 358.

44. *A New Dialogue between The Horse at Charing-Cross, and The Horse at Stocks-Market* (London, 1703), p. 1.

45. *The Tryal and Conviction of several Reputed Sodomites, before the Right Honourable the Lord Mayor, and Recorder of London, at Guild-hall, the 20th Day of October, 1707.* A single Miscellaneous Sheet in the British Library, shelfmark 515.1.2.(205).

46. *The London Spy* for January, 1699, Part III, p. 14.

47. No copy exists of the 1707 edition, but the 4th edition is reprinted in Dunton's *Athenianism* (London, 1710), vol. 2, pp. 93–99.

48. The verses are reproduced in full by Rubini, pp. 379–380. The illustrations are reproduced by Alan Bray, *Homosexuality in Renaissance England* (London: Gay Men's Press, 1982).

49. *For God or For Satan*, p. 30, cited by Rubini, p. 352.

50. *A Full and True Account of the Discovery and Apprehending A Notorious Gang of Sodomites in St. James's* (London, 1709). This is a single sheet, incorrectly bound with an unrelated trial, in a collection of Miscellaneous Sheets in the British Library, shelfmark 515.1.2.(209).

51. *The Fifteenth Account of the Progress made toward suppressing profaneness and debauchery* (London, 1710), cited by Randolph Trumbach, 'Modern Prostitution and Gender in *Fanny Hill*', in *Sexual Underworlds of the Enlightenment*, ed. G.S. Rousseau and Roy Porter (Manchester University Press, 1987), p. 74.

52. E.J. Burford, *The Orrible Synne: A Look at London Lechery from Roman to Cromwellian Times* (London: Calder and Boyars, 1973) p. 133.

53. Letter from 'Decius' to Abel Boyer, *Political State* for June 1721, vol. 21, p. 622.

54. Boyer, *Political State* for May 1721, vol. 21, pp. 522–533.

Chapter 3: Mother Clap's Molly House

1. Most of the material in this chapter is found in *Select Trials for Murders, Robberies, Rapes, Sodomy . . . To which are added, Genuine Accounts of the Lives . . . of the most eminent Convicts* (London, 1742, 2nd ed.), 4 vols. The relevant trials, from which I have drawn together a consecutive narrative, are those of Margaret Clap (3.37–38), William Brown (3.39–40), William Griffin (2.365–366), George Kedger (2.366–367), Gabriel Lawrence (2.362–364), Martin Mackintosh (3.36–37), George Whittle (2.369–372) and Thomas Wright (2.367–369). Most of these trials are also recorded in the following with minor variations in details: *Select Trials for Murders, Robberies, Rape, Sodomy . . . To which are added Genuine Accounts of the Lives . . . of the most eminent Convicts. From the year 1720 to 1724* [and 1724 to 1732] (London, 1734–35), 2 vols.; *Select Trials at the Session-House in the Old Bailey . . . From . . . 1720, to this time, etc* (Dublin, 1742, 1743), 4 vols.; and *Select Trials for Murder, Robbery, &c at the Sessions House in the Old Bailey from 1720* [to 1741] (London, 1742), 4 vols.

2. [Edward Ward], *The History of the London Clubs* (London, 1709). This is a 'facsimile reprint' of 100 copies, by F[red] M[archmont], n.d.

3. See Lawrence's trial.

4. See Wright's trial.

5. See the trials of Clap and Lawrence.

6. See the trials of Clap, Lawrence and Griffin.

7. See Clap's trial.

8. See the trials of Wright, Griffin and Mackintosh.

9. Most of the information about Newton is in Lawrence's trial.

10. Most of the information about Courtney is in Kedger's trial.

11. *The London Journal*, 23 April 1726.

12. Eric Partridge, *A Dictionary of Slang and Unconventional English* (London: Routledge & Kegan Paul, 1937; repr. 1961), vol. 1, p. 770.

13. Joseph Cam, M.D., *A Practical Treatise: Or, Second Thoughts on the Consequences of the Venereal Disease* (London, 1729), and *A Dissertation on the Pox* (London, 1731).

14. Ikey Solomons (pseud. William Makepeace Thackeray), *Catherine*, in *Fraser's Magazine*, serialised from vol. XIX, no. CXIII (May, 1839) to vol. XXI, no. CXXII (February, 1840). The concluding chapter describes her execution but does not mention the hangings of the sodomites just minutes before; in the event, the description of the execution has been entirely omitted from all subsequent editions of the novel.

15. See Andrew Knapp and William Baldwin, *The Newgate Calendar* (London, 1810 ff.), 1.347–364; and *The Tyburn Chronicle* (London, c. 1769, 4 vols.), 2.252–293.

16. *The London Journal*, 14 May 1726.

17. *Select Trials* (1734–35), 2.208–209.

18. *The London Journal*, 30 July 1726.

19. *Weekly Journal, British Gazetteer*, and *London Journal*, 17 December 1726.

20. See Eric Partridge, *A Dictionary of Slang and Unconventional English*, vol. 1, p. 422.
21. Francis Grose, *The Classical Dictionary of the Vulgar Tongue* (London, 1785), entry under 'Game Pullet'.
22. *The London Spy* for December 1698, p. 9.
23. *Reformation necessary to prevent Our Ruine: A Sermon Preached to the Societies for Reformation of Manners, at St. Mary-le-Bow, on Wednesday, January 10th, 1727* (London, 1728), p. 30.
24. The Account is appended to Smalbroke's sermon.
25. Ned Ward, *The Field-Spy* (London, 1714), p. 16, cited by Bahlman, p. 47.
26. George Smyth, *A Sermon To the Societies for Reformation of Manners, Preach'd at Salter'-Hall, On Monday, June 26, 1727* (London, 1727), pp. 19–20 and 31–33.
27. Bahlman, pp. 65–66.
28. Alan Bray, *Homosexuality in Renaissance England* (London: Gay Men's Press, 1982), p. 90.

Chapter 4: The Sodomites' Walk in Moorfields

1. *Weekly Journal*, 7 May 1726.
2. E.J. Burford, *The Orrible Synne* (London: Calder and Boyars, 1973), pp. 67, 121, 174, 218, 220, 239.
3. Hanway, *Citizen's Monitor* (London, 1780), p. xvi.
4. *Proceedings . . . at the Old Bailey*, 7th Sessions, October 1731, case of David Hall, p. 9.
5. *The Annual Register* (1763), Chronicle, p. 51; *Chambers' Guide to London the Secret City* (London: Ocean Books Ltd., n.d.), pp. 32–33.
6. *Select Trials* (1734–1735), 1.309–310.
7. *Characters of Gentlemen That have* put in *to The Ladies Invention*, no. 1, probably printed in February 1699, in a collection of broadside ballads in the British Library, shelfmark 816.m.19.18x.
8. *Select Trials* (1734–1735), 2.39–45; also in *Select Trials* (1742–1743), 1.315–316, *Select Trials* (1742), 1.329–330, and *Proceedings . . . at the Old Bailey*, 1st Sessions, December 1730, p. 8.
9. *The Weekly Journal*, 7 and 14 January 1726/7.
10. *Times*, 17 July 1810.
11. *Select Trials* (1734–1735), 2.378.
12. M.R. Holmes, *Moorfields in 1559* (London: HMSO, 1963).
13. *Select Trials* (1734–1735), 1.239–240; *Select Trials* (1742), 1.280–283.
14. 'To the Author of a Play call'd Sodom', repr. in *Sodom, or The Quintessence of Debauchery*, introd. by Albert Ellis (North Hollywood, Calif.: Brandon House, 1966), p. xlii.
15. *Times*, 17 July 1810.
16. See the reports of the Council meetings held on 19 June 1689, 12 and 17 February, 1 July, 6 November 1691, 17 February, 19 April, 27 October 1692,

13 July 1693, 14 June 1703, 16 June, 27 July 1726, *The Records of the Honorable Society of Lincoln's Inn. The Black Books,* vol. III (Lincoln's Inn, 1899).

17. Charles William Heckethorn, *Lincoln's Inn Fields and The Localities Adjacent* (London: Elliot Stock, 1896), p. 52.

18. Tried at King's Bench, Westminster, 17 July 1728, as reported in *The London Journal,* 20 July 1728, and *The Country Journal: or, The Craftsman,* 20 July 1728.

19. *Select Trials* (1742, 2nd ed.), 3.36.

20. [James Dalton], *A Genuine Narrative of All the Street Robberies Committed since October last, by James Dalton, And his Accomplices* (London, 1728), p. 38.

21. *The London Journal,* 4 March 1726/7.

22. *Select Trials* (1734–1735), 1.150–151; also in *Select Trials* (1742), 1.152–153, and *Select Trials* (1742–1743, 2nd ed.), 1.158–160. See also *The Tyburn Chronicle: or, Villainy Display'd* (1769), vol. 1, pp. 386–388.

23. *Select Trials* (1734–1735), 2.243–244; *The Weekly Journal,* 15 April 1727. See also *Select Trials* (1742–1743), 3.71–73; *Select Trials* (1742), 3.74–75; and *Mist's Weekly Journal,* 15 April 1727.

24. *The Weekly Journal,* 6 May 1727.

25. *The Weekly Journal,* 8 November and 11 November 1727.

26. *The Malefactor's Register: or, New Newgate and Tyburn Calendar* (n.d., late 18th cent.), selected as *The Newgate Calendar,* ed. Sir Norman Birkett (London: Folio Press, J.M. Dent, 1974), p. 80.

27. *Mist's Weekly Journal,* 15 April 1727.

28. Gerald Howson, *Thief-Taker General: The Rise and Fall of Jonathan Wild* (London: Hutchinson, 1970), pp. 49–53, 23–24, *et passim.*

29. Reprinted in the same year, as *The Regulator: or a Discovery of Thieves, Thief-Takers &c,* in *The Malefactor's Register,* pp. 80–84.

30. Ibid. pp. 84–86.

31. Howson, pp. 62–63.

32. *Proceedings . . . in the Old Bailey,* 4th Session, April 1730, p. 14.

33. *Hell upon Earth* (London, 1729), p. 42.

34. *The Weekly Journal,* 26 August 1727.

35. *The Weekly Journal,* 14 January 1726.

36. *Times,* 25 July 1810.

37. *The Weekly Journal,* 23 April 1726.

38. *The Weekly Journal,* 9 September, 21 October, 28 October 1727.

39. *The Weekly Journal,* 5 August 1727.

40. Dalton, pp. 38–39.

41. Ibid. pp. 40, 41.

42. *The Weekly Journal,* 9 September 1727.

43. [Robert Holloway], *The Phoenix of Sodom* (London, 1813), pp. 14–15.

44. Quoted in Bernhardt J. Hurwood, *The Golden Age of Erotica* (London: Tandem, 1968), p. 32.

Chapter 5: Maiden Names and Little Sports

1. Bruce Rodgers, *The Queen's Vernacular* (London: Blond and Briggs, 1972).
2. See, for example, *Select Trials* (1734–1735), 2.208–209.
3. [James Dalton], *A Genuine Narrative of All the Street Robberies Committed since October last, by James Dalton, And his Accomplices* (London, 1728), p. 37.
4. Ibid. pp. 37, 40.
5. Ibid. p. 38.
6. Ibid. pp. 38–39.
7. Ibid. pp. 37–40.
8. Ibid. pp. 38–40.
9. Ibid. p. 37.
10. Robert Holloway, *The Phoenix of Sodom* (London, 1813), pp. 12–13.
11. *Select Trials*, 2.208–209.
12. Dalton, pp. 37–40.
13. Ibid.
14. *Proceedings . . . in the Old Bailey*, Session 4, April 1730, p. 14.
15. Holloway, pp. 12–13.
16. *Proceedings . . . in the Old Bailey*, Session 6, 5–8 July 1732, case no. 37, pp. 166–170.
17. Terry Castle, 'The culture of travesty: sexuality and masquerade in eighteenth-century England', in *Sexual Underworlds of the Enlightenment*, ed. G.S. Rousseau and Roy Porter (Manchester University Press, 1987), pp. 156–180.
18. See *The London Spy*, 1704, cited in Bernhardt J. Hurwood, *The Golden Age of Erotica* (London: Tandem, 1965), p. 34.
19. E.g., Arno Karlen in *Sexuality and Homosexuality*, and Randolph Trumbach, 'The Birth of the Queen: Sodomy and the Emergence of Gender Equality in Modern Culture, 1660–1750', in *Hidden from History: Reclaiming the Gay and Lesbian Past*, ed. by Martin Duberman, Martha Vicinus, and George Chauncey, Jr (New York: Penguin, 1990), pp. 129–140.
20. *The British Journal*, 2 and 23 January 1725.
21. *Hell upon Earth: Or The Town in an Uproar* (London, 1729), pp. 36–37.
22. [Edward Ward], *The History of the London Clubs* (London, 1709), p. 29.
23. *Select Trials* (1742, 2nd ed.), 3.37.
24. Humphrey Nettle, (pseud. for Rev. William Jackson), *Sodom and Onan* (London, 1776), p. 15.
25. Dalton, pp. 38–39.
26. Ward, *London Clubs*, p. 29.
27. Dalton, p. 40.
28. Geza Roheim, *Psychoanalysis and Anthropology* (New York: International Universities Press, 1950).
29. Margaret A. Murray, *The God of the Witches* (Oxford University Press, 1931; repr. 1973), p. 154. Her source for the anecdote is Arthur Wilson, *The Life and Reign of James the First* (London, 1706).
30. Holloway, p. 28.

31. *Select Trials* (1742, 2nd ed.), 3.37–38.

32. Dalton, p. 37.

33. *Hell upon Earth*, p. 42.

34. *Select Trials* (1734–1735), 2.57–59.

35. See *A New Canting Dictionary* (London, 1725).

36. *Select Trials*, 2.196–199.

37. See Eric Partridge, *A Dictionary of Slang and Unconventional English* (London: Routledge & Kegan Paul, 1937; 1961), vol. 1, pp. 197, 526.

38. *Select Trials*, 2.209–210; *Hell upon Earth*, p. 43; *The Weekly Journal*, 7 May 1726.

39. *Hell upon Earth* (London, 1729), p. 43.

40. *The Sins of the Cities of the Plain; or The Recollections of a Mary-Ann* (London, 1881). Jack Saul is the Mary-Ann in this authentic autobiography.

Chapter 6: Caterwauling

1. [James Dalton], *A Genuine Narrative of All the Street Robberies Committed since October last, by James Dalton, And his Accomplices* (London, 1728), p. 43.

2. *Select Trials* (1734–1735), 2.196.

3. *The Weekly Journal*, 7 May 1726.

4. Used in the pamphlets *Sodom and Onan* (1776) and *The Phoenix of Sodom* (1813).

5. See these entries in Francis Grose, *The Classical Dictionary of the Vulgar Tongue* (London, 1785).

6. *The Weekly Journal*, 7 May 1726.

7. *Hell upon Earth: Or The Town in an Uproar* (London, 1729), p. 43.

8. See this entry in *A New Canting Dictionary* (London, 1725).

9. *Select Trials* (1734–1735), 2.210–211.

10. Dalton, p. 42.

11. *The Weekly Journal*, 7 May 1726.

12. See Grose, *Classical Dictionary of the Vulgar Tongue*.

13. *The Weekly Journal*, 7 May 1726. But according to *A New Canting Dictionary* 'He has bit his Blow' means 'he has done his feat; he has stollen the Goods.'

14. *Select Trials* (1734–1735), 2.198–199.

15. Cited by Randolph Trumbach, 'The Birth of the Queen: Sodomy and the Emergence of Gender Equality in Modern Culture, 1660–1750', in *Hidden from History*, ed. Martin Duberman, Martha Vicinus and George Chauncey, Jr (New York: Meridian, 1989), p. 136.

16. *Proceedings . . . in the Old Bailey*, Sessions 5, 22–24 May 1735, case no. 50, p. 82.

17. Cited by Polly Morris, 'Sodomy and Male Honor: The Case of Somerset, 1740–1850', in *The Pursuit of Sodomy: Male Homosexuality in Renaissance and Enlightenment Europe*, ed. Kent Gerard and Gert Hekma (New York and London: Harrington Park Press, 1989), pp. 395–397.

18. Pisanus Fraxi [Henry Spencer Ashbee], *Bibliography of Prohibited Books* (London,

1885; New York, 1962), vol. 3, pp. 60–61.

19. *Proceedings . . . in the Old Bailey*, Sessions 7, 6–11 September 1732, case no. 85, pp. 217–219.

20. *Select Trials* (1734–1735), 2.367-371; *Proceedings . . . in the Old Bailey*, Sessions 5, August 1730, pp. 10–13.

21. *Select Trials* (1734–1735), 2.193-194; also in *Select Trials* (1742), 2.349–351; and 1742, 2nd ed., 2.362–364.

22. *Select Trials* (1734–1735), 1.83–85; also in *Select Trials* (1742), 1.101–103; and 1742, 2nd ed., 1.105–108.

23. *Select Trials* (1734–1735), 1.239–240; also in *Select Trials* (1742), 1.269–271; and 1742, 2nd ed., 1.280–282.

24. *Proceedings . . . in the Old Bailey*, Sessions 6, July 1732, case no. 51, p. 171.

25. Randolph Trumbach, 'Sodomitical Assaults, Gender Role, and Sexual Development in Eighteenth-Century London', in *The Pursuit of Sodomy: Male Homosexuality in Renaissance and Enlightenment Europe*, ed. Kent Gerard and Gert Hekma (New York and London: Harrington Park, 1989), p. 426.

26. *The Exquisite*, c.1842, no. 31, p. 366.

Chapter 7: Popular Rage

1. *Select Trials* (1734–1735), 2.210–211.

2. Ibid. 1.150–151.

3. Ibid. 2.367–371.

4. Robert Holloway, *The Phoenix of Sodom, or the Vere Street Coterie* (London, 1813), p. 13.

5. Quoted in *The Fruit Shop* (London, 1766), pp. 160–165. In fact these lines are lifted from Charles Churchill's poem 'The Times', first published in 1764; see *The Works of C. Churchill* (London, 1774), vol. III, pp. 170–171.

6. *Satan's Harvest Home* (London, 1749), p. 55.

7. *A Sapphick Epistle* (London, sometime between 1771 and 1781), p. 7.

8. James Dalton, *A Genuine Narrative* (London, 1728), pp. 42–43.

9. 'Jeremy Bentham's Essay on "Paederasty"' introduced and edited by Louis Crompton, *Journal of Homosexuality*, vol. 3 (1978), pp. 383–405, and vol. 4 (1978), pp. 91–107.

10. *The Trial of Richard Branson for An Attempt to commit Sodomy, On the Body of James Fassett* (London, 1760); he was tried on 18 January 1760, though the incident occurred in August 1759.

11. Quoted by Pisanus Fraxi [pseud. of Henry Spencer Ashbee], *Bibliography of Prohibited Books* (London, 1879; repr. New York: Jack Brussel, 1962), vol. 2, p. 125.

12. *Satan's Harvest Home*, Ch. II, p. 51.

13. Humphrey Nettle, (pseud. for Rev. William Jackson), *Sodom and Onan* (London, 1776), p. 12.

14. From 'Œconomy of Love', in *The Fruit Shop*.

15. See *The Fruit Shop*, Part 2, Ch. VII, pp. 160–165.

16. *Satan's Harvest Home*, pp. 58–59.

17. *Clod-Pate's Ghost: Or a Dialogue Between Justice Clod-Pate, and his (quondam) Clerk Honest Tom Ticklefoot* (London, n.d.), p. 2.

18. *Satan's Harvest Home*, p. 50.

19. Ibid. p. 53.

20. Ibid. p. 54.

21. Ibid. p. 50.

22. Quoted in *Satan's Harvest Home*, p. 61.

23. Holloway, *Phoenix of Sodom*, pp. 12–13.

24. *The Weekly Journal*, 14 May 1726.

25. *Satan's Harvest Home*, pp. 53–54.

26. W. Bornemann, *Einblicke in England und London im Jahre 1818* (Berlin, 1819), p. 179, cited by Ivan Bloch, *Sexual Life in England Past and Present*, trans. William H. Forstern (London, 1938), p. 399.

27. Ibid. p. 52.

28. Holloway, p. 16.

29. *Sodom and Onan*, pp. 26–28.

30. *Times*, 25 July 1810.

31. *Times*, 16 October 1810.

32. *Times*, 9 October 1810.

33. *The Weekly Journal*, 6 May and 11 November, 1727.

34. *The Weekly Journal*, 9 September, 21 October, and 28 October, 1727.

35. *Annual Register* (1763), Chronicle, entry for 3 April, p. 67.

36. Dated by hand April 1763. Reproduced by Peter Wagner, *Eros Revived* (London: Secker and Warburg, 1988), p. 38.

37. *Times*, 2 August 1810.

38. *Phoenix of Sodom*, p. 8.

39. Ibid. p. 32.

40. Cases in *Select Trials* (1734–1735), vol. 1, pp. 20–23, 97–98, 100–104, 179–181, 280–281, 281–282, 327–328, 360–361; vol. 2, pp. 37–38, 119–120, 120–121, 121–123, 142–144, 211–212, 218–220, 238–239, 244–245, 261–262, 338–339, 372–374, 381–382, 395–396, 429–430.

41. Ibid. 1.211–212; *British Journal*, 4 June 1726.

42. Antony E. Simpson, 'Vulnerability and the age of female consent', in *Sexual Underworlds of the Enlightenment* (Manchester University Press, 1987), pp. 181–205.

43. H. Montgomery Hyde, *The Other Love* (London: Mayflower Books, 1972), pp. 93–94.

44. *Report from the Select Committee on Criminal Laws* (House of Commons, 1819), Appendix I, Table VI, p. 132.

45. *Tables Showing the Number of Criminal Offenders Committed for Trial or Bailed ... in the Year 1836* (London, 1837), first page of 'Statements on Criminal Law, Prepared by the Direction of the Secretary of State for the Home Department.'

46. *Times*, 24 September 1810.

Chapter 8: Blackmail

1. See J. Bellamy, *Crime and Public Order in England in The Later Middle Ages* (London: Routledge & Kegan Paul, 1973).

2. Bellamy, *Crime and Public Order . . .*; L. Radzinowicz, *A History of English Criminal Law and Its Administration From 1750* (London: Stevens, 1948), vol. I; Mike Hepworth, *Blackmail: Publicity and Secrecy in Everyday Life* (London: Routledge & Kegan Paul, 1975).

3. *Select Trials* (1734–1735), 1.61–66; *Select Trials* (1742), 1.75–82.

4. *Select Trials* (1734–1735), 1.152–153, 208–210.

5. Ibid. 2.17–19.

6. Ibid. 2.196; *The London Journal*, 23 April 1726.

7. Ibid. 2.396–397; also *Proceedings . . . in the Old Bailey*, Sessions 1, December 1730, pp. 9–10.

8. *Proceedings . . . in the Old Bailey*, Sessions 2, 16–20 January 1730, pp. 15–16.

9. *The Weekly Journal*, 20 May 1727.

10. *The London Journal*, 2 September 1727.

11. *Proceedings . . . in the Old Bailey*, Sessions 4, April 1734, case no. 62, p. 119.

12. *Account of the Life and Actions of Joseph Powis, by himself, given to the Ordinary of Newgate* and published in *The Ordinary of Newgate, His Account of the Behaviour, Confession, and Dying Words, of the Malefactors, Who were Executed at Tyburn, on Monday the 9th of this Instant October, 1732*, pp. 21–29. His trial and conviction is in *Proceedings . . . in the Old Bailey*, Sessions 7, September 1732, case no. 16, pp. 177–178.

13. *The Whole Proceedings On the wicked Conspiracy Carried on against the Hon. Edward Walpole, Esq., By John Cather, Adam Nixon, Daniel Alexander, Patrick Cane alias Kane, and others* (London, 1751).

14. *The Adventures of Peregrine Pickle*, ed. James L. Clifford (Oxford University Press), Chap. 73, p. 366.

15. *Annual Register* (1759), Chronicle, pp. 99–100.

16. W.H.D. Winder, 'The Development of Blackmail', *Modern Law Review*, vol. IV (1941).

17. Cited in Winder, as above.

18. *Annual Register* (1779), Chronicle, pp. 199–200, 208–209; *The Complete Newgate Calendar*, ed. G.T. Crook (London: Navarre Society, 1926), vol. 4.

19. Robert Holloway, *The Phoenix of Sodom, or the Vere Street Coterie* (London, 1813), pp. 37–38.

20. C.J. Fielding, *The Brothers. An Eclogue* (London, 1782).

21. *Annual Register* (1779), Chronicle, p. 237.

22. Cited in Winder, 'The Development of Blackmail'.

23. *Times*, 18 July 1810.

24. *Proceedings . . . in the Old Bailey*, 1810 Sessions, case no. 604, pp. 323–331.

25. This is made clear in another report on the case, in Jackson, vol. VIII, pp. 270–275.

26. William Benbow, *The Crimes of the Clergy* (London, 1823), pp. 222–224.

27. *The Guardian*, 23 March 1972.
28. *Final Commitment of Allison, for a Detestable Crime*, single broadside sheet in a collection of Tracts in the British Library, shelfmark Cup.363.gg.31.(6). These tracts were assembled as a result of the Clogher scandal of 1822, and the latest dated contents are for December 1824.
29. Holloway, *Phoenix of Sodom* (1813), p. 18.
30. Ibid. pp. 38–39.
31. By Polly Morris, 'Sodomy and Male Honor: The Case of Somerset, 1740–1850', in *The Pursuit of Sodomy: Male Homosexuality in Renaissance and Enlightenment Europe*, ed. Kent Gerard and Gert Hekma (New York and London: Harrington Park Press, 1989), pp. 383–406. The case of Tyler is reviewed on pp. 393–394.
32. Morris, p. 389.

Chapter 9: The Third Sex

1. 'An Epistle from Mr Pope to Dr Arbuthnot', *The Twickenham Edition of the Poems of Alexander Pope*, General Editor John Butt (London, 1939), vol. IV, p. 95.
2. Robert Halsband, *Lord Hervey; Eighteenth-Century Courtier* (Oxford: Clarendon Press, 1973); Robert Halsband, *Life of Lady Mary Wortley Montagu* (Oxford, 1956); Robert Halsband, *The Complete Letters of Lady Mary Wortley Montagu* (Oxford, 1965–1967).
3. *A Proper Reply to a Late Scurrilous Libel* (London, 1731).
4. *Observations on the Writings of the Craftsman* (London, 1731).
5. Honoré Gabriel Riqueti, Comte de Mirabeau, *The Secret History of the Court of Berlin* (London: H.S. Nichols, 1895). See also A.L. Rowse, *Homosexuals in History* (London: Weidenfeld and Nicolson, 1977), pp. 91–99.

Chapter 10: The Warden of Wadham

1. *The Diary of Dudley Rider 1715–1716*, ed. W. Matthews (London, 1939), p. 143.
2. Most of the material in this chapter is drawn from *A Faithful Narrative of the Proceedings . . . against Robert Thistlethwayte, Late Doctor of Divinity, and Warden of Wadham College for a sodomitical Attempt upon Mr W. French, Commoner of the same College* (London, 1739). A hand-written note in the copy in the British Library ascribes its authorship to Charles D'Oyly, a friend of French. A few extra details concerning Swinton are in *A Faithful Narrative of the Proceedings In a late Affair between The Rev. Mr. John Swinton, and Mr. George Baker* (London, 1739).
3. Robert Barlow Gardiner, ed., *The Registers of Wadham College, Oxford*, 2 vols. (London, 1889, 1895).

4. Ibid.

5. *The State of Rome, Under Nero and Domitian* (London, 1739), pp. 7, 9. In a collection of Poems in the British Library, shelfmark 840.m.1.(35).

6. Trial of Mary Blandy, in Andrew Knapp and William Baldwin, *The Newgate Calendar* (London, 1810), II.473–484; see also Rayner Heppenstall, *Reflections on the Newgate Calendar* (London: W.H. Allen, 1975), pp. 56–57.

7. Heppenstall, p. 113.

Chapter 11: The Age of Scandal

1. *The London Chronicle: or, Universal Evening Post*, 4 and 6 January, 1757.

2. *The Tyburn Chronicle*, (c. 1769), vol. 4, pp. 137–142.

3. *The Malefactor's Register* (London, 1779) , vol. IV, pp. 203–205.

4. Cutting from an unidentified periodical, dated 20 July, in a collection of Tracts at the British Library, shelfmark Cup.363.gg.31.

5. *A new Treatise on artificial fireworks, etc* (London, 1765), with editions in 1766 and 1776; *A treatise on Skating* (London, 1772), with editions in 1775, 1780, 1797, 1823, 1825, 1855, etc.

6. *Annual Register* (1772), Chronicle, entry for 11 August, p. 121, and 7 September, p. 126.

7. *Malefactor's Register*, vol. V, p. 104. Also reported by William Jackson, *The New and Complete Newgate Calendar* (London, 1818), vol. V, pp. 102–104.

8. Unidentified newspaper cutting, dated by hand as July 1773, in the collection of Tracts cited above.

9. Cutting from an unidentified newspaper, dated by hand as 15 June 1773, in the collection of Tracts cited above.

10. Peter A. Tasch, *The Dramatic Cobbler: The Life and Works of Isaac Bickerstaff* (Lewisburg: Bucknell University Press, 1971).

11. *Love in the Suds; A Town Eclogue. Being the Lamentation of Roscius for the Loss of his Nyky*, with a prefatory *Letter to David Garrick, Esq. From William Kenrick* (London, 1772).

12. Jon Bee, *The Works of Samuel Foote, Esq., with . . . An Essay on the Life, Genius, and Writings of the Author*, 3 vols. (London, 1830), vol. I.

13. Bee, I.lxv.

14. The complete trial is reported in the *Annual Register* (1776), as an Appendix to the Chronicle, pp. 231–236.

15. The date of publication is established by an advertisement which appeared in *The Morning Post, and Daily Advertiser* for 22 June 1776: 'This Day is published, Price 2s. Sodom and Onan, A Satire. Embellished with a striking likeness of the patron, engraved by an eminent Artist.'

16. *The Middlesex Journal* for 13 January 1771, though he is merely identified as 'a man of genteel appearance'.

17. The original etching upon which this was based, in reverse, is a portrait of 'Ganymede' alone, holding a cane, and without manacles; it is of finer quality

but less interest. Both etchings are by M. Darly, and one has obviously been copied from the other. In vol. IV of the *Catalogue of Political and Personal Satires* (British Museum Publications, 1978 reprint), first published in 1883, the satirical etching titled 'Ganymede & Jack-Catch' was incorrectly identified as a portrait of Samuel Vaughan, tried in 1769 for trying to bribe the Duke of Grafton into disposing of a reversion of a place in favour of his son in Jamaica, a political misdemeanour for which there was not the slightest reason to call him Ganymede. But Mary Dorothy George in vol. V of this *Catalogue*, first published in 1935, corrects this identification to Drybutter, not Vaughan (p. 40). The portrait titled 'Ganymede', dated 1771, looks as though it was etched before the satirical print, because it is full of very carefully engraved details, evincing the kind of skill usually reserved for the original rather than the copy. In the satirical etching, the hat and clothes are only lightly sketched in, the legs have been repositioned to accommodate the manacles, which look as though they have been stuck on rather than part of the original design, and the cane has been omitted together with part of the hand which held it.

18. *The Middlesex Journal* for 1719 January 1771.

19. *Proceedings . . . in the Old Bailey*, January 1771, Session 2, case nos. 77 and 78, pp. 71–74.

20. Alan Chester Valentine, *Lord George Germain* (Oxford: Clarendon Press, 1962), pp. 472–475.

21. *The Poetical Works of Charles Churchill*, ed. Douglas Grant (Oxford, 1956), p. 404.

22. See Charles Durnford and E.H. East, *Term Reports* (London, 1817), vol. IV, pp. 126–130.

23. *Gazetteer*, 23 May 1776.

24. The trial is fully reported in *Lloyd's Evening Post*, vol. 39, no. 3036, 9–11 December 1776; see also the *Annual Register* (1776), Chronicle, p. 199.

25. See T. Baine's *The Theatre Licentious. A Sermon*, London, 1770.

26. *Autobiography Letters and Literary Remains of Mrs Piozzi (Thrale)*, ed. A. Hayward (London, 1861), vol. 1, pp. 310–311.

27. Bee, I. clxiii.

28. Bee, ibid.

29. William Cooke, ed., *The Table-Talk and Bon-Mots of Samuel Foote* (London, 1902), p. 9.

30. William Cowper, 'Tirocinium', originally published in 1784, in *The Works of William Cowper*, ed. Robert Southey (London, 1864), vol. VI, p. 185.

31. Newspaper cutting of about 1785 cited in *Survey of London*. vol. XXXV. *The Theatre Royal, Drury Lane, and The Royal Opera House Covent Garden* (The Athlone Press, University of London, 1970), p. 48.

32. George Parker, *Views of Society and Manners in High and Low Life* (London, 1781), II.87–88, cited by Randolph Trumbach, 'London's Sodomites: Homosexual Behavior and Western Culture in the 18th Century', *Journal of Social History*, vol. 11, no. 1 (1977), pp. 133.

33. *The Trials at Large of the Felons, in the Castle of York* (York, 1775), case no. 13.

34. Robert Holloway, *The Phoenix of Sodom, or the Vere Street Coterie* (London, 1813), p. 27.

35. *Annual Register* (1806), Chronicle, entry for 25 August, pp. 438–439.

36. Newspaper cutting in the collection of Tracts cited above, dated 6 November but no year. The raid is discussed by Archenholtz, *Originalzüge aus dem Charakter englischer Sonderlinge* (Leipzig, 1796), pp. 158–160, cited by Ivan Bloch, *Sexual Life in England Past and Present*, trans. William H. Forstern (London, 1938), pp. 400–401.

Chapter 12: The Vere Street Coterie

1. Old Bailey Sessions Book, no. X. 24; William Jackson, *New and Complete Newgate Calendar; or Malefactor's Universal Register* (London, 1818), vol. VII, pp. 200–201.

2. Old Bailey Sessions Book, no. X. 25.

3. Andrew Knapp and William Baldwin, *The Newgate Calendar: Being Interesting Memoirs of Notorious Characters* (London, 1810–1812), vol. V, pp. 64–65.

4. The estimate given by Andrew Knapp and William Baldwin, *The Newgate Calendar: Being Interesting Memoirs of Notorious Characters, Who have been convicted of Outrages on The Laws of England* (London, 1810) vol. 1, p. 50.

5. William Jackson, *The New and Complete Newgate Calendar; or Malefactor's Universal Register* (London, 1818), vol. VII, pp. 370–371.

6. Robert Holloway, *The Phoenix of Sodom, or The Vere Street Coterie* (London, 1813). Much of the material in this chapter comes from this source.

7. Jackson, vol. VIII, p. 273.

8. *The Weekly Dispatch* for 8 April 1813 refers to the long-past event, but is unsure whether six or seven men were placed in the pillory, and incorrectly says that it took place in October.

9. *Annual Register* (1810), Chronicle, 27 September, pp. 280–281; *Times*, 28 September 1810; *Times*, 28 September 1810; see also Bernhardt J. Hurwood, *The Golden Age of Erotica* (London: Tandem, 1965), p. 165.

10. *Times*, 29 September 1810.

11. Old Bailey Sessions Roll, 19 September 1810.

12. Old Bailey Sessions Book, no. X. 26; see also the *Times*, 20 September 1810.

13. Jackson, vol. VIII, p. 275–276. The *Times*, 6 November 1810, incorrectly reported that Hepburn was granted this order from the War Office, and that White was the person to be called back from Portugal in order to testify.

14. The details are noted by Jackson, vol. VIII, pp. 275–280.

15. First Sessions, Middlesex, Mr Justice Grose president, case no. 1 (*Times*, 6 December 1810).

16. Old Bailey Sessions Book, no. X. 26.

17. Jackson, p. 280. Confirmed by the *Annual Register* (1810), Chronicle, 11 December, p 293.

18. See H. Montgomery Hyde, *The Other Love*, pp. 94–95.

19. *Annual Register* (1833), Chronicle, Part 2, pp. 90–96.
20. *Times*, 26 July 1810; see also Pisanus Fraxi [Henry Spencer Ashbee], *Bibliography of Prohibited Books* (London, 1877; New York, 1962), vol. I, p. 212.
21. Old Bailey Sessions Roll, 19 September 1810.
22. Old Bailey Sessions Book, no. X. 26; and *Proceedings . . . in the Old Bailey*, 1810 Sessions, case no. 641, p. 347.
23. Ibid.
24. *Times*, 1 August 1810.
25. *Times*, 11 August 1810.

Chapter 13: A Child of Peculiar Providence

1. This chapter draws upon the following sources: *The Infamous Life of John Church* (1817); *The Trial and Conviction of John Church* (1817); *The Sentence and Affidavit of John Church* (1817); Rev. T. Latham, *The Rod in Pickle* (1817); *The Trial and Conviction of that Infamous Hypocrite John Church* (1817); *Religion and Morality Vindicated* (1813); [Robert Holloway], *The Phoenix of Sodom* (1813); William Benbow, *The Crimes of the Clergy, or The Pillars of Priest-Craft Shaken* (1823), pp. 19–21; *The Weekly Dispatch*, 18 April, 25 April, 2 May, 9 May, 1813; *Morning Chronicle*, 20 April 1813 *et passim*; and the autobiography and sermons of John Church: *The Foundling; or, The Child of Providence* (1823), *The Morning of Spiritual Youth* (1814), *A Feast for Serpents* (1813), *The Thirteen Names of the First Patriarchs* (1814), *The Sacrifice of Life* (1814), *The Glorious Law-Giver* (c.1814), *The Nature of a Gospel Church* (c.1814), *The Living Letter* (1814), *Christ the True Melchisedec* (1813). Oakden's trial is in the Old Bailey Sessions Book, no. X. 25.
2. *The Bishop! Particulars of the Charge against the Hon. Percy Jocelyn, Bishop of Clogher* (London, c.1822), p. 6.

Chapter 14: Men of Rank and Fortune

1. *Annual Register* (1809), Chronicle, pp. 346–350.
2. G.E.C., *The Complete Peerage*, vol. XII, Part 1 (London: The St Catherine Press, 1953), pp. 812–813. See also H. Montgomery Hyde, *The Other Love* (London: Heinemann, 1970; Mayflower edition, 1972), p. 92.
3. William Benbow, *The Crimes of the Clergy, or The Pillars of Priest-Craft Shaken* (London, 1823), p. 230.
4. Pisanus Fraxi [pseud. of Henry Spencer Ashbee], *Bibliography of Prohibited Books* (London, 1879; repr. New York: Jack Brussel, 1962), vol. II, p. 50.
5. Benbow, pp. 8–14.
6. Benbow, pp. 229–230.
7. Benbow, pp. 238–239.

8. Pisanus Fraxi, vol. I, pp. 340–342.
9. *Lion in Tears, Or the Church's Lament for Dr Greenfield*, published as a result of the Clogher affair in 1822, in a collection of Tracts in the British Library, shelfmark Cup.363.gg.31.
10. Some of the contemporary documents are gathered together in a collection of Tracts in the British Library, shelfmark Cup.363.gg.31, which includes newspaper cuttings, a handwritten epigram, the ballad *Lion in Tears*, and *A Correct Account of the Horrible Occurrence Which took place at a Public-house in St. James's Market, in which it was discovered that . . . The Bishop of Clogher . . . was a principal actor with A Common Soldier!* [1822]. More details are found in *The Bishop!! Particulars of the Charge against the Hon. Percy Jocelyn, Bishop of Clogher* [1822], and in Benbow, *Crimes of the Clergy* (1823), pp. 41–44. See also H. Montgomery Hyde, *The Other Love*, pp. 99–101.
11. The British Library once had the single sheet of the *Subscription for James Byrne* with a list of subscribers, and a 36-page *Sketch of the Life, and Unparalleled Sufferings of James Byrne, late coachman to the Honourable John Jocelyn, brother to . . . the Lord Bishop of Clogher. Together with some observations on the conduct of the Jocelyn family* (1822). These were in a collection of documents about Byrne which was destroyed by bombing during World War II, and I have not located other copies.
12. The complete record of the proceedings appears as an Appendix to the *Annual Register* (1822), Chronicle, pp. 425–432. The case is reviewed in the entries for 20 July 1822, p. 126, and 7 August 1822, p. 138. The selling of the tithes is confirmed by Benbow, p. 140.
13. 'Court of King's Bench, Westminster. Byrne v. Parkins. 16 February 1824', reprinted in the *Annual Register* (1824), Chronicle, pp. 55–62.
14. Benbow, p. 44.
15. *The Bishop!!*, pp. 67.
16. Ibid. pp. 79.
17. William Jackson, *The New and Complete Newgate Calendar; or Malefactor's Universal Register* (London, 1818), vol. VII, p. 371.
18. This survey of Beckford's life is based primarily upon Boyd Alexander, ed., *Life at Fonthill 1807–1822, with Interludes in Paris and London from the Correspondence of William Beckford* (London, 1954), and Brian Fothergill, *Beckford of Fonthill* (London and Boston: Faber and Faber, 1979).
19. Benbow, p. 230.
20. Unrecognised newspaper, 17 March 1828, Bodleian MS.Beckford c.75, fol. 58.
21. *The Age*, 31 August 1834, MS.Beckford c.75, fol. 132.
22. Wrapper; *News*, 14 November 1826; *John Bull*, 7 May 1826; MS.Beckford c.83, fols. 64, 72–73.
23. *Morning Chronicle*, 14 February 1826, MS.Beckford c.83, fol. 131.
24. *News*, 23 September 1827, MS.Beckford c.83, fol. 139.
25. *Morning Chronicle*, 17 and 19 April 1830, MS.Beckford c.67, fols. 178 and 181.
26. *Examiner*, 1 April 1827, MS.Beckford c.75, fol. 23.

27. *News*, 29 April 1832, MS.Beckford c.83, fol. 81.

28. *Morning Chronicle*, 23 March 1825, and an unidentified newspaper, 4 May 1825, MS.Beckford c.83, fols. 129–130.

29. *News*, 22 March 1833, MS.Beckford c.83, fol. 84.

30. *News*, 4 May 1828, MS.Beckford c.74, fol. 273.

31. *Morning Chronicle*, 22 October 1825, 27 July 1829, MS.Beckford c.75, fols. 68–69; *The Age*, September 1825, MS.Beckford c.71, fol. 34.

Chapter 15: Tommies and the Game of Flats

1. Judith C. Brown, *Immodest Acts: The Life of a Lesbian Nun in Renaissance Italy* (Oxford University Press, 1986).

2. Cited by Arno Karlen, *Sexuality and Homosexuality* (London: Macdonald, 1971), p. 145.

3. D. Martino Schurigio, *Muliebria Historico-Medica* (Dresdae & Lipsiae, 1729), pp. 90–107; and *Gynæcologia Historico-Medica* (Dresdae & Lipsiae, 1730), pp. 377–378.

4. [William Walsh], *A Dialogue Concerning Women, Being a Defence of the Sex* (London, 1691), pp. 34–35, 58–59, 103–104.

5. A.G. Busbequius, *Travels into Turkey*, English translation (London, 1744). The original book was invariably cited whenever lesbianism was mentioned, e.g. William Walsh's *A Dialogue Concerning Women* (London, 1691) and in Martin Schurig's *Muliebria Historico-Medica* (1729).

6. *A Sapphick Epistle, from Jack Cavendish to the Honourable and most beautiful Mrs. D—*, London, c.1781. The recipient is called 'Mrs D–R' on p. 5, and 'Dame' is used conspicuously.

7. *The Whig Club, or a Sketch of Modern Patriotism*, cited by Brian Fothergill, *The Strawberry Hill Set: Horace Walpole and His Circle* (Faber and Faber, 1983), pp. 201–202.

8. Fothergill, pp. 193–198.

9. Letter to George Montague, 26 July 1755, *The Yale Edition of Horace Walpole's Correspondence*, ed. W.S. Lewis, vol. 9 (London: Oxford University Press; New Haven: Yale University Press, 1941), p. 171.

10. See *The Bagford Ballads*, ed. Joseph Woodfall Ebsworth, 2 vols. (Hertford, 1878): 'The Woman-Warrior', I.323–325; 'The female Warrior', I.326–329; 'The Blind Beggar's Daughter of Bednall Green', I.308–310. Mary Frith (1584–c.1660), known as Moll Cutpurse, is celebrated in numerous ballads and plays, as was the less well known Mary Carlton, or Kentish Moll (Bagford Ballads, I.309–310; Roxburgh Collection, III.35).

11. *The Counterfeit Bridegroom*, undated broadside ballad, British Library shelfmark 816.m.19.(21.).

12. Mary Turner, 'Two entries from the marriage register of Taxal, Cheshire', *Local Population Studies*, no. 21 (Autumn 1978), p. 64.

13. *Annual Register* (1766), Chronicle, entry for week of 21 October, p. 144.

14. *Annual Register* (1766), Chronicle, entry for 16 June.
15. This story is related as 'A Curious Married Couple', in the American journal *Fincher's Trades' Review*, vol. 1, no. 8 (Philadelphia, 25 July 1863), p. 29, col. 6; reprinted by Jonathan Katz, *Gay American History* (New York: Thomas Y. Crowell Company, 1976), p. 226.
16. *The Female Soldier, or The Surprising Life and Adventures of Hannah Snell* (London, 1750); see also Marian West, 'Women Who Have Passed as Men', *Munzey's Magazine* (New York, 1901), vol. 25, p. 280, reprinted in Jonathan Katz, p. 226. Her autobiography is reprinted in *Women Adventurers*, ed. Menie Muriel Dowie (London: Unwin, 1893).
17. The following summary is from Henry Fielding's *The Female Husband: or, The Surprising History of Mrs Mary, alias Mr George Hamilton* (London, 1746).
18. Cited by Lynne Friedli, '"Passing women" — A study of gender boundaries in the eighteenth century', in *Sexual Underworlds of the Enlightenment*, ed. G.S. Rousseau and Roy Porter (Manchester University Press, 1987), pp. 238–239.
19. Fielding, p. 21.
20. *Bath Journal*, 22 September 1746; see also *The Gentleman's Magazine*, 28 November 1746; *Daily Advertiser*, 7 November 1746; *St James's Evening Post*, 8 November 1746.
21. Andrew Knapp and William Baldwin, *The Newgate Calendar: Being Interesting Memoirs of Notorious Characters, Who have been convicted of Outrages on The Laws of England*, 5 vols. (London, 1810?), II.125126.
22. Fielding, pp. 22–23.
23. Knapp and Baldwin, III.395.
24. *Annual Register* (1822), Chronicle, entry for April, pp. 72–74.
25. *A Narrative of the Life of Mrs Charlotte Charke* (London, 1755). Written by Herself. 2nd ed.
26. Friedli, pp. 240–242.
27. The following details are based upon Captain Charles Johnson (probably a pseudonym for Daniel Defoe), *A General History of the Robberies and Murders of the Most Notorious Pirates* (1724), *Historie der Engelsche Zee-Roovers* (1725), and Charles Ellms, *The Pirates' Own Book* (1837); see also Philip Gosse, *The History of Piracy* (1932), Neville Williams, *Captains Outrageous: Seven Centuries of Piracy* (1961), Alfred Sternbeck, *Filibusters and Buccaneers* (1930), David Mitchell, *Pirates* (1976), and Susan Baker, 'Anne Bonny & Mary Read', in *Women Remembered*, ed. Nancy Myron and Charlotte Bunch (Diana Press, 1974), C.J.S. Thompson, *The Cruel Mysteries of Sex* (1974).
28. Lillian Faderman, *Surpassing the Love of Men* (New York: William Morrow and Company, 1981), pp. 103–106.
29. See Faderman, p. 123.
30. Quoted by Michael Brander, *The Georgian Gentleman* (Farnborough: Saxon House, 1973), p. 133.
31. Cited by Faderman, p. 110.
32. *The Exquisite* (London, c. 1842), no. 7, pp. 82–83; no. 8, pp. 88–89; no. 9, pp.

106–107; no. 10, p. 118; no. 11, pp. 130–131; no. 12, pp. 142–144; no. 13, pp. 149–151.

33. According to *The Bon Ton Magazine* for December 1792, cited by Arno Karlen, *Sexuality and Homosexuality*, p. 142; and by Lillian Faderman, *Surpassing the Love of Men*, p. 40.

34. Quoted in Paul Tabori, *Secret and Forbidden* (London: New English Library, 1969), pp. 63–64.

Chapter 16: From Twickenham to Turkey

1. *The Rare Adventures and Painful Peregrinations of William Lithgow*, ed. Gilbert Phelps (London: The Folio Society, 1974), p. 222.
2. Lithgow, pp. 209–210.
3. Lithgow, p. 57.
4. *The Bishop!! Particulars of the Charge against the Hon. Percy Jocelyn, Bishop of Clogher* (London, [1822]), p. 9.
5. Lithgow, p. 43.
6. *Schouwtooneel soo der Geexecuteerde als Ingedaagde Over de verfoeielijke Misdaad van Sodomie*, 1730, reviewed by Louis Crompton, 'Gay Genocide: From Leviticus to Hitler', in *The Gay Academic*, ed. Louie Crew (Palm Springs, CA: ETC Publication, 1978), pp. 85–91.
7. Arend H. Huussen, Jr, 'Sodomy in the Dutch Republic During the Eighteenth Century', in *Hidden from History: Reclaiming the Gay and Lesbian Past*, ed. Martin Duberman, Martha Vicinus, and George Chauncey, Jr (New York: Meridian, 1989), pp. 141–149.
8. Paul Tabori, *Secret and Forbidden* (London: New English Library, 1969), pp. 65–66.
9. *Letters from Liselotte*, trans. and ed. Maria Kroll (New York: McCall, 1974), pp. 121–122.
10. Tabori, p. 52.
11. *Le nuits de Paris* (Paris: Hachette, 1960).
12. 'Francis Higgeson's Journal' in *The Founding of Massachusetts*, ed. Stuart Mitchell (Boston: Massachusetts Historical Society, 1930), p. 71; reprinted by Jonathan Katz, *Gay American History: Lesbians and Gay Men in the U.S.A.* (New York: Thomas Y. Crowell, 1976), p. 20.
13. The case is reprinted by Katz, pp. 1619.
14. John Winthrop, *History of New England from 1630 to 1649*, ed. James Savage (Boston: Little, Brown, 1853), vol. 2, p. 324; repr. by Katz, p. 22.
15. E.B. O'Callaghan, ed., *Calendar of Historical Manuscripts in the Office of the Secretary of State, Albany, N. Y.* (Albany: Week, Parsons, 1865), p. 103; see Katz, pp. 22–23.
16. O'Callaghan, *Calendar of Historical Manuscripts*, pp. 201, 213.
17. Samuel Danforth, *The Cry of Sodom Enquired into, Upon the Arraignment and Condemnation of Benjamin Goad* (Cambridge, Mass., 1674).

18. Katz, p. 570 n.

19. *The Writings of George Washington*, ed. John C. Fitzpatrick (Washington, D.C.: U.S. Government Printing Office, 1934), vol. 11, pp. 83–84; repr. by Katz, p. 24.

20. Helen Hornbeck Tanner, *Zespedes in East Florida, 1784–1790, Hispanic-American Studies*, no. 19 (Coral Gables, Fla.: University of Miami, 1963), pp. 167–168; repr. by Katz, pp. 24–25.

21. *St. Méry's American Journey*, trans. and ed. Kenneth Roberts and Anna M. Roberts (Garden City, N.Y.: Doubleday, 1947), pp. 284, 286; repr. by Katz, pp. 25–26.

22. Thomas Harris and Reverdy Johnson, *Reports of Cases Argued and Determined in the Court of Appeals of Maryland, In 1810, 1811, 1812, 1813, 1814, & 1815* (Annapolis, Md.: Jonas Green, 1826), vol. 3, pp. 154–158; repr. by Katz, pp. 26–27.

23. Katz, pp. 27–28, 572 n.

24. The following survey is based upon Martin Smith, 'Our Australian Gay Heritage', *Campaign*, no. 19 (April 1977), pp. 13–15, 42, 46.

Bibliography

Trial Records

Account of the Life and Actions of Joseph Powis, by himself, given to the Ordinary of Newgate, in *The Ordinary of Newgate, His Account of the Behaviour, Confession, and Dying Words, of the Malefactors, Who were Executed at Tyburn, on Monday the 9th of this Instant October, 1732.*

An Account of the Proceedings Against Capt. Edward Rigby. London, 1698.

A Complete Collection of State Trials, ed. T.B. Howell. London, 1816.

A Complete Narrative of all the prisoners who were try'd . . . at the Sessions-House in the Old Bailey. London, c.1740.

The Complete Newgate Calendar, ed. G.T. Crook. London: Navarre Society, 1926.

Durnford, Charles, and E.H. East. *Term Reports.* London, 1817.

Final Commitment of Allison, for a Detestable Crime. (London, c.1822).

A Full and True Account of the Discovery and Apprehending A Notorious Gang of Sodomites in St. James's. London, 1709.

Jackson, William. *The New and Complete Newgate Calendar; or Malefactor's Universal Register*, 8 vols. London, 1818.

Janssen, Sir Stephen Theodore. *This Sheet contains three Tables from 1749 to 1771 . . . showing the Number of Sessions at the Old Bailey . . . with the Number of Persons sentenced to die, & for what crimes, 2d The Number of Persons Executed . . ., 3d The Numbers . . . either Pardoned, Transported, or Died in Newgate . . .* 1 August 1772. Republished 1784.

Knapp, Andrew, and William Baldwin. *The Newgate Calendar: Being Interesting Memoirs of Notorious Characters, Who have been convicted of Outrages on The Laws of England*, 5 vols. London, 1810–1812.

The Malefactor's Register; or, The Newgate and Tyburn Calendar . . . from the Year 1700 to Lady-Day 1779, 5 vols. London, c.1779.

The Malefactor's Register: or, New Newgate and Tyburn Calendar (n.d., late 18th cent.), selected as *The Newgate Calendar*, ed. Sir Norman Birkett. London: Folio Press, J.M. Dent, 1974.

The Proceedings on the King's Commission of the Peace, and Oyer and Terminer, and Jail-Delivery of Newgate. Incomplete collection of trials from 1722–1726. British Library shelfmark L.21.aa.2.

Select Trials at the Session-House in the Old Bailey . . . From . . . 1720, to this time, etc, 4 vols. Dublin: W. Smith, G. Ewing, 1742, 1743.

Select Trials for Murder, Robbery, &c at the Sessions House in the Old Bailey from 1720 [–1741], 4 vols. London, 1742.

Select Trials for Murders, Robberies, Rapes, Sodomy . . . To which are added, Genuine Accounts of the Lives . . . of the most eminent Convicts . . . 1720–1723, 2nd ed., 4 vols. London: L. Gulliver, J. Huggonson, 1742.

Select Trials for Murders, Robberies, Rape, Sodomy . . . To which are added Genuine Accounts of the lives . . . of the most eminent Convicts. From the year 1720 to 1724 (1724 to 1732) inclusive, 2 vols. London, 1734, 1735.

The Sentence and Affidavit of John Church (Court of King's Bench, 24 November 1817). London: Hay & Turner, 1817.

Tables Showing the Number of Criminal Offenders Committed for Trial or Bailed . . . in the Year 1836. London, 1837.

The Trial and Conviction of that Infamous Hypocrite John Church. London, 1817.

The Trial and Conviction of John Church. London, 1817.

Trial of John Lawe. Proceedings at the Old Bailey for 1820 April 1694. British Library shelfmark 515.l.2.(154).

The Trial of Richard Branson for An Attempt to commit Sodomy, On the Body of James Fassett. London, 1760.

The Trials at Large of the Felons, in the Castle of York. York, 1775.

A True Narrative of the Sentence of Titus Oats for Perjury at the Kings-Bench-Barr at Westminster. London, 1685.

The Tryal and Condemnation of Mervin, Lord Audley Earl of Castle-Haven. London, 1699.

The Tryal and Conviction of several Reputed Sodomites. London, 1707.

The Tyburn Chronicle, 4 vols. London, c.1769.

The Whole Proceedings. On the King's Commission of the Peace, Oyer and Terminer, and Gaol Delivery . . . in the Old Bailey. 1714–1830.

The Whole Proceedings On the wicked Conspiracy Carried on against the Hon. Edward Walpole, Esp., By John Cather, Adam Nixon, Daniel Alexander, Patrick Cane alias Kane, and others. London, 1751.

Books and Pamphlets

Alexander, Boyd, ed. *Life at Fonthill 1807–1822, with Interludes in Paris and London from the Correspondence of William Beckford*. London, 1954.

Aubrey, John. *Brief Lives*, ed. Andrew Clark. Oxford, 1898.

Bacon, Sir Francis. *The Works of Sir Francis Bacon*, ed. James Spedding *et al*, 14 vols. London, 1857–1874.

The Bagford Ballads, ed. Joseph Woodfall Ebsworth, 2 vols. Hertford, 1878.

Bahlman, Dudley W.R. *The Moral Revolution of 1688*. New Haven: Yale University Press, 1957.

Bailey, Derrick Sherwin. *Homosexuality and the Western Christian Tradition*. London and New York: Longmans, Green, 1955.

Baine, T. *The Theatre Licentious. A Sermon.* London, 1770.

Barnard, Nicolas. *The Case of John Atherton.* London, 1710.

Bellamy, J. *Crime and Public Order in England in The Later Middle Ages.* London: Routledge & Kegan Paul, 1973.

Benbow, William. *The Crimes of the Clergy, or The Pillars of Priest-Craft Shaken.* London, 1823.

Bentham, Jeremy. 'Jeremy Bentham's Essay on "Paederasty"' introduced and edited by Louis Crompton, *Journal of Homosexuality*, vol. 3 (1978), pp. 383–405, and vol. 4 (1978), pp. 91–107.

The Bishop!! Particulars of the Charge against the Hon. Percy Jocelyn, Bishop of Clogher. London [1822].

Blackstone, William. *Commentaries on the Laws of England.* Oxford, 1750.

Bloch, Ivan. *Sexual Life in England Past and Present*, trans. William H. Forstern. London, 1938.

Boyer, Abel. *The Political State*, vols. 21–23. London, 1721–1722.

Brander, Michael. *The Georgian Gentleman.* Farnborough: Saxon House, 1973.

Bray, Alan. *Homosexuality in Renaissance England.* London: Gay Men's Press, 1982.

Bretonne, Restif De La, Nicolas-Edmé. *The Nights of Paris*, trans. Nicholas Deaken. London: New English Library, 1968.

Brown, Judith C. *Immodest Acts: The Life of a Lesbian Nun in Renaissance Italy.* New York and Oxford: Oxford University Press, 1986.

Bullough, Vern L. 'Heresy, Witchcraft, and Sexuality', *Journal of Homosexuality*, 1, 2 (1974), 183–201.

Burford, E.J. *The Orrible Synne: A Look at London Lechery from Roman to Cromwellian Times.* London: Calder & Boyars, 1973.

Busbequius, A.G. *Travels into Turkey.* London, 1744.

C., G.E. *The Complete Peerage*, 13 vols. London: The St Catherine Press, 1910–1940, 1953.

Cam, Joseph, M.D. *A Dissertation on the Pox.* London, 1731.

Cam, Joseph, M.D. *A Practical Treatise: Or, Second Thoughts on the Consequences of the Venereal Disease.* London, 1729.

The Case of John Atherton . . . Fairly Represented. London, 1710.

Cavendish, Jack (pseud.). *A Sapphick Epistle, from Jack Cavendish to the Honourable and most beautiful Mrs. D—.* London [?1771 or 1781].

Chambers' Guide to London the Secret City. London: Ocean Books Ltd., n.d.

Characters of Gentlemen That have put in to The Ladies Invention. London (1699).

Charke, Charlotte. *A Narrative of the Life of Mrs Charlotte Charke.* London, 1755.

Charnock, John. *Biographia Navalis*, 6 vols. London, 1795.

Church, John. *Christ the True Melchisedec.* London, 1813.

Church, John. *A Feast for Serpents.* London, 1813.

Church, John. *The Foundling; or, The Child of Providence.* London 1823.

Church, John. *The Glorious Law-Giver.* London [1814].

Church, John. *The Living Letter.* London, 1814.

Church, John. *The Morning of Spiritual Youth.* London, 1814.

Church, John. *The Nature of a Gospel Church.* London [1814].

Church, John. *The Sacrifice of Life.* London, 1814.

Church, John. *The Thirteen Names of the First Patriarchs*. London, 1814.

Churchill, Charles. *The Poetical Works of Charles Churchill*, ed. Douglas Grant. Oxford, 1956.

Churchill, Charles. *The Works of C. Churchill*, 4 vols. London, 1774.

Clod-Pate's Ghost: Or a Dialogue Between Justice Clod-Pate, and his (quondam) Clerk Honest Tom Ticklefoot. [London, n.d.].

Clowes, Wm. Laird. *The Royal Navy, A History*, 7 vols. London, 1898; repr. New York: AMS Press, 1966.

Cooper, Rev. William M. *Flagellation and the Flagellants: A History of the Rod*. London, c.1885.

A Correct Account of the Horrible Occurrence Which took place at a Public-house in St. James's Market, in which it was discovered that . . . The Bishop of Clogher . . . was a principal actor with A Common Soldier! London [1822].

The Counterfeit Bridegroom. London [1720].

Cowper, William. *The Works of William Cowper*, ed. Robert Southey, 8 vols. London, 1864.

Crompton, Louis. 'Gay Genocide: From Leviticus to Hitler', in *The Gay Academic*, ed. Louie Crew (Palm Springs, CA: ETC Publication, 1978), pp. 85–91.

Crompton, Louis. 'Homosexuals and the Death Penalty in Colonial America', *Journal of Homosexuality*, 1, 3 (1976), 277–293.

[Dalton, James]. *A Genuine Narrative of All the Street Robberies Committed since October last, by James Dalton, And his Accomplices*. London, 1728.

D'Ewes, Sir Simonds. *Autobiography and Correspondence*, ed. James Orchard Halliwell, 2 vols. London, 1845.

D'Ewes, Sir Simonds. 'The Fall and Great Vices of Sir Francis Bacon', bound up as an appendix to Thomas Hearne, *Historia Vitae et Regni Ricardi II; Prince Charles's Journey into Spain* (London, 1729), pp. 387–388.

[D'Oyly, Charles]. *A Faithful Narrative of the Proceedings . . . against Robert Thistlethwayte*. London, 1739.

Dowie, Ménie Muriel, ed. *Women Adventurers*. London: Unwin, 1893.

du Maurier, Daphne. *Golden Lads: A Study of Anthony Bacon, Francis, and their friends*. London: Victor Gollancz, 1975.

du Maurier, Daphne. *The Winding Stair: Francis Bacon, His Rise and Fall*. London: Victor Gollancz, 1976.

Duberman, Martin, Martha Vicinus, and George Chauncey, Jr eds. *Hidden from History: Reclaiming the Gay and Lesbian Past*. New York: Penguin, 1990.

Edgerton, William L. *Nicholas Udall*. New York, 1965.

Eglinton, J.Z. (pseud.). *Greek Love*. London: Neville Spearman, 1971.

An Elegy On the much Lamented Death of Charles Earl of Sunderland, Who Died April, 1722.

Evelyn, John. *The Diary of John Evelyn*, ed. E.S. De Beer, 6 vols. Oxford: Clarendon Press, 1955.

Faderman, Lillian. *Surpassing the Love of Men*. New York: William Morrow and Company, 1981.

A Faithful Narrative of the Proceedings In a late Affair between The Rev. Mr. John Swinton, and Mr. George Baker. London, 1739.

The Female Soldier, or The Surprising Life and Adventures of Hannah Snell. London, 1750.

Fielding, C.J. *The Brothers. An Eclogue.* (London, 1782).

[Fielding, Henry]. *The Female Husband: or, The Surprising History of Mrs. Mary, alias Mr. George Hamilton.* Taken from her own Mouth since her Confinement. London, 1746.

Foote, William. *The Table-Talk and Bon-Mots of Samuel Foote.* ed. William Cooke. London, 1902.

Foote, Samuel. *The Works of Samuel Foote, Esq., with . . . An Essay on the Life, Genius, and Writings of the Author,* ed. Jon Bee, 3 vols. London, 1830.

Fothergill, Brian. *Beckford of Fonthill.* London and Boston: Faber and Faber, 1979.

Fothergill, Brian. *The Strawberry Hill Set: Horace Walpole and His Circle.* London: Faber and Faber, 1983.

Fraser, Antonia. *King James.* London: Weidenfeld and Nicolson, 1974.

Fraxi, Pisanus [pseud. of Henry Spencer Ashbee]. *Bibliography of Prohibited Books,* 3 vols. London, 1877, 1879, 1885; repr. New York: Jack Brussel, 1962.

The Fruit-Shop, A Tale; Or, A Companion to St. James's Street, 2 vols. London, 1765, 1766.

Garde, Noel I. (pseud.). *Jonathan To Gide: The Homosexual in History.* New York: Vantage, 1964.

Gardiner, Robert Barlow, ed. *The Registers of Wadham College,* Oxford, 2 vols. London, 1889, 1895.

Gerard, Kent, and Gert Hekma, eds. *The Pursuit of Sodomy: Male Homosexuality in Renaissance and Enlightenment Europe.* New York and London: Harrington Park, 1989.

Goodich, Michael. 'Sodomy in Ecclesiastical Law and Theory', *Journal of Homosexuality* 1, 4 (1976), 427–434.

Goodich, Michael. 'Sodomy in Medieval Secular Law', *Journal of Homosexuality,* 1, 3 (1976), 295–302.

[Gordon, Thomas] Britannicus. *The Conspirators: Or, The Case of Catiline.* London, 1721.

[Gordon, Thomas] Britannicus. *The Conspirators, Or, The Case of Catiline.* Part II. London, 1721.

Grose, Francis. *The Classical Dictionary of the Vulgar Tongue.* London, 1785.

Halsband, Robert. *The Complete Letters of Lady Mary Wortley Montagu.* Oxford, 1965–1967.

Halsband, Robert. *Life of Lady Mary Wortley Montagu.* Oxford, 1956.

Halsband, Robert. *Lord Hervey; Eighteenth-Century Courtier.* Oxford: Clarendon Press, 1973.

Heckethorn, Charles William. *Lincoln's Inn Fields and The Localities Adjacent.* London: Elliot Stock, 1896.

The Hell-Fire-Club: Kept by a Society of Blasphemers. A Satyr. London, 1721.

Hell upon Earth: Or The Town in an Uproar. Occasion'd by The late horrible Scenes of Forgery, Perjury, Street-Robbery, Murder, Sodomy, and other shocking Impieties. London, 1729.

Heppenstall, Rayner. *Reflections on the Newgate Calendar.* London: W.H. Allen, 1975.

Hepworth, Mike. *Blackmail: Publicity and Secrecy in Everyday Life.* London: Routledge & Kegan Paul, 1975.

Historical Account of the Origin, Progress, and Present State of Bethlehem Hospital. London, 1783.

[Holloway, Robert]. *The Phoenix of Sodom, or the Vere Street Coterie, Being an Exhibition of the Gambols Practised by the Ancient Lechers of Sodom and Gomorrah, embellished and improved with the Modern Refinements in Sodomitical Practices, by the members of the Vere Street Coterie, of detestable memory.* Sold by J. Cook. London, 1813.

Holmes, M.R. *Moorfields in 1559.* London: HMSO, 1963.

Howson, Gerald. *Thief-Taker General: The Rise and Fall of Jonathan Wild.* London: Hutchinson, 1970.

Hurwood, Bernhardt J. *The Golden Age of Erotica.* London: Tandem, 1968.

Hyde, H. Montgomery. *The Other Love: An Historical and Contemporary Survey of Homosexuality in Britain.* London: Heinemann, 1970 (Mayflower edition, 1972).

The Infamous Life of John Church. London, 1817.

[Jackson, William] Humphrey Nettle. *Sodom and Onan.* London [1776].

Johnson, Captain Charles. *General History of the . . . most famous Highwaymen, Murderers, Street Robbers, and . . . Pirates.* London, 1734.

Johnson, Captain Charles. *A General History of the Robberies and Murders of the Most Notorious Pirates.* London, 1724.

Jones, Robert. *A new Treatise on artificial fireworks.* London, 1765.

Jones, Robert. *A treatise on Skating.* London, 1772.

Karlen, Arno. *Sexuality and Homosexuality.* London: Macdonald, 1971.

Katz, Jonathan. *Gay American History: Lesbians and Gay Men in the U.S.A.* New York: Thomas Y. Crowell, 1976.

Kearney, Patrick J. *The Private Case.* London: Jay Landesman, 1981.

Kenrick, William. *Love in the Suds; A Town Eclogue. Being the Lamentation of Roscius for the Loss of his Nyky.* London, 1772.

Latham, Rev. T. *The Rod in Pickle; or, An Answer to the Appeal of John Church, The Obelisk Preacher.* London, 1817.

Lithgow, William. *The Rare Adventures and Painful Peregrinations of William Lithgow,* ed. Gilbert Phelps. London: The Folio Society, 1974.

Lion in Tears, Or the Church's Lament for Dr Greenfield. [London, 1822].

Love-Letters Between a certain late Nobleman And the famous Mr. Wilson. London [1723].

Luttrell, Narcissus. *A Brief Historical Relation of State Affairs from September 1678 to April 1714,* 6 vols. Oxford University Press, 1857.

Mairobert, Pidansat de. *L'Espion anglois, ou Correspondance Secrete entre Milord All'Eye et Milord All'Ear,* 10 vols. London, 1784, 1785.

Marston, John. *The Poems of John Marston,* ed. Arnold Davenport. Liverpool, 1961.

McNeill SJ, John J. *The Church and the Homosexual.* London: Darton, Longman and Todd, 1977.

M[iddleton], T[homas]. *Micro-cynicon. Sixe Snarling Satyres*. London, 1599.

Miller, Joe. *Joe Miller's Jestbook*. London, 1739.

Mirabeau, Comte de, Honoré Gabriel Riqueti. *The Secret History of the Court of Berlin*, 2 vols. London: H.S. Nichols, 1895.

Myron, Nancy, and Charlotte Bunch, eds. *Women Remembered*. London: Diana Press, 1974.

A New Canting Dictionary. London, 1725.

A New Dialogue between The Horse at Charing-Cross, and The Horse at Stocks-Market. London, 1703.

Norton, Rictor. *The Homosexual Literary Tradition*. New York: Revisionist Press, 1974.

An Ode Inscribed to the Right Honourable the Earl of Sunderland at Windsor. London, 1720.

Orleans, Elisabeth Charlotte, Duchesse D'. *Letters from Liselotte*, trans. and ed. by Maria Kroll. New York: McCall, 1970.

Partridge, Eric. *A Dictionary of Slang and Unconventional English*, 2 vols. London: Routledge & Kegan Paul, 1937; repr. with supplement, 1961.

Philautus (pseud., possibly for Nathaniel Lancaster). *The Pretty Gentleman: or, Softness of Manners Vindicated*. London, 1747.

The Plot Discover'd: Or Captain Wilson's Intrigues laid Open . . . Together with an Account of the Mysterious Papers he left behind him. London, 1694.

Pope, Alexander. *The Twickenham Edition of the Poems of Alexander Pope*, General Editor John Butt. London, 1939.

Pulteney, William. *Observations on the Writings of the Craftsman*. London, 1731.

Pulteney, William. *A Proper Reply to a Late Scurrious Libel*. London, 1731.

Radzinowicz, L. *A History of English Criminal Law and Its Administration From 1750*. London: Stevens, 1948.

The Records of the Honorable Society of Lincoln's Inn. The Black Books. Lincoln's Inn, 1899.

Religion & Morality Vindicated, Against Hypocrisy and Pollution; or, an account of the Life and Character of John Church the Obelisk Preacher, Who Was Formerly A Frequenter of Vere-Street, etc. London, 1813.

Rider, Dudley. *The Diary of Dudley Rider 1715–1716*, ed. W. Matthews. London, 1939.

Rodgers, Bruce. *The Queen's Vernacular*. London: Blond and Briggs, 1972.

Roheim, Geza. *Psychoanalysis and Anthropology*. New York: International Universities Press, 1950.

Rousseau, G.S., and Roy Porter, eds. *Sexual Underworlds of the Enlightment*. Manchester University Press, 1987.

Rowse, A.L. *Homosexuals in History*. London: Weidenfeld and Nicolson, 1977.

Satan's Harvest Home: or the Present State of Whorecraft, Adultery, Fornication, Procuring, Pimping, Sodomy, And the Game at Flatts. Collected from the Memoirs of an intimate Comrade of the Hon. Jack S–n–r. London, 1749.

[Saul, Jack]. *The Sins of the Cities of the Plain; or The Recollections of a Mary-Ann*. London, 1881.

Schurigio, D. Martino. *Gynæcologia Historico-Medica. Dresdae & Lipsiae*, 1730.

Schurigio, D. Martino. *Muliebria Historico-Medica. Dresdae & Lipsiae*, 1729.

Smalbroke, Richard. *Reformation necessary to prevent Our Ruine: A Sermon Preached to the Societies for Reformation of Manners*. London, 1728.

Smith, Martin. 'Our Australian Gay Heritage', *Campaign*, no. 19 (April 1977), pp. 13–15, 42, 46.

Smyth, George. *A Sermon To the Societies for Reformation of Manners*. London, 1727.

Sodom and Onan, A Satire. London (1776).

Tabori, Paul. *Secret and Forbidden*. London: New English Library, 1969.

Tasch, Peter A. *The Dramatic Cobbler: The Life and Works of Isaac Bickerstaff*. Lewisburg: Bucknell University Press, 1971.

Taylor, Gordon Rattray. 'Historical and Mythological Aspects of Homosexuality', in *Sexual Inversion*, ed. Judd Marmor (New York and London: Basic Books, 1965), pp. 140–164.

Thackeray, William Makepeace. *Catherine*, in *Fraser's Magazine*, serialised from vol. XIX, no. CXIII (May, 1839) to vol. XXI, no. CXXII (February, 1840).

Titus's Exultation to the Pillory, upon his Conviction of Perjury. A Ballad. London, 1685.

Trumbach, Randolph. 'London's Sodomites: Homosexual Behavior and Western Culture in the 18th Century', *Journal of Social History*, vol. 11, no. 1 (1977), pp. 1–33.

Turner, E.S. *The Court of St. James's*. New York, 1959.

Turner, Mary. 'Two entries from the marriage register of Taxal, Cheshire', *Local Population Studies*, no. 21 (Autumn 1978), p. 64.

Udall, Nicholas. *Nicholas Udall's Roister Doister*, ed. G. Scheurweghs, in *Materials for the Study of Old English Drama*, vol. 16, ed. Henry De Vocht. Louvain, 1939; repr. Vaduz, 1963.

Walpole, Horace. *The Yale Edition of Horace Walpole's Correspondence*, ed. W.S. Lewis. London: Oxford University Press; New Haven: Yale University Press, 1937 and following.

[Walsh, William]. *A Dialogue Concerning Women, Being a Defence of the Sex*, with a Preface by John Dryden. London, 1691.

[Ward, Edward]. *The History of the London Clubs*. London, 1709. A reissue by F[red] M[archmont] of 100 copies, n.d.

[Ward, Edward]. *The Second Part of the History of the London Clubs*. London [1720?].

Ward, Ned. *Compleat & Humourous Account of all the Remarkable Clubs and Societies*. London, 1705.

Weeks, Jeffrey. *Coming Out: Homosexual Politics in Britain, from the Nineteenth Century to the Present*. London: Quartet Books, 1977.

Weldon, Anthony. *The Court and Character of King James*. London, 1651. Repr. in Francis Osborne, *Secret History of the Court of James the First*. Edinburgh, 1811.

Wilmot, John. *Sodom, or The Quintessence of Debauchery*, introd. by Albert Ellis. North Hollywood, Calif.: Brandon House, 1966.

Winder, W.H.D. 'The Development of Blackmail', *Modern Law Review*, vol. IV (1941).

Wodrow, Robert. *Analecta*, 4 vols. Maitland Club, 1842–1843.

Index

Other non-fiction titles from GMP — The Gay Men's Press

Alan Bray
Homosexuality in Renaissance England
This ground-breaking study, surveys the transition from the duality of 'sodomy' and 'friendship' to the beginnings of a gay identity.
ISBN 0 85449 095 7 pbk UK £7.95 US $15.00 AUS $19.95

Michael Elliman and Frederick Roll
The Pink Plaque Guide to London
Thoroughly researched and illustrated, this unique compendium of gay history contains a wealth of information on a hundred major figures — from Erasmus and Christopher Marlowe through to Radclyffe Hall and Mary Renault.
ISBN 0 85449 026 4 pbk UK £7.95 US $12.50 AUS $19.95

GMP books can be ordered from any bookshop in the UK, and from specialised bookshops overseas. If you prefer to order by mail, please send full retail price plus £2.00 for postage and packing to:

GMP Publishers Ltd (GB), P O Box 247, London N17 9QR.

For payment by Access/Eurocard/Mastercard/American Express/Visa, please give number and signature.
A comprehensive mail-order catalogue is also available.

In North America order from Alyson Publications Inc.,
40 Plympton St, Boston, MA 02118, USA.
(American Express not accepted)

In Australia order from Bulldog Books,
P O Box 155, Broadway, NSW 2007, Australia.

Name and Address in block letters please:

Name
_____

Address
_____

_____

_____